EVERYDAY AESTHETICS

To the Memory of my Father, Gheorghe Mándoki

Everyday Aesthetics
Prosaics, the Play of Culture and Social Identities

KATYA MANDOKI
Universidad Autónoma Metropolitana, Mexico

ASHGATE

© Katya Mandoki 2007

All rights reserved. No part of this publication may be reproduced, stored in a retrieval system or transmitted in any form or by any means, electronic, mechanical, photocopying, recording or otherwise without the prior permission of the publisher.

Katya Mandoki has asserted her right under the Copyright, Designs and Patents Act, 1988, to be identified as the author of this work.

Published by
Ashgate Publishing Limited
Gower House
Croft Road
Aldershot
Hampshire GU11 3HR
England

Ashgate Publishing Company
Suite 420
101 Cherry Street
Burlington, VT 05401-4405
USA

Ashgate website: http://www.ashgate.com

British Library Cataloguing in Publication Data
Mandoki, Katya
  Everyday aesthetics : prosaics, the play of culture and
  social identities
  1. Aesthetics
  I. Title
  111.8'5

Library of Congress Cataloging-in-Publication Data
Mandoki, Katya, 1947-
  Everyday aesthetics : prosaics, the play of culture, and social identities / Katya
Mandoki.
      p. cm.
  Includes bibliographical references and index.
  ISBN: 978-0-7546-5889-4 (hardcover)
  1. Aesthetics. I. Title.

  BH39.M38 2007
  111'.85--dc22

2006019740

ISBN: 978-0-7546-5889-4

Printed and bound in Great Britain by Antony Rowe Ltd, Chippenham, Wiltshire.

Contents

List of Tables	*x*
Glossary	*xi*
Preface	*xv*
Acknowledgement	*xviii*

PART 1	**THE LABYRINTHS OF AESTHETICS**	**1**
Chapter 1	**The Problems of Aesthetics**	**3**
	Problems of definition	3
	Problems of location	3
	Problems of distinction	5
Chapter 2	**The Fetishes of Aesthetics**	**7**
	The fetish of beauty	7
	The fetish of the artwork	8
	The fetish of the aesthetic object	10
Chapter 3	**The Myths of Aesthetics**	**15**
	The myth of the opposition art/reality and aesthetics/everyday life	15
	The myth of aesthetic disinterest	17
	The myth of aesthetic distance	19
	The myth of the aesthetic attitude	22
	The myth of aesthetic aspects or qualities	24
	The myth of the universality of beauty	26
	The myth of the opposition between the aesthetic and the intellectual	27
	The myth of the synonymity of art and aesthetics	29
	The myth of the aesthetic potentiality of artworks	30
	The myth of the aesthetic experience	31
Chapter 4	**The Fears of Aesthetics**	**37**
	The fear of the undesirable	37
	The fear of everyday impurities	38
	The fear of psychologism	39
	The fear of the immoral	40

vi *Everyday Aesthetics*

PART 2	**ON AESTHESIS**	**43**
Chapter 5	**Demarcating Aesthetics**	**45**
	A genealogical perspective for a bio-aesthetics	47
	Bio-aesthetics	49
	Socio-aesthetics	50
Chapter 6	**Basic Categories for Aesthetic Analysis**	**53**
	Aesthetic subject and aesthetic object	53
	Objectivity, objectuality, and objectivation	55
	Subjectivity, individuality, identity, role	57
Chapter 7	**Conditions of Possibility of Aesthesis: The *A Priori***	**61**
	Space-time	61
	The body	62
	Vital energy	63
	Cultural conventions	64
Chapter 8	**The Phenomenology of Aesthesis: Aesthetic Latching-On and Latched-By**	**67**
PART 3	**TOWARDS PROSAICS**	**73**
	Prosaics and panaestheticism	73
Chapter 9	**Prosaics and Poetics**	**75**
	Poesics and prosics	79
Chapter 10	**The Tangents of Prosaics**	**81**
Chapter 11	**The Nutrients of Prosaics**	**87**
	Mikhail Bakhtin	87
	John Dewey	88
	Johan Huizinga	90
Chapter 12	**The Play of Culture**	**93**
	Categorization of games by Caillois	94
Chapter 13	**The Horizons of Prosaics**	**97**
PART 4	**SEMIO-AESTHETICS**	**101**
	Semio-aesthetics and aesthesio-semiotics	101
Chapter 14	**Thresholds of Semiotic Perception: Sensation, Discernment and Regard**	**105**

Chapter 15	**The Axis of the Signic**	**109**
	Signifier	111
	Signified	112
Chapter 16	**The Axis of the Symbolic**	**115**
Chapter 17	**Comparative View of Both Axes: The Symbolic and the Signic**	**119**
Chapter 18	**The Non-Axis of the Obtuse**	**125**
Chapter 19	**Beyond Semiosis to Aesthesis**	**127**
Chapter 20	**Aesthetic Enunciation and its Dialogical Character**	**131**
	Aesthetic syntagm and paradigm	133
PART 5	**OCTADIC MODEL FOR AESTHETIC ANALYSIS**	**135**
	The projection of the semiotic axes to the aesthetic	136
Chapter 21	**Rhetoric and its Registers**	**139**
	Lexic register	142
	Acoustic register	143
	Somatic register	144
	Scopic register	146
Chapter 22	**Dramatics and its Modalities**	**149**
	Proxemics	149
	Kinetics	151
	Emphatics	152
	Fluxion	152
Chapter 23	**The Rhetoric-Dramatic Coupling**	**155**
	Lexic proxemics	155
	Acoustic proxemics	156
	Somatic proxemics	156
	Scopic proxemics	157
	Lexic kinetics	157
	Acoustic kinetics	158
	Somatic kinetics	158
	Scopic kinetics	158
	Lexic emphatics	159
	Acoustic emphatics	160
	Somatic emphatics	161
	Scopic emphatics	161
	Lexic fluxion	162
	Acoustic fluxion	163

viii *Everyday Aesthetics*

	Somatic fluxion	164
	Scopic fluxion	164

Chapter 24 Con-Formations of the Rhetoric-Dramatic Coupling **169**
Heteroglossia 170
Polyphony 172
Hybridization 173
Ex-pression, im-pression, com-pression, de-pression 173

PART 6 MATRIXES AND IDENTITIES **177**

Chapter 25 The Matrixes: A General Approach **179**
Matrixes and paradigms 182

Chapter 26 Diachronic and Synchronic Perspective of Cultural Matrixes **185**
Diachronic perspective of the matrixes 186
Synchronic perspective of the matrixes 187

Chapter 27 The Family Matrix **195**
The registers of rhetorics in the family matrix 196
The modalities of the dramatic in the family matrix 198
Family proxemics 198
Family kinetics 199
Family emphatics 200
Family fluxion 201
Paradigmatic projections in the family matrix 203

Chapter 28 The Religion Matrix **205**
Judaic religious matrix 207
Christian religious matrix 213
Islamic religious matrix 219
A parallel approach to dramatics in the religious matrix 226
Religious fluxion 233
Final considerations of the religious matrix 234
Paradigmatic projection of and in the religious matrix 235

Chapter 29 The School Matrix **237**
School rhetorics 238
School dramatics 239
Paradigmatic projection of the school matrix 246

Chapter 30 The Medical Matrix **247**
Medical rhetorics 247
Medical dramatics 250
Medical emphatics 252
Paradigmatic projection in and from the medical matrix 255

Chapter 31	**The Occultist Matrix**	**257**
	Occultist rhetorics	258
	Occultist dramatics	261
	Paradigmatic projection in the occultist matrix	266
Chapter 32	**The Arts Matrix**	**269**
	The registers of the rhetoric in the artistic matrix	273
	Modalities of artistic dramatics	283
	Paradigm projections related to the artistic matrix	293
Conclusions	**Matricial Symbols and Aesthetic Games**	**295**
References		*301*
Index		*313*

List of Tables

Table 5.1	The Branches of Aesthetics	49
Table 5.2	Bio-aesthetics and Socio-aesthetics	52
Table 6.1	Object-Related Distinctions	57
Table 6.2	Phases of Subjectivity	60
Table 9.1	Prosics and Poesics	80
Table 12.1	Types of Games	94
Table 12.2	Latching-on/by Games	95
Table 14.1	Types and Strata	106
Table 14.2	Phases, Thresholds, Interactions, Processes and Attributes	108
Table 15.1	Strata	110
Table 16.1	Strata, Planes and Axes	117
Table 17.1	Axes	123
Table 19.1	Semiosic and Aesthesic Processes	128
Table 21.1	Strata, Axes and Coordinates	137
Table 21.2	Registers and Sub-registers of Rhetoric	148
Table 22.1	Dramatic Modalities and their Grades	153
Table 23.1	Rhetoric-Dramatic Coupling	156
Table 23.2	Scheme of Correspondences for the Octadic Model	166
Table 24.1	Military Funerals	170
Table 24.2	Types of Pressure	175
Table C.1	Matrixes' Symbols	296

Glossary[1]

Acoustics: communication by means of sound.
Aesthesiology: study of the physical operation of the senses.
Aesthesio-semiotics: semiotics of the senses or of taste.
Aestheticism: a position that considers aesthetic values above all others.
Aesthetics: the study of aesthesic processes.
Aesthetology: study of aesthetic theories.
Aesthesis: processes that involve the subject as a live being open and receptive to the world.
Alliteration: rhetorical figure that means repetition of similar elements (sounds, figures, words, spaces).
Alterity: to be other, synonymous of otherness.
Anacoluthon: rhetorical figure that means a sudden fracture of speech.
Antiphrasis: rhetorical figure that means a change of meaning.

Biome: complex of communities characterized by a distinctive type of flora and fauna, and maintained under climatic conditions of the region.

Captivate: a condition of subjectivity that consists in having a disposition to be delighted and fascinated by other people, objects, events or situations.
Captivity: a condition of subjectivity that makes it susceptible to being absorbed by other people, objects, events or situations.
Catachresis: rhetorical figure in which an absent element is replaced by another.
Com-pression: reciprocal pressure between the dramatics and rhetorics.
Corpo-reality: corporeal reality.
Co-subjectivity: form of subjectivity in relation to others, a shared subjectivity.
Chronotope: for Bakhtin, space-time definition of an event or object.
Culturome: complex of matrixes characterized by distinctive type of activities and habits maintained under particular semiosic and material production partly depending on the regional biome.

De-pression: emptiness by dissipation of the dramatic in the rhetoric.
Dramatic: axis of prosaics in which the attitude of the subject unfolds.

---

1 Since there is a variation in the meanings given to the rhetorical figures among diverse authors, this glossary only tries to define the sense in which they have been used in this text. Definitions given by Barthes (1974), Beristáin (1992) and Ducrot and Todorov (1972) have been consulted.

Ellipsis: rhetorical figure that means suppression of elements.

Emphatics: accentuation of an element upon others in enunciation.

Enunciation/interpretation: dual process that happens in each subject since enouncers interpret at the time they enunciate, and their interlocutors not only interpret but construct and enunciate a version of what they understand.

Ex-pression: activity from the dramatic to the rhetoric.

Exotopy: placed outside.

Fluxion: dramatic modality that points to the flow of enunciation from and towards the subject by retention or expulsion of energy, time or matter.

Heteroglossia: diversity of registers or subregisters in a statement, namely, mixed syntagms.

Hybridization: interpenetration of subjectivities or consciences.

Hyperbole: rhetorical figure by increase or exaggeration.

Identity: matricial construction of the personal or collective image.

Im-pression: activity directed from the rhetoric to the dramatic.

Individuality: singularity of being.

Institution: collective, social organism consolidated by explicit rules.

Kinetics: modality of the dramatic in the display of dynamism or immobility.

Latched-by: passive condition of being clutched or held by something against one's will.

Latching-on: activity of being absorbed or captivated by something or someone.

Lexics: communication by means of verbal syntagms.

Matrix: collective human organism or spontaneously emerged anthropomorphic unit of third order.

Mattergy: abbreviation of matter and energy.

Objective subjectivation: act of the subject to apprehend aspects of the intersubjective reality.

Objective subjectivism: relative to the subject in as much constituted from the objectivity of the social.

Objectivity: intersubjectivity.

Obtuse: outside all orders or expectations, unusual.

Paradigm: context or system of selection in the enunciation or interpretation.

Periphrasis: rhetorical figure that means deflection of language to avoid a taboo.

Phaneroscopy: Peircean term to refer to phenomenology.

Poesics: referred to poetry, artistic or everyday.

Poetics: referred to art, elitist or of the masses.

Polyphony: multiplicity of voices.

Presence: mode of being in life.

Glossary   xiii

Presentation: staging of the self through identity (Goffman).
Prosaics: referred to the aesthetics of daily life.
Prosics: referred to prose, artistic or everyday.
Proxemics: dramatic modality denoting to distance or proximity.

Re-presentation: to present again, another presentation.
Reticence: rhetorical figure that means sudden interruption of speech by a change of mood.
Rhetoric: the axis of prosaics for discursive configuration.
Role: anonymous function of the person determined by the context or circumstance.

Scopics: communication by means of visual and space syntagms.
Semio-aesthetics: aesthetics of communication or of semiosis.
Semio-arts: arts that focus (in form or content) upon processes of semiosis or signification and symbolization.
Semiosis: processes of exchange of signs.
Semiotics: the study of semiosic processes.
Sign: element of the semiosic process that operates by oppositions and differentiation.
Signic: axis relative to the production of signs by oppositions and differentiation.
Signified: effect of signification of a semiosic event in the signifying subject, whether as enouncer or interpreter.
Signifier: subject that enacts and signifies a semiosic event.
Socio-aesthetics: the study of aesthesis in the social context.
Somatics: communication by means of corporeal syntagms.
Sub-ob-jectivism: integrated vision of subjectivism and objectivism as proposed here.
Subjective objectivation: act to make perceivable aspects of one's subjectivity towards the addressee.
Subjective objectivity: processes of intersubjectivity in the subject.
Subjectivity: condition of all live beings in their capacity of perception.
Suspension: rhetorical figure in which the statement is slowed down.
Symbol: element of the semiosic process that operates by association of loads of time, matter or energy.
Syntagm: network of elements present in the enunciation.

Unlatched-by: process of being set free from an involuntary grip over one's senses or sensibility.
Un-latching-onto: Losing hold of something or someone to which one was significantly adhered or attached.

Preface

Aesthetics dazzles. It holds the mystery of fascination whose power can be sometimes so overwhelming as to abruptly transform a social order from one moment to the next. For this very reason, the study of aesthetics can no longer justify circumscribing itself to the narrow limits of the "Fine Arts" or to a few categories such as "beauty" or "the sublime" to which mainstream aesthetic theory habitually restricts it. Nor should it be confined exclusively to the analysis of fashion, design, interior decoration, handicrafts and folklore where the aesthetic intention is quite obvious. As live creatures, we are susceptible of being captivated and also captured by the aesthetic to the degree that it exerts a constituent role in a variety of activities among which the production of imaginaries, the legitimization of power, the construction of knowledge and, particularly, the presentation of identities are most salient.

Through the aesthetic lens the dramaturgical presentation of identities proposed by Goffman acquires a new hue in its dynamics of persuasion, seduction, and negotiation. Every presentation of the self not only informs who we are or pretend to be, but also tries to persuade, affect, fortify, or debilitate others by aesthetic strategies. Thus, when exploring the presentation of identities, we must necessarily arrive at its germinal or breeding locus: the social matrixes. The pertinence of analyzing aesthetics in social interactions became more tangible to me the more I realized that strategies of an aesthetic nature are deliberately wielded in areas as different as politics, marketing, sports, religion, war, and the family, not only in art and entertainment. Society is not an abstract conglomerate of beings piled up or ironed over geographic territories, as often implied in purely statistical approaches. Social organizations take shape through immense qualitative differences: they can be hard and soft, comprise nuclei and edges, provoke attraction and aversion, and are susceptible or resilient to contagion. Matrixes are the formations by which social groups unfold, each and every one entwined by semiosic and aesthesic fibers in a process of increasing diversification.

By aesthetic devices, identities for commodities are fabricated to tempt the consumer, for nation states to achieve cohesion, for religions to instill devotion, and for professionals to persuade upon their credibility. Aesthetics have a definitive role also in arguing for the innocence or guilt of a defendant, in favoring one political candidate over another and certainly in recruiting volunteers for virulent organizations. There is no social group that does not generate some form or another of aesthetics. These quite conspicuous strategies have been, strangely enough, neglected precisely by the school system, wasting a wealth of aesthetic potential for engaging students with their learning process more integrally. More surprising even is that all these manifestations have been totally overlooked by aesthetic theory.

Given the amplitude of its spectrum, the main problem was how to approach these multifarious phenomena without losing the specificity of the aesthetic along the way or arriving at the dead end of panaestheticism. From here arose the need to construct a model that would allow distinguishing the deployment of aesthesis as a basic ingredient in all social interchanges, since human beings relate to one another not merely as functional machines but, with more or less depth, from our condition of sensibility. The octadic model of two coordinates each with four categories here elaborated is intended as a map to guide observation of these interchanges. This effort to integrate all registers of human communication for their simultaneous analysis in a single intersemiotic model (namely the corporeal, verbal, visual-spatial, and acoustic) is essential so as not to lose the complexity and meaning in interactions when a single register, two at most, is focused on, which almost amounts to trying to take pleasure in a symphony through a single instrument.

I was forced to rework the notion of "faculty of sensibility" since it always seemed to me too slippery and elusive a term. What distinguishes it from other human faculties has been the great question that concerned specialists in aesthetics for more than two centuries. The main problem with this notion, inherited mainly from Baumgarten and Kant, is that it implicitly carries the erroneous idea of the compartmentalization of the mind into distinct faculties: intuition, reason, understanding, sensibility, and so on. Neurological research has proved that there is indeed a certain compartmentalization of the cortex, but not in the Kantian sense, since different sensorial and neural operations such as sight, hearing, psychomotor, and language functions are each located in different areas of the brain. Although it is necessary to bring this notion of "sensibility" up to date by contributions from cognitive sciences, I examine it under a concretely corporeal, phenomenological light. The double concept of "*latching-on/by*" developed and applied in this text comes as a result of this approach.

While mainstream aesthetics insists in coping with the same traditional problems such as the ontological status of the work of art and the objectivity of beauty, in everyday life we must face in utter conceptual defenselessness the development of a real technocracy of sensitivity, psycho engineering of subjectivity, and the flourishing of the aesthetics of violence. For that reason, it will be more difficult to rebut that many of the most serious problems of contemporary highly technological societies could be directly, if not exclusively, related to aesthetics. I am referring to drug addiction, racism, delinquency, suicide, alcoholism, domestic violence, child pornography, obesity and even emotional diseases like the chronic depression, obsessive and compulsive disorders, anorexia and bulimia. They are related to an individual's aesthetic dignity and sensibility. Physical and psychological violence that derives into crime, militant fanaticism, and social pathology breaks through a wounded sensitivity.

What is unequivocal after this endeavor is that the field of aesthetics can never become a science in the strict sense of the term, since it is totally bound to subjectivity not only as its object of inquiry, but also as its place of enunciation, interpretation and analysis. If the principle of verifiability of science requires of any observer to corroborate a phenomenon under the same conditions, in studying aesthetics observations vary depending upon the matricial location of the subject.

Preface   xvii

This does not condemn us to sheer solipsism, as there will be coincidences with other observers given the shared interpretative communities and overlapping matrixes in which we stand. Thus, I invite readers to look at everyday life focusing upon aspects not previously considered as related to the aesthetic, and to explore from their own matricial configuration the fascinating manifold of aesthetic activities. What this book offers is a map for this adventure.

We will thus begin by examining many of the basic theoretical problems that have concerned and still obsess aestheticians, most of which have become definite epistemological obstacles for the advancement of aesthetics. We will end in the all too ordinary activities practiced in our culture, from our way of living, our language and bearing, the way we adorn ourselves, how we pay tribute to what we admire and worship, to the ways of legitimizing power, celebrating our triumphs and remembering our dead. The central thesis of this book is that it is not only possible but indispensable to open up aesthetics towards the wealth and complexity of everyday life in its different manifestations. That is exactly what prosaics is about: simply, everyday aesthetics.

We have now realized that Saussure's linguistics were but the tip of the iceberg of an unlimited, pervasive semiosis. I hold that art is no less the tip of a vast and wide ranging aesthesis. Being a communicative process, aesthetics necessarily is linked to semiotics, yet there are key differences between them: from semiotics we obtain meaning and sense, from aesthetics openness and sensitivity; from the former coherence, from the latter adherence. I hope to be able to prove it.

Katya Mandoki
Universidad Autónoma Metropolitana
Mexico, April 2007

Acknowledgement

Once again, I wish to express my gratitude to the Universidad Autónoma Metropolitana in Mexico for its unrelenting support in the carrying out of this work.

PART 1
THE LABYRINTHS OF AESTHETICS

It's super, it's grand, it's a beaut, it's swell, it's peachy, it's the real McCoy, it's nifty, it's gorgeous, it's cool … are not just ordinary words; they are everyday aesthetic judgments. In daily life we constantly and unknowingly pass aesthetic judgments on a variety of situations, people, and incidents. Aesthetic theory, however, ignored these commonplace expressions to concentrate only on the pompous judgments of a group of specialists concerning the relatively minute universe of the artworld. Is the theoretical edifice inhabited by aestheticians really solid enough to justify their contempt for everyday aesthetic judgments? Far from it!

I will first acquaint the reader with the main issues in aesthetics being debated today. My approach will be critical without pretending the complete dismantling of its conceptual scaffold. Such an approach would divert us from the goal set here, namely, to explore aesthetics in everyday life. For that purpose, a concise and synthetic review of ideas inherited principally from Baumgarten and Kant is necessary to clear the way towards the construction of a theoretical frame for observing everyday aesthetic phenomena.

Chapter 1

The Problems of Aesthetics

Problems of definition

The term "aesthetic" has been used to designate an experience, the quality of an object, a feeling of pleasure, classicism in art, a judgment of taste, the capacity of perception, a value, an attitude, the theory of art, the doctrine of beauty, a state of the spirit, contemplative receptivity, an emotion, an intention, a way of life, the faculty of sensibility, a branch of philosophy, a type of subjectivity, the merit of certain forms, or an act of expression. What this large heterogeneous list clearly indicates is that aesthetics has not been able to define its object. In some cases it refers to certain characteristics of the subjects or effects on them. In others, it deals with the qualities of the object, the qualities of an act, or the analysis of a social practice such as art, and even of a certain period or style of that practice.

The definition of a concept like "aesthetics" is even more problematic after the questions Wittgenstein (1958 § 66–72) raised concerning the act of defining. In his example of the concept of "game", he claims there is no common characteristic among the various usages of this word; there are only similarities or *family resemblances* and blurred boundaries. For Wittgenstein: "The meaning of a word is in its use in language." (§ 43) From this approach, if the concept of aesthetics were in its use, then we would have to admit that it is related to unisex aesthetics, aesthetic surgery, or dental aesthetics. It is evident in all these usages that aesthetics refers to beauty and similar ideas such as the pretty, the cute, the agreeable, the elegant, the nice. It is not my intention to restrict the terminologies utilized by dentists or dog and hair stylists, but to establish a theoretical starting point, at least a demarcation, for the term "aesthetic".

Problems of location

There is, on the one hand, the problem set forth by Wittgenstein and applied to aesthetics by Weitz (1989), of whether a definition is at all possible, and on the other hand, whether aesthetics is a discipline. To regard aesthetics as a discipline may be a problem for some, for example Diffey (1984), who considers (but unfortunately does not prove) that aesthetics is not a discipline but a multidisciplinary or an interdisciplinary field. For Diffey there exist disciplines like philosophy, sociology, and psychology that may focus occasionally on aesthetic questions. Aesthetics would then be, for the author, a multidisciplinary problem or object.

Despite Diffey's very brief argumentation in this regard, he pointed out a real problem that has not received enough attention in aesthetic theory, which simply

4 *Everyday Aesthetics*

considers aesthetics as a branch of philosophy. However, there still remains an ambiguity with regard to whether aesthetics is a *discipline*, the objects of which are art and beauty (or significant form, symbolic expression, sensuous experience), or whether it is an *object* of various disciplines like psychology, sociology, philosophy, and history of art.

If aesthetics were an object of various disciplines, we would possess a theoretical corpus from psychology, sociology, semiotics or history, focused on aesthetics. This corpus exists in a fragmentary state only. There is no history of aesthetics, but only of aesthetic theories (for example, Bayer 1984). There is no sociology of aesthetics, but sociological views of artistic phenomena (for example, Hauser 1969), or psychological approaches to the perception of form (Arnheim 1985). If we were to define aesthetics exclusively as the study of art (decidedly not the position taken here) we could agree, and very partially so, with a conception of aesthetics as the object of various disciplines, since there is sociology of art, history of art, and theory of art. This definition of aesthetics as the study of art would not, however, be acceptable to a large number of aestheticians who prefer to define it as the study of beauty, whereas art would be the subject of another discipline namely, art theory: Nwodo (1984), for example.

On the other hand, if aesthetics were a discipline, there would be a department of aesthetics at virtually every university (most disciplines exist first and foremost as departments in universities). Since that is not the case, students interested in aesthetics come from departments like philosophy, and in rare cases from art history. Aesthetics has thus been a branch of another discipline, philosophy, and not a discipline in the proper sense, the same as ontology, ethics, or metaphysics. As Berleant has argued (1991, 1): "Nor again can aesthetics claim independence as a discipline, for many of its leading ideas have been transplanted from broader philosophical ground. Moreover, for a variety of reasons the study we call aesthetics is not exclusively philosophical."

The criticism that Wolff (1983) directs at aesthetics for its lack of a sociological dimension proves that this branch of philosophy is adamant in not converting itself into a multidiscipline. So far, there have been almost no non-philosophical approaches to aesthetics, and these have always been marginal. One such is Bourdieu's (1987) critique of aesthetics based upon this point. He even accuses aesthetics of plagiarizing categories of social sciences and disguising them as its own. He criticizes the ahistorical character of aesthetic categories and aesthetic experience, which ignores the social conditions that allow the emergence of such categories and experiences.

The traditional approach to the study of aesthetics is related to philosophical tendencies from which various theories arise.[1] To the best of my knowledge, none of

---

1 Analytical philosophy, based upon Russell, Moore, Weitz, and Goodman, is prevalent nowadays mainly among Anglo-American aestheticians. Other approaches are, in very general terms: a) phenomenology inherited from Husserl, Heidegger, Merleau Ponty, and Dufrenne; b) theories of language and semiotics backed by Cassirer, Shapiro, Wittgenstein, Jakobson, Eco, and Mukarovský; c) Kantian developments taken by Schaper, Guyer, and Crowther; d) Marxist aesthetics imposed by Zhdanov, fathered by Lukacs, and followed by Sánchez Vázquez, Bujarin, Kosik, Della Volpe, Gramsci, Lunacharsky, Benjamin, Adorno, and Eagleton; e)

The Problems of Aesthetics 5

these theories or tendencies constitutes a discipline; rather, each views art, aesthetics and beauty from its own methodological perspective.

Currently, aesthetics is not multidisciplinary precisely because it rejects any non-philosophical challenge (in some cases, even a challenge from non-analytic aesthetics) be it sociological (as claimed by Wolff), anthropological, biological, psychological, semiotic, economic or political. One cannot blame aesthetics for being so hermetic. Viewed as a branch of philosophy, it cannot do otherwise. Its limitations could be removed by means of another orientation, not as a branch of philosophy, but as the interdiscipline that Diffey apparently had in mind.

Aesthetics is not only a philosophical problem. It is also a social, symbolic, communicative, political, historical, anthropological, even neurological and especially pedagogical one as well. It therefore requires an interdisciplinary, comprehensive orientation. I am proposing an interdisciplinary rather than a transdisciplinary aesthetics since the purpose is to integrate and not to transcend disciplinary approaches, many of which have managed to construct methodological tools that are indispensable for dealing with aesthetic problems. To sum up, aesthetics should not be treated as a branch of philosophy but requires a multidisciplinary approach. As I will contend in Part II, the aesthetic is not only about the ontological status of artworks or beauty but a complex dimension that cuts across social life in a manner similar to the political, economic, technological or semiotic.

Problems of distinction

There have been numerous attempts to define aesthetics and to distinguish it from the philosophy of art. With the provocative title of "Philosophy of art versus aesthetics" Christopher S. Nwodo (1984) made a historical investigation beginning with Plato, passing through Thomas Aquinas, continuing with Kant, and culminating with Heidegger, Kovacs, Maritain, Steinkraus, and Lipman to contend that these are two distinct disciplines. The proposal as such is not new, since more than half a century ago Wilhelm Worringer, Max Dessoir and Emil Utitz proposed the *Allgemeine Kunstwissenschaft* or general science of the arts as independent from aesthetics. In fact, art history is becoming increasingly more and more unconnected to aesthetics since philosophical problems are rarely addressed in this field. Proof of this are the publications and clearly differentiated interests of each area: there are very few art historians interested in problems of aesthetic theory, while philosophers of aesthetics rarely consult textbooks by art historians.

For Nwodo, aesthetics would be the theory that studies beauty, leaving art to the theory of art. He eludes the objections regarding the pertinence of the concept of beauty for aesthetic theory and the arguments about its uselessness (like those posed

---

idealism in Croce, Schopenhauer, Collingwood, Schiller, and Fichte; f) intentionalists or expressivists such as Langer, Ayer; g) essentialists such as Kainz; h) deconstructionists like Derrida, Culler, and so on; i) analytic-institutionalists such as Danto and Dickie, j) pragmatists like Dewey followed by Shusterman; k) feminists, namely Korsmeyer, Hine, Brand, and Langer (Cassandra) among others; and l) environmental aesthetics initiated by Berleant and Carlson, as well as Haapala, and von Bonsdorff.

6 *Everyday Aesthetics*

by John Dewey, Richard Hamann, and Mikel Dufrenne). The problem with Nwodo's proposal is not so much that, in contemporary art, beauty progressively lost the dominant role it played in traditional academic art, although this seems to be one of the reasons for the distinctions pointed out. The problem is that, as a category, beauty lacks sufficient relevance in itself for establishing a whole disciplinary field around it, say "beautology". If that were to be the case, then there is no reason why other disciplines such as "uglology", "sublimology", "tragicology", "grotesqueology", "sordidology", "comicology", and "triviology" could not be equally established. With this reduction to the absurd it is evident that it is not possible to establish a discipline upon one of the various aesthetic categories. Anyway, in principle we can agree with Nwodo about the importance of differentiating aesthetics (if not as the theory of beauty) from philosophy of art.

Art is a technique for the production of sensitive effects, and, thus, constitutes a part of aesthetics. At this point, the role sensibility has for Baumgarten and orthodox aesthetics is still valid, except that by aesthetics we may not understand the study of beauty and art, but of activities related to our sensibility as live beings.[2] Beauty is only one of the many, many categories in the production of sensitive effects. There are almost as many aesthetic categories as there are adjectives in a language, and art is only one of its manifestations. Besides, not only art, but also science involves aesthetic considerations (cf. Osborne 1981, 1982, 1984, 1986; Heisenberg 1974, Engler 1990, Wechsler 1978).

Aesthetics is definitely an elusive phenomenon difficult to define by the traditional philosophical procedure of necessary and sufficient reasons. It is difficult to locate as a specialized discipline or a multidisciplinary object, and hard to distinguish from related fields, such as philosophy of art, art history and art criticism. What remains possible, however, is marking its boundaries despite its blurred edges. I shall attempt to do that in Part II.

---

2   Rubert de Ventós (1969) and John Dewey ([1934] 1980) also understood aesthetics as basically related to sensibility, following Baumgarten's initiative. All three philosophers, however, limited the aesthetic to the artistic.

Chapter 2

The Fetishes of Aesthetics

The fetish of beauty

The notion of beauty has been, and continues to be, the cornerstone of aesthetic theory. As such, it has generated numerous problems. Consequently, Nwodo (among other authors) proposed a distinction between aesthetics and philosophy of art that defines the former centering on beauty as its main disciplinary object, whereas the artistic would pertain exclusively to the latter. It must be emphasized, however, that beauty (as truth, justice or goodness) is an effect of language and not an ontological fact: it results from the conversion of an evaluative adjective (beautiful, true, just, and good) into a noun (beauty, truth, justice, and goodness). It thus appears to have been existing on its own, independently from the subject who, in fact, originally judged something as being good, just, true, and beautiful. This is how beauty becomes a fetish, appearing to have powers of its own and to exist independently of the subject.

All these evaluations are made by persons who depend on certain conventions to decode the meanings that "good", "beautiful", and "just" can take and to select the objects these may be attributed to. This explains why the deformation of the lower lip among the people of certain African tribes, the flattening of the forehead among the Mayans, the malformation of Chinese women's feet, the silicone injection into the breasts and of collagen into the lips among Western women, the eyelid surgery among oriental women, tattoos, laceration, piercing and lifting can be considered by some as beautiful. In similar terms, the hand amputation of those accused of theft among orthodox Moslems, pouring acid over Pakistani women's faces, the death penalty in several states of the USA, the sale of children and women into prostitution and slavery in many countries are considered justifiable in their respective social contexts. The existence of the phlogiston or of ether in the universe has also been taken as truth during certain periods in the history of science.

I am not trying here to argue for total relativism: on the contrary, whereas beauty is context dependent, justice is definitely not as it involves the absolute principle of life and of individual integrity. Rather, my point is that, whereas justice is absolute concerning human life, since its consequences are irreversible, beauty is relative and does not exist in itself. Beauty is a linguistic effect used by a particular subject to describe personal experiences and social conventions, not things that exist independently of perception. The notion of beauty is a linguistic categorization of a non-linguistic experience, although it can be provoked by language (in the case of literature and poetry), or provoke the production of language (the typical case, art criticism). Beauty subsists only in the subjects who experience it, just as life only exists in live beings.

8 *Everyday Aesthetics*

It is not enough, however, to declare that beauty is a fetish in order to get rid of it in aesthetic theory. Mikel Dufrenne (1973, 1viii), for one, warns us: "we shall avoid invoking the concept of the beautiful, because it is a notion that, depending on the extension we give it, seems either useless for our purposes or dangerous". But then he ends up declaring: "Basically, it is not we who decide what is beautiful. The object itself decides, and it does so by manifesting itself. The aesthetic judgment is passed from within the object rather than within us. We do not define the beautiful, we ascertain what the object is." (Dufrenne 1973, lxii)

The author questions the fetishism of beauty, but ends up inventing another even worse: objects that "decide by themselves", are capable of establishing "an aesthetic judgment from within", and define themselves as beautiful. In something he is right, namely in the danger of the notion of beauty, that, in his case, laid out this snare for him.

For John Dewey too, the notion of beauty, for theoretical ends, becomes an obstructive term.

> Beauty is at the furthest remove from an analytic term, and hence from a conception that can figure in theory as a means of explanation or classification. Unfortunately, it has been hardened into a peculiar object; emotional rapture has been subjected to what philosophy calls hypostatization, and the concept of beauty as an essence of intuition has resulted. For purposes of theory, it then becomes and obstructive term. (Dewey [1934] 1980, 129–30)

Thus we might follow Dewey's more coherent direction and assert that beauty is not a quality of objects in themselves but an effect of the relation that a subject establishes with a particular object from a particular social context of evaluation and interpretation. It is the subject's sensibility that discovers its objects and sees in them what it has put into them, not according to a personal whim but depending on its socio-cultural, perceptive, and evaluative conditions. In this sense, we return to the starting point from which philosopher David Hume began to reflect by the eighteenth century on the problems of taste and beauty to settle them respectively as diverse and relative.

The fetish of the artwork

I do not intend to criticize here the exaggerated importance given to artistic production in aesthetic theory. What interests me in this section is analyzing fetishism in its literal sense: the work of art converted into a fetish, possessor of human and superhuman powers and capacities, or even magical attributes. From a Marxist point of view, Terry Eagleton (1990) detects with great perspicuity that the work of art has been for aesthetic theory a sort of subject that embodies all the values the bourgeoisie sought to legitimize since the Enlightenment. Values like autonomy, self-regulation, self-determination, lawless legality, self-management, and the individual as an end-in-itself (all attributed to the work of art by aesthetic theory) provide the perfect model of subjectivity that the early capitalist society required. This idea became so effective that art acquired greater rights than the very subject it tried to resemble or constitute in what Eagleton denominates as "ideology of the aesthetic". In other words, the

The Fetishes of Aesthetics

bourgeoisie of the eighteenth century imagined a subject whose characteristics were metaphorically projected into the work of art, but all subsequent aesthetic theory took this image literally. Hence, the emergence of views of the artistic artifact as in itself capable of expression, of autonomy, of meaning, of attitudes, and of values. Kant clearly indicated that the harmony we ascribe to the object is, in fact, the projection of our cognitive faculties of imagination and understanding upon it, and not a specific factor within the work itself. Analytical aesthetics, however, have taken literally what in its origin was a metaphorical expression, and thoroughly tries to prove the ontological status of beauty and of the work of art as existing by themselves, independently of the subject.

The idea that a work of art "expresses" is an effect of language. It can be said; I have just said it. Picasso's *Guernica* "expresses" the terror of a massacre that occurred in 1937. There it is, said. This doesn't mean, however, that because something is enunciable, it is possible (I can say: the griffon is eating lentils; enunciable albeit impossible) and much less real. This is to conflate language with reality (although reality is, in fact, basically constituted by language). To invoke is not so easy, nor is magic so accessible. To say that art expresses does not imply that this is indeed the case. Works of art don't talk; language is the ability of the subject only, not of inanimate objects. A text doesn't say anything. It is the subject who, through the text, produces certain meanings. This mechanism of fetishization, of attributing powers and capacities to objects, is the same Marx saw in the relation of the worker with the commodities he himself produces seeing only relations among objects, rather than social relations between human beings mediated by commodities. It's true that there are ways of speaking that allow us to envision an object being expressive. In this case, however, the expression that seems to be found in a work of art is only that of the artist, coagulated as a trace in the object. Whoever is expressing is always and only a subject who is then interpreted by another subject.

There is, however, no symmetry between aesthetic enunciation and aesthetic interpretation, since the former depends on the latter and not vice versa. An act of enunciation is aesthetic if, and only if, it is interpreted as such, even if only by the enouncers themselves. On the other hand, objects, events, persons, acts that did not emerge with any aesthetic intention can nonetheless become aesthetic as a result of interpretation. A murmuring voice can have no meaning to a certain subject but be intensely seductive or evocative to another. Gadamer was right in claiming that aesthetics is mainly an act of interpretation, since appreciation and valuation are always interpretative. As for Dewey, "the word 'esthetic' refers ... to experience as appreciative, perceiving, enjoying. It denotes the consumer's rather than the producer's standpoint" ([1934] 1980, 47), it is an act of reception.

Among the best-known theoreticians who ground aesthetic theory on the notion of "expression" is Susanne Langer (1979, 240). She understands art as symbolic expression created for our perception through form expressing human feelings directed to our senses or imagination. Even if what she says sounds reasonable, art, however, does not "express" any human feeling but it is the artist's feelings and thoughts that are interpreted by the spectator through the work of art, and who lets herself be emotionally aroused by it. Allow me once more to insist that it is not art, artworks or forms that express; it is artists who do, just as it is not language that signifies but the subject who articulates it to produce signification. Art is not the expression of emotions; there are spectators who perceive and interpret certain properties of objects like sounds, colors or brush strokes as an expression of emotions stemming from their own experience with that object.

Things are not capable of acting; a medicine does not cure, nor does a text please (as Barthes would imply by "the pleasures of the text"). It is the patient who cures himself by taking the medicine, and a reader who delights herself by reading a text. This effect of fetishization is a habit so deeply rooted in language, that it would be a titanic enterprise, if not an impossible one, trying to defeat it. What is worth emphasizing, however, is that we are dealing with an effect of language, and not a real fact; it is a way of speaking, not of being. When one and the other are confused, there appear aberrations like the "objectivity of beauty", the "expression of the work of art", the "pleasures of the text" (and not through the text), and the "sensual objects", or "aesthetic objects" (literally objects—not subjects—capable of experience or sensibility).

Dufrenne acknowledges that an object is only an object for a subject, but a few paragraphs later he says: "The aesthetic object is nothing more than sensuous in all its glory, whose form, ordering it, manifests plenitude and necessity, and that carries within itself and immediately reveals the meaning that animates it." (Dufrenne 1987, 5) He is suggesting that an object can be sensuous, capable of sensuality and animated by meaning. Fetishism in aesthetics is similar to that of religion and witchcraft: if the statue of a saint can make miracles or a doll can summon an evil spell, a work of art can express. It is only a matter of faith.

Let me warn the reader that whenever "language betrays me" in cases of conventional fetishization, please read instead something like "in case I betray myself through language". We must be careful about magical thinking: it is fine for the child who perceives that he is followed by the moon, that toys break, clothes get dirty, and trees move away from the car window. If language "engenders" concepts, it also "disguises" its effects as being part of reality. We all practice a form of animism in language that anthropomorphizes things and invests them with human qualities. In an artwork, this animism is more tempting since it is created to exhibit the traces of human activity, of the artist's emotions and attitudes. In theory, nevertheless, this linguistic animism must be avoided whenever possible, because a theoretical construction can collapse by confusing facts with words.

The fetish of the aesthetic object

This is by far the most deep-rooted and problem-ridden fetish of aesthetics. To begin with, the term "aesthetic object" is already an oxymoron since the aesthetic denotes, by definition and etymology, the capacity to perceive, appreciate, enjoy, and experience. How then, taken literally, can an object perceive, appreciate, enjoy, or experience? Dufrenne, for example, starts his discussion of aesthetic experience and aesthetic object by confronting the problem of the circularity of definitions, namely: the aesthetic object is that which is captured through aesthetic experience, and an aesthetic experience is that which is established in relation to the aesthetic object. He

The Fetishes of Aesthetics

states that by aesthetic experience he will refer to the spectator's and not the artist's, although it may exist in both. This distinction appears to me totally irrelevant to the problem he intends to face, since the artist is always already (as deconstructionists love to say) a spectator, the very first concerning his own work. Dufrenne tries to evade the idealism and the psychologism implied in his approach when he affirms that:

> [P]erception, aesthetic or non-aesthetic, does not create a new object, and that object as aesthetically perceived is not different from the thing objectively known or created that solicits this perception (in this case, the perception of the work of art). Within the aesthetic experience that unites them, we can therefore distinguish the object from its perception in order to study each separately. (Dufrenne 1973, xlix)

I think, however, that Dufrenne is mistaken when he states that "perception, aesthetic or non-aesthetic, doesn't create a new object". It definitely creates it! If we consider that the object is only something physical, a thing, his statement is true: we do not produce physically a thing only by perceiving it (even though we do produce it mentally qua object of perception, we produce a synaptic map so to say). But any object, say a urinal for Duchamp, when aesthetically perceived becomes an aesthetic object, and when presented in an artistic institution becomes a work of art. Here we witness a metamorphosis of a physical, functional and commercial object into a sensorially or formally appreciated object (even if that was not Duchamp's point, I was surprised to find that so it seems for some aestheticians who estimate the urinal for its form, color and texture!) and then into an artistic object.

Dufrenne's mistake results from his lack of differentiation between the aesthetic and the non-aesthetic, and between the aesthetic and the artistic. The object qua aesthetic depends upon the subject's aesthetic appreciation. Its physical existence, on the other hand, does not depend on this judgment. The object perceived aesthetically is indeed qualitatively different from the thing used functionally. A urinal proposed by Duchamp as *Fountain* and exhibited in a museum as a work of art is different from a urinal solely appreciated by its shape and texture in a bathroom furniture store, and different again from the one utilized to soothe a physiological urgency. We are talking here about three distinct types of objects: the artistic, the aesthetic, and the functional. All three are objects only to a subject who interprets them as such depending on the code used and the context of observation.

Supposing that instead of the *Brillo* boxes which Warhol replicated in wood to present them as artworks (Danto's recurrent example), he would have used real ones (that is, the same cardboard boxes for packaging materials taken from a supermarket). These boxes might physically be the same supermarket items, but as aesthetic objects they are qualitatively different from the boxes as functional objects because they are solemnly presented within the consecrating spaces of museums and art galleries, and thus acquire a particular social value.[1] It is necessary to distinguish,

---

1   It reminds me of the scaffolding I rented from a company to elaborate and present my artwork *Histogram* at the gallery of the Auditorio Nacional in 1985 in Mexico City. The work got the prize at a national contest and exhibition of alternative art—thus conferred the status of art. So, was the scaffolding used art?

12 *Everyday Aesthetics*

therefore, between the *utilitarian object* that depends on its being put to use, the *artistic object* that depends on an institution to be classified as such (cf. Dickie 1974, Danto 1964), and the *aesthetic object* that depends on the aptitude of a subject to enjoy, appreciate, or endure it.

The circularity in the definition of aesthetic object-aesthetic experience that frightens Dufrenne must certainly be faced and resolved. Its solution lies not with regard to the aesthetic object, but in relation to the subject apt for aesthetic appreciation. To deny that the aesthetic originates in the subject—psychologism or not—equals to denying that knowledge originates in the subject. Here we have the positivistic dream of some aestheticians who believe that all problems of aesthetic theory would dissolve as soon as specific objects, features or qualities could be established so distinctly that they automatically, inescapably, produce an aesthetic experience in any subject exposed to them. This concept leads them to emit ideas like "What the artwork expects from the spectator" and "What the artwork brings to the spectator" (Dufrenne 1973, Part 1 and 2 of Chapter 3). Similar sentences can be found in other texts by the same author, for whom: "the aesthetic object incessantly exercises a demand on the one who performs or observes it; through this demand it reveals a desire-to-be that somehow warrants its being." (Dufrenne 1987, 6) Dufrenne passes from fetishism of beauty to fetishism of the aesthetic object, namely, from fetishism that hipostasizes an idea to one that anthropomorphizes the object. In both cases, the object is endowed, albeit metaphorically (but ends up taken literally), with the human capacities of perception, joy, assessment of beauty, emotionality, expression, sensibility, and sensuality. The aptitudes of the subject and the relations that can be established with the object are hallucinated as aptitudes of the object itself and the relations that it would establish with the subject.

The conclusion set forth here diverges from that of Dufrenne: it is indeed necessary to distinguish the physical object from the aesthetic object, since the latter depends on sensibility, whereas the former does not necessarily do so. Dufrenne's goal in his analysis is the distinction between aesthetic experience and aesthetic object. This can only be established by considering the aesthetic object a product of an aesthetic relation that a subject establishes with it, and not the reverse (the subject is not the product of the object). Dufrenne wanted to elude the psychologism implicit in this definition; and yet, the positivism that permeates his writing (strange for a phenomenologist, as it seems a metaphorical positivism) is equally dangerous. We cannot deny that we are impinging upon the field of psychology when we talk of emotions, perception, and sensibility. But what is the problem with having objects common to aesthetics and psychology? Infection perhaps? Analytic aestheticians tenaciously defend their discipline from psychologism for fear of being absorbed into it (see Chapter 4). That is why they hold on fast and steady to the aesthetic object, to beauty, and to the work of art understanding them as "objective aesthetic objects". In their endeavor to distance themselves from psychologism, they increasingly subordinate the subject to the object. That is exactly what Dufrenne (1973, l–li) proposes to do when he asserts that the definition of aesthetic experience is too wobbly "because we do not introduce enough precision into the definition of the aesthetic object. And how shall we introduce it?—by subordinating the experience

The Fetishes of Aesthetics

to the object instead of the object to the experience, and by defining the object itself through the work of art."[2]

This type of conceptual endeavor seeks a touchstone or a definite object from which to construct its theory. However, in this attempt it is easily forgotten that, after all, it was originally art, aesthetic objects, qualities and shapes that this theory intended to explain, judge, evaluate, justify, and legitimize; these are its problems rather than its foundations. Mainstream aesthetics will corroborate the privileged status of certain objects, artworks and, by contagion, of certain subjects who are in contact with them, namely, aestheticians and art historians, although there are many other objects, subjects, and events pertinent to aesthetics. Aestheticians continue to work alone in the museums, libraries and art galleries with their coffee table books and academic journals so as not to be disturbed by the smell, heat, and sweat of everyday life.

---

2 Another author, who not only shares this belief of the independent existence of the aesthetic object, but of the "aesthetic qualities", is A. MacC. Armstrong (1987, 7), who even states that "the configuration (*shapeliness*) has proven to be a quality that is a real quality, a quality inherent to the object, and a quality that is normative or different from morality, as well as from utility".

Chapter 3

The Myths of Aesthetics

The myth of the opposition art/reality and aesthetics/everyday life

Despite John Dewey's insistence on the continuity of art and reality and his arguments against the "museum view" of the aesthetic, it is still common to find in aesthetic theory the presupposition that art and beauty are spheres separated from the ordinary world and, therefore, those who write about them have a secret access to them. By applying categories like "the autonomy of art" and "distanced contemplation", mainstream aesthetics separates the aesthetic from ordinary life and art from reality invoking essentialist and supra-historic truths often with strongly religious hues. This idealization of aesthetics is common to romanticists, philosophical idealists, and Marxists alike.

Such contrast between art and reality, echoed in the separation between aesthetics and everyday life, is one of the most common problems posed by artists, critics, and art theoricians. Marxist aesthetics—as well as the diatribe prevalent up to the mid-twentieth century between artists in favor of "art for art's sake" versus those siding with "committed art"—were based on this false problem. Underlying this is the myth of the disconnection between art and life, art and society, and aesthetics and the everyday. In the first case, art was supposedly able to afford a total separation from reality, while in the latter it had to search for an active connection towards social change. Art, however, no matter how elitist it may be, is and has always been a social product and is linked to society. Even the position of "art for art's sake" implies social commitment, namely a commitment to non-commitment with certain political or social groups, and consequently to remain tacitly committed to others.

Socialist realism (such as Brecht's theater and Mexican muralism) believed in the direct connection between art and reality to the degree that it postulated the transformation of reality by means of art. This tendency was concerned with the problem of whether to elevate the masses toward art or to lower art to the masses. The relation art–reality was soon substituted by the need to resolve the elitism in the fine arts for its propagandistic instrumentation. The point was to transform highbrow art— a manifestation of the aristocracy and the bourgeoisie—into a cultural manifestation that included the masses and the proletariat. It failed because the masses have their own artists, conventions, and genres, while these elite artists simply transplanted their own conventions into another, quite foreign, horizon of expectations. What must be noted is that art and reality, like aesthetics and the everyday, are totally entwined, not thanks to the explicit will of the artist, but because there is nothing further, beneath or beyond reality. Even dreams are real, as dreams. The effort to unite art-reality is, therefore, unnecessary. Moreover, when art manifests itself as a mechanism for evasion or for emancipation (what the Frankfurt School intended

16   *Everyday Aesthetics*

to promote) it is fatally and irremediably immersed in reality, whether indexically pointing at it by the evasion itself (silence is very eloquent) or by assuming particular sides for criticism or emancipation.

By contrast, Mijail Bakhtin and Walter Benjamin recognize the insertion of the artistic into reality, though the former understands this relation in ethical terms when he states that: "A poet must recognize that his poetry is guilty of the triviality of life, and the man in life must know that his lack of demand and seriousness in his existential problems are guilty of the sterility of art. Art and life are not the same, but they must be united in me, within the unit of my responsibility." (Bakhtin 1990, 11–12)[1]

In his classic essay "The work of art in the era of mechanical reproduction", Benjamin recognizes that technologies of industrial production correspond directly with the production of artistic images, and that there is no such separation between art and reality. Adorno criticizes Benjamin for his lack of mediation and his reduction of artistic phenomena to the technical and social. Nonetheless, Benjamin was right in detecting the intimacy in the relation between art and its technological environment. Contemporary visual production of great aesthetic quality in film and video attests to this fact. Similarly, recorded music or Vasareli's visual artworks reproduced by thousands through mechanical processes as in an art factory do not invalidate their artistic status. Even science fiction and genres of the fantastic are always anchored in some region of reality and knitted with the very fabric of the real so as to maintain a significant degree of plausibility.

It is true, as Adorno denounced, that there is alienation, reification, and dogmatism in everyday life. But artistic reality, if one could separate it from everyday life, also exhibits alienation from less agreeable aspects of reality, reification of beauty, and the tendency to dogmatically reproduce its own values, ideology, categories, and established hierarchies. To seek refuge within the confines of art and beauty is the typical resort of a puritanical gesture that nonetheless always fails, because the world of art is the same world of everybody else with its meanness and greatness, its refinement and its coarseness. Greatness and refinement are part of ordinary extra-artistic reality, as meanness and vulgarity are part of the arts.

Art is an activity with various facets and uses; it may be pecuniary, linguistic, ethical, cathartic, libidinal, aimed at affirming the author's or the owner's prestige in the process of social distinction, and political in the forging of national and ethnic identities. Nowadays, artists' names and signatures circulate within the artistic matrix by conventions and hierarchies similar to credit cards or paper money in the market. The value of a signed plastic card, like that of an artist's signature on a paper napkin with a doodle or a urinal in a museum, are purely conventional, and they function as signs and symbols by a system of differences and oppositions. Not that art has prostituted herself since she was never a virgin; and this despite of, or rather due to, her intimate relations with religion.

To insist on the separation between art and life equals to believing in the separation between science, technology, philosophy, and life. All are ways for the appropriation of reality, ways of seeing and understanding life, and of transforming it. Just as a "butterfly effect" that could cause, by successive effects, a hurricane on

---

1   All translations from Spanish texts to English are mine.

The Myths of Aesthetics 17

the other side of the planet, the alterations in one area of social life generate changes in many other spheres, among them, of course, art.

This myth of the opposition of aesthetics and everyday life is so deep-rooted that philosophers of aesthetics don't even consider it necessary to make it explicit. When they accidentally collide with the relation between the aesthetic and the everyday without the alibi of beauty, they simply ignore it, as does Dickie in his criticism of Stolnitz, or evade it; and if they face it, they contradict themselves. Let me refer to the curious case of Jerome Stolnitz (1992, 10), who defines the aesthetic attitude as "disinterested and sympathetic attention to and contemplation of *any object of awareness whatsoever*, exclusively for its own sake alone" (emphasis mine). Notice that he states that *any object* is apt for an aesthetic contemplation, but then he recants when he mentions the possibility of an aesthetic experience in a dirty market of a run-down suburb. Stolnitz comments "Evidence of this kind [of an aesthetic experience in a shabby market] cannot establish that *all* objects can be aesthetic objects. When such evidence is multiplied, however, it makes this assumption a reasonable one at the outset of aesthetic inquiry." (Stolnitz 1992, 13) This affirmation is very much surprising for two reasons: first, because, as mentioned before, it flagrantly contradicts his definition that includes "any object", to deny it later; and second, because no philosopher, much less an aesthetician, has until now depended on a quantitative approach like "the multiplication of evidence" to make a statement. Stolnitz contradicts himself again at the end of his article, reaffirming that "anything at all, whether sensed or perceived, whether it is the product of imagination or conceptual thought, can become the object of aesthetic attention". Still, he does not develop the idea any further, but just drops it like a hot potato on the lap of the reader. Dickie (1992) mercilessly analyzes Stolnitz's position, yet he does not make any reference to this most controversial affirmation, nor does he comment on this contradiction, since he takes for granted (and his examples prove it), that the aesthetic is limited to the artistic.

Extending the aesthetic to the everyday results in really threatening specialists, since it exposes the field of aesthetics to the risk of collapse when divested from its object, be it beauty or art. If aesthetics is not confined to art and beauty, it vanishes right before the terrified eyes of aestheticians. (cf. Chapter 16 on panaestheticism)

The myth of aesthetic disinterest

The idea of aesthetic disinterest already appears in Shaftesbury and Hume as a reaction against bourgeois' egotism and coarse instrumentality, but it was consolidated precisely with Kant's *Critique of Judgment* § 2. He defines aesthetic experience as a "disinterested delight" in beauty to differentiate it from interested delight in the agreeable and the good. For Kant there is neither practical interest in the object or through it in aesthetic experience, nor in the existence of the object or owning it. Kant, as Shaftesbury and Hume, institutes the concept of "disinterest" to prevent "tarnishing" the judgment of beauty with worldly preoccupations and to differentiate aesthetic delight (as disinterested) from the delight in the good or the agreeable (considered as interested).

18   *Everyday Aesthetics*

It is necessary to recognize, however, that if the concept of "disinterested delight" would hold, it should encompass as well the delight in the good, and in the agreeable. In other words, it is possible to feel "disinterested delight" not only in beauty, but also in an agreeable conversation or a kind deed. One can also enjoy the representation of Iago's wickedness, or the disagreeable appearance of the hunchback of Notre Dame. Additionally, one must admit, no matter how shameful, that there can be "disinterested delight" in evil when it is enjoyed for its own sake alone, since human beings are capable of disinterest in the Kantian sense not only with regard to beauty but also to ugliness and depravity. We cannot take the easy way out of dismissing these real cases on the ground that they are immoral. We are aestheticians, not moralists, and it is our duty to understand them, even if morally repugnant, or rather precisely because of it. In any case, it is not so easy to differentiate objects that provide disinterested delight from those of interested delight, as Kant pretended, and even less to prove that there is disinterest in this and not in that delight, since to experience delight already involves an interest due to its pleasurable effects.

This myth of Kantian disinterest is still upheld by many contemporary authors like Stolnitz, Crowther (1987), and others. Berleant (1986 I, II, 1991) and Dickie (1974), on the other hand, question it and propose respectively the term "engagement", or "focused attention". For Berleant (1992, 18) "the notion of unitary perception in aesthetic experience has thus gradually taken form as an alternative to the theory of disinterestedness". For Dickie, what counts is exclusively the attention given to an object;[2] disinterest (a mere synonym to attention), becomes consequently an irrelevant notion. It may be worth noting that, oddly enough, when discussing the concept of Kantian "disinterest", many Anglo-American aestheticians relate it to "attention" rather than to "delight", which was the original sense used by Kant.

For reasons different from those of Dickie, and more akin to Berleant's, I maintain that aesthetic appreciation is never disinterested. There is always an interest of the subject on the object, whether to derive pleasure, satisfy curiosity, understand or explore it, get emotional nourishment, be excited, involved, or aroused. Crowther (1987) finds an excellent example to illustrate Kantian disinterest and advocate on its behalf: a mirage in the desert. According to him, we aesthetically appreciate the mirage of an oasis without having the least interest in its physical existence. We could have a utilitarian interest in its existence if we were dead thirsty (that for Crowther is not aesthetic interest), but to appreciate the beauty of that imaginary landscape we don't need its material existence. This example is so good that it not only invalidates Kantian disinterest, despite Crowther's intentions, but also involuntarily refutes the notion of "aesthetic aspects" proposed by Crowther. Let us see how that happens. Obviously in the mirage there is no objective aspect to detect, regardless of the amount of attention paid to it, because there is no "aesthetic object" as understood by the naïve realism of analytic aesthetics. What, then, are

---

2   Dickie argues that there is only one way of listening or attending to music in his example of Jones who listens to it to take an exam the next day, and Smith, who does not have an ulterior motive. He does, I insist: Smith's ulterior motive could be his satisfaction. There are as many ways to listen to music or to see a painting as there are subjects that relate to them, but in all of them there exists an interest.

The Myths of Aesthetics

the "aesthetic aspects" that attention detects in this case? In fact, aspects only exist through a perceptive or aspectual activity of the subject (call it the "aspector"). As far as disinterest goes when perceiving that imaginary landscape, find a single spectator who would not prefer the landscape to exist physically in order to enter it and increase the delight it can provide: to smell its aromas, taste the refreshing water, and feel the cool shade of its palm trees. (This refutes, unwillingly, also the myth of the aesthetic distancing, which will be dealt with in the next section.) The mirage as such is purely visual, but it "seduces" the subject who is certainly interested in its physical existence for achieving a more integral, intense experience. Crowther is fascinated by the mirage of the mirage because he shares the prevailing idea in aesthetic theory that contemplation from a distance is the aesthetic experience par excellence. He forgets that aesthetic delight in a landscape, as that in architecture, depends also on exploring it from the inside, smelling the wood, brick, leather .... You do not enjoy equally the façade of a building when reproduced by photography as you do the architectonic work in its entirety.

The strongest argument against this idea of disinterest lies in the worldwide reaction to the vandalism against Michelangelo's *Pieta* some years ago, the indignation against the destruction of monumental Buddha by the Talibans in Afghanistan and the looting of cultural treasures from the Baghdad museum during the war on Iraq. We cannot remain indifferent to the destruction of beautiful designs and works of art precisely because of the aesthetic value they have for us. There is no doubt that aesthetic appreciation demands the existence of the objects that provide it; and it is impossible to remain detached from their existence or destruction.

Kant's concept of disinterest can be applicable not to the aesthetic relation but to the semiotic import of an object or event. In other words, when the semiosic process is substituted by aesthetic appreciation, the subject may be disinterested in *what* an object means to concentrate instead on *how* it is presented, namely the aesthetic value it acquires for him. When encountering a friend, after semiotically recognizing who she is, the subject will focus on *how* she looks, speaks, appears to be, and so on, that is, on her aesthetic presence. On seeing a cactus and after re-cognizing it as, say, an Opuntia, semiosic disinterest can give way to aesthetic appreciation: we will then perceive its shape and color, how thorns emerge symmetrically, how the gray on its skin contrasts with the green, its texture and composition. Thus, the semiosic process passes from the front stage of perception (in recognition) to the backstage as disinterest gives way to aesthetic dis-covery. To sum it up, in aesthetic appreciation there is no aesthetic disinterest, but only, and to a certain degree, semiosic disinterest at the moment when semiosis passes to a secondary plane in perception for the emergence of aesthetic appreciation.

The myth of aesthetic distance

With the concept of *psychical distance*, Edward Bullough (1979) leans on a long philosophical tradition that seems more preoccupied with legitimizing the distance of the aesthete with regard to the masses and of educated taste with respect to the vulgar one, than to advance the understanding of the aesthetic. Bullough's concept

20 *Everyday Aesthetics*

of aesthetic distancing actually echoes Kantian disinterest and inherits for us the same problems.[3]

The example that Bullough presents to argue his case is that of a jealous husband who aspires to the representation of Othello and identifies himself to such an extent with the storyline, thinking of his personal problems, that he loses the necessary distance to aesthetically enjoy the drama. On the other hand, it could be argued that his emotional state might even intensify the experience of the drama, and not necessarily impair it. Contrarily, an eight-year-old child who attends the performance will be so remote from the problem of marital jealousy, that it could hardly generate the necessary empathy to enjoy it. What would then be the adequate distance?

Dickie (1988, 12) proposes the term *sharply focused* instead of *detached* to define aesthetic appreciation. For him, lack of detachment would simply mean lack of attention to the artwork, being absorbed with one's own thoughts. The Dickiean concept of "focus" does not consider, however, that such focus can be not only sharp, but blurred, convergent or divergent, and even wide-angle or telephoto as well. Blurred focus reminds me of the idea of distracted aesthetic perception that Benjamin (1968) talked about with regard to movie-goers; there are different degrees of attention or dispersed foci as in aesthetic reception typical of soap operas or musical programs in television. Dickie, of course, would never concede that in this case you could talk of aesthetic appreciation, because, as we shall see later, for the author there is only the dichotomy attention/no attention. Neither would Bullough, but for other reasons, because since the soap opera viewer and movie-goers need to identify themselves with the protagonists, weep at their woes and be happy at their joy, they cancel the necessary contemplative distance. Nonetheless, Aristotle clearly claimed that to share the feeling of "fear and pity" with the protagonists through identification is the condition for the cathartic process provided by an artwork; psychical distance would thus cancel catharsis.

It is Bertolt Brecht (1985, 327) who takes the concept of distancing as the key technique of his epic theater. He calls it *Verfremdungseffekt* or the effect of distancing that "has the purpose of placing the spectator in an inquisitive, critical attitude before the process being represented". Brecht does not seek identification with the events on stage by the public and its resultant Aristotelian catharsis. On the contrary, he tries to break the "hypnotic field" of the theatrical illusion. He interposes a distance guided by the gestures of the actor to make the spectator conscious of his social circumstances. Brecht's effort to create distancing techniques shows that this effect is far from automatic; rather to the contrary, he understands that the natural relation of the theater-goer with the plays is usually the lack of distancing, identification.

---

3   Lawrence W. Hyman (1986), in his attack on Dickie, tries to vindicate the concept of aesthetic experience, and insists on notions of disinterest and distanciation. Nonetheless, he contributes little in his intent, since he concludes that if the value of a novel "is not cognitive or moral, how could the experience that produces such a value be called, but aesthetic experience?" There are many ways to answer him. Hyman's argument presupposes that there exist only three types of values a) cognitive, b) moral, and c) aesthetic, somewhat like Kant in his three Critiques. If x is neither a nor b, it must be c. But the premises are false, since there can be d or e and so on; namely, there can be other types of values: d) political, e) economical, f) linguistic, g) personal, n) and so on. Thus, the conclusion is false.

Greek drama did not seek distancing, but rather catharsis and identification; hence, could it be denied that, for lack of distancing, the Greeks did not enjoy their marvelous tragedies and comedies? Present day soap opera hunts for the maximum hypnotic effect possible, the state of dramatic illusion that Brecht would have frowned upon, and although the interruption by commercial messages and the serialization in chapters inevitably provide distancing, the spectator insists on returning to the state of identification with the characters. The dreamlike effect of movies that the film-makers cultivate with such zeal is a result of non-distancing that the public greatly enjoys. None of these cases of lack of distancing can be explained as simply lack of attention, as Dickie would characterize them. It is just the opposite: the movie-goer's attention is nailed on the film to such an extent that distance disappears, and he totally identifies himself with what the character is undergoing.

Just as distancing is not a sufficient condition to define what is aesthetic, the absence of distance isn't either. Aesthetic appreciation is not static with observers remaining at a fixed and adequate distance from the object, but, rather, as in everyday life, they *swing* at different distances from their object. The example of distancing given by Brecht comes from *Les Misérables* by Victor Hugo, when a man talks to a gardener who says that they are waiting for the king, whence the man retorts "I am the King". Dickie's (1992) example is the moment in which TinkerBell in *Peter Pan* addresses the children and asks them "who believes in fairies?" thus the spell of illusion on the stage is broken. In both cases the spectator is put in motion: he *swings* back and forth from his seat toward the stage, from fantasy to actuality. Brecht knew it so well that he resorted to *Verfremdungseffekt* only *after* having perfectly achieved the illusion on stage and the identification of the spectator through theatrical resources and his dexterity as a playwright. Otherwise, distancing would not even be necessary, as there simply would be plain reality.

Arnold Berleant attempts to destroy three myths (he accurately calls them "axioms") that predominate in mainstream aesthetics: "that art consists primarily of objects, that these objects possess a special status, and that they must be regarded in a unique way." (1986, 1991: 11) Berleant's healthy criticism is based not only on their obstruction for accounting non-material art like the *happening*, the *ready made*, and conceptual art, but in disregarding the continuity of experience, and its holistic character, that joins the perceiver and the world.[4] Moreover, he disapproves notions such as Bullough's "psychic distance" (1979), to which we may add "prehension" in Aldrich that stem from Kant's approach based on the notions of contemplation and disinterested delight. Thus, he proposes to substitute the work of art by "*situations* in which experiences occur and that frequently, but not invariably, include identifiable objects" (Berleant 1986 II, 200). For Berleant, aesthetic experience is not disinterested, neither contemplative nor distanced. He proposes the concept of "engagement" when he argues that there is indeed a distinctive characteristic both in traditional and in contemporary art, namely "appreciative engagement" (Berleant

---

4   Osborne (1980) illustrates in part Berleant's object of criticism. Faced with works of body art, land art, happenings, conceptual art, and so on, his course of action is, rather than try to adapt aesthetic theory to the works, as Berleant does, to eliminate the works from the theory declaring that they are not art.

22   *Everyday Aesthetics*

1986 II, 199; 1991). Along with Wittgenstein we shall ask ourselves about the use of the word "engagement" and find appreciative engagement in love, in politics, in religion, in business, and in sports. Consequently, the notion of "engagement" seems to me insufficient to define the specificity of the aesthetic. Nonetheless, Berleant's efforts to overcome traditional fetishes and dogmas by pointing out the preponderance of the subject's activity in aesthetic related processes are badly needed (even if he disputes the subject-object dichotomy).

Indirectly connected to distancing, Bakhtin proposes a basic concept for aesthetic analysis, namely "alterity" (Bajtín 1990, 13–92) or "exotopy", as Todorov (1984) translates it.[5] This concept means that the spectator is other with regard to an artwork or, specifically, with regard to the hero of a novel in the same way as the author is other with regard to the hero he creates. By being other, the object is viewed from a different place and time. The concept of exotopy does not necessarily imply psychological distance because there is a moment of empathy or *Einfühlung* (Lipps 1924), of closeness to the other. Bullough's "psychical distance", on the other hand, is so remote that it does not participate or communicate with the other, or have anything in common with it.

To sum it up, "aesthetic distance" lacks theoretical value, and its substitution by "attention" proposed by Dickie does not solve the problem. Berleant's term of "engagement" does shorten such distance, perhaps too much. I thus propose the concept of *aesthetic swinging* that Brecht practiced with mastery when he attracted the spectator toward the play by identification, and then distanced him by the *Verfremdungseffekt*. Painters, sculptors and architects also make use of this swinging when they provide a detailed view of the work seen at a close distance complemented by the overall view seen from afar. This swinging is evident when one observes a painter or a sculptor in action: we continuously move back and forth, away and near the work to better appreciate it. The spectator will later emulate this movement. Without aesthetic swinging it would be impossible to perceive what Monroe C. Beardsley, following Hutcheson, calls "unity in diversity", since the first requires distance and the second, nearness. Talented musicians also sway us far away and then close to the theme by variations in volume and musical motifs, elaborating an acoustic landscape for exploration. These dynamics of varying distances are required for aesthetic appreciation: a vision of the whole and of its parts.

The myth of the aesthetic attitude

In one of the most widely reproduced texts of Anglo-American analytical aesthetics, George Dickie (1992) disputes as a mere myth the notion of the "aesthetic attitude" proposed by Jerome Stolnitz who, as mentioned before, defined it as "disinterested and sympathetic attention to and contemplation of any object of awareness whatever, for its own sake alone". (Stolnitz 1992, 10) Along this line, Stolnitz compared the aesthetic attitude to practical perception, the latter focusing upon particular aspects

---

5   It can be said that this discovery is compatible to the concept of "desfamiliarization" or estrangement (*ostranenie*) proposed by Victor Shklovsky like a key function of the art, as far as it suspends the automatic classification of percepts.

The Myths of Aesthetics 23

of the object for ulterior motives, thus ceasing to be disinterested and, consequently, aesthetic. In somehow similar terms, Beardsley (1987) also proposed the "aesthetic point of view" he defined as "the adoption of the point of view in regard to X is to be interested in any aesthetic value that X might possess" (1987, 13), a definition he continued refining, so as to be able, subsequently, to establish the concept of "aesthetic value". Virgil Aldrich (1963) made the distinction also between two modes of perception, the ordinary and the aesthetic; the former aimed at the physical aspect of the object, and the latter to its aesthetic aspect. Jan Mukarovský's (1977, 146–7) "aesthetic posture" (which he distinguishes from the religious, the practical, and the theoretical postures), and the idea of "aesthetic position" by the Mexican philosopher Samuel Ramos ([1950] 1976) are other versions along this line. How are we to choose between these interpretations of aesthetic phenomena as resulting from a point of view, attitude, posture, position, value, or perception?

Dickie (1974, 1992) questions the idea that there could be different modes of perception, and calls the notion of "aesthetic attitude" a useless myth that diverts aesthetic theory from its objectives of elucidating genuinely aesthetic phenomena. For Dickie, such "aesthetic attitude" is simply attention and lacks any theoretical value whatsoever. He acknowledges, not without some irony, that this notion might have the practical value of fostering in the spectator a more unbiased attitude toward the appreciation of, for instance, abstract art. If, however, this practical value could be proven, wouldn't this be reason enough for recognizing its theoretical value?

The exact point of Dickie's (1992, 35) criticism is that "Stolnitz confuses a perceptual distinction with a motivational one". For Dickie, there are no distinct modes of perception, but distinct motives or intentions in a perception that is nothing other than mere attention. I concur with Dickie that the aesthetic does not depend on whether or not an aesthetic attitude is adopted, but, as I will argue in the next section, the problem is not solved by the simple dichotomy attention/non-attention. Something else happens in aesthetic phenomena that cannot be reduced to mere attention, even if it doesn't depend on the adoption of an attitude.

The best result of Dickie's position is that he disentangles himself from the notion of "disinterest" by pointing out that it is simply a question of inattention. In Bullough's example, repeated by Dickie, the person who attends an interpretation of *Othello* and keeps lamenting his wife's unfaithfulness doesn't lack distanced or disinterested perception of the play; for Dickie he simply is not paying the necessary attention because he is wrapped up in his personal problems.

Although Dickie's examples avoid the notions of disinterest and distancing, they also overvalue the role of intention and motivation. This is tantamount to saying that having a personal or practical intention with regard to an artwork would automatically cancel the possibility of enjoying it. Another fallacy in his proposal is the presumption that having an aesthetic motivation is enough to guarantee full aesthetic appreciation. We might pay a lot of attention to a painting that has great quality and prestige according to the consensus of the artworld and yet not be moved by it. Then, in an unexpected situation in everyday life, an intense aesthetic encounter with an uncommon object might occur, without our ever having sought it.

If aesthetic attention is defined by intention or motivation, as set forth by Dickie, the demystifying thrust he is wielding against the "aesthetic attitude" does not do

24 *Everyday Aesthetics*

anything but change one term for another, leaving the essence of the problem intact: the "aesthetic attitude" of Stolnitz is now denominated by Dickie "attention with aesthetic intention". In other words, Dickie unwillingly continues to qualify the act of perception, which he doesn't call "aesthetic attitude" anymore but "attention with aesthetic purposes or motivations". Stolnitz could therefore reply, appropriately, that this motivational attention already establishes a perceptual difference, and consequently there are different modes of perception. Combining both versions we would have a spectator so concentrated on having an attention with aesthetic intentions or motivations, or in adopting an aesthetic attitude, that no energy would be left to enjoy the artwork.

If there really existed such a thing as an "aesthetic attitude", the right place to verify it is at gallery and museum openings illustrated by the affectation and pretentiousness members of the *artworld* usually strike, and that results somehow hilarious to the uninitiated public: it is the attitude of the snob. Observers who are not convinced of this parameter should better look for other explanations in more commonplace situations. There they might find that more than an *attitude*, aesthetic appreciation is a particular *activity* of the subject, an activity of appreciation and fascination (as will be explained in detail in Part II).

The myth of aesthetic aspects or qualities

If the aesthetic attitude is a myth, as Dickie correctly proclaims, simply substituting the term "attention" for "attitude" will not jettison it. It is now Dickie's attention/ inattention myth that requires dismantling. Stolnitz may argue that his own definition includes Dickie's "attention" and is even able to qualify it further (as sympathetic and disinterested, and so on). Dickie, on his part, might argue that it is unnecessary to complicate matters too much, and that Occam's razor is perfectly applicable in this case.

However, Dickie's contention that there is nothing but attention/inattention involved in aesthetic appreciation depends upon the existence of certain entities denominated "aesthetic aspects" or "aesthetic qualities". That is why, in his opinion, attention is always the same, and what vary are these aspects or qualities where attention is placed. This approach to the problem presupposes that objects are multidimensional having all these different aspects or qualities whereas subjects are one-dimensional, capable only of detecting or not detecting them depending on their motivation, like automats, shifting attention to different aspects.

If those entities called "aesthetic aspects" were not to exist objectively and separately, Dickie's contention of a single type of attention would crumble, since there would be nothing to typify aesthetic phenomena or connect a judgment to. This battle to prove the existence of aesthetic aspects or qualities would perhaps have a better prognosis if fought instead for *artistic* (rather than aesthetic) aspects, and that would consist in what spectators perceive in artworks. Artistic aspects are Van Gogh's strong, visible brush strokes, Tamayo's rich, colorful textures, and Orozco's vehement linear rhythms, and so on because they are deliberate signifiers elaborated by each artist. As there are artistic aspects that enable us to distinguish one author

The Myths of Aesthetics   25

from another, there are also practical, cognitive, financial, or political aspects in an artwork. Aspects, like percepts and concepts, are not things in themselves or entities objectively existing in the world, but a linguistic conversion of verbs into nouns, namely, of the action of "aspecting" (like percepts of perceiving and "concepts" of conceptualizing). In other words, they are perceptual or conceptual constructs which result from an act of perception or conceptualization. An "aspect" is a noun from the Latin verbs *aspicere* or *aspectare*, namely perceive, indicating that it is an effect of an action performed by the subject who perceives or "aspécts". Equally, a "quality" is the substantivation of the act of qualifying. This action performed by the subject upon the object has gradually been reified, creating the illusion that the naive realists take for reality; namely the existence of aspects, concepts and percepts (or qualities) independently from the subject. As time goes by, reified terms seem "to create" a strange effect of authority and independent existence.

The philosophical illusion that aesthetic aspects exist objectively and independently of the subject or observer is the result of various subjects carrying out in common the activity of aspectation. For example in ballet, a dancer, a choreographer, and the public will coincide in the appreciation of the grace in the performance because they are aspecting and judging it from the same interpretative community. That is why Kant sought universal consensus to the judgment of beauty, in order to render its objective existence despite its incurable subjective origin. Kant, however, openly requests this consensus, he even demands it, but he does not take it for granted based on a supposed empirical objectivity of beauty or on a supposedly factual existence of aesthetic aspects.

Based on this belief on objective aspects or qualities, and on a single type of attention, Dickie now depends on various motivations that draw the attention to the object. The question then emerges if those different motivations do not already alter the manner of paying attention. There are notable differences in the types of attention paid to different activities: we display rational attention in handling concepts and consistency in an argument, psychomotor attention when driving a car or playing video-games, kinaesthetic attention on a roller-coaster or bicycle ride, haptic and olfactory attention during sexual intercourse, or practical attention in performing a task. Attention is not the same when listening to a concert as when checking the phone bill and the difference lies not only in *what* one pays attention to, but also in *how* one does.

It is necessary to emphasize also that "attention with aesthetic motivation" is not always deliberate, nor is it one-dimensional, and not even in all cases of the same order. Many of us have involuntarily suffered the aesthetic intrusion of a noisy neighbor who sets his stereo full-blast and sequesters our attention against our will, to the extent that we cannot avoid listening to it. Our inability to not pay attention makes this experience so irritating. Without a doubt, the aesthetic has to do with attention, and the negative aesthetic experience in this case has to do with this seizure of attention, but the value of this experience definitely depends on the nature of the attention.

Consequently, just as aesthetic attention is not always voluntary and intentional, it is not one-dimensional either. We don't go to the movies with the intention of listening to the background music, but we perceive distractedly the emotional effect with which the director and musicians stress the mood of the scene by the music. There are aesthetic perceptions that never surface to conscious attention, such as the scents of a park we hurriedly cross to work, the songs of the birds that surround us at dawn without our being aware of them generating a feeling of calmness. There are also acts that we automatically perform without paying any particular attention to them and that can still give us a satisfaction we might call "aesthetic"; for example riding a bicycle.

There is a lot more and a lot less to aesthetic appreciation than mere attention. More than attention when we consider a basketball player in love with a violinist, who attends a concert of classical music just to please her. Having no musical education, he truly makes a huge attention effort during the two hours the concert lasts, with the firm desire to find the "aesthetic qualities" that attract his girlfriend so much. And yet, he doesn't succeed, and suffers through those two endless hours. If aesthetic appreciation were, as Dickie says, attention with aesthetic motivations, the motivations of our athlete are amorous but also aesthetic since he genuinely wishes to appreciate the music as his fiancée does, but where is the flaw? The lover feels betrayed, since much more than attention is required to enjoy the music. At least, artistic education is needed as well as auditory training (Dickie would correctly define artistic education as attention training). On the other hand, there is also much less than attention such as when one is receptive to a stimulus in a relaxed and distracted manner. An infant who falls asleep soothed by his mother's voice (without paying any particular attention to the words or the melody, but merely as a sensation of comfort and drowsiness), does, in my view, keep an aesthetic relation.

That aesthetic appreciation requires attention is obvious, since one needs to pay some degree of attention to something to perceive it. Nevertheless, attention differs in quality. I do not pretend to say that every individual owns a supply of perfectly differentiated and catalogued modes of perception, readily available for whatever the occasion might require. Perception is a capacity that not only humans possess, but all living beings from the most elemental to the most complex. It involves diverse operations in which focusing particular senses or organs, be they cellular membranes or an educated ear, is only the beginning of a process that engages different motor and sensory abilities. In human beings these functions are highly multifaceted, since different regions of the brain are constituted and activated throughout an individual's lifetime. The corporeal complexity of our species has also mental and perceptual sophistication, in contrast to one-dimensional receptiveness of unicellular organisms, or the pseudo-perception of computers which only we can translate into images, sounds, or words. That is why human perception is not a matter of paying or not paying attention to this or that aspect, but of the complexity and diversity of processes that depend on our particular species' morphology, in addition to our culture. To reduce these processes to simple attention almost equals to reducing humans to protozoa.

The myth of the universality of beauty

"Beauty is that which, without concept, pleases universally." This is the classical definition of beauty with which Kant ends the Second Moment of his *Critique of Judgment*. He requests universal adhesion to the judgment of taste because, being

The Myths of Aesthetics

aesthetic, it is subjective by definition; no objective evidence may be claimed for it. This subjectivity makes it impossible to prove that an object is beautiful; but it is possible, according to Kant, to demand adhesion to the universal subjective validity upon "the total sphere of those who judge". This myth of universality as expectation and demand has galloped on the back of aesthetics for more than two centuries. Marx himself, despite his obstinate socio-historical view and his conviction of structural determinants, had to make an exception in this case and succumb to this myth of the universality of beauty when he asked himself how was it possible for classical Greek art to still be valid and move us. Its validity for Marx (1968) was based upon, yes, its universality. The reason he found was that it reminds us of "humankind's childhood".

The myth of the universality of beauty has been in fact a disguise for another myth: the universality of Western culture. The philosopher believed to be hoisting Thought, through which he could have access to Truth, Goodness, and Beauty. The contact with Truth would inebriate him because he could see above the common man miserably deceived by appearances. Everything was ruled by a vertical perspective in which Reason hierarchically arranged the positions of everything that exists toward the centripetal focus of The Absolute. However, at this beginning of a new millennium, we have to take this will for universality for what it is, namely, a will for power. At the bottom and in the light of ethnographic studies, we can recognize that such "Universal Beauty" is simply Western conventions on beauty. The myth of the universality of beauty results from the Euro-centrist projection of its values over non-Western aesthetic manifestations in its pretension to uphold, precisely, that universality.

As empirical investigations on the judgment of taste in different cultures and social classes progress (along the line initiated by the International Association of Empirical Aesthetics), what may come out badly bruised will be this universality of beauty. The universality of the aesthetic, on the other hand, will remain unharmed, as all human beings, regardless of our culture or space-time situation, are basically sensitive, open creatures.

The myth of the opposition between the aesthetic and the intellectual

One of the foundations and clichés in aesthetic discourse has been the opposition between the aesthetic and the intellectual. Since its beginnings with "clear and distinct ideas" of reason as opposed to "clear but confused ideas" of sensibility in Baumgarten, to "beauty without concept" in Kant and his incisive division of the three critiques (of thinking, of acting, and of judging), examples of this myth are countless.

One of the rare exceptions to this formula is John Dewey, who points out that:

> [... T]here is emotionalized thinking, and there are feelings whose substance consists of appreciated ideas and senses.... The only significant distinction concerns the kind of material to which emotionalized imagination adheres. Those who are called artists have for their subject matter the qualities of things of direct experience; "intellectual" inquirers deal with these qualities at one remove, through the medium of symbols that stand for qualities but are not significant in their immediate presence. The ultimate difference is

28 *Everyday Aesthetics*

enormous as far as the technique of thought and emotion are concerned. But there is no difference as far as the dependence on emotionalized ideas and subconscious maturing are concerned. (Dewey [1934] 1980, 73)

In concert with Dewey, I do not believe in the conceptual purity of scientific thought; neither do I believe in the emotional purity of the aesthetic. There is a plurality of activities, capacities, and interactions that occur in aesthetic phenomena. I don't see it as a cataleptic state of ecstasy almost implied by the use of the term "contemplation". Neither is it a purely emotive experience because intellectual, corporeal, and sensorial activities also come into play. Guiraud unknowingly illustrates this contraposition between aesthetics and logic when he states:

> The fundamental distinction that opposes two antithetic modes of experience and two types of corresponding semiotic codes: the logical experience and the affective or aesthetic experience. The former refers to the objective perception of the outside world, the elements of which are encompassed by reason in a system of relations. The latter corresponds to a purely subjective intimate feeling that the soul emits in the face of reality. (Guiraud 1989, 87)

These "emissions of the soul" are not as "purely subjective" as Guiraud thinks, since even emotionality, like reasoning, is ruled and produced by social contexts and conventions. That is why the attitude of *The Stranger* by Camus at his mother's funeral is so shocking: the character did not produce the emotion that social conventions establish for that situation. Our contemporary mass culture entails a set of rules for emotions since, for example, love is perfectly coded so that one must feel love and sexual desire in situations similar to those presented by the media. An intimate dinner by candlelight, soft music background, wine, ladies' black or red underwear trimmed with lace, perfumes, and silken bed-sheets, preferably black, are among the recommended techniques to produce sexual fantasies and erotic effects, not to speak of the new theatrical games announced for sexual arousal. This not only proves that the emotional and the conventional are intimately linked in experience, but to what degree social codes and standards rebound in the emotional production of desire. The idea is to restrict reactions to the emotionally correct.

To consider the aesthetic as opposite to the intellectual may be useful for understanding certain operative distinctions in theory, but certainly not as a substantial opposition. That is why we may focus aesthetic analysis in terms of the conformations that can produce the most diverse effects such as truth, justice, beauty, horror, or uncontrollable laughter. From this perspective, "the intellectual" or "the aesthetic", are not essences, entities, or sections of reality valid for themselves, but processes by which the subject produces effects of truth or delight.

In conclusion, the difference between the intellectual and the aesthetic could be established not as an essentialist question as Guiraud does, nor as a metaphysical or epistemological question as presented by Baumgarten in his distinction between "distinct" and "confused" ideas. We are dealing with diverse human activities and abilities that come into play and merge in aesthetic related experiences. Kant himself saw that in aesthetic experience the mental function is not excluded when

The Myths of Aesthetics

29

he conceived it as the "free interplay of imagination and understanding". This description, more than two centuries later, continues to be perfectly valid.

The myth of the synonymity of art and aesthetics

There are three positions that question the predominant relation between aesthetics and art. The first is opposed to the idea that all art must *necessarily* be aesthetic. The second questions art as *exclusively* aesthetic. The third, main target of this text, impugns the *artistic exclusivity* of aesthetics.

One of the main critics of the first version, namely, the aestheticity of art, is Noël Carroll (1986, 57–63), who questions whether aesthetic reception is definitive in our relation with art, and if it should be characterized only in terms of the production of aesthetic effects. He proposes that there are ways of interaction with art that are not aesthetic and yet are equally or more satisfying, like interpretation, discovery of structures and latent meanings, of enigmas and puzzles. He attacks, in sum, the aesthetic definition of art or its over-aesthetization, since, for Carroll, the relation with art can also be intellectual. The reader may now recognize that Carroll's objection is a result of succumbing to the previous myth, namely, the opposition of the aesthetic and the intellectual, as if by being intellectual, art can no longer be aesthetic.

Another critic against the over-aesthetization of art is Timothy Binkley ([1977] 1987), who considers that being aesthetic is not a sufficient condition, and not even a necessary one, for something to be art. He says that not everything in art is aesthetic, and that upon seeing its marriage with aesthetics as a forced union, art seeks meaning beyond the skin-deep glances. That is why, for Binkley, art is *indexing* according to certain conventions established by the "artworld" or artistic institution (along the line of Danto).

Note that in Binkley as in Carroll there is an underlying presupposition of the aesthetic as related to perception. For this reason, aesthetics seems to them irrelevant in conceptual art such as Marcel Duchamp's *Fountain*, since perceiving the urinal is really beside the point. In other words, because both Carroll and Binkley subsume the aesthetic as perception, obviously sensorial reception of conceptual art does not have the same importance as the intellectual process it arouses, and they consequently deny the aestheticity of art. On the other hand, if we don't limit aesthetics to sheer perception, as these authors do, but include sensibility in a wider sense (implicit in Kant's "free interplay of imagination and understanding"), then we must acknowledge that the aesthetic dimension is a necessary condition for the artistic. If the intellectual process that conceptual art generates is unable to produce effects on the subject's sensibility, then it cannot be considered to have any artistic value. Every work considered artistic, even conceptual works like Duchamp's *L.H.O.O.Q.* or *Fountain*, is appreciated by the sensitive (not merely sensual) effects that the spectator generates in relation to the work.

In sum, it is not necessary to de-aesthetize art in order to admit the intellectual dimension in experiencing artworks. There are concepts with enormous emotive charge and feelings of great conceptual complexity (as in Dewey's quote a few pages earlier). Therefore, I do not share this criticism to the first version of the myth of

30 *Everyday Aesthetics*

the aesthetics of art in terms of the *necessity* of aesthetics in the artistic: Art *must* be aesthetic.

It is the second version of this myth of the aesthetic in art that is of interest here, namely, that of the exclusivity of the aesthetic in art. I maintain that art is not exclusively aesthetic because not all relations with art are aesthetic. Art is also technical as when verifying its authenticity, epistemological as a way to explore the world, political as means of propaganda and definitely semiotic as it communicates something from the author to the audience, reader, or spectator. Additionally, art is also psychological and therapeutic in its cathartic function (as in psychodrama), financial for speculation in pecuniary investments, and, above all, economic for the sustenance of the artist. Thus art is not exclusively aesthetic, although it necessarily is so. It has been presented as exclusively aesthetic for marketing reasons to magnify its myth as an almost superhuman creation of a genius.

Finally, we have the third version of the artistic exclusivity of aesthetics, which asserts that aesthetics must refer exclusively to art. Today this myth completely dominates theoretical production in aesthetics, to the degree that approaches such as the aesthetics of landscapes, gardens, weather, smell, and tea ceremonies, and so on are presented only marginally and taken to be rather exotic. Even Kant's discourse on the sublime in nature and mathematics remains somehow subterranean, while the sublime has been incorporated as yet another category in aesthetic theory referring, once again, to artworks. This myth has blocked the emergence of inquiries dealing with everyday aesthetics and will likely segregate them for a long time in the periphery of aesthetic debate. Although art is not the theme of this book, the myth of the aesthetic exclusivity of art mirrors the artistic exclusivity of aesthetics. This has long been an epistemological obstacle that is urgent to counteract for analyzing aesthetics in all its bewildering non-artistic ramifications.

Summing up, the ideology of art seals off all non-aesthetic aspects of artistic production making it appear as if it were exclusively aesthetic, when in fact it is *also* aesthetic, among other things (economic, political, semiotic, technological, public relational, therapeutic, etc). More mundane topics are delegated to studies by ethnologists and economists, while aesthetic theory (as seen in the first Chapter) refuses to be "polluted" by conceptual tools from other disciplines and by non-artistic objects in the same manner as the theory of art separates itself from non-aesthetic concepts. This is a curious symbiosis that threatens both of them to imminent extinction.

The myth of the aesthetic potentiality of artworks

Derived from the fetish of the aesthetic object, the myth of the aesthetic potentiality of artworks consists in supposing that the "aesthetic object" has the potential of arousing an aesthetic experience. Most art theoreticians tend to share this widespread myth, illustrated by Sánchez Vázquez's eloquent description of how Velazquez's *Meninas* waits to accomplish its aesthetic potential when observed by the spectator: "Since it was painted and exhibited in 1656, the picture realizes again and again its potential or disposition to be contemplated, converting itself always, at any given

The Myths of Aesthetics   31

moment, into an aesthetic object. But there are also moments when the picture remains in the hall, silent and engrossed, in expectation of new contemplations, of an endless consumption, that will never mean its consummation." (Sánchez Vázquez 1992, 112)

Of course, Sánchez Vázquez speaks metaphorically and he acknowledges that the object becomes an aesthetic object only when the spectator is contemplating it. Still, given the tendency in aesthetic theory to center around objects rather than subjects, many will interpret this statement literally, as if the object would actually convert itself into an aesthetic object or has a disposition to be contemplated. The picture, however, does not convert into anything; it is the subject that establishes a relation with it who changes his perception of it from, say, something hanging from a wall to something aesthetically significant. Nothing happens to the object; to whom something happens in relation to the object is the subject only.

Language is treacherous and makes Sánchez Vázquez appear to anthropomorphize the object instead of the subject, since a painting is not something with dispositions and expectations but a coagulated objectification of subjectivity, be it the painter's or the spectator's. In other words, the *Meninas* do not have the disposition to be observed; the only disposition is that of the subject to observe the picture or of the painter to paint it. A painting does not have an aesthetic potential; it is only the enunciator, Velazquez in this case, who has given the spectators the opportunity of constructing meanings and forms by inviting them to play a game of interpretative strategies with it, as Fish (1976, 1980, 183) would say. This invitation is only effective for those who already have the disposition and the interpretative strategies with which to construct the meaning of the picture. Foucault (1984) accepts the invitation, and the meaning he produces of *Meninas* (as a representation of representation, or as the play of representations of the "classic episteme") is the result of the interpretative strategy he exerts upon the picture. From other strategies, different from Foucault's, other meanings can be construed.

The well-known Aristotelian dichotomy potentiality-actuality functions only in aesthetics in relation to a subject, not an object. It refers to the potentiality of the spectator to exercise certain interpretative strategies as regards to the object, the potentiality of the author to display a discourse, or the potentiality of communication between author and spectator through an artwork. The picture, on the other hand, is not a potential idea or aesthetic experience, but the trace or result of an act of enunciation by its author, and thereafter the result of an act of interpretation by other spectators. Sure, an act of enunciation could remain as a potential act of interpretation, but then also the whole universe.

The myth of the aesthetic experience

Directly or indirectly, the notion of "aesthetic experience" has a very long history and a large family of resemblances. Even if, strictly speaking, it began during the eighteenth century (cf. Townsend 1992), Plato's contemplation of the idea of Beauty, and the dangerous consequences to the soul of poetry and music, as well as Aristotle's concept of "catharsis of pity and fear", have implicit the idea of aesthetic experience.

32 *Everyday Aesthetics*

Classical and modern versions of aesthetic experience emerge from Kant's "free play of imagination and understanding", Lipps's *Einfühlung*, Dewey's *an experience* ("when the material experienced runs its course to fulfillment ... integrated within and demarcated in the general stream of experience from other experiences"), Dilthey, Gadamer and Wellek's *Erlebnis* (in opposition to *erfahrung*) to Beardsley's "sense of actively exercising constructive powers of the mind" in unified and coherent experiences, Parret's (1993) "euphony and synaesthesia", Berleant's "appreciative engagement" to Shusterman's (1999) reminder of "heightened, meaningful, and valuable phenomenological experience".

Discussions oscillate between objectivist versions that define the aesthetic experience by the object experienced, and the subjectivists who define it by the quality of the experience. The former go hunting for aesthetically relevant qualities, concepts, aspects, features, properties, attributes, and so on in the object (for example order, harmony, unity, coherence, proportion, rhythm, elegance, and so on) to prove their position. The subjectivists, on the other hand, must undergo the embarrassment of describing these qualities of the experience in an intimate tone sometimes bordering the sentimental.

Following Kant's "disinterested delight" and Baumgarten's "clear but confused ideas", subjectivism attempts to describe and qualify the subject's experience by introspection or reconstruction *a posteriori*. However, the very moment in which something that may be qualified as "aesthetic experience" occurs, it is instantly nullified by becoming a descriptive non-aesthetic process. This is the aporia facing all attempts to define aesthetic experience from pure subjectivism. To escape it, one enters another, namely being ensnared in circular definitions that define the object as aesthetic by the "aestheticity" of experience it arouses, or qualifying as such the experience by the aestheticity of the object (Dufrenne, for instance).

No wonder Dickie (1965) set forth to denounce the idea of "aesthetic experience" conceived by Beardsley as a mere phantom. For Dickie, the aesthetic experience is an empty term that transposes qualities of the object, namely being unified and coherent, to the subject.[6] Michael Mitias (1982, 158) in turn tried to defend the viability of the aesthetic experience against Dickie's attack by asking under what conditions can an object be perceived as an aesthetic object.[7] By those conditions, however, he understands something like "creative imagination" which is another way of naming or describing aesthetic experience. Mitias's argumentative effort to justify the ontological validity of aesthetic experience against his opponents' fails because he seems more concerned to defend Beardsley's position against Dickie's attack than to validate aesthetic experience. Against the argument that aesthetic experience cannot be qualified, Mitias responds that it can by having the qualities attributed to it by Beardsley, namely: unity, coherence, and completeness.

This debate, however, cannot be won from Beardsley's perspective because we still lack technical or empirical tools to test any such qualities in experience. And

---

6   See also Shusterman's (1999) account of this debate.

7   The issue, however, is far from solved and not a matter of describing the aesthetic experience *a posteriori*, or of invoking and recapturing its taste, but of understanding its conditions of possibility, as will be argued in Chapter 7.

The Myths of Aesthetics   33

even if this qualification of an experience were possible, it is not reason enough to validate aesthetic experience itself, since we can surely find "coherent, unified, and complete" experiences that are not particularly aesthetic since, as stated by Dickie, all normal experience is coherent. Consider, for example, going to the butchers' to buy a pound of veal. It is coherent because we do whatever is necessary for that purpose; it is unified because it integrates all our acts in that direction; and it is complete because it starts when we decide to buy the pound of veal, and ends when we have done so. And yet, it is not necessarily aesthetic. In addition, this qualification would take us into psychological labyrinths to determine if these qualities are inferred before (by autosuggestion), during (by introspection), or after (by retrospection) the experience.

It is not a question of performing taxonomies of experiences classifying on one side those that are coherent, unitary, and complete, and on the other those that are not. Of course, Mitias does not recommend such taxonomy, but it would be the logical consequence of his distinction between the aesthetic and non-aesthetic experience from the point of view of their qualities. He goes even further to suggest that what makes an experience aesthetic is the experienced object's "aesthetic qualities". In other words, according to Mitias, aesthetic experience is that which is permeated and endowed with structure by the aesthetic object; and the aesthetic object is that which enables such experience by possessing "aesthetic qualities". Surprisingly, Mitias suddenly becomes an objectivist in his intent to defend the subjectivistic position of the aesthetic experience. Exactly the opposite happens to Dickie (1992) as he strives from a recalcitrant objectivism to demystify the aesthetic experience by defining it simply as attention, but ends up by settling on the subject who has the aesthetic "motivations" or "intentions" to observe and judge the qualities of the object. Ironically, Mitias finally defines the aesthetic experience by the aesthetic object, as Dickie defines the aesthetic object by the subject's aesthetic motivation. Again, all we have are circular definitions.

Since the question has only been displaced, not solved, it would then be necessary to ask which are the qualities of the aesthetic attitude, that define the aesthetic object, that cause the aesthetic experience, that distinguish the aesthetic subject, that detect the aesthetic aspects, that structure the aesthetic experience, that differentiate the aesthetic subject from the non-aesthetic one ... (As in the traditional Jewish song for Passover in which the Saintly, blessed be He, killed the angel of death, that killed the butcher, that slay the ox, that drank the water, that extinguished the fire, that burned the stick, that hit the dog, that bit the cat, that ate the goat that the father bought for two zuzim).

Richard Shusterman (1999) is ready to defend the viability of aesthetic experience, because in his view it constitutes the "general background condition for art". Using Danto's "indiscernibles argument" in a sci-fi scenario, he justifies aesthetic experience because it allows us a more serious matter than to differentiate art from non-art, namely cyborgs from humans. I think Shusterman goes too far in his defense, and yet falls too short. Too far because cyborgs and humans are very easy to differentiate on multiple and by far more objective accounts than aesthetic experiences, but he falls too short in proposing the aesthetic experience not for formal definition [Dewey's basic mistake using aesthetic experience to define art, as stressed

34 *Everyday Aesthetics*

by Shusterman,] "but for art's reorientation toward values and populations that could restore its vitality and sense of purpose". If art has traditionally been produced for the sake of providing aesthetic experiences to spectators, now it appears that aesthetic experiences have to be produced to justify art. It is true that contemporary museumized visual arts wander rather purposelessly and lack significant social grounding, but the public has no difficulty in finding alternative aesthetic delight through many other artistic and nonartistic phenomena like movies, video-games, telenovelas, weekend hobbies, pets, and sports.

We have seen how the question "what are the qualities of an aesthetic experience?" carries a circular response, where the aestheticity of the experience derives from the aestheticity of the object, and this, in turn, from the aestheticity of the attitude or motivation taken. According to Mitias and Stolnitz, even to Dickie, it is the intention of the subject in his or her adoption of the "aesthetic attitude" or the "attention with aesthetic motivations", what actualizes the object's potential "aesthetic qualities" producing (by contagion, osmosis, infiltration, or whatever) the aesthetic experience or the detection of the aesthetically relevant. What these philosophers are all concerned about, as Shusterman points out, are the services that the notion of aesthetic experience can perform for the definition or demarcation of art. Does achieving a correct inventory of artworks require their triggering aesthetic experiences, or is it enough being interpreted (Danto) and simply classified (Binkley) as such?

My concern here is not whether an aesthetic experience is a sufficient or even necessary condition to distinguish the artistic from the non-artistic, but it is certainly indispensable to distinguish the aesthetic from the non-aesthetic. Here I shall attempt not precisely to deny or affirm the theoretical viability of the concept of aesthetic experience in regards to the classification of artworks, but to approach it through a corporeal and phenomenological perspective (see Chapter 8). The problem lies in an erroneous account of the concept of "aesthetic experience". It is not the intention, nor the attention, neither the aesthetic aspects nor the attitude or involvement that define aesthetic experience. Neither is it pertinent to ask what causes an experience to be aesthetic in one case and not in another. The main question to be asked is: what are the conditions of possibility for an aesthetic experience, just as Kant [1781] did not ask what makes knowledge true, but how is it possible. Our task is, consequently, not to describe, qualify, define, or redefine aesthetic experience but instead to: a) establish the conditions for the possibility of aesthesis, b) explore its genealogy, and c) phenomenologically delineate it by a metaphorical projection of a basic experience. This we shall do in Chapters 7 and 8.

Finally, if the aesthesis is the aptitude for experience, all experience would be aesthetic and all aesthesis experiencial. Consequently the notion of "aesthetic experience" is a redundancy as "aesthetic object" an oxymoron and discussion around them an aporia. Quite a problem!

Perhaps there is way out: Let us speak instead of *artistic experience* (taking on Dewey's paradigmatic "an experience" related always with art, as well as Shusterman's (1999) defense of it against Dickie and other philosophers who tried to reject it). We can consider as well that there are sport experiences, sexual, religious, touristic experiences we may have when practicing sport, sex, religion, or traveling.

The Myths of Aesthetics   35

It is not necessary to qualify these experiences in themselves to recognize them: simply, their objects are different by two criteria: 1) the real or imaginary, the context in which they occur, and 2) the objects to which they relate. From my point of view (and which I will argue in the following chapters), all experience is aesthetic by definition because to experience is equivalent to aesthesis. But not all experience is artistic which only happens in relation to artworks. Briefly, we must distinguish between "artistic experience" which is the generalized sense used in aesthetic theory, and "aesthetic experience", a mere redundancy.

Chapter 4

The Fears of Aesthetics

Peeping behind the stage of mainstream aesthetics' discourse, we will come across a real anxiety concerning the implications of panaestheticism and, with it, of the loss of discursive privileges exclusive to aestheticians. Aesthetics is afraid of the recognition of aesthetic legitimacy in the experience of any subject with any object, and consequently the relativization of aesthetic values and their democratization. There is, in addition, the problem of art's demystification (even if during this past century artists have tried a thousand times, and failed just as often, to demystify art, particularly Dada). The risk of such demystification has a serious impact upon museums, curators, donations, foundations, and other art related institutions and practices. These are the reasons why dogmatic aesthetics would rather end up "legislating itself into irrelevance" by attempting to decree the acceptable modes of artistic action and appreciative response in Berleant's (1991, 15) eloquent terms, than evince its secret fears.

The fear of the undesirable

From the dreads of aesthetics, and as a mechanism of defense, emerges what could be defined as the "Pangloss Syndrome". I define this syndrome, in honor of Voltaire's character that caricaturized Leibniz, as the tendency to deal only with things that are nice and worthy, good and beautiful.

> Master Pangloss taught the metaphysico-theologo-cosmolonigology. He could prove to admiration that there is no effect without a cause; and, that in this best of all possible worlds, the Baron's castle was the most magnificent of all castles, and My Lady the best of all possible baronesses.
>
> "It is demonstrable," said he, "that things cannot be otherwise than as they are: for all things having been created for some end, they must consequently be created for the best. Observe, that the nose is formed for spectacles, and therefore we come to wear spectacles. The legs are visibly designed for stockings, and therefore we come to wear stockings [...]; and they who assert, that every thing is right, do not express themselves correctly; they should say that every thing is for the best." (Voltaire, Candide chap. 1)

That is why, from the eighteenth century with Baumgarten and the Anglo-American theorists of taste, to this day, aesthetics has performed a surgical operation of systematic exclusion of all phenomena that are not positive and useful in their supply of pleasure and nice thoughts. Here becomes finally obvious that Kantian disinterest was not, after all, such. The "Pangloss Syndrome" explains why aesthetics has dealt only with art and beauty, so when other qualities that are not as pleasing become

38   *Everyday Aesthetics*

apparent, they are either only mentioned superficially or swept under the rug. That is also why the disgusting, the obscene, the coarse, the insignificant, the banal, the ugly, the sordid, have not been considered relevant to aesthetics, even though our sensibility confronts them every day. Exceptions worth mentioning are Karl Rosenkranz's classic *Aesthetics of Ugliness* (1853) and Aurel Kolnai (cf. Korsmeyer and Smith eds 2004) who proposes disgust as a philosophical category, as well as William Ian Miller (1997) concerning disgust and Giesz (1973), Broch (1979), Moles (1990), and other theorists of *kitsch*.[1]

The "Pangloss Syndrome" prevents us from considering the very opposite of Aristotelian catharsis, namely aesthetic poisoning, much more socially relevant than spiritual purification. The concept of "alienation", that so much worried the theoreticians of the Frankfurt School, particularly Adorno, can be seen not only as a political phenomenon but also as aesthetic poisoning. The escalation of violence in many industrialized countries might be due not only to the easy acquisition of firearms by civilians, but to a systematic aesthetic poisoning and daily aggression to the sensibility of the citizen, where objects are increasingly worth more than the subjects. Cruelty is not only a moral category but an aesthetic one: it always targets sensibility.

The fear of everyday impurities

At the vacillation of facing the aesthetic in the everyday, in nature, in others, in the world—a quandary that Kant confronted in relation to the sublime—Dufrenne returns to the domesticated comfort of the artistic, perfectly tamed, civilized, and codified. This horror of mundane aesthetics simply emanates from a prudery that disdains the "impurities" imported from our common, ordinary world:

> This is the path that we shall follow, and its advantage is immediately apparent. As no one doubts the presence of works of art and the genuineness of the finest works, the aesthetic object, if we define it in relation to them, can be easily located [sic]. And at the same time, the aesthetic experience to be described will be an exemplary one, free of the impurities [sic] sometimes imported into the perception of an aesthetic object stemming from the world of nature, as when the contemplation of an alpine landscape is blended with the pleasant feelings awakened by the fresh air or the scent of hay, by the pleasure of solitude, the joy of climbing, or the heightened feeling of freedom. But one may also regret that the investigation of the natural aesthetic object is then deferred. However, we think our method is the right one, because aesthetic experience derived directly from the work of art is surely the purest and perhaps also the first historically... [sic!!] (Dufrenne 1973, li)

In sum, Dufrenne believes that perception of fresh air or the scent of hay, the pleasure of solitude or the joy in climbing are too impure to deal with, whereas only art is pure. He supposes that it is necessary to gather a handful of experts that should define art, so that the human being may be capable of aesthetic experiences. Dufrenne's maneuver is almost paradigmatic in traditional and contemporary aesthetics of

---

    1   Korsmeyer has continued this investigation on disgust as an aesthetic category, also Radford (1999) in Dali's work.

The Fears of Aesthetics

this evasion in examining the aesthetic dimension outside this domesticated, pre-aestheticized and almost anesthetized realm, the artistic. Such fear of the impurities of the everyday will have to be overcome if we want to explore aesthetics beyond its present restriction to an inoffensive theory of beauty and art.

Moreover, unyielding with regard to Kant's exclusions in his *Third Critique*, it is necessary to include not only the agreeable into aesthetic appreciation, but the disagreeable, since, far from missing our objective, it would allow us to explore the aesthetic dimension through all corporeal senses, not only seeing and hearing, but taste, touch, smell, as well as synaesthesia and kinesthesia, in addition to all categories, whether pleasant or unpleasant, excruciating or delightful.

The fear of psychologism

Another fear of aesthetics is to be absorbed by psychology. When aesthetic theory refers to feelings or emotions to clarify sensibility, psychology is in fact stepping over its heels. That is why Dickie (1968, 312–335) takes on to question whether psychology is relevant to aesthetics. His perfectly predictable answer is: of course it is not! For our already well-known polemic author who, as a true philosopher, provides better questions than answers, the idea of a psychological aesthetics is futile since he considers that an empirical science such as psychology can contribute nothing to the understanding of aesthetics. Arnheim (1985), on the contrary, incorporated Gestalt psychology to artistic analysis and Berlyne (1971) proposed precisely a biological, empirical, and psychological approach, presently followed by his group at The International Association of Empirical Aesthetics with Albert Wellek, Robert Francès, Carmelo Genovese, and others.

Dickie, however, has partly a case here. Aesthetic theories that are defined in terms of effects as pleasure or pain, faithful to their Kantian heritage, are certainly threatened to become psychological studies. Bakhtin was concerned about this distinction when he made the following statement: "the problem of the soul is methodologically an aesthetic problem, and cannot be one of psychology, which is a causal science lacking evaluation, since the soul, despite developing and shaping in time, is an individual totality, evaluative and free". (Bajtín 1990, 93) He again deals with the problem in the following manner: "That which is mine in the experience of the object is studied by psychology, but in an absolute abstraction of the evaluative weight of the I and of the other, of their uniqueness; psychology only knows of 'possible individuality' (*Ebbinghaus*). The internal givenness is not contemplated, but is studied in the supposed unity of the psychological law in a context deprived of values." (Bajtín 1990, 104) In other words, while psychology incorporates the particular into the general and uses a causal non-evaluative criterion except in therapeutic terms, aesthetics, on the other hand, does consider the particular and the concrete and establishes valuations, but it does not operate from a cause-effect criterion.

Ever since Kant, the effects of pleasure and pain have been set forth as relevant to and characterizing aesthetics. We speak of the comical as causing an effect of laughter, of the tragic as provoking the emotion of pity and compassion, of the

40 *Everyday Aesthetics*

sublime as causing wonder and awe, of the grotesque provoking a feeling of disgust. However, the tragic can cause laughter and the comical, sadness; the sublime can provoke horror and the grotesque, pleasure. The specificity and classification of emotional effects by themselves pertain to the field of psychology, not aesthetics. While the relation that Othello establishes with the beauty of Desdemona and with the words of Iago can be considered aesthetic because it is based on the appreciation of her beauty and is captivated by Iago's rhetorics, Othello's emotional reactions of love, rage, and jealousy are psychological effects, not aesthetic. We, on the other hand, appreciate aesthetically the representation of these emotions on the stage, but the emotional effects this representation provokes in us, like sympathy, pity, sadness or pleasure, are psychological.

For that reason, to exorcise the fear of psychologism, aesthetics must stop worrying about qualifying the emotional effects generated by aesthetic relations. It is not that these effects lack importance, on the contrary. Yet aesthetics is not concerned with specific emotional effects that change from one subject to another, but with the means and conditions by which those effects are produced.

The fear of the immoral

Sánchez Vázquez intends to include the realm of the everyday into his aesthetic theory and applies categories such as the ugly, the comical, the sublime, the grotesque, and the beautiful to art as well as to everyday life. He states that man can have aesthetic relations in the everyday through these categories. Nevertheless, when he confronts the tragic, his pen, like a frightened horse, refuses to continue.

> To convert the fire in a building, in which a man is being devoured by the flames, into a spectacle or an object of contemplation, and to enjoy the shapes, the colors or the expression of the terrified face, would not only be immoral, but a human perversion. In this sense, the tragic loses its aesthetic dimension in real life, a dimension that we do find when we consider it from the categories of the beautiful, the ugly, or the sublime. (Sánchez Vázquez 1992, 214)

That someone can watch death, pain, or a conflagration as a spectacle and feel pleasure is, unfortunately, a fact. The proof is their repeated display in films and television. This attraction to the tragic in real life explains the crowds that gather at traffic accidents or similar events, the repeated transmission of tragic and violent images in the mass media and even the existence of something as monstrous as snuff. This attraction, perverse or not, amoral or immoral, is aesthetic, embarrassing as it may be. Sánchez Vázquez cannot accept it; that is why he prefers to deny that the tragic in real life can be considered aesthetic. He affirms: "With this limitation that, as we see, is more moral than aesthetic, it can be stated that the tragic occurs in real life, in human existence, without it necessarily having an aesthetic dimension." In spite of what Sánchez Vázquez would wish to find, the tragic in real life will necessarily have an aesthetic dimension as long as the sensibility of the subject comes into play by judging something as being "tragic".

The Fears of Aesthetics

Sánchez Vázquez's horror to accept the tragic as aesthetic in everyday life is morally understandable, but theoretically inconsistent. The problem he faces here stems from the ambiguous definition of aesthetics carrying the burden of antiquated ideas such as "contemplation", "feeling of pleasure", and "disinterested delight". Thus, instead of getting rid of these connotations about the aesthetic (that precisely in this example prove their uselessness), Sánchez Vázquez preferred to jettison everyday tragedies from having an aesthetic dimension. The tendency to automatically attribute a virtuous character and a morally positive connotation to everything related to the aesthetic, again the Pangloss Syndrome, works here once more as an epistemological obstacle. Aesthetic phenomena needs not be immoral, but also not moral. We must overcome the Pangloss Syndrome if we really want to understand human sensibility.

Sánchez Vázquez's observation is highly interesting because it sends us back to the previous section, that of the fear of psychologism, but by another route. To feel fear, repugnance, morbidity, pain, or panic about something does not make it, by definition, aesthetic. In the previous section I explained that while the conditions to produce emotional effects are pertinent to aesthetics, the specificity of their emotional effects is relevant to psychology. The presence of emotion does not define the aesthetic (since it can be produced be chemical stimulants or internal body processes). Also, categorizing something as tragic, comical, or grotesque, is not equivalent to experiencing them as an aesthetic, since it could be a purely taxonomic judgment. A premature death will not be tragic for someone who does not apprehend it sensitively. We have the case of a forensic doctor who simply reports "female, 17, died from congestion of the digestive system ...." On the other hand, a trivial but profoundly touching object, like "the obtuse" for Barthes (1986), that is practically non-categorizable (like the image of an insignificant character with a cap in a scene of a film by Eisenstein) is full of aesthetic significance for him.[2]

Summing up, that the tragic in everyday life may be contemplated with pleasure is certainly a perversion, and it certainly occurs, but should not for that reason be invalidated as pertinent to aesthetic inquiry. On the contrary, it is our duty as aestheticians to understand how it occurs. It is aesthetic not because it involves contemplation or pleasure but because it impinges upon the subject's sensibility. The tragic in the everyday or in art is definitely aesthetic whenever it moves or touches us, and is not when it is a simple categorization, lacking sensitive appraisal. From understanding this responsive disposition or its blockage we could explore its imbrication with ethics in Kant's enigmatic paragraph 59 of the *Critique of Judgment* referring to "beauty as the symbol of morality". But this topic is beyond the scope of this text, and will have to be dealt with elsewhere, sometime.

It is necessary to confront the fear of the immoral in the research of aesthetic phenomena, and overcome the calculated naïveté of attributing it an exclusively virtuous character if we ever want to understand the complete range of its manifestations. Phenomena like the current aesthetics of violence, snuff or classical music played at the gates of the gas chambers in Auschwitz require a rigorous examination without the ballast of naïve aestheticism and its Pangloss Syndrome.

2　See Chapter 13.

In due time, the theory of aesthetics will have to account not only for the delight in Kantian beauty and the sublime, but for phenomena like aesthetic violence and the aesthetization of violence, of aesthetic abuse and intrusion, the blunting of sensibility, its perversion, and its poisoning.

In conclusion, the fears of aesthetics facing the precipices of relativism, subjectivism, psychologism, of the prosaic and mundane, of the undesirable and the immoral have functioned as real epistemological obstacles in the zeal of aestheticians who hold on to art and beauty as privileged, and exclusive, objects of their discipline. If they let loose of the fetish of beauty, it is only to immediately grab another: art.

PART 2
ON AESTHESIS

Not too victorious, one might say, was our exit from the labyrinths of aesthetics. We came out of it without a sufficiently clear concept of the aesthetic, of its limitations, scope, and particular modes of manifestation. Venturing into its problems, myths, and fetishes allowed us at least to recognize that the dimension of the aesthetic is not as simple as might be suggested if taken as a mere synonym of art and beauty.

Mainstream aesthetic theory considers that the purpose of this discipline is to discover the special characteristics proper to aesthetic objects, particularly of certain objects classified as "artworks", and to elucidate what criteria would validate such classification. Analytic aesthetics, for example, yearns to proceed by the standard for hard sciences in order to purge philosophic discourse from logical weaknesses, define objects that would be specific to its field, and isolate them in their supposedly independent and observable reality for verifying if the propositions of the theory are well–founded and "match reality". This imitation of scientific procedures hides the fact that what we are dealing with here are not the objects but the subjects that relate in a particular manner to their surroundings in terms of their sensibility. These subjects exceed the limited confines of the artistic precisely because it is from them whom the aesthetic dimension is projected.

Everyday aesthetics is as volatile as it is persistent. It does not materialize into finite and durable items like artworks, even if it permeates all regions of social reality. The fact that it is not spectacular or extraordinary explains why it hasn't called the attention of aesthetic theory. Yet, the study of the aesthetics of everyday life becomes possible precisely now, when social sciences and humanities have converged towards examining simple facts and ordinary practices, as does ethnography, human ethology, conversational analysis, and micro–sociology or symbolic interactionism. The goal is no longer to elaborate great theoretical abstractions or grandiose treaties but to explore the minute network of concrete social exchanges.

In this second part, Ariadne's thread is being spun allowing us to exit this labyrinth. A broader yet no less precise demarcation of aesthetics will be elaborated with sufficient amplitude to encompass both the everyday and the artistic, and yet with enough caution so as not to lose on the way the specificity that differentiates the aesthetic from the non–aesthetic. After this demarcation we will be able to stand on a firmer ground for undertaking our longed for exploration of the aesthetics of everyday life.

Chapter 5

Demarcating Aesthetics

Each new book on aesthetics goes on to define once again what the author understands by the term "aesthetics". Other disciplines like physics or mathematics do not need to begin by defining physics or mathematics in each new publication. What seems evident from the labyrinths we have explored so far is that there is no agreement on what can be understood by "aesthetics", and as long as this situation continues, a more solid development of its theory is impossible. An attempt of definition at hand, among hundreds of possible others, is that proposed by Adolfo Sánchez Vázquez (1992, 57): "Our definition is the following: aesthetics is the science of appropriating reality in a specific manner, associated with other ways of human appropriation of the world, in given historical, social, and cultural conditions."

The author, however, does not say what that "specific manner" is, and what the "other ways" are. Besides, the definition of Sánchez Vázquez can also be applied to sociology, politics, or economics. Consequently, it is not operative. Moreover, is aesthetics really a science? Why? What methodology does it use? Have aesthetic theories really advanced to such an extent as to grant them scientific status? As I mentioned in the Preface, while the principle of verifiability in science demands that any observer, wherever situated, can corroborate a phenomenon under the same conditions, in aesthetic studies observations wholly depend upon the matricial location of the subject. What is more, aesthetic theory does not look for laws in nature nor has any possibility of prediction over the phenomena been observed. This is the reason why aesthetics has no hope of ever becoming a science in the strict sense of the term, as there can never be two subjects located exactly in the same matricial configuration given the absolute uniqueness of each one as an individual. We can, however, develop aesthetics not as a science but as a theory by constructing analytical categories, tools and models—as did Freud for the psychoanalytical study of the subject—and demarcating its field of pertinence. Note that we are not looking for a definition as much as for a demarcation.

I have quoted precisely Sánchez Vázquez because it is remarkable that when he sets out to define aesthetics, he arrives at a very imprecise proposal and, yet, when he only tries to describe aesthetics, he targets with notable finesse upon a specifically aesthetic ingredient, namely the idea of "excess", rendering a heuristically fertile concept (developed in Chapter 18; see also Mandoki 2001).

In finding a clue to the primordial sense with which the term "aesthetic" emerged, it is necessary to go back to its etymological origin. From the Greek etymology, aesthetics specifically refers to the *subject of sensibility* or *perception* (*aisthe* perception or sensibility derived from *aisthenasthai*, and the suffix *tes* agent or subject). It does not refer to any particular category of objects or their relation to beauty, much less to art despite the fact that these have been the meanings selected

46 *Everyday Aesthetics*

and established by aesthetic theory and art history for more than a quarter of a millennium already.

Credit is given to Baumgarten in his *Metaphysics* (1739), where the word "aesthetics" appears for the first time as a specific concept denoting a branch of philosophy (before his enormous unfinished treatise *Aesthetics* of 1750–58) and refers to the "science of sensitive knowledge": *Aesthetica est scientia cognitionis sensitivae.* Thus for Baumgarten human beings have a special kind of knowledge that is sensitive because it is characterized by its link to the senses.

But what is the "sensitive"? It invokes a kin of terms which exhibit *family resemblances* with the common root *"sen"* (cf. Dewey [1934] 1980, 22) all of which are related to the basic concept of sensibility: *sen*timent, *sen*sation, *sen*sual, *sen*sitive, *sen*sible, *sen*tient, *sen*sorial, *sen*sational, *sen*suous, (common) *sen*se, *sen*se as meaning, *sen*se as reason, *sen*sing as feeling, and so on. All these terms are invoked, but the sensitive is not limited to any of them in particular. This family of similar terms has caused headaches to aestheticians that intend to apprehend concepts from their essence and define aesthetics by necessary and sufficient reasons, or by proximate genus and specific difference.

From the point of view of rationalist ideology of the eighteenth century it is understandable that Baumgarten would hierarchically claim: "the things are known by a superior capacity as objects of logic, whereas the things perceived must be by an inferior capacity as its object or aesthetics". (Baumgarten [1735] 1975, 9) One must acknowledge his great merit of proposing precisely then, in the midst of rationalism, the differentiated study of sensitive knowledge. Nevertheless, the Cartesian vein of his specification of sensible representations as "clear but confused" compared to the "clear and distinct" cognitive representations becomes irrelevant today.

Terry Eagleton (1990, 15) points out, to the contrary, that with this movement Baumgarten tried less to project the world of the body and the sensible to the forefront of philosophical discussion, than to subject it to the colonization of reason. Eagleton is right, but having failed under the adamant resistance of the object to be confined in these rational categories, Baumgarten effectively managed to situate it at the center of philosophical debate, where it is still located today.

At the very beginning of the *Critique of Pure Reason* § 1, in his "Transcendental Aesthetics", Kant defines the aesthetic as relative to sensibility: "I call transcendental aesthetics the science of all a priori principles of sensibility." By the term "sensibility" Kant understands "the capacity of receiving (receptivity) representations according to the manner of how the objects affect us". But at the beginning of the *Critique of Judgment* § 1 there is a slight change of signification in what Kant defines as aesthetic, emphasizing the subjective: "The judgment of taste is, therefore, not a judgment of knowledge; thus, it is not logical, but aesthetic, if we understand by this that the determining base of which cannot be but *subjective*. If in a judgment [...] [the representations] [...] are only referred to the *subject* (his feeling), this judgment is always aesthetic." (Emphasis added)

Following Baumgarten, Kant contrasts the aesthetic to the logical, except that his valuation is not hierarchic as in the former. What is clear so far is that in both, the Greek meaning of the term *aisthetes* and the Kantian definition, we are dealing first and foremost with the *subject*. And yet, the subject of perception is the starting point not only of aesthetics, but of different disciplines; they all differ, however, in the points of arrival. Neurology studies the subject of perception with regard to the brain and its neural processes. Epistemology focuses the mechanisms with which the subject builds knowledge and legitimizes its validity. In psychology the subject of perception is focused according to its social adjustment and well-being. By and large, ethics is concerned with the subject's decisions and acts in accordance to social and personal values. Aesthetics studies the subject in its openness to life. Thus, epistemology and aesthetics overlap as they both are interested in perception, but they diverge in that one accentuates cognitive effects of perception whereas aesthetics highlights its appreciative effects. By both cognitive and aesthetic processes, the subjects constitute realities that are factual and imaginary, social and personal; but while denotation predominates in the cognitive, connotation is more connected to the aesthetic. Ethics and aesthetics also overlap when focusing subjects in terms of their sensibility; however, in ethics what matters are the decisions taken by the subject, whereas for aesthetics what predominates is their adhesion (as I will explain in Chapter 8).

Valuation is an activity that subjects perform according to different criteria. We may appraise, as cognitive subjects, the truth value in a proposition, or, as ethical subjects, assess the demand and consequences of an action. As aesthetic subjects we may consider the lure or repulsion that a person, object or event can inspire. In each case appraisals depend on social conventions with regard to truth, goodness or attractiveness.

A genealogical perspective for a bio-aesthetics

In the *History of Sexuality*, Foucault (1986) wrote about "aesthetics of existence" with regards to ways for accomplishing a harmonious and beautiful life. He was referring to classical Greece's ideal of maintaining balance and self-control over one's life (implying the synonymity of aesthetics and beauty). It is not this sense that I am concerned with here, but rather with Foucault's interest on the genealogy of the subject and power that develop from Nietzsche's genealogy of morality. Thus we shall explore the aesthetic subject from a genealogical approach related to what Foucault intended to elaborate, particularly in his last writings (although he focused this genealogy on power, not precisely aesthetics, as a constituent of the subject). This genealogical perspective in the formation of subjectivity (linked to an enigmatic term, "sensibility") derives both from the etymological meaning of *aisthetes* and the Kantian definition of aesthetics in both Critiques, reinforcing the subject as the node of convergence from which aesthetic theory emerges.

Weitz (1987, 153) affirmed that it is not possible to define either aesthetics or sensibility in an absolute manner; consequently the function of aesthetic theory cannot be definitional, which he believed to be logically condemned to failure. Instead, he proposed to read it as summaries of serious recommendations for paying attention to certain manners and aspects of art. I disagree with Weitz; we must understand defining, or at least demarcating, as a constitutive act necessary for theory in preventing terminological ambiguities. Accurately, Weitz (1987) emphasized a

48 *Everyday Aesthetics*

distinction between the evaluative and the descriptive use of the word "art" which, applied to aesthetics, is very significant since when something is referred to as "aesthetic" it is not always clear whether it is with the intention of describing it or of praising it. Let me affirm that, along this text, the use of the term "aesthetic", as well as the term "artistic" will be exclusively descriptive. Moreover, I contend that there is good and bad art, as there are good and bad aesthetics (namely sensitive interactions that do not nourish but enfeeble the subject, or blockage of sensibility). From now on, when I refer to an event as "aesthetic" it will mean not that it is beautiful or artistic, but only that it is pertinent to the study of aesthetics.

From the start, one of the problems that aesthetics has been dragging along is the conflation between the object of analysis and the theory that analyzes it. It brings to mind the common case when news anchors announce that in a certain region there are "meteorological problems", literally problems with the study of meteors, instead of saying that there are climatic or atmospheric problems. That is why authors interested in this field often speak of "aesthetic objects", meaning literally objects that are sensitive (when what they really mean is "objects of aesthetics").

Because a definition is not about catching the ultimate essence of its object but instead of making theoretical constructions and operations explicit, we must state what precisely we are going to understand here by this term. It is then useful to apply to aesthetics the same distinction Morris (quoted by Pelc 2000, 426) made between semiosis and semiotics: "Semiosis: process of signs, e.g. a process in which something is a sign for some organism. It has to be distinguished from semiotics as the study of semiosis. The terms 'semiosic' and 'semiotic' must be distinguished in the same manner."

Equally, by "aesthetics" we will understand the study of the condition of aesthesis. Aesthesis refers to the particular nature of subjectivity that makes it sensitive, receptive, or porous to its environment. Subjectivity implies sensibility. Consequently, if we focus upon the human scale only, we will no longer consider the aesthetic experience as its central problem (which would literally mean a beautiful experience in the evaluative sense or an experience that results from studying art) but instead the condition of being open and exposed to life. What is worth exploring here are not those privileged moments denominated "aesthetic experiences" but this condition of being alive that consists of openness and permeability to the world. There is no aesthesis without life, and no life without aesthesis. What is at stake for aesthetic studies is the basic condition of any live being.

Adopting a genealogical perspective forces us to admit that there is no reason why aesthetics should be confined exclusively to the human species, as this openness to the world occurs throughout various levels of organism complexity among all live creatures at any stage of evolution. A thirsty animal that finds water to quench its thirst may also enjoy its freshness. This fact allows us to understand better what we are referring to when we use the enigmatic word "sensibility", namely, this porous condition that, as a membrane, protects as well as exposes every live creature. Such membrane is the contour that separates and at the same time connects the subject with its world or *umwelt* at any scale: Monera, Protista, Fungi, Plantae up to Animalia. At a cellular level, aesthesis depends on the cellular wall of bacteria and protozoa and the plasmatic membrane in cells. In the pluricellular order of mammals, this condition

Demarcating Aesthetics   49

Table 5.1   The Branches of Aesthetics

AESTHETICS	
BIO-AESTHETICS	SOCIO-AESTHETICS
Cyto-Aesthetics	Prosaics (Medical, Religion Family School,
Phyto-Aesthetics	Military, National, Juridical, Sports)
Zoo-Aesthetics	Poetics (Music, Literature, Sculpture,
Anthropo-Aesthetics	Painting, Film, Photography)

depends on their epithelial membranes like the skin or epidermis, the timpani membrane that allows us to hear, membranes like the cornea and photoreceptors in retinal cones for seeing, the olfactory epithelium in the nasal cavity and taste receptor cells at the tongue conducted through the nervous system. This porosity to stimuli from the environment is the condition of aesthesis or sensibility in all live beings before, during and after triggering processes of semiosis.

Maturana and Varela (1992, 43) explored live creatures from unicellular to pluricellular up to pluri-individual or social organisms in terms of their inner organization they defined as *autopoiesis*. "Our proposition is that living beings are characterized in that, literally, they are continually self-producing. We indicate this process when we call the organization that defines them an *autopoietic organization*." They emphasized that at a cellular level, the most elemental organism generates a border by its membrane to separate it from the environment in a particular dynamic. It must be added that aesthesis is essential for autopoiesis to take place, since no self-production is possible without openness to its habitat. In the cell, this condition of autopoiesis permits it to close and individualize itself for performing the metabolism basic for its self-production, and at the same time to open for detecting nutrients and assimilating them or getting rid of toxic elements for its survival. Aesthesis and autopoiesis are coupled.

We could then consider the field of aesthetic studies as developing into a bio-aesthetics, namely an inquiry on live creatures as membraned and exposed to the world. In this text we will explore only the anthropological level, namely the human being in its interaction with the world, with itself and others at the scale of anthropo-aesthesis. The aesthetics of art, that traditionally has been equivalent to the whole field of aesthetic studies, is merely one part of it circumscribed to the artistic matrix. What is of interest here is what this condition of aesthesis implies to the human being as a vulnerable creature and susceptible to pleasure and pain, open to fascination and repulsion. (See Table 5.1.)

Bio-aesthetics

One fresh morning, a sluggish cat enjoys its siesta at the sunniest spot of the couch. By observing animal behavior it is easy to be convinced of the viability of a zoo-aesthetics. My cat Nu and her son spend the whole day sleeping, playing under the carpets, exploring the house and the garden, licking themselves and grooming each other. They play three types of games: locomotive play (jumping, running, climbing),

50 *Everyday Aesthetics*

predatory (they simulate attacking each other and hunt small lizards and humming birds), and object play (they roll balls, threads, and cables) (cf. Bekoff and Byers 1998). Their pleasure is evident.

These behaviors illustrate what Levinas understood by "sensitivity" when he affirmed: "Sensibility is enjoyment" and added: "sensibility is therefore to be described not as a moment of representation, but as the instance of enjoyment ... Sensibility is not an inferior theoretical knowledge bound however intimately to affective states: in its very gnosis, sensitivity is enjoyment; it is satisfied with the given, it is contented." (Levinas [1969] 1998, 136) We may consequently understand aesthesis etymologically as perception and phenomenologically as enjoyment.

It is, therefore, easier to find an illustration of sensitivity in cats playing than in galleries and museums of the contemporary metropolitan cities where it is sometimes necessary to wait in long lines in order to hurry through jammed museum halls only to listen to a frequently trivial explanation of an artwork (and finally sigh of relief after this obligatory bath of highbrow culture). Although it is possible to speak of animal sensitivity by observing them, it is, however, at a conjecture level to explore vegetal sensitivity.

The possibility of empathy or *einfühlung*, key concept of Lipps's aesthetic philosophy, could be re-examined under the light of the recent findings by Giacomo Rizzolatti, Leonardo Fogassi and Vittorio Gallese (2006) with respect to the monkey's pre-motor ventral area which has the peculiarity that certain neurons are fired not only when the monkey performs physical action like pushing, hauling, grabbing, or chewing a peanut, but also when perceiving that another monkey (and even the human researcher), performs them. In other words, those neurons are activated in the performance of an action as much as in the perception of such action, and could give significant hints to explain the phenomenon of emotional contagion.

We can project an additional distinction from the semiotics of Thure von Uexküll et al. (1993), who propose the categories of *endosemiosis* and *exosemiosis* from which we could derive the concepts of endo-aesthesis and the exo-aesthesis, understanding by the former inherent sensitivity and by the latter interactional sensibility. Endo-aesthesis can occur in cases such as sensitivity during prenatal stage of the fetus or feeling in the oneiric or coma state. Exo-aesthesis may be an adequate term to denote aesthesis during animal mating rituals, awareness of danger and social interactions. Artistic production may well include both: inner sensitivity to creative imagination and finding vehicles or idiolects to communicate and share this sensibility with others.

Socio-aesthetics

From bio-aesthetics as the enjoyment of the mere fact of being alive, we pass to socio-aesthetics. Here is where, occupied in everyday activities for the cultural production of commodities, services and linguistic work (as Rossi-Landi has called it) a surplus pops up that is consumed and produced not only as a physical object and as a sign, but as something else: a significative object of pleasure or pain. As individuals, we always crave for pleasure despite years of education that have persuaded us that pleasure should be sacrificed under the weight of duty. We lack the luxury life of cats and yet, in everyday life, we constantly produce and receive an aesthetic surplus in our interactions with the social environment. Things have meaning, but they also convey joy, or pain.

We will thus demarcate socio-aesthetics as the study of the processes of aesthesis in the midst social life (echoing Saussure's definition semiology as "the study of signs in the midst of social life"). Socio-aesthetics will focus on two particular fields of study: poetics as the aesthetic production and reception of the artistic, and prosaics as the aesthetic dimension in everyday life. This book is not about socio-aesthetics because it does not include the whole scope of Poetics. Our center of attention will be exclusively prosaics, although we will include the prosaics of art, namely, artistic modus operandi seen as a social practice in everyday life. prosaics will analyze art as a social matrix from the outside, whereas Poetics analyzes artistic invention from within, according to its own idiolects and rules of configuration. Since practically all aesthetic theory, art criticism and philosophy of art have been dedicated to this subject, we will not deal with it in this work.

Prosaics is particularly at stake through the strategies of constitution of and interaction with personal and collective identities. The aesthetics of art, traditionally understood as equivalent to the whole field of aesthetics, is part of socio-aesthetics that centers around the production within the artistic matrix well-known as "artworld". As a tip of the aesthetic iceberg, poetics has been the most conspicuous of all aesthetic activities as the action of making artifacts deliberately directed towards human sensibility for mental and sensorial enjoyment. It is an institutionalized practice (cf. Dickie, Danto) taken to be synonymous to the whole field of aesthetics. I want to stress the limited role that Poetics plays within the aesthetic spectrum, and despite it, the reason it has usurped the whole aesthetic theory is due to not only its spectacular artistic achievements but its important role in strategies for social distinction and status legitimization. (cf. Bourdieu 1984, Eagleton 1990)

In conclusion let us establish aesthetics as the study of the condition of aesthesis, and as such having two lines of inquiry: bio-aesthetics as the study of aesthesis in live creatures, and socio-aesthetics as the study of aesthetic practices in social life. Socio-aesthetics will focus on two particular objects of study: poetics as the theory of artistic activity, events and artifacts, and prosaics as aesthetic activity, events and artifacts in daily life. If *signification* or semiosis depends upon, as Bateson once said, "a difference that makes a difference", the *significative* or aesthesis depends on how such difference affects our propensity for joy or woe.

As human beings we may move along the aesthetic spectrum from our basic bio-aesthetic condition of live creatures undergoing enjoyment or pain, to our prosaic, everyday labor of dramaturgically presenting our identities to survive socially, on to the more refined artistic aesthetics in poetics creating literary, musical or visual artifacts and imaginary worlds by mapping routes we can travel as spectators or readers to interpret and enjoy these inventions. (See Table 5.2.)

Table 5.2   Bio-aesthetics and Socio-aesthetics

Main aspects	Bio-aesthetics	Prosaics	Poetics
Activity	Undergoing	Laboring	Working
Appearance	Presence	Presentation	Re–presentation
Condition	Person	Persona	Personage (character)
Subjective phase	Individuality	Identity	Personality

Chapter 6

Basic Categories for Aesthetic Analysis

Aesthetic subject and aesthetic object

It is necessary to begin from the "orthodox" subject-object dichotomy as a point of departure for our analysis (despite Heidegger and many other postmodernist authors' objection to it for considering it a metaphysical idea).[1] Rather than metaphysical, the subject-object distinction is operative as a necessary theoretical tool for focusing with more precision problems here discussed. The whole debate upon the aesthetic object-subject partly proves how problematic this distinction still is, as well as how unavoidable it remains for the field of aesthetics.

Aesthetic theory has oscillated between objectivism (of beauty, of the text and its meaning, of the work of art and its concepts, properties, features, or aspects[2]) and a more or less assumed subjectivism from the theory of reception, negative hermeneutics, idealistic aesthetics, theories of empathy (*Einfühlung*) or experience (*Erlebnis*), and literary deconstruction. Deciding on one of these alternatives has been perhaps a question, as Feyerabend (1974, 72) would have it, of an almost visceral or temperamental decision rather than a result of objective rational thinking. So I must make explicit that the text I am elaborating here is written from the objectivism of the subject and the subjectivism of the object. I understand the subject as necessarily constituted by the dense objectivity of the social (and, therefore, a relatively objective subject), and the object as necessarily existing solely by the perception of the subject (as an object of perception), a subjectivated object. In other words, I start from an *objective subjectivity*—that of a subject always and necessarily constituted from social objectivity—and from *subjective objectivity*—an object that exists inasmuch as it is subjectivated by the subject. This integrated vision of subjectivism-objectivism (which we may designate with the ugly but precise term of "*sub-ob-jectivism*") is a dynamic, complex, and fluid process. The effect of stability and objectivity of the object becomes less a result of the material permanence of the object than of the subject's common social, semiotic, and anatomic conditioning

---

1 Since Heidegger to postmodern philosophers like Lyotard and Derrida, the notion of metaphysics has become a derogative term. Nevertheless, although this is not the place to discuss it, thought cannot proceed without some metaphysical presuppositions. Not everything is perfectly refutable and verifiable; the same exigency of verifiability is itself metaphysical. The most logical, rational and rigorous mathematical axiom of A=A, is based on the metaphysical assumption of the identity.

2 See Sibley "Aesthetic Concepts" in Margolis (1987, 29–52) and Crowther "Aesthetic Aspects" (1987).

54 *Everyday Aesthetics*

that enable it to interpret as "sameness" perceptions that differ in time, form, and place.[3]

Objectivity is understood here as intersubjectivity or co-subjectivity generated by conventions, debates, and negotiations among subjects in their shared social production of reality.[4] This subject-object relation is a social relation, inasmuch as subjects always constitute themselves from the social, and from there also they constitute their objects. In the *Third Critique*, the subject seeks universal consensus to his judgment of taste, but Kant is not aware that this judgment was already conditioned by the subject's insertion in society. This subject was already, even before expressing his judgment, part of the *sensus communis*, the communal sense, to which he then appeals to obtain universal consensus. Such transcendental subject is in fact, against Kant, a social and historical subject rather than a metaindividual one. This does not mean that it should be reduced to a particular position determined by the system, as was supposed by antihumanistic trends in Marxism, or to a monadic point of view as in Leibnizian metaphysics. It is not the original Cartesian subject either, the cogito, from whom thought and certainty originate in isolation. There are conditions for the possibility and emergence of the aesthetic subject within particular historical situations. The subject that aesthetics deals with is always historically, corporeally, and socially constituted.

There are various modes of the subject-object relation, depending on the capacities put into play. Among these relations is the technical (operating with the object), the cognitive (knowing the characteristics of the object), the aesthetic (appreciating or enduring the object), economic (profiting from the object) relations that overlap and entangle with each other, but that can nevertheless be differentiated. In medicine, for instance, the relations that the subject (a surgeon) establishes with his object (the patient) may be: technical in performing surgery, cognitive in medical research and diagnosis of an illness, or ethical when in assuming responsibility over the life and well-being of the patient. Other relations are the economic as a source of income and expense, linguistic as a translation of symptoms (indexical signs) into language (symbolic signs in Peircean terms), and psychological when emotionally affecting or being affected by the condition of the patient. There can also be an aesthetic relation when, in a face-to-face communication, appreciation or delight in the interaction become salient.

There is usually no reciprocity in aesthetic relations between subject and object as a waterfall, a cave, or paintings do not respond to our admiration. The sensation that an object responds or that it is possible to dialogue with it is an effect of the anthropomorphization of the objects. The supposed "dialogue with art" never really takes place with an artwork but with the artist mediated by the artwork and in a deferred non-reciprocal process. Even in theater performances, where there seems to be a dialogue between actors and the public, that dialogue is partly illusory since the reaction of the public was more or less calculated beforehand. Nonetheless, it is

---

3 This sub-objectivism is somehow compatible with the concept of "interpretative communities" proposed by Stanley Fish (1980) for whom the stability of the text is an effect of the stability of interpretative strategies.

4 Herman Parret (1995, 6–7) felicitously proposed this concept of co-subjectivity.

Basic Categories for Aesthetic Analysis

undeniable that theater performances are affected by the reactions of the public at each show, and that dialogical variation may occur. But not even here can we speak of true reciprocity. A dialogue is a woven logos by two or more speakers affecting one another. When the expression of one does not affect the other, when it does not produce any effects, there is no dialogue but two successive or overlapping monologues.

Each process of aesthesis is a particular event determined by the relation of a specific subject with a specific object. Dewey points this out when stating that:

> But the object of—or better in—perception is not one of a kind in general, a sample of a cloud or river, but this individual thing existing here and now with all the unrepeatable particularities that accompany and mark such existences. In its capacity of object-of-perception, it exists exactly in the same interaction with the living creature that constitutes the activity of perceiving. (Dewey [1934] 1980, 177)

Therefore, it is possible to speak of aesthetic objects only in terms of subjects relating to them from their sensible disposition as aesthetic subjects. Perceiving an object does not affect the object as such, but it does affect the subjects and their perception of it. The object does not respond nor does it seduce: Subjects allow themselves to be seduced by their perceptions or provoke seductions. By the same token, only subjects perceive an artist's inscriptions through an object.[5] Art does not express as words do not speak. It is subjects who express themselves through art and speak by means of words in their relation with other subjects, who in turn interpret the words and respond to art mediated expression.

I denote "aesthetic subject" the creature open to the world and alert to its oscillations (as described by John Dewey), the place where the organism opens up to life for nurturing or recoils from it for protection. The subject that aesthetics deals with is sensitive to art and beauty, as traditional aesthetics has underlined, but is also sensitive to science and to justice, to the reasonable and the worthy, to nature and to life. It is a subject equally exposed to the grandiose and to the despicable, to the grotesque and to the elegant, to the vulgar and to the refined, to the sublime and to the banal. We can thus aesthetically appreciate both the ethical and cognitive dimensions when observing a noble act or a well-elaborated concept.

Objectivity, objectuality, and objectivation

To keep it simple, I will understand "objectivity" as synonymous of intersubjectivity; by "objectuality" the nature of the object as a mere thing; and by "objectivation" the processes through which subjects manifest themselves and communicate with each other. It is then possible to speak of different types of objectivations among which are the linguistic, scientific, or aesthetic options each of them differentiated by the particular codes and processes involved.

---

5   Baudrillard (1984) proposes the objects' activity of seduction, but it is not the object, but the subject behind the object, who seduces, namely the designer and the advertiser who seduce the consumer who in turn accedes or not to let himself be seduced. The objects are only mediators in this process, not agents.

Science has intended to work at a level of pure objectuality of the referent, of the thing as such, of the object in its intrinsic constitution independently of man, until it was forced to admit that even in a hard science such as physics, the intervention of the subject is inevitable and should be taken into account while observing a phenomenon. The specific conditions of measurement in Einstein's relativistic physics and Heisenberg's Principle of Uncertainty confront us not only with the limits of pure objectuality, but with those of objectivity in science, as well as with the inescapable presence of the subject. It is always human beings and only us who observe, build, explain, predict, point out, focus, and positions ourselves. The inexorable presence of the subject is even more salient in aesthetic investigation than in hard sciences. Nevertheless, tenacious positivistic aestheticians still persist in their attempts to prove the objectuality of the aesthetic and its objectivity independently of the subject, as if aesthetics would reside in certain qualities or aspects whose inventory the theory would have to elaborate. In fact, this naïve realistic aesthetics pretends to be examining the objectivity of the aesthetic object when what it actually describes is the consensus among different subjects in regards to their particular artistic taste. Considering that the subject is socially constituted, such objectivity is found less in the objectuality of the object, than in the conditions of perception shared by the subjects. Their intersubjectivity qua subjects manifests itself as expectations and interpretations of what they perceive common to all of them. Subjects constitute themselves through and by social density, as well as by their corporeal or biological configuration the result of which is this effect of objectivity in perceptions.

I understand subjects as nodes in dynamic and interactive processes of objectivation/subjectivation from morpho-biological and socio-cultural conditions. Subjects operate in relation to their *umwelt* (Uexküll 1982) or "horizons of expectations" (Jauss 1978) and "interpretative strategies" (Fish 1976, 1980), ideologies, semiotic codes, *zeitgeist*, or *weltanschauung*. When we coincide in an interpretation or a perception, we believe to be sharing the same text or object, when what we are really sharing is a common region of intersubjectivity, a bio-cultural *a priori*. We believe to have objects in common when in fact we are sharing our manner of being subjects. Consequently, by aesthetic objectivity I understand the conditions from which the aesthetic subject as such is constituted, that is, the matrixes of subjectivity and the *a priori* of aesthetics.

The disquisitions about the truth of art, the aesthetic aspects, the qualities of an artwork, the concretion of values or of feelings in the artwork, its form or beauty presuppose the objectuality of the aesthetic object. From this supposed objectuality it is assumed that the function of theory would consist of detecting the aesthetic aspects as material elements of the work as if they would pre-exist perception. This is how the fetishes of aesthetics tenaciously spring forth attributing aesthetic or sensitive qualities to an object and converting it into a pseudo-subject.

In conclusion, to distinguish between object, objectivity, objectivation, and objectuality in aesthetics, let's first point out that we can speak of an aesthetic object only in relation to the aesthetic subject. Its being aesthetic is the product of the relation that a subject establishes with it at a given moment. Objectivity, on the other hand, has nothing to do with the object but only with the subject, since it is a result of intersubjective and social conditions of subjectivity. Objectivation is a

Basic Categories for Aesthetic Analysis

Table 6.1   Object-Related Distinctions

Objectivity	Intersubjectivity
Objectuality	Thingness
Objectivation	Subject's exteriorization
Subjectivation	Subject's interiorization

process complementary to subjectivation: while in objectivation subjects manifest themselves, produce and transform social reality, in subjectivation it is social reality that produces, constitutes, and transforms the subjects. Subjectivity is permeability. Finally, objectuality, differing from objectivity, does have to do with the object, but is not objective since it refers to the thing-as-such, to its thingness; it is not objective because it does not pass through the subject and therefore is not inter or co-subjective. Consequently, we can refer to objectuality as language refers to the extra-linguistic and Kant referred to the *noumena*. Objectuality is the outside of knowledge and perception which nevertheless limits them, resists and opposes them, imposing a territory relatively closed to knowledge: that of thingness. With a tragic and passionate love, a devotion never reciprocated, knowledge pursues objectuality which is forever evasive; he is willing to sacrifice his honor for a wink, for the least insinuation by which he may position himself for penetrating, at last, all her secrets. He fools himself.

Subjectivity, individuality, identity, role

As we are already embarked on the task of establishing methodological distinctions, and since aesthetics revolves mainly around processes related to subjectivity, we must examine both the *objectus* (thrown forth) and the *subjectus* (thrown below). Here we must distinguish four profoundly interlocked concepts: subjectivity, individuality, identity, and role. Subjectivity is the condition of openness or being exposed to the world which in human beings is displayed by three phases: individuality, identity, and role. Subjectivity is what distinguishes a live creature from inanimate matter in any level of nature.

By individuality I understand the visceral, corporeal, energetical condition of the subject, that is, its character and singularity. Individuality is our biological substrate that belongs to us from birth while sustaining ourselves in life until we lose it at death. Esoteric and mystic teachings appear to target individuality in an attempt to penetrate the primordial inner self in this elemental relation with life and death. From individuality emerge temperament and character, the impulse for life, the thrust, and the vigor.

Identity, on the other hand, is always social and depends on others for its consolidation, although it is built and projected by the subject and even outlives him. Identity is granted to us by others since it is the product of negotiations and presentation of the self. Identity is what begins at the "mirror phase" pointed out by Lacan, the discovery by the infant of his or her image as an object in the mirror, the sense of being seen from the outside. Later it evolves in the awareness of owning a certain appearance,

58   *Everyday Aesthetics*

exercising a profession, belonging to a certain family or ethnic group, nation or religion. It has to do with prestige, accomplishments, and reputation. Identities may be personal or collective and we become members of society only through them. They are essential for social survival, as the shell of a snail for its biological subsistence.

The fact that identities are granted does not mean that we remain passive to them. On the contrary: we are exposed to continuous processes of construction and negotiation employing strategic games to establish credibility or influence others. These games were pointed out by Goffman's ([1959] 1981) dramaturgical analysis of the presentation of self in "face to face" interactions. Precisely in identity construction, aesthetic strategies play a fundamental role. The production of identity is, then, not only a semiosic activity as a display of signs of who we are or what we want, but also aesthetic, since it is aimed at achieving appreciation by and for others. As Berger and Luckmann (1986, 217) point out, identity is a phenomenon that emerges from the dialectics between an individual and society and not an isolated or pre-established item. Identity is made by acts of enunciation and interpretation that are performative when words transcend to acts, and constitutive of the person when appreciated and appraised positively or negatively by others.

Subjectivity is the condition of possibility of identity, just as individuality for subjectivity. From individuality, subjectivity emerges to become objectivated through identities. The collective conditions of possibility for the construction of identities are the matrixes or institutions that establish each of their conventional rules and values. The function of subjectivity, however, is not limited to be only the substratum of identities, since it functions as the point of integration of realities internal and external, private and public, personal and social, and above all, present, past, and future enabling one to recognize oneself as the same being through time. Subjectivity is equally intrasubjectivity (Wiley's 1994 I-you-me), inter-identity within the subject, and intersubjectivity among various subjects. The instability resulting from the multiplicity of identities as discrete entities displayed by the person in different settings according to Goffman's ([1959] 1981) dramaturgical analysis is controlled and balanced by subjectivity. While highly dynamic in its continuous interchange with social reality, subjectivity binds identities together and maintains the memory and continuity that allows one to recognize oneself within these identities regardless of how variable the contexts of enunciation may be.

Throughout the processes of objectivation and subjectivation (as cardiac systole and diastole) subjectivity stays alive, and in continuous movement and exchange with the environment. By objectivation it constitutes identities of its own, and by subjectivation it appreciates or validates others' identities, while reinforcing, creating, and recreating its own subjectivity. Therefore, contrarily to what could be supposed, there is no symmetry between identity and subjectivity because while subjectivity is heterogeneous, relatively stable and unique in its being rooted on individuality (although highly dynamic in each individual), identity is multiple, homogeneous, and ephemeral in each case, according to the context. The consistency and credibility of an identity depend on homogeneity since this enables necessary predictability, in contrast to the mode of subjectivity which, if it were homogeneous, would seriously limit the possibilities of survival by imbuing excessive rigidity to the range of action and reaction necessary to cope with varying circumstances. Cases

Basic Categories for Aesthetic Analysis 59

of rigid subjectivity require medical intervention, particularly when one identity usurps the place of subjectivity as a whole (as with workaholics and fanatics), or when individuality usurps it, as in drug addiction where the bodily impulses take over the whole range of action of the person. Multiple personality syndrome is so painful because diverse identities tear apart an individual's subjectivity, thus causing her to lose the basic anchor for a unified direction of experience.

From the conception of symbolic interactionism as set forth by Goffman, it is worth examining a term repeatedly mentioned by the author and frequently confused with identity, namely, the role. While identity is personal and specific, role is anonymous and general. Identity is built, whereas role is assumed; in identity the subject is active, but in the role he is passive. By identities let us understand those that have to do with family, religion, school, national, professional all of which are personally and collectively constructed. By roles I understand circumstantial conditions such as being a passenger in a vehicle, buyer in a supermarket, client in a bank, customer in a restaurant, user of a service.

Jean Paul Sartre describes how the waiter in a café plays and presents his role as café waiter:

> But what is he playing? It isn't necessary to watch him a long time to see: he plays he is a waiter in a café. There is nothing there that can astonish us: play is a sort of discovery and investigation. The child plays with his body to explore it, to establish his inventory. The waiter in the café plays with his condition to achieve it. This obligation does not differ from that imposed on all merchants; all its condition is that of ceremony, the public demands from them that they perform it as a ceremony. There is the dance of the shopkeeper, the dressmaker, the auctioneer through which they endeavor to persuade their customers that they are nothing more than a shopkeeper, an auctioneer, a dressmaker.[6]

To illustrate these three levels of subjectivity, consider the subject as a cell whose nucleus corresponds to individuality, and its cellular membrane to identity, whereas its location and function within the tissue or organ would correspond to its role. Cerebral death or the state of coma is the death of the subject, but not of the individual while it maintains its vital functions, nor of its role as patient. His identity also remains because he will still continue being father, son or brother to somebody.

In certain situations it is possible to substitute identity for role, and even subvert the role with identity. As an example, instead of resigning oneself to the role of patient delegating on the physician, the whole weight of the decision in regards to surgical intervention (with the risks of anonymity and dehumanization it implies), a person may choose to constitute a personal identity facing a doctor. He will formulate questions regarding the diagnosis and deploy an inquisitive attitude about the treatment to better appraise the doctor's credibility. Thus he will veer the interaction of the role of passive patient toward the identity of an alert, intelligent person that directly questions and shares the responsibility of the treatment. It would be desirable if we could do the same interactional veering as citizens in relation to professional politicians.

---

6   Jean-Paul Sartre in *L'Etre et le Néant*, Gallimard, p. 99 quoted by Joseph (1999, 58–59).

Table 6.2 Phases of Subjectivity

Subjectivity	Inter-intrasubjective	Node of the three phases
Individuality	Intrapersonal	Singularity, uniqueness
Identity	Interpersonal	Objectivation of subjectivity
Role	Impersonal	Anonymous and circumstantial

It has been supposed that subjectivity is mainly a concern for the field of psychology rather than for aesthetics, so that these three phases of individuality, identity, and role would respectively correspond to the id, the ego, and the superego in Freudian psychoanalysis. Psychology, however, intervenes in cases of disturbance of the relation between these phases, whereas aesthetics is not interested in pathological or borderline cases, but instead in the genealogy of the subject and its condition and display of sensibility (as Foucault proposed it with relation to power). That is why subjectivity and identity are of direct concern to aesthetics. Both the strategies of constitution of the identity through objectivation as well as the activity of subjectivity by subjectivation, unequivocally involve aesthetic processes since they require mechanisms of appraisal. Such assessment is accomplished via seduction, repulsion, or fascination, rather than by argumentation, logic, or weighing evidence (as the validation of a scientific theory or deciding upon a criminal case). Aesthetics contributes to explain why and how certain practices, images, or discourses culminate as group or personal identities sensibly appraised and displayed. Aesthetics does not take the subject for granted, but converts him or her into a question to be examined from a dynamic and genealogical perspective.

Conflicting identities occur when our identity as parents overlaps with our identity as son or daughter so that our parental authority may be compromised by our compliance as descendants. The contradiction between our role when waiting in line for some bureaucratic requirement and the impulse to subvert our anonymity and display our identity is a transgression that, at least where I come from, is frequently punished with the disapproving gaze of the other people obeying in line. There is also the attack on individuality by identity when a subject frustrated in trying to attain a goal as lover, or professional assaults or kills himself (as illustrated by a character in the film *The Hours* trapped within an asphyxiating identity of wife, and ends up contemplating suicide as the only possibility of liberation). As categories proposed for analytical purposes only and not discrete ontological entities, it is worth remembering that these three phases of subjectivity flow through the continuum of social semiosis and personal experience.

Chapter 7

Conditions of Possibility of Aesthesis: The *A Priori*

Just as knowledge is an effect of our capacity to know, the aesthetic is an effect of our ability to feel. As with Kant, one should inquire about the conditions of human sensibility, a task as complex as it is necessary, and of which I will only propose the basic elements. Consequently, more than asking what is beauty or art, the question for aesthetics lies in understanding the conditions of possibility for sensibility.

In "Transcendental Aesthetics" Kant states in his first *Critique* that *intuition* is our immediate relation with objects that surround us. Such intuition depends on and is displayed through two pure *a priori* forms: *space* as internal sense, and *time* as external sense. These two *a priori* are necessary but insufficient conditions for the aesthetic. We also need the material sensation of the object or the *corporeal a priori* and the *context a priori* constituted by cultural codes and social conventions of formal perception and signification. Finally, for the aesthetic to occur it is necessary the vitality of the subject, the *a priori* of *energy* stratum as the body is its material stratum.

Experiencing music presupposes the intuition of time during which the sounds occur, overlap and follow one another, of the space in which they vibrate, of the body capable of perceiving them, of culture from which they signify as signs and acquire meaning through recognizable patterns, and of the vital energy capable of responding emotionally to them. In contrast, the situation of anesthesia is precisely the elimination of space and time intuition, of body sensations and physical pain, of any formal perception and emotion.

Of the four conditions for the possibility of aesthetic appreciation, Dewey deals mainly with the last two. He describes how the long line of animal ancestry remains in human beings and conditions our experience and interaction with the environment. Thence arises the experience of harmony as a solution to conflict, the sense of order and form, balance and rhythm, consummation, unity, and intensity. "In a world like ours, every living creature that attains sensibility welcomes order with a response of harmonious feeling whenever it finds a congruous order about it." (Dewey [1934] 1980, 15)

Space-time

There are two situations, according to Dewey, where aesthetic experience is impossible. One is in a world that is absolutely static, the other in an absolutely chaotic world, lacking any kind of order, rhythm, or form. In one case the intuition of

62 *Everyday Aesthetics*

time would be lost; in the other that of space by simultaneous explosion of immediate and amorphous sensations. Every view of the world is necessarily shaped from a spatial-temporal location; it is a chronotopical view, as Bakhtin would say.

The category of space-time is not understood here as an ontological category but a phenomenological one, a condition of the possibility for experience. (Berger and Luckmann 1989, 39–46) Without it, it is not only impossible to conceive everyday life as an orderly universe, but it could not even be conceived as a universe. Starting from space-time, intersubjectivity becomes possible when temporal and spatial dimensions are shared with others. Although the spatio-temporal intuition is obvious as a condition for aesthesis, it is necessary to mention it because it is generally overlooked in aesthetic theory. We perceive space-time with our sense organs, the brain, the cerebellum, the basal ganglia, and the hippocampus that deal with the succession of movement, time, and memory. Even visual perception is organically segmented in different areas of the brain to distinguish shape, depth, volume, color. (Edelman 1992, 105) In other words, space and time intuition is not purely mental, nor totally conformed from birth, as implied by the Kantian transcendental view, but depend on body and culture and are developed both from phylogenetic and ontogenetic processes. Although spatio-temporal intuition is transformed by experience as Piaget has shown by observing its development in children, it does not cease to be *a priori*, since it may change its configuration but not its irrevocability in every perception.

Space constitutes the "here" of my body and is constituted by it, as time constitutes and is constituted by the "now" of my conscience and the moment of perception or sensation. Bodily space-time extend beyond the here to the near, far, and remote, and beyond the now of the present to yesterday and tomorrow, from the present to the absent.

Being an experience and not a theoretical abstraction, we are dealing with a topological and concrete experiential space in opposition to abstract Euclidean space. (cf. Saint-Martin 1992, 90–1) Time is thus less a fixed objective quantity than a rhythmic sentient background for everyday activities and patterns of temporal regularity with which we endow our everyday life with a sense of order. (Zerubavel 1985 Chapter 1) Subjective space may thus be infinitely vast, as when a mother becomes inaccessible to the child despite being in the same room, or infinitely small, when the infant feels suffocated by her overprotection. In short, contrary to Kant's ahistorical view, space-time intuition has been radically transformed in the twentieth century by aerodynamics, as well as by scientific and technological breakthroughs like nanotechnology and astronomy, shrinking our sense of time through obsessive acceleration in our lives, and significantly expanding our concept of space. Yet they remain *a priori* as inescapable conditions for any perception.

The body

With the enigmatic phrase "aesthetics is born as a discourse of the body" Eagleton (1990, 13) begins his conceptual itinerary through aesthetic ideology. The centrality of the body for aesthetics is a reality that Kant tried to evade, but that obsessively reappeared along his *Third Critique*. For Dewey, on the other hand, in his radically

Conditions of Possibility of Aesthesis: The A Priori 63

anti-Kantian position, the body is always at the origin of any aesthetic experience. Sense is the raw material of subjectivity, and exists not only in the so-called body organs, but also as a mental sense, namely the emotional, relational, and sensorial meaning. The body has come to the fore of philosophical thought, particularly with feminism and biologically based studies. Lakoff and Johnson (1999) have extensively argued how the mind, language, and philosophy are intrinsically embodied so that spatial as well as temporal relations are understood in terms of corporeal schemes.

Berger and Luckmann (1986, 71) also point out that, as human beings, we not only *are* a body that defines us, but also *have* a body that we utilize. Human bodies define senses as specifically human senses, and therefore their social and historical character, as Marx pointed out. Human bodies have suffered transformations in dimensions and proportions, in their resistance to diseases, in the range, specialization and distinction of their senses, and in the partial atrophy of others (for example olfactory sense), as well as in their motor and mental capacities, life span, and territorial necessities.

From here it could be inferred that if we accept the specificity and morphology of the body as a condition for the possibility of aesthetics, this would take us, by extension, to the possibility of a feminine aesthetics in contrast to a masculine aesthetics. We would also have aesthetics from the obese and from the emaciated (as in anorexia), the heterosexual and homosexual, from scarcity to abundance, an aesthetics of illness and of health, and from the lascivious to the puritan. We shall consequently have to accept the fact that the diversity of bodies and their practices will condition a diversity of aesthetic perspectives. There are different ways to apprehend reality depending on the different ways of living the body.

Vital energy

Although the concept of "energy" in human sciences is still problematic and sometimes used as synonymous of power, libido, will, impetus, force (work force in economy and illocutionary force in speech act theory), it is a necessary concept for the analysis of aesthetic phenomena because it underlies experience. The energy of live beings is expressed as vitality, and can be vegetal, animal, and, in general, biological. Our body, however, is only human: socially and historically human. By vitality we must understand the drive or intentionality animating and encouraging us qua live beings. Although there can be a non-conscious intentionality, all conscience is always intentional, directed, and focused from its energy.

> In the esthetic object, the object operates [...] to pull together energies that had been separately occupied in dealing with many different things on different occasions, and give them that particular rhythmic organization that we have called [...] clarification, intensification, concentration. Energies that remain in a potential state with respect to one another [...] evoke and reinforce one another directly for the sake of the experience that results. (Dewey [1934] 1980, 176–7)

As the human being partakes in the global process of circulation and interchange of energies in Dewey's biological approach (Chapter VIII), I will use the concept of

64 *Everyday Aesthetics*

"energy" to designate vitality, vigor, impetus, having certain affinity with the idea of "soul" in Plato, Aristotle's "entelechy", "archeus" in Paracelsus, "the will-to-live" in Schopenhauer, and the "élan vital" in Bergson.

Cultural conventions

Cultural conventions are material and mental collective constructions that lend stability and solidity to our life. Unstable and mortal creatures as we are, we depend on culture and its conventions for our shelter and coexistence. (Arendt [1958] 1998, 136) The configurations culture can acquire are diverse, as attested by historical, anthropological, and ethnographic research. Culture modifies the *a priori* of the body and of space-time while these modify culture. As in space-time, culture does not cease to be an *a priori* even if it undergoes historical transformation, as there is no human group, remote or near, past or modern, that had not constituted culture. From the most primitive hordes of hunter and gatherer nomads to contemporary hordes that bunch up at beaches and urban stadiums, they all act according to their own culture. Earliest evidence of culture as *a priori* is witnessed through cave paintings since the Paleolithic age and even among primates, where certain agreements for coexistence are established within each group. In this sense, if culture is perhaps not exclusive of the human species, it is definitely inherent to it, as Robinson Crusoe illustrates it. Every human group necessarily creates culture.

Through processes of habituation, cultural conventions provide the basic order, direction, and stability for coexistence. (Berger and Luckmann 1986, 74) This habituation is gradually institutionalized into shared and ever more complex versions of reality. From conventions like language, use of space and body, as well as the time-bound rhythm of activities through sacred and profane rituals, the individual enters a reality constructed by and inherited from his ancestors as if it were natural and everlasting. Berger and Luckmann illustrate the genesis of cultural conventions in the processes of construction of reality through mechanisms like typification, objectivation, sedimentation, internalization, identification, and legitimation up to what they call "alternance" in critical moments, namely the permutation of one system of conventions for another. Thus, I shall not inquire further into this theme, and refer instead the reader to that text.

Space-time intuition, cultural conventions, corporeal, and energetic conditions spill out into one another constituting sensibility. The condition of being human, which is a bio-social condition, lies at the origin of the space-temporal, corporeal, vital, and cultural *a priori*. Therefore, scientific knowledge and aesthetic awareness have several things in common: a) *intuition* of space and time; b) *perception* from cultural conventions or "interpretative communities" (matrixes of subjectivity in case of aesthetics and logical-mathematical codes and paradigms in case of science); c) *sensation*, the condition of which is the corporeal *a priori* of the subject in the detection of matter (even with technological prosthesis in sciences like the telescope, the microscope, X-rays and laser and so on); lastly d) vital *impulse* that propels us toward aesthetic and cognitive activities.

The structures to which intuition, sensation, perception, and impulse are submitted in the scientific process are, obviously, not the same as in the aesthetic. Logic and analysis regulate the operations for the production of concepts, in addition to the systematic observation and recording of data, their verification and scientific proof. The orders that condition the aesthetic do not produce concepts and are not subjected to a systematic logical analysis, although they obey matrix structures that regulate modes of enunciation and interpretation for the establishment of values and categories as part of a common sense. In other words, while the conditions of subjectivation of reality are similar in scientific activities as in aesthetic ones, they differ radically in the mode of processing subjectivation and in their strategies of objectivation.

Chapter 8

The Phenomenology of Aesthesis: Aesthetic Latching-On and Latched-By

To define an aesthetic experience as "contemplation" already involves the more or less unknowing metaphorical projection of a religious, mystical situation towards aesthetics. By this theoretical tactic, a great part of society is automatically excluded from recognizing this kind of experiences in their life. Is the aesthetic really as extraordinary? Quite the contrary: the aesthetic is, in fact, the most common, everyday and indispensable activity we perform throughout our life. The very first impulse we have from the moment we are born is related to the aesthetic. I am referring to the act of *latching-on* to the nipple and thriving from it. Instead of the mystic "contemplation" that cancels the somatic condition of the subject, I will metaphorically project to aesthetics' theoretical domain this primordial archetype of bonding between mother and child that starts at this corporeal experience of the infant *latching-on* to the mother's nipple. What makes this coupling possible is the morphological affinity between the subject and the object. This morphological, and thus formal, coupling between the mouth of a mammal and the mother's nipple permits *adhesion*. Precisely, as we shall see later, adhesion is the essential aesthetic operation both at an individual and at a collective level.

The judgment of taste, for Kant (*CJ* § 8), demands adhesion of others for its confirmation, but that adhesion is the result of a formal adherence of the subject to the object of judgment as well as the social conformation of the subject to *sensus communis.* In the act of *latching-on*, subjects are coupled to their objects by their form in diverse registers of experience (visual, aural, corporeal, or verbal). If reality can be understood as a semiosic intersubjective network that we share with others, aesthetics is that cohesive structure that allows us to adhere to it, somewhat like the sticky filaments of spider cobwebs for insects to adhere to.

From birth, this process begins in *sensation* (hunger), where *perception* is generated (of the breast, the gradual recognition of the mother by smell, touch, visual image). The baby eloquently expresses being *latched-onto* and absorbed by the rhythm of sucking, pressing the breast with her little hands, immersing her face in it, and moving her leg or arm out of sheer pleasure. From this primeval experience of every human as a mammal, all our future aesthetic experiences take root.

Aesthetic *latching-on* sharpens one or several senses simultaneously: hearing is tuned more than any other sense when we are captivated by music; sight is sharpened when we are *latched-onto* a beautiful landscape or interesting object, smell becomes more keen at a delightful aroma, taste at a delicious flavor, and touch at a soft, silky texture. There is certain orality, metaphorically speaking, in aesthesis when we nourish ourselves through the world.

68 *Everyday Aesthetics*

Latching-on is an act through which we extract the vigor to live, like the seed that adheres and *latches-on* to the earth generating roots to absorb its nutrients and thrive. Therefore, the notion of "disinterested delight" so common in aesthetic theory, is denied by the concrete experience of the vehement appetite in aesthesis. Let us imagine for a moment what our life would be like without any opportunity for *latching-on*, without the possibility of being captivated by something: someone we love, a landscape, a cup of coffee, an animal, music, religious beliefs, projects, dreams, art, friends, and so on. This state of lack of *latching-on* or affective deprivation characterizes the mentally ill who, even without enough firm soil to be rooted and adhered to an intersubjective reality, still desperately extend roots for adhering at least to the nebulous ideas of their fantasies. We are captivated by what is affectionately significant, valued, and brimful of meaning.

Not only since we are born, but also when we wake up every morning, moment by moment we seek objects for *latching-on*. We listen to the singing of the birds, watch the hues of the sky at dawn, feel the freshness of the shower, smell the scent of the soap, touch the clean clothes, savor the coffee, listen to some music, read the newspaper, and so forth. By *latching-onto* one object or another we weave with small pleasures our daily existence as the bee *latches-onto* one flower and another to extract pollen. If our aesthetic appetite were to depend solely on artistic masterpieces, we would starve and hardly survive the simple and sometimes difficult act of getting up every morning.

In contrast to the term "engagement" proposed by Berleant and "attention" by Dickie, both of which may be applied to extra-aesthetic situations losing their specifically aesthetic import, the term *"latching-on"* implies fascination, seduction, impetus, nutrition, and appetite, more closely related to the phenomenon that interests us. *Latching-on* is also an alternative concept to "contemplation" criticized by Dewey, and that has remained in mainstream aesthetics as the attitude or aesthetic experience par excellence, including all its religious connotations erroneously associated to a purely mental state. The prevalence of this notion of "contemplation" is partly attributable to the disqualification by aesthetic theory of the everyday realm, as the typical objection against an aesthetic of the everyday because it cannot figure out what the hell could be worth contemplating in the plain and ordinary. Sánchez Vázquez's refusal to include the tragic in everyday aesthetics is due to this definition of the aesthetic involving contemplation. Among the consequences of this obtrusive notion are: a) the exaggerated weight granted to the visual, to the exclusion of the other senses; b) overlooking the crucial role of the body for aesthetics; c) tacitly denying that intellectual activity also participates in the aesthetic (contrary to its clear indication in Kant's formula *CJ* § 9 of "free play of imagination and understanding); d) ignoring that aesthetics implies activity, making it seem purely receptive. Whereas the term "contemplation" metaphorically projects a religious experience to the aesthetic, that of *"latching-on"* projects it from a corporeal experience common not only to all human beings but to mammals as well.

Accepting Weitz's (1987, 1989) proposal when he advocated an aesthetic theory of open and flexible concepts allows us to delineate the domain of the aesthetic as an aperture to the world with the act of *latching-on* as its dynamic principle. *Latching-on* is an activity, not an attitude (in contrast to Stolnitz's "aesthetic attitude") and

The Phenomenology of Aesthesis: Aesthetic Latching-On and Latched-By 69

extends along a spectrum of different ranges from a slight, pleasant drowsiness to a passionate and voracious aesthetic appetite. It is imperative to secularize and embody the concept of the aesthetic, even though its feasibility will have to be proven in subsequent applications. *Latching-on* implies a rhythm in nature that Dewey ([1934] 1980, 162) emphasized by stating: "Only as these rhythms even if embodied in an outer object that is itself a product of art, become a rhythm in experience itself are they esthetic." It is not random that the baby *latching-on* to the nipple performs an eminently rhythmic activity.

On the opposite pole in the spectrum of the aesthetic is the contrary to *latching-on*, namely the passivity of being *latched-by*. In this case the subject feels not captivated but captured by the object in situations of intrusion. In *latching-on* there is intentionality, impetus toward an object, Kant's "free play between imagination and understanding", whereas in *being latched-by* there is aesthetic poisoning, loss of capacity for "free play", and the numbing or lesion of sensibility by aesthetic violence. *Latched-by* is therefore equally relevant to aesthetic theory as a depletive condition of sensibility.

Just as the subject is established for Althusser in two ways, namely as *subject of* and as *subject by* (subject of subjectivation and subjected by), the aesthetic subject is equally constituted in subject of *latching-on* and subjected in *latched-by*. *Latching-on* is an opening, an act of amplitude, while aesthetic *latched-by* is enclosure and narrowness of sensibility in its impotence. In one case the subject *latches-on* and thrives; in the other it is held captive and depleted.

Aesthetic activity understood as *latching-on*, far from being disinterested, fulfills itself to thrive and extract force for living. Subjects may be captivated by music and feel energized or solaced, or by a novel to enrich themselves with the situations narrated, but also by religion to feel sheltered within its world-view, by medicine hoping to be cured, by a profession to satisfy a vocation of service or a necessity for recognition. What we are looking for is vigor, not only pleasure.

Sensibility can have various degrees of fluidity. In this fluidity lies another difference between *latching-on* and *latched-by*. Normally sensibility should flow freely at each opportunity that presents itself, since joy is our natural disposition to life. Aesthetic violence, however, blocks sensibility when it ceases to be a source of joy causing only pain. Those who lead a privileged life of aesthetic nourishment and stimuli in benevolent environments can maintain their sensibility open. On the other hand, those who are continually exposed to aesthetic violence by inhabiting sordid, noisy, malodorous spaces, or lead a stressful and aggressively competitive life are *latched-by* and forced to block their sensibility to avoid suffering. Many among us who must commute to work every day for hours in overcrowded cars of the metro or lanes in a stuck "freeway" during rush hours to arrive at an unsatisfying and stressful day's work block our sensibility for sheer adaptation to this hostile environment. Something similar, although much more intense, happens in political, ethnic, economic, and religious conflicts where aesthetic violence is exerted against others to offend, humiliate, or cause pain.

When sensibility is *latched-by* aesthetic sordidness, the subject seeks to unblock it. Defensive numbness of the senses is a reaction of survival and resistance to aesthetic *latched-by*. We could add the case of those who, in the face of an adverse reality,

70 *Everyday Aesthetics*

look for a strong discharge of alcohol or drugs aiming to *latch-on* to something by chemical-neuronal hyperactivity yet end up *latched-by* them. This intense need for *latching-on* is indicative of the degree of contemporary sensitive blockage, since the voracious consumption of violence in mass entertainment is not by mere chance. The aesthetics for the masses organize ever more spectacular displays to unblock sensibility by hyper stimulation, creating further numbness that increasingly needs greater and greater impact to react.

Aesthetic *latching-on* is *eros* in intentionality or craving for life, impetus. Thus, there are different forms of *latching-on*: not only by artistic contemplation when the subject is entranced by the beauty he attributes to an object, but also in mass *latching-on* that Parret (1993) calls "intercorporeality and euphony" occurring during political gatherings in the streets or among fans of a showbiz celebrity and a sport team at the stadium. Parret's idealized "affective being together" in *latching-on* can easily turn into a *latched-by* due to manipulation, resentment, radicalism, prejudice, and guilt. It might be worth mentioning religious *latching-on* whose extreme is mystics' ecstasy. Intense levels of *latching-on* can change into *latched-by* when they are no longer voluntary, as in cases of political or religious fanaticism where the devotee stops being nurtured by his faith to be devoured by it.

Latching-on also occurs towards knowledge through learning and research when we passionately cling to a problem or puzzle until we solve it. In Socratic *wonder* the philosopher *latches-onto* an enigma with the same appetite as the infant to the nipple. This is why I have insisted that the difference between intellectual and aesthetic activity does not warrant the compartmentalization effected by Kant, since the process of learning imbricates intimately with aesthetic *latching-on*. All institutions or social matrixes display aesthetic strategies destined to individual or collective *latching-on*. Their goal is not only to obtain collective assent regarding the feasibility and legitimacy of the realities proposed, but the adherence of subjects, and therefore their acquiescence to constitute identities and realities in relation to them.

We can propose the additional complementary concepts of *unlatching-to* as a rupture of the condition of *latching-onto*, and the *unlatched-by* as liberation from being *latched-by*.

Unlatched-to is a well-known situation that happens after having been fully immersed in a project that finally crystallizes and we suddenly realize that our efforts in that direction are no longer necessary. It is a feeling of momentary disorientation until we find a new object for *latching-on*. The same happens when we lose by death or rupture a beloved friend, lover, or member of the family. By contrast, when we have been *latched-by* a consuming or suffocating relationship and we have the strength to break up, we welcome the *unlatching-by* with a sigh of relief and a sense of freedom and well-being. Note that both *latching-onto* and *unlatching-by* are active, whereas *latched-by* and *unlatched-on* are passive.

We conclude that aesthesis is a condition of aperture to the world that generates an act of *latching-on* or is undergone in being *latched-by*. This act of *latching-on* nourishes the subject, whereas being *latched-by* weakens, confuses, and harms him. It is certainly not enough for solving a problem to simply change the name of "aesthetic experience" or "engagement" for "aesthetic *latching-on*", since these are terms to be elucidated, not answers, and a purely nominal or semantic operation does not solve anything. Still, the concept of *latching-on* as a metaphoric projection from the primordial experience of suckling, does contribute a phenomenological basis to outline the concept of aesthesis.

PART 3
TOWARDS PROSAICS

Prosaics and panaestheticism

We must face from the very beginning the almost automatic condemnation that conservative aestheticians will thrust against the proposal here elaborated: the allegation of panaestheticism. Such imputation would go more or less along the following lines: if the concept of aesthetics is extended beyond art and beauty, then everything would end up being aesthetic and, therefore, the object of study would totally disperse. Indeed, when saying that everything is aesthetic, the aesthetic ceases to be pertinent. This objection is absolutely compelling and indisputable. Yet there is no such claim that everything is aesthetic for prosaics' perspective. On the contrary, the opposite assumption is the case: no thing is aesthetic, not even artworks or beautiful things. The only aesthesis resides in the subjects, not in things. The formulation of an aesthetics of everyday life elaborated here cannot be more innocent of any charge of panaestheticism for the simple fact that when enunciating that "all the things are aesthetic" aesthetic objetualism is presupposed, a sin of which prosaics must be acquitted.

Aesthesis is a condition of live beings. Moreover, it is not "a condition" but "the condition" of life. To live implies aesthesis (which does not mean that everything in life is aesthesis). By the same token, if the concept of "art" is applied to everything (as the art of loving, the art of deceiving, of talking, of betting, or of drinking), then it also loses relevance (in this latter case the term is simply used in a metaphorical sense).

I owe to Jan Mukarovský this precaution against the accusation of panaestheticism (who assumes that any object and any action—whether the result of a natural process or of human activity—can become vehicle for the aesthetic function).[1] In his effort to extend the borders of aesthetic analysis, Mukarovský quotes Guyau who proposes: "To breathe deeply, to feel how our blood is purified in contact with the air, is this not an intoxicating sensation to which it would be difficult denying aesthetic value?" (*Les problèmes de l'estétique contemporaine*). Dessoir is also quoted in saying: "Designating a machine, the solution of a mathematical problem, the organization of a certain social group as beautiful things is something more than a form of expression" (*Ästhetik und allgemeine Kunstwissenschaft*). Note the different meanings for the

---

1   He warns that "this does not imply a panaestheticist affirmation, since: 1) it does not affirm the necessity, but solely the general possibility of the aesthetic function; 2) it does not question the dominant position of the aesthetic function among the remaining functions of given phenomena; 3) one is not to conflate the aesthetic function with other functions, nor to conceive other functions as mere variants of the aesthetic function." (Mukarovský 1977, 47)

aesthetic implied by each of these thinkers: while in Guyau's phrase the concept of the aesthetic is linked to pleasure, in Dessoir it is tied to beauty.

In prosaics, however, the aesthetic is related to experience as the live dimension of reality without necessarily implying any relation to beauty or pleasure. For that reason, prosaics can be considered close to a philosophical and anthropological aesthesiology (for example, as the study of the cultural operation of the senses) or part of a socio-aesthetics (as the unfolding of aesthesis in social life). Prosaics is concerned both with aesthetic mechanisms and with their effects upon sensitivity.

Chapter 9

Prosaics and Poetics

Having established the terms from which we will conceptualize aesthetic phenomena, we may now undertake the exploration of one of its most perplexing and least explored manifestations: those of everyday life. To the Western ear, the mere idea of "everyday aesthetics" seems an oxymoron despite the fact that, etymologically, the aesthetic refers to the most basic and indispensable activity for survival in every live being: perception. To the same degree that philosophy began by inquiring first about the vastness of the universe than about the uniqueness of the human being, aesthetics also pondered upon an extraordinary phenomenon, art, before considering its more primordial, everyday manifestations.

Poetics, defined by Aristotle as the study of art in general (*Poetics* 1447) has been retrospectively understood as coextensive to aesthetic theory. The first attempts to define aesthetics as a particular branch of philosophical studies during the mid-eighteenth century also linked it to the extraordinary phenomena of art and beauty. The borders of one have corresponded exactly with those of the other. Yet art is, in fact, the tip of an iceberg beneath which the vast world of the prosaic is pulsating.

I have chosen the term "prosaics" to distinguish it from "poetics" and to point towards a variety of aesthetic activities with which we constitute our everyday life. The term "prosaics" is derived from the Latin verb *provertere* (throw forward) and seems adequate to encompass the great number of social and individual processes that are presented and re-presented by aesthetic mediations. The prosaic or everyday aesthetics is thus not opposite to, but underlying, artistic enunciation.

In a little known text, Aristotle appears to have designated as "prosaics" the requirements for a good comedy and the secret of a good joke, in contrast to poetics that is concerned with pity and fear in Tragedy.[1] Nevertheless, in his *Poetics* (1449b) he includes comedy when examining a ridiculous situation, an ugly thing, and humorous poets like Epicharmus, Phormis, and Crates who competed at the archon (486-440 A.C.). Before the development of the arts in prose such as novels or short stories, this term had relation with the fact that a Tragedy's high status characters expressed themselves in poetry whereas common people did it in prose (as in Shakespeare's plays). Aristotle dedicated most of his *Poetics* to the analysis of Tragedy, but has since then been used to designate the study of the art in general, comedy included.

"The mountain tops do not float without support; they don't even just rest on the earth: They *are* the earth in one of its manifest operations." (Dewey [1934] 1980, 3) With this metaphor, Dewey points out that art does not rise by its own strength,

---

1   Cf. "A Brief History of Laughter", Adrienne Kress, http://www.library.utoronto.ca/uc/ucdp/buffo/laughter.html. 3/29/2005.

76 *Everyday Aesthetics*

nor does it only lean on or reflect the everyday, but is one of its most remarkable manifestations, constituted by the very same matter that conforms the everyday. Such continuity between artworks and everyday events Dewey refers here to is, however, far from clear.

While both, the poetic and prosaic, demand valuation, the latter is not as aware of this appeal for estimation and recognition as the former. Poetics, on the other hand, explicitly presents, as Dickie and Danto have argued, candidates for aesthetic appreciation within the specific context of the "artworld". It is a specialized area of prosaics that studies professional poiesis in the production and reception of the artistic. Another point from which we can situate prosaics is considering it as part of a broader field, namely socio-aesthetics or the study of aesthetic phenomena in social life. (See Table 5.1)

Prosaics views life aesthetically, as poetics views prosaics aesthetically. Aesthesis is not reduced to perception although it is a *sine qua non* condition which starts by *presence* in everyday life, to its *presentation* in prosaics, and its *re-presentation* in poetics. Picasso's *Guernica* or any figurative painting, novel or theater, re-present (present again) its characters or situations in poetics out of the material that emerges from their presentation to sensibility and their presence to the sensation in everyday life. It also *presents* the identity of the author qua artist and human being, his gesture of selecting certain topics for artistic expression and not others, and his indignation towards the massacre perpetrated by the Germans during the bombing against the Basque town in April of 1937. The painting in turn *re-presents* through austere chromatism and black and white contrasts, vertiginous dynamism and a heart rendering expressivity of human and animal bodies, the horror Picasso imagined of this massacre. Poetics is the way by which aesthetics tries to evade the volatility of prosaics. For that reason it resorts to this impressive capability of representation. But such *presentation* of prosaics in the witness of an event is not equivalent to its *presence* among the Guernica victims whose lives were snatched by the Nazis.

As antecedents to the use of the term of "prosaic" it is worth mentioning two cases: One is classical studies' designation of prose writing as opposed to metrics— for example, *1648 Nobiliss. virginis Annae Mariae a Schurman, opuscula Hebraea, Graeca, Latina, et Gallica. Prosaica et Metrica*. The other, quite similar but much more recent in the field of aesthetics, is Morson and Emerson's book entitled *Mikhail Bakhtin, Creation of a Prosaics*. Here they define the term as follows: "Prosaics encompasses two related but distinct, concepts. First, as opposed to 'poetics', prosaics designates a theory of literature that privileges prose in general and the novel in particular over the poetic genres. Prosaics in the second sense is far broader than theory of literature: it is a form of thinking that presumes the importance of the everyday, the ordinary, the 'prosaic." (Morson and Emerson 1990, 15) I quote this definition for two reasons: first, because it reflects the common usage given to the word "prosaic", and second because it is the first time that the term is mentioned for theoretical purposes not in a derogatory sense. The authors nevertheless turn aside this sense to focus in Bakhtin's theory of the novel and use it in the same traditional sense as Annae Mariae a Schurman and others.

Although I understand prosaics as "what assumes the importance of the everyday, the commonplace, the 'prosaic', it is not the everyday in itself or the commonplace

Prosaics and Poetics 77

as such that would constitute the object of prosaics but its aesthetic dimension. In daily life we sleep, we make love, we eat, we speak, and we work. Through all these acts, prosaics as a theory points exclusively at the manners in which our sensibility is involved and expressed. Even if our daily tasks depend on perception and constitute the "life world" or *Lebenswelt* (Schütz and Luckmann 1973), prosaics focuses specifically on the way in which we perform them in order to generate or receive sensible effects. Schütz and Luckmann (1977, 25) define the *lebenswelt* as follows: "By world of everyday life must be understood that scope of the reality that the normal alert adult estimates simply in the attitude of common sense. We designate by this presupposition everything that we experience as unquestionable ...." Prosaics does not focus on the *lebenswelt* by itself but on how the aesthetic dimension conditions it. By the same token, we will not analyze everyday life as a sociologist, psychologist, political philosopher, or anthropologist would do (among which are many distinguished authors who have contributed to its study, cf. Lefebvre 1972, Heller 1972, Certeau 1988, Schütz 1976, Schütz and Luckmann 1973). Nor am I proposing a "thick interpretation" of the everyday in the sense proposed by Clifford Geertz (1997), since, as I clarified in Chapter 14, prosaics goes beyond a semiotic decoding of everyday life.[2]

The everyday is, indeed, "the prose of the world" as Merleau-Ponty once said. The quotidian, etymologically related to the term "day" (of the Latin *quotidie*), is not a simple fact given once and for all since it is continuously constituted on the basis of negotiated agreements and shared rules where personal and collective identities are presented/displayed to the sensibility of participants. Prosaics deals with styles of rhetorical and dramaturgical presentation of these identities in their social context (Goffman [1959] 1981). Since sensibility is involved, these presentations require strategies of persuasion and adhesion. We will concentrate here exclusively in the social practices in which aesthetics acquire a preeminent strategic function to captivate or to subjugate, and those practices have to do with the identities.

In agreement with Peter Berger and Thomas Luckmann (1986, 36) I understand that "everyday life presents itself as a reality interpreted by people, and that for them it has the subjective significance of a coherent world." Such social construction of reality partly depends on social identities that are also elaborated and negotiated in relation to those realities. The dramaturgy in the display of personal identities studied by Goffman and the means by which certain social constructs acquire the necessary legitimacy and credibility, namely, the adherence stressed by Berger and Luckmann, both depend upon aesthetic processes. So, if realities and identities are social constructions, as amply stated by these authors, the thesis proposed here is

---

2   My appreciation to Heinz Paetzold for bringing to my attention the relation between prosaics and Clifford Geertz's thick anthropological interpretation. Although in both cases the context of interpretation is crucial and a semiotic approach is basic (particularly in grasping the grounding symbols in each matrix) prosaics goes beyond semiosis as it refers not only to the social meaning of certain activities, but to their constitutive role and affective relevance. Geertz leaves interpretation open to each observer and does not really operate with semiotic tools, whereas in this case, a concrete semiotic model is designed to help the reader explore environments not as remote as the cock fights in Bali, but his own, proximate contexts.

that the materials, the structures and the instruments with which they are constructed for the subjects' adherence to them are, to a considerable degree, aesthetic.

The everyday has numerous aspects that have been examined by different disciplines (economics, politics, linguistics, sociology, ecology, etc.). Here we shall concentrate exclusively on social practices in which the aesthetic function is dominant, similarly to what Jakobson (1963) and Mukarovský (1977) pointed at in all cases when the form of the message became the key aspect of communication. This does not imply assuming a formalist stance but rather a pragmatic one because forms are elaborated precisely for their effects upon the *destinataire* or addressee. In other words, signifiers are conformed for the sake of their signifying effect, and not for their sake alone. We will thus demarcate prosaics as an inquiry into the processes of aesthesis in the midst of social life (in a similar fashion as Saussure defined semiology as the "study of signs in midst of social life"). Prosaics deals with the ways in which such aesthetic constitution in everyday life is displayed and the type of activities it is involved in. It begins precisely where Berger and Luckmann, as well as Goffman arrived and ended, since our purpose is not to explore what processes occur in the construction of social realities and identities but how they captivate the subjects to *latch-onto* and adhere to them in particular social contexts.

We will consequently have to veer 180 degrees the traditional approach to aesthetics by focusing not on the *aesthetic effects of social practices* such as art, fashion, or design, but on the *social effects of aesthetic practices* performed throughout a wide array of social institutions such as the family, the school, religion, the State, a prison. The nature of specific aesthetic practices within each of these institutions is precisely the question that prosaics will have to answer. The purpose is, thus, to study aesthetics not as the effect of art and beauty, but as constitutive of social effects. The emphasis in this constitutive function proper to aesthetics can only be theoretically dealt by the analysis of the processes of enunciation and interpretation in which sensibility is objectified and subjectified.

This turn requires examining aesthetics not through a purely philosophical approach, whether speculative as in idealistic tendencies or trans-disciplinary as the postmodernist trends. The predominant analytic aesthetics' approach that scrutinizes the logic of the propositions and their matching to reality is also not suitable for this purpose, since it erases context and subject alike. Because we are dealing with the subject of enunciation and its contextualized positioning as conditions of perception and valuation, an interdisciplinary approach is necessary involving semiotics, sociology, phenomenology, psychology, epistemology and whatever theoretical tools may show heuristic value. Beginning from symbolic interactionism, particularly Goffman's work ([1959] 1981, 1963) and his incursion into micro-sociology, it is possible to achieve qualitative analyses of common practices where the relevance of everyday aesthetics becomes salient.[3]

---

3   This micro-sociology of prosaics contrasts to the macrosocial theory of art elaborated by numerous authors like Hauser (1969) and Wolff (1983, 1993) since our goal is to understand the diverse aesthetic practices in their social scope, not only the works of art in their social context.

Prosaics and Poetics 79

The metaphor of "social cement" has been often used to explain the function of ideology in a particular society. Ideology, however, helps merge people together due less to its informational import than its emotional appeal, less to its denotational character than to the connotational. Marxist analyses of a few decades ago emphasized ideology as social agglutinant. What they did not explain then is how this cohesion is achieved with such effectiveness, because to maintain relatively unified a society of extremely antagonistic classes requires powerful mechanisms. There is a sensitive component in how ideology is constructed and propagated to the degree that its cohesive function happens to be a result of aesthetic strategies for adherence and identification of subjects involved.

Poesics and prosics

In order to avoid such ambiguous statements as: "... the novel, the most prosaic of the prosaic forms" (Morson and Emerson 1990, 27), a change in terminology might be useful. To designate the theory of literature that refers to prose (or the study of prose genres like the novel and short stories), allow me to propose the neologism of "*prosics*" hoping it will be justified by the imprecision it may evict. "Prosics" could thus also be distinguished from prosaics, whose definition in dictionaries refers both to prose and to the trivial. By the same token, literary theory of poetry could be called "*poesics*" which would be distinguished from poetics, the meaning of which is also ambiguous (poetics as poetry and as artistic activity). Poetics will be understood in this last sense exclusively as art, including all forms of artistic activity in its various genres independently of their quality, social origin, style conventions or highbrow/lowbrow extraction. In poetics we can find manifestations of both *prosics* and *poesics*. *Prosics* in highbrow *poetics* can be found in novels, dramatic literature, short stories, and so on, and in lowbrow in soap-operas, romantic stories, and so on. *Poesics* in highbrow *poetics* is manifested by sonnets, stanzas, or verses, and in rap, ballads, pop, and rock lyrics for mass arts.

In prosaics we can also find manifestations of both of these terms: *prosaic prosics* are present in a variety of verbal conventions close to what Bakhtin (1990, 248–293) calls genres: reports, orders, applications, scientific treatises, philosophical essays, love letters, and parlor talks. *Prosaic poesics* are rhymed prayers, sport cheers, political or commercial slogans, and rhymed duels (like those practiced by Turkish children described in Dundes, Leach et al. 1972).

There are two key differences between aesthetic activities in poetics and in prosaics. Notice that poetics always involves a finite and consummated character of enunciation that contrasts to the intermittent, continuous, and unfinished character of prosaics. The qualities of unity, coherence, and completeness that Beardsley attributed to aesthetic experience may be applied to the *products* of poetics rather than to aesthetic experience itself. Every illocution in poetics, independently of its quality and range, is always finite (although, as Eco 1974, 1978, 1991 points out, it remains open to interpretation). A picture, a film, a soap opera, a compact disc album are enunciations with a clearly established beginning and end according to genre conventions. By contrast, in prosaics unity, coherence, and completion are

Table 9.1   Prosics and Poesics

Prosaic prosics	Reports, orders, applications, scientific treatises, philosophical essays, love letters, conversations
Poetic prosics	Elite art: novel, dramatic literature, short stories
	Mass art: romance stories, soap-operas
Prosaic poesics	Rhymed prayers, sport cheers, political or commercial slogans, rhymed duels
Poetic poesics	Elite art: sonnets, stanzas, or verses
	Mass art: rap, ballads, pop, and rock lyrics

not as definitive as in poetics, since they continue pause after pause, turn after turn, altering and alternating with time. There is an ongoing process of autopoiesis in the subject's identity to seduce and convince, be accepted and cherished by others; never a finished, complete or perfectly coherent product.

The second difference between prosaics and poetics is that the latter is based on social division of work. Given its professionalization, only very few can learn and practice artistic expression, while in prosaics all of us, without exception, are enunciators (even if the matrixes from which we enunciate may vary). We shall thus explore how institutions are established to achieve the necessary adhesion and feasibility, and how personal and collective identities are conformed.

Although there is a theoretical as well as a political risk in the concept of collective identities such as the hypostatization in Durkheim's theory of the "collective conscience" (to which one may add Nazism's *Volksgeist* or "spirit of the people", or the Jung's "collective unconscious"), I share the position well presented by Gilberto Gimenez (1991, 199) when he states: "This risk would only exist if the collective identity of a group were conceived as something totally different and external to the personal identities of its members. The collective identity does not plan over individuals, but results from the way in which the individuals relate among themselves within a group or a social collectivity. I have already said that the identity is not 'essence' but a system of relations and representations."[4]

The observation point we are occupying for prosaics is not so much the place where subjectivity sheds towards individuality, since this concerns especially ethics and mysticism. Neither is it of the relation between identity and role that concerns sociology, but particularly, yet not exclusively, that of subjectivity with identity. (cf. Chapter 6)

Summing up, I have distinguished the term "prosaics" to denote exclusively the aesthetic dimension in everyday activities. Other meanings of the term as the trite, the vulgar, or the insignificant, are applicable to both poetics and prosaics, since there is vulgarity and triviality in art as well as in everyday life. It must be clear that prosaics is an area of research that does not carry any axiological load; it is not an adjective nor a value, but merely the examination of the aesthetic dimension in everyday life.

---

4   Giménez quotes the concept of collective identity from Pérez Agote, 1986, pp. 76–90.

Chapter 10

The Tangents of Prosaics

Since the publication of the first edition of *Prosaics* in 1994, four books came to my hands that attempt to deal directly or indirectly with aesthetics of the everyday. One is *Homo Aestheticus* by Ellen Dissanayake (1996) who proposes a Darwinian explanation of art and, without too much modesty, qualifies her work as a Copernican revolution in the field of aesthetics (curiously, there is another book with the exact same title, published six years earlier: Luc Ferry's *Homo Aestheticus* 1990). In her subtitle she promises to explain where art comes from and why, and her solution is that art is a behavior for the purpose of survival. For the author, the "species-centric regards art not as an entity or quality but instead as a behavioral tendency, a way of doing things. This behavioral tendency is inherited and thus both indelible and universal." (Dissanayake 1996, 34) There are numerous problems with her proposal, beginning with its title: since it deals with art, and only indirectly with aesthetics (although a clear distinction between both is not given), her book would be best entitled "homo artisticus". But this is the least of its problems among which considering art as a behavior and, more problematic even, stating that such artistic behavior is inherited, are salient. It would be reasonable to expect that a statement with scientific pretensions based on the Darwinian paradigm would provide some empirical evidence. This not being the case, we have evidence against her claim in all those objects that the artistic matrix has collected for centuries and jealously guards in museums and private collections. These objects may not be aesthetic as such (as I have argued in Chapter 2, the notion of "aesthetic objects" is an oxymoron), but they are definitely artistic by the simple reason of having been categorized, inventoried, quoted, analyzed, collected, and enjoyed as such. Artworks are *objects for* various intellectual, hedonistic, economic, political, semiotic, or erotic behaviors, but certainly not behaviors in themselves. Literally, only live beings can have behaviors, (and perhaps particles also, but only metaphorically).

What "behavioral tendency" does the author speak of? She defines it as "making special". According to her, "the biological core of art, the stain that is deeply dyed in the behavioral marrow of humans everywhere, is something I have elsewhere called 'making special'". (1996, 42) In that manner Dissanayake easily appears to solve the problem that has long troubled philosophers and art critics. This formula would be wonderful if it would really work. There are, however, so many cases of "making special" very difficult to categorize as artistic. We can recollect several instances of "making special" particular individuals or groups which do not conform to the common denominator; and are separated from the rest for gender, race, ethnicity, political, religious differences. "Making special" as a category needs, I think, more polishing.

Everyday Aesthetics

For Dissanayake (1996, 35) "by calling art a behavior, one also suggests that in the evolution of the human species, art-inclined individuals, those who possessed this behavior of art, survived better than those who did not. That is to say, a behavior of art had 'selective' or 'survival' value: it was a biological necessity." One cannot but profoundly deplore the fact that Mozart, Beethoven, Van Gogh, Modigliani, Manet, Kafka, Proust, and more recently Basquiat and so many other martyrs of art did not know this well kept secret, as it would have made their frequently painful and brief existence much easier. If anything characterized these great artists is that they didn't do too well in managing to survive.

In sum, Dissanayake believes she has proved the Darwinian universality of art. Evidently art does not require justifications, Darwinian or whatever. Strangely enough, if there is a common characteristic in what has been denominated "art", from the Paleolithic to the postmodern, from Dada to Orlan's body art, is its artificiality. Contrary to Dissanayake's claim, I contend that art is unnatural by nature. Aesthetics, on the other hand, is integrated to, and forms part of, nature not only human but also animal, as in a cat's delight in the sun or playing with yarn, and in the bower bird trimming and decorating its nest. Despite very interesting and suggestive examples indeed, Dissanayake's endeavor unfortunately fails among other reasons because she does not distinguish between aesthetics and art. If aesthetics are, in fact, universal and transcend the human species, art on the other hand is exclusively human and apparently also exclusively Western (this polemic assertion liable to Eurocentrism will be explained in Chapter 31).

Another text in this direction is Ossi Naukkarinen's (1998) *Aesthetics of the Unavoidable*. Naukkarinen states that there are many types of aesthetics. Each particular case of aesthetics can be characterized according to a spatial three-dimensional model composed of three polar coordinates that go from the explicit to the tacit, from the original to the commonplace, and from the volatile to the stable. Why he chooses these rather than other categories is not sufficiently explained. He defines the aesthetic as that which is "always linked to a tradition, amplifying or repudiating its characteristics". Unfortunately, as Dissanayake, Naukkarinen also conflates the artistic, that is indeed linked to tradition, with the aesthetic, that is not necessarily so, even if linked to a context. What is peculiar about his proposition is that he chose to define it as an "aesthetics of the unavoidable" referring to everyday objects like "advertisements, cars, hairdos, clothes, other people, household utensils, credit cards, eyeglasses, CD players, computers, shoes, pencils, neon lights, wallets, lighters, beer bottles, traffic lights, etc." (1998, 12), all of which are neither necessarily unavoidable nor necessarily aesthetic. These objects may be common within a certain social and cultural class in contemporary urban societies, but utterly foreign in other contexts. Yet the main interest in Naukkarinen's approach is his attempt to explore aesthetics of non-art, an attempt worth pursuing but requires more specification of what is meant by "aesthetic", "non-art" and "unavoidable".

The third attempt towards an aesthetics of the everyday is much more coherent and sets forth much fewer problems. I am referring to Yi-Fu Tuan's *Passing Strange and Wonderful; Aesthetics, Nature and Culture* (1995) a delightful book that understands aesthetics as synonymous to beauty. Tuan simply applies aesthetic traditional categories, namely "contemplation", "disinterestedness", and "distancing", to daily life. The book is nicely illustrated with literary fragments and appeals to those fortunate enough to achieve such an aesthetic quality of life. Tuan understands aesthetics as a special access for remembering that life is beautiful and worth living. We cannot, however, continue reproducing this Pangloss Syndrome in the terrain of theory construction. That the aesthetic in everyday life is not only found in beauty but also in quite grotesque and violent manifestations is a fact. Tuan succeeds in seeing beauty beyond art, even in everyday life, but the twilight that surrounds it and the darkness into which it sinks when aesthetic violence is exerted and when other categories unfold, remain alien to the prospect of his theory. The luminous filament of art keeps blinding aestheticians and conceals from them whole territories that are perhaps gloomier but no less socially relevant.

Along this same line we can situate Crispin Sartwell's *The Art of Living: Aesthetics of the Ordinary in World Spiritual Traditions* (1995), and to a certain extent Yuriko Saito's (2005) reflection on the aesthetics of weather. Saito's clear prose forms part of the compilation of 11 articles that Andrew Light has just published with Jonathan M. Smith entitled *Aesthetics of Everyday Life* (2005). Saito takes on Japanese tradition where weather aesthetics are much appreciated and very sophisticated, as expressed by haiku poetry and tea ceremonies, two forms of specifically Japanese art. Without a doubt, a beautifully elaborated reflection on the sensitive relation that we establish with nature through weather. How poignant it can be for human sensitivity, in the East or the West alike, has been eloquently expressed by its significant presence in novels and other genres as film, poetry and indirectly, music. In another text, Yuriko Saito (2001) approached the aesthetic from the point of view of artistic and non-artistic objects in the Japanese culture as the tea ceremony or the bath, the packings and the food in an attempt to get rid of the Western artisto-centric perspective in aesthetics. Like Yi-fu Tuan, Saito feeds from non-Western aesthetics to shake a little the narrowness of the art centristic perspective to find new horizons for the aesthetic experience.

In this compilation Leddy contributes with respect to contemplation of objects not conventionally considered artistic but with "aesthetic" and properties associated to "beauty". As an analytical philosopher, Leddy (2005, 19) analyzes language applied to aesthetic objects asserting that: "a one more fruitful way to explore the aesthetics of everyday life is through discussion of aesthetic terms" and is sorry that some of them like "neatness", "messiness", "looks good", "smells nice" have been neglected (I cannot but think that this type of analysis corresponds more to linguistic semantics than to aesthetics). In a previous text, Leddy's (1995) attempt to demonstrate that categories such as "clean", "dirty", "messy", or "neat" can be considered as relevant "everyday surface aesthetic qualities" makes me wonder why select these rather moralistic categories instead of so many other possibles like the frumpy, the dowdy, the sleek, the creepy, the dull, and so on. In these texts Leddy stayed at the surface of an everyday aesthetics.

Another author in this anthology is Arnold Berleant who, continuing from Schiller, looks for a social aesthetics from categories like acceptance, perception, sensuality, discovery, unicity, reciprocity, continuity, involvement, and multiplicity. Berleant considers that we can find beauty in forms and human relations within the family or friendship and finds a parallel between the beauty and love or between art and love.

84 *Everyday Aesthetics*

Berleant proposes to replace conflicts and aesthetic violence by a social model of love for a more human community. With the deep respect and esteem that I have for Berleant, I cannot but corroborate clear symptoms of the Pangloss syndrome in this proposal since aesthetics does not necessarily have to be the remedy for conflict or violence; as it can equally be a constituent of violence. (cf. Mandoki 1999)

In this anthology, Arto Haapala starts off from another text by Tuan (1974) to argue that a place can express aesthetic properties. He mentions that "strangeness creates a basis for sensitive aesthetic appreciation" (2005, 50) (similar to the distinction I proposed between re-cognition and dis-covery) and distinguishes between the aesthetic of the habitual and of the extraordinary. He proposes the term of "attachment" as a central concept for understanding the aesthetics of the everyday, a term that can also relate to *latching-on*. Allen Carlson focuses aesthetic appreciation of the landscape from the traditional concepts of "contemplation" and "aesthetic object" to regulate and consider (under the assumption that a landscape is to aesthetics what the text to literary postmodern theory) which are the acceptable forms to appreciate a landscape. He proposes five topics for which he denominates "correct curriculum for the appreciation of the landscape": forms, common knowledge, science, history, and contemporary use. (2005, 105) I believe that the reader knows my position with respect to similar approaches well enough, so I will not abound in this proposal. Glenn Kuehn's attempt (2005) to argue that food is art, was preceded by Quinet (1981) and Kafka (1989 Barbara not Franz) with the same point but different arguments. Emily Brady (2005) does not need to resort to art centrism for arguing that smell and taste belong to the scope of aesthetics. In fact we can affirm that, by definition, what is sensed belongs aesthesiology and, in the cultural context, to aesthetics. From Sibley, predecessor of the discussion on the aesthetics of these two senses (and against their exclusion by Thomas Aquinas), Brady argues that sniffing and savoring are aesthetic objects in the full sense of the term. I agree with Brady's aim, but keep wondering why it is necessary to insist on their character of "objects" instead of faculties of the subject, paths for aesthesis? The fetish of the aesthetic object disguises as qualities of the objects what are exclusively qualities or aptitudes of the subjects. The scents and flavors are effects of aesthesis, not only human but in various creatures, none of which exist without the mediation of the subject.

With a solid bibliographical corpus but not as much in the argumentative, Welsch proposes sport as art and concludes that "the sport is a species of art. Art (in the usual sense) is another one [species of art]." (Welsch 1999, 236; 2005, 150) How many species of art exist, according to Welsch, is not sufficiently specified because it would require a scrupulous taxonomy of the arts. As I objected to him during a recent congress, Welsch does not tell between "aesthetic" and "art", which thwarts him to realize that sport, in effect, is aesthetic; but there is no fantasy, artifice, or meaning in the artistic sense we inherited since the origins of Greek classic art. Sports being aesthetic does not make it artistic. They both are very much alike: sport, like the art, is a professional public performance for contemplation and enthusiastic, even empathic, participation of the public. There is even a poiesis of the body by the artifice of training, as in body building and the sculptoric surgery of the body, but that is not precisely sports. Also, there are certain hybrid art-sports like gymnastics and figure skating that *imitate* art, but are not. Welsch cites Hegel's authority who

The Tangents of Prosaics 85

supposes that sport preceded Greek art, but where are the historical evidences? Sport is doubtlessly aesthetic and is practiced for the aesthesis it is able to convey (otherwise it would not attract the masses) but it is definitively not artistic since already from his origin the Greeks perfectly distinguished the *amphitheatron* for the arts from the *stadion* for sports.

In all the aforementioned authors, there has been an attempt to legitimize diverse aesthetic activities by greater or smaller reference to the art centric paradigm. In others, as in the case of Zúñiga (1989) and Sánchez Vázquez (1992), the idea of an everyday aesthetics remains a side remark rather than a real theoretical enterprise. Gillo Dorfles entitled a chapter "Aesthetics of the Quotidian" in his book *Praise to Disharmony*, where he proposes "the chromatic explosion in the youthful dress, a typographical lay-out or television transmissions in a timid and superficial aesthetic outline of the everyday". In fact, rather than being interested in the prosaic, Dorfles (1989, 172) brings about the "everydayness of the artistic phenomenon" in a typical conflation between the aesthetic and the artistic.

The luminous, spectacular character of art blinds aestheticians from perceiving the aesthetic irradiation in nature, everyday life, and other fields of human experience that are crucial to explore. Tuan, Saito, Brady and Berleant manage to gaze at it beyond art and make evident that interest in the aesthetics of everyday life has grown during the last decade or so. Nevertheless, not only the indifference of traditional aesthetics regarding everyday life, but the few efforts to approach it demonstrate the difficulty of the task of elaborating a theory of the aesthetic beyond the category of beauty and the art centristic paradigm. Tuan's beautification of the everyday, Naukkarinen's discovery of the aesthetics in design and in human appearance and Dissanayake's making art an inherited behavior exemplify the degree in which art and beauty keep haunting every endeavor that infringes canonical aesthetics' dogmas.

Chapter 11

The Nutrients of Prosaics

The attempt to transcend aesthetic theory beyond the artistic was initiated by Kant in his reflections about nature and the sublime and, at the beginning of the twentieth century, by Max Dessoir in *Asthetik und allgemeine kunstwissenschaft*, a distinction between aesthetics and a general science of art. Dessoir proposed an "aesthetic nature" and tried to explore extra artistic aesthetics in everyday and cultural life.[1] However, in his attempt to go beyond the *Einfühlung* principle and to establish this approach as a scientific enterprise, he tried a more objetualistic approach looking for the aesthetic in the objects themselves. This fetishism, I think, paralyzed his effort. Guyau also proposed the idea of a non-artistic aesthetics of experience when stating: "To breathe deeply, to feel how the blood is purified in contact with the air, is this not an intoxicating sensation indeed, to which it would be difficult to deny aesthetic value?" (*Les problèmes de l'estétique contemporaine*) Since then, these efforts were totally forgotten and left pending. There are three authors, however, that did not deliberately intend to elaborate a non-artistic aesthetics yet collaborated in paving the way towards this purpose, each from a totally different approach, as we shall see.

Mikhail Bakhtin

Morson and Emerson (1990, 23) consider Bakhtin to be the first in formulating a comprehensive theory of prosaics understood as a theory of prose (or prosic poetics), while he was only one among other "prosaic" thinkers or philosophers of the ordinary, Tolstoy among them. Bakhtin, however, is certainly a pioneer in prosaics for his insistence in focusing aesthetic problems from the very density of the everyday. He also looks at literature from people's everyday language, instead of starting from theoretical generalizations of the artist's genius, his personal style or from a formalist approach to exclusively artistic languages. Like the prophet Moses who led the people of Israel toward the Promised Land but never got there, Bakhtin pointed the direction toward prosaics but only saw it from afar.

> We very keenly and subtly hear all those nuances in the speech of people surrounding us, and we ourselves work very skillfully with all these colors on the verbal palette. We very sensitively catch the smallest shift in intonation, the slightest interruption or voices in anything of importance to us in another person's practical everyday discourse. All those verbal sideward glances, reservations, loopholes, hints, thrusts do not slip past our ear, are not foreign to our lips. *All the more astonishing, then, that up to now all this has found*

---

1 In Mukarovský, 1977, 104.

no precise theoretical cognizance, nor the assessment it deserves! (Cited by Morson and Emerson 1990, 34; the emphasis is mine)

This "precise theoretical cognizance" is what prosaics has to undertake, not being limited to the information conveyed but encompassing also the intermittent flutters and subtle nuances of sensibility. In his analysis of the genres, in his vision of the carnival, in his concepts of the "chronotope", "dialogism", "polyphony", and "heteroglossia", Bakhtin constantly encountered the prosaic. What he dealt with was prosic poetics in the novel (mainly Rabelais and Dostoyevsky), within which various genres intertwine and merge. Although the concept of prosaics does not exist in Bakhtin, he repeatedly mentions everyday life (*byt*), the casual and ordinary (*bytovoj*), the extra-artistic (*vnexudozestvennyj*), and everyday genres (*bytovoj zanr*).

In the same way as, for Bakhtin (1990, 13–92), the look of the other produces our aesthetic image in relation to a horizon, and the look of the author produces the aesthetic image of the character related to a narrative context, the look of prosaics projects an aesthetic image of the everyday by the way in which it is presented and lived. The artist objectivates aesthetically a view on life through poetics by an artwork, like the common man aesthetically objectivates a view on life through prosaics by his way of living it. I do not mean a philosophical view, but a sensorial, sensitive one.

For Bakhtin, there is a border, though blurred, between the everyday and the artistic. He sees the carnival as an ambiguous case located on the border between art and life itself, presented with elements characteristic of the play. Yet at the same time it is organized and fabricated, planned during the rest of the year for this purpose. In that sense, it is not life itself but an artifice. Carnival constitutes a subversive look upon social institutions from humor and desacralization, and not being part of poetics, it is clearly prosaics in its shaking up social roles and dissolving conventions.

Polyphony, hybridization, and heteroglossia, terms that acquire a particular sense in Bakhtin, appear in the novel precisely because they are part of prosaics. If we follow the conceptualization of the everyday genres established by Bakhtin (where he includes love letters, ordinary conversations, employment applications, memoranda, scientific treatises, philosophical essays, and so on) it is clear that his theory of the genres is written from prosaics towards poetics. It seems that for Bakhtin, prosaics was an implicit embryo for the development of his philosophical and literary theory, since the various themes he discussed are united in their origin to the aesthetic configuration in the everyday. Therefore Bakhtin is a nutrient of prosaics, though his main focus was upon prosic poetics.

John Dewey

Another nutrient of prosaics is John Dewey, who set out to explore the aesthetic from an ample view of experience, not only everyday but also organic and vital. His main concern was to explain aesthetic experience generated by the work of art as emerging from the basics of experience, instead of exploring the implications of this bio-aesthetic approach beyond the artistic. In his monistic view of aesthetic experience,

The Nutrients of Prosaics

sensibility is of organic or biological and cultural origin. Despite declaring himself anti-Kantian, Dewey inquires about the conditions for the possibility of the aesthetic and artistic experience, as Kant inquired about the conditions for the possibility of knowledge and the judgment of taste.

> How is it that the everyday making of things grows into that form of making that is genuinely artistic? How is it that our everyday enjoyment of scenes and situations develops into the peculiar satisfaction that attends the experience that is emphatically esthetic? These are the questions that the theory must answer. The answer cannot be found, unless we are willing to find the germs and roots in matters of experience that we do not currently regard as esthetic. (Dewey [1934] 1980, 12)

To answer these questions Dewey ([1934] 1980, 3) tries to "recover the continuity between the types of refined and intensified experience, like the works of art, and the everyday events, doings and sufferings that are universally recognized as the elements of the experience". It is not by analyzing objects sequestered in museums and theaters, in galleries and private collections that one can find answers concerning aesthetics, as Dewey points out. Many works of the past, today out of context in restricted spaces for the arts, had a very different social function from mere contemplation, namely, that of elevating the dignity and intensifying the emotion and adherence of the community in which they were created. This is why he states that:

> In order to understand the esthetic in its ultimate and approved forms, one must begin with it in the raw; in the events and scenes that hold the attentive eye and ear of man, arousing his interest and affording him enjoyment as he looks and listens: the sights that hold the crowd—the fire-engine rushing by; the machines excavating enormous holes in the earth, the human fly climbing a steeple-side .... (Dewey [1934] 1980, 4–5)

Medieval communities created the visibilities of the sacred through integration of ritual, music, architecture, incense, lighting, and feast. This does not occur today with the art of the elite, amputated as it is from the collective and everyday. Therefore, for Dewey, there is a greater vitality for the satisfaction of the aesthetic thirst of society in aesthetic manifestations not considered artistic, like movies, jazz, comics, and tabloid papers, than in the fine arts. To this list I would add rock, television, sports, fashion, and video-games.[2]

Dewey encompasses a great variety of aesthetic manifestations, very remote from the orthodox concept of art:

> Bodily scarification, waving feathers, gaudy robes, shining ornaments of gold and silver, of emerald and jade, formed the contents of esthetic arts, and, presumably, without the vulgarity of class exhibitionism that attends their analogues today. Domestic utensils,

---

2   Dewey also inspired Richard Shusterman (1992) to propose a pragmatist approach to aesthetics. In fact, Shusterman is much more faithful to Dewey's intentions by incorporating to his theory contemporary art genres in popular art and theoretical debates (postmodernism and deconstruction) than my somehow forcing it to remain in the organic, raw basis he originally explored. Zúñiga (1989) also proposed a Dewey-based analysis of everyday aesthetics but unfortunately, does not seem to have pursued it.

90 *Everyday Aesthetics*

furnishings of tent and house, rugs, mats, jars, pots, bows, spears, were wrought with such delighted care that today we hunt them out and give them places of honor in our art museums. Yet, in their own time and place, such things were enhancements of the processes of everyday life. Instead of being elevated to a niche apart, they belonged to display of prowess, the manifestation of group and clan membership, the worship of gods, feasting and fasting, fighting and hunting, and all the rhythmic crises that punctuate the stream of living. (Dewey [1934] 1980, 6–7)

All of this belongs to the sphere of prosaics.

Johan Huizinga

The third nutrient of prosaics is Johan Huizinga. In his classical work *Homo Ludens*, Huizinga insists that his goal is not to show the element of play *in* culture, but rather the play *of* culture. Civilization is constituted beginning from play, and not as an aspect among others of cultural life. Without play there is no culture, since, for Huizinga, play precedes culture. "Play is a voluntary activity or occupation executed within certain fixed limits of time and place, according to rules freely accepted but absolutely binding, having its aim in itself and accompanied by a feeling of tension, joy, and the consciousness that it is 'different' from 'ordinary life'." (Huizinga 1955, 28)

He mentions different types of play as those of strength and dexterity, games of invention, of riddles and puzzles, of chance, exhibitions, and acting of all types. Huizinga recognizes the profound aesthetic quality of play, in which delight is produced and the subject remains in a state of "absorption" (another term for "*latching-on*"). He finds play in all social activities like language, myths and rituals, where subsequently other practices such as law, trade, craftsmanship and arts, knowledge and science, emerge. For Huizinga all these activities are rooted in the original soil of play.

"The object of this essay is to demonstrate that there is more than a rhetorical comparison to view culture *sub specie ludi*." (1955, 5) In fact, for the author to say that culture originates from the playing is not metaphorical but literal. Huizinga remits us to Calderón, Shakespeare, and Racine who used the metaphor of life being like theater with a strong moral emphasis pointing to the vanity of all things and echoing Neo-Platonism. Huizinga, on the contrary, does not say that culture is *like* a game, but that it *is* playing.

What Huizinga wants to demonstrate is *how* we can recognize the ludic element in diverse cultural and social activities, and *where* play is to be found within such serious activities as the religious, the legal, and the cognitive. On the other hand, *why* culture is constituted by play is not dealt with by the author but we may perhaps propose an answer: it seems to me the cognitive function Lakoff and Johnson (1980, 1999) attributed to metaphors, namely as a projection of something concrete and experiential to understand something more abstract, is closely related to play. As in cognition we understand something abstract by analogy with something more concrete, in social life we understand the significance of something by playing. Human beings understand significant activities in terms of play, an experience

The Nutrients of Prosaics 91

projected from the vital to the cultural. Those who have not played cannot understand their acts in broader cultural terms than their immediate utility.

It is interesting to note that the traditional conflation of the aesthetic with beauty makes Huizinga hesitate in associating aesthetics and play, and he ends up separating them, despite their very obvious affinities:

> If, therefore, play cannot be directly referred to the categories of truth and goodness, can it be included perhaps in the realm of the aesthetic? Here our judgment wavers. For although the attribute of beauty does not attach to play as such, play nevertheless tends to assume marked elements of beauty. Mirth and grace adhere at the outset to the more primitive forms of play. In play beauty of the human body in motion reaches its zenith. In its most developed forms, it is saturated with rhythm and harmony, the noblest gifts of aesthetic perception known to man. Many and close are the links that connect play with beauty. All the same we cannot say that beauty is inherent in play as such; so we must leave it at that: play is a function of the living, but is not susceptible of exact definition either logically, biologically, or aesthetically. (1955, 7)

Despite Huizinga's hesitation, it is impossible to overlook the remarkable affinities between the ludic and the aesthetic such as the difficulty in defining them, the "rapture" or process of "absorption" (mentioned by Huizinga) or *"latching-on"* generated in both, the importance of rhythm (see the emphasis in this respect stressed by Dewey no less than by Huizinga), and a delight and integral commitment of the subject in both situations. More importantly, in both sensibility is involved. Both draw a magic circle in space-time; in both participate subjectivity, imaginaries, and illusion (from *inlusio, illudere*, or *inludere*, that means "in play"). And lastly, in both cases there is a display of constituted identities and realities. Huizinga (1955, 9) affirms concerning play that: "it adorns life, it broadens it, and to that extent it is a necessity both for the individual, as a function of life, and for society, because of the meaning it has, its significance, its expressive value, its spiritual and social associations, in brief, as a function of culture". Those words apply exactly to aesthetics. How, then, can aesthetics and play be distinguished? Could it be that aesthetics is play, or that play is always aesthetic? In fact, play belongs to aesthetics as our arteries and heart belong to our body. Ludics as the study of play is no less essential to the understanding of the aesthetic than poetics as the study of the arts, since both focus on human disposition to *latching-on* and our susceptibility of being *latched-by*.

At this point the perspicacious reader may suspect that to a certain extent I am abusing the intentions of these authors by recruiting them into the unsuspected adventure of prosaics and projecting them far beyond their original purposes. After all, what Dewey was concerned with was art, rather than with everyday life, that was only the basis from which he tried to explain artistic, not everyday phenomena. Bakhtin also was interested in literature, and in the same manner observes the everyday that supports the production of this genre. His interest was not to search for the aesthetics of the everyday, but the leak of the everyday into art. Huizinga, despite the fact that the proximity of aesthetics and play did not escape him, bestows aesthetics an excessively restricted sense. It would then appear as if I am looking for renowned godfathers for an undertaking as marginal as the aesthetics of the everyday and to legitimize it with the childish zeal of overlooking its incurable orphanage. I cannot adduce anything in my defense.

Chapter 12

The Play of Culture

Huizinga's insistence to see play through the most diverse manifestations in everyday life, and not as one more element of culture, links us directly with his undertaking. In an identical sense, prosaics does not explore aesthetics *in* culture focusing on artistic displays or decorative elements in daily life, but the aesthetics *of* culture, namely, how culture is inherently woven by aesthetic games. If for Huizinga "without play there is no culture", we can affirm with equal vehemence that without aesthetics there is no culture. Play, as aesthetics, cuts across the density of the social. After Huizinga, and from prosaics, we can understand that social reality in all its domains is constituted by play.

As Goffman ([1959] 1981) repeatedly indicates, identities are also constituted by games. The function of aesthetics in what I shall call "scopics" resides in the manufacture of social toys (props and wardrobes) and of toy-stores or magic circles (scenery or *setting* in Goffman's terms). In "lexics" the rules of the games are explicitly established and in the "acoustics" one displays the sounds accompanying games (cheers, shouts, laughter, whistling). "Somatics", as the corporeal activity involved in playing is also present. There is no play without the aesthetic, as there are no aesthetics without play. Kant was well aware of it when he talked of "free *play* of imagination and understanding" to describe aesthetic experience. Play is aesthetic, as aesthetics are ludic.

Through his historical approach, Huizinga privileges particularly one type of game, the *agon* or competence, above a variety of other possible games. Nevertheless, it is less his choice of this particular game than his tenacity and clarity in emphasizing the core of the ludic element as constitutive of culture and social reality, which makes his endeavor worth following. As the opposite of aesthetics is not ugliness but apathy, the opposite to play is not seriousness but the automatic. Machines do not play, even if they seem to do so, as chess by computer: they simply perform movements by programmed instructions.

Dewey emphasizes the importance of order, harmony, and rhythm with the same vehemence regarding aesthetics as Huizinga does regarding play when he states:

> The profound affinity between game and order is perhaps the reason why play [...] seems to lie to such a large extent in the field of aesthetics. Play has the tendency to be beautiful. It may be that this aesthetic factor is identical to the impulse to create orderly form, which animates play in all its aspects. The words that we use to denote the elements of play belong for the most part to aesthetics, terms with which we try to describe the effects of beauty: tension, poise, balance, contrast, variation, solution, resolution, and so on. Play casts a spell over us; it is "enchanting", "captivating". It is invested with the noblest qualities we are capable of perceiving in things: rhythm and harmony. (Huizinga 1955, 10)

94 *Everyday Aesthetics*

Table 12.1   Types of Games

Games	Action	Condition	Main property
Agon	Challenge	Rivalry	Contest
Alea	Gamble	Tremor	Chance
Mimicry	Imitation	Simulation	Disguise
Ilinx	Frolic	Vertigo	Balance
Peripatos	Exploration	Adventure	Conjecture

Summing up, Huizinga traverses culture with the eyes set on play as a constituent element. We shall explore it observing aesthetics also as a constituent, pointing out the elements it utilizes and the games it displays.

Categorization of games by Caillois

Probably based on Huizinga's work, a decade and a half later Caillois ([1986] 1994) proposed four categories of games he classified as *agon* or competition, *ilinx* or games of vertigo, *mimicry* or games of masquerade and imitation, and *alea* or games of chance.[1] This classification is indeed interesting and helpful in penetrating further the dimensions of play. Despite the perfect symmetry of the Caillois system, it is necessary, however, to add another category of games overlooked by the author that I shall name *"peripatos"*, and that differs from mimicry by not being generated by imitation or *"as if"*, but by exploration or *"what if"*. The game *peripatos,* that encompasses those mentioned by Huizinga as "games of invention, of riddles or puzzles", participates in science and art, in the construction of theories and conjectures. We always enter these undertakings with the ludic spirit of learning what would happen if this or that possibility, idea or act was to materialize.

Peripatos rests on playful curiosity. When painting a picture, writing a story, or elaborating a theory, the game we play is exploratory: we play *what if.* The term *"peripatos"* comes from the Greek *peripatein* meaning to traverse, to roam. The school of Aristotle was called "peripatetic school" because of the teacher's habit of pacing while teaching. The corporeal *peripatos* of Aristotle and his pupils is an exact metaphor of the intellectual *peripatos* they were engaged in. It is, however, necessary to distinguish *"peripatos"* from *"peripetia"* or vicissitude, which for Aristotle was the abrupt change of events in a Tragedy. Thus to the taxonomy of games by Caillois I shall add one more line.

Games do not always present themselves in such a pure state as the above table may imply since ones often overlap others. The ludic effects of different games vary between the re-creation of *mimicry*, the frolic of *ilinx*, the palpitation of *alea*, the emulation of *agon*, and the adventure of *peripatos*. Competition implies challenge

---

1   My gratefulness to Lauro Zavala for bringing to my attention Caillois's text. The author adds another distinction worth considering for further elaboration in the two axes that traverse each of these categories going from *paideia* or chaotic games to *ludus* or orderly games. Without using Caillois terms, we can recognize playful *latching-on* in his "ludus" and play *latched-by* in his "paideia".

The Play of Culture

Table 12.2   Latching-on/by Games

Games	Latching-on	Latched-by
Agon	Athletics	Animosity
Alea	Betting	Addictive gambling
Mimicry	Playful disguise	Deliberate deceit
Ilinx	Vertigo	Madness
Peripatos	Perplexity	Quandary

that always results in a winner and a loser: the goal of *agon* is always triumph. Frolic in *ilinx* generates vertigo and the sharpening of one of the senses struggling to maintain balance. The adventure of *peripatos* consists in exploring another path, in deviating from the routine towards a different option.

The process of re-creation so common in religious rituals results, as its name indicates, from the repetition and imitation of events, namely, by creating again in *mimicry* some significant event of the past. In the military, sports, national or governmental events, it is mainly competition or *agon* that is played, where identities are not only maintained, but exalted, exhibited, and risked for prestige. In the artistic and scientific matrixes, as well as in tourism, the coveted effect is that of adventure for the explorer, although *agon* and *mimicry* are not absent as we shall see when we analyze each matrix in Part 5.

Due to the Pangloss Syndrome, none of these authors dares to recognize that there are also cruel games. I refer to children torturing animals that are later reproduced in soldiers, wardens, and teachers who play torturing inmates, subordinates, and pupils or even their own children and spouse with different degrees of cruelty. No matter how shameful these may appear to the theoretician, such repulsion does not entitle one to ignore them. The difference between the cruel and the cordial game depends on this link to *latching-on* or *by* as can be seen in Table 12.2. In one case there is good faith, in the other bad faith, linked not only to a moral category but also an aesthetic one. Thus aesthetic violence is exerted against oneself or others in games where the condition of being *latched-by* prevails.

Chapter 13

The Horizons of Prosaics

Traditional aesthetics restricted itself by definition to the study of art and beauty. It still remains, as Passmore (1951) affirmed half a century ago, quite a dreary discipline, particularly through today's Anglo-American analytical philosophy obsession of trying to match words with worlds and translating it all to the simple formula of "If P then Q". That a field of research that pretends to study human sensibility ends up reduced to a mere classification, description, evaluation or justification of objects denominated "artworks", to the exclusion of the rest of its manifestations, is astonishing. Heirs of Baumgarten and Hume, aestheticians should have originally occupied themselves with the standards of taste and the science of sensitive knowledge (*scientia cognitionis sensitivae*) to defend the importance of human sensibility (*Sinnlichkeit* in Kantian terms) throughout the various aspects of culture, but they forgot to do so. Engrossed with art and beauty, looking for their place and influence in the academia and the artworld to arbitrate what is and is not art (when obviously the market, the curators, collectors, and artists are the ones deciding it *ad hoc* and *ad libitum*), we as aestheticians have evaded our social responsibility of contributing to the knowledge of human beings from our particular perspective, and thus lost for this field of inquiry the relevance it deserves.

Some of the most serious problems of contemporary technological urban societies are directly (although not exclusively) related to the aesthetic. Drug addiction, racism, delinquency, and hypertension, even physical and emotional illnesses like chronic depression, cancer, anorexia, and obesity have to do with human sensibility. Whoever constantly requires drugs or food is desperately looking for something pleasant or comforting to *latch-on*. By trying to flee from aesthetic misery, people yearn for sensations and emotions difficult for them to obtain otherwise. Even racism, we have to admit, has to do with excluding others partly because of aesthetic reactions: the racist rejects the other for his skin color and odor, sound of voice and manner of speaking, physical appearance, behavior, and so on.

Genealogical and aesthetic analyses of subjectivity and identity can significantly contribute to the understanding of many of these complex contemporary social phenomena. Thus, to suppose that aesthetics only refers to art and beauty is at this stage an indolent evasion. Berleant (1991, 211) proposes going beyond aesthetics as we have learned it and inquire into non-Western and pre-literate cultures to have some fresh insights into its nature. This is, indeed, a healthy and necessary proposal, but we need not go so far for answers, since consequences of our aesthetic ignorance are right next to us, in the sheer aesthetic violence of contemporary urban life. Aesthetic theory has to deal with social reality here and now to safeguard the quality of life and the respect for the integrity of human sensibility, not merely to evaluate and legitimize artworks in the market for their investors' pecuniary safety.

98 *Everyday Aesthetics*

Psychological violence that leads to crime and to social pathology passes through an abused and injured subjectivity. Aesthetic violence is not merely a personal question that an individual may or may not solve by psychotherapy: it is a systematic socially reproduced problem.

More than half a century after the Nazi genocide, we still have not been able to understand how such inconceivable cruelty towards human beings and the complicity of civil German population with the NSDAP and the Gestapo was possible. What cultural conditions could produce subjects whose sensibility allowed them to act with such indifference towards extreme human pain? As Ulrich Herbert argues (2000, 43) the so-called "final solution" was accomplished not as a result of a sudden rapture of mass hysteria, but with a remarkable indifference, disinterestedness (one could add that even with a Bulloughian "psychical distance") that moralized genocide demoralizing morals. In other words, there was a serious obstruction of human sensibility whose roots we still do not fully grasp. How can we explain the genocides perpetrated by the Turks against the Armenians, the Hutus against the Tutsis, and the Iraqis against the Kurds? Under what conditions are Islamist suicide killers produced today whose instinct of survival is substituted by the aesthetics of death for the sake of slaughtering innocent people? Their "farewell videos" show that it is a question less of politics or morality than of the production of forms of sensibility that aestheticize death to a mythical, grandiose image.

We partly depend on our sensibility to orient ourselves regarding others, our values and answers to life's mysteries, and sometimes also for judging what is true or false. Rational argumentation is less relevant to influence the common man than unconscious persuasion in its appeal to sensitivity and emotion. Little we know of human sensibility, although unfortunately, those who study it more thoroughly do it with the intention of manipulating it. Cosmeticized, disguised and rehearsed politicians use their manufactured images in political representations to seduce voters. Their image advisors are experts in a not very imaginative *mise-en-scène*, but given the mediocrity of the political debate, highly effective in supplanting it. The advantages of aesthetics for manipulating behavior and opinion surprise no one any more. The odd habit of fabricating identities to commodities in advertising campaigns results from their findings on the necessity of identification and acceptance of the potential client, as well as of the mechanisms of adhesion and loyalty to certain images. Aesthetic strategies are thus deliberately used to catch consumers' attention at the tiniest, most volatile opportunity of trademark exposure, and seduce them.

The media networks compete by aesthetic mechanisms to obtain higher ratings: the news are broadcasted today with sentimental music backgrounds to win the audience's sympathy for their pre-established victims, instead of triggering thought and debate on these problems. Worldwide predicaments are displayed under the genre of melodrama for their fast digestion so that the public immediately identifies the good and the evil side to extract politically correct opinions according to their socially convenient political identity. Infuriated masses, delirious fanatics, screaming women, bleeding bodies, soldiers and policemen in action are scenes coveted for their impact upon the audience's sensitivity. It is not a matter of reasoning over the facts, but of being touched by the yellowish aesthetics in the news. The capacity to be in another's situation diminishes in direct proportion to the saturation of sensibility and the tendency towards indifference. In this condition, and more relevant than beauty, apathy becomes an aesthetic problem. While philosophers debate over the ontological status of beauty, the legions of people living in a state of aesthetic misery and violence, indigence and exclusion, grow every day.

When I initiated this inquiry more than a decade ago, I asked myself if the attempt to theorize everyday aesthetics was simply quixotic. Since these problems need to be addressed, quixotically or not, prosaics can contribute significantly to their understanding. Obviously, not all social problems are a result of aesthetic negligence, but some of them are, much more than previously supposed.

PART 4
SEMIO-AESTHETICS

How to proceed now without having "the artwork" as paradigmatic, "beauty" as an objective judgment, "the aesthetic object" as ultimate referent, "the faculty of taste" as a standard, not even a technique such as "painting" or "sculpting" for a sense of direction through this enterprise? These ideas have conducted preceding studies in this field but, as was argued in Part One, at a very high theoretical cost. What, then, are we going to speak about now if we no longer consider theater or music, romanticism or classicism, tragedy and comedy as indispensable categories and values for defining the aesthetic?

I have certainly renounced to a great deal of clues that have guided previous philosophical studies in distinguishing what may or may not be understood as "aesthetic phenomena", yet what I am not willing to give up is a conceptual foundation for this endeavor. True, to propose a foundation for a theoretical enterprise is no longer a very "intellectually correct" position in these so-called postmodern, deconstructionist times. I would, nevertheless, really like to see how deconstructionist proposals—both theoretical and architectural—can do without any foundations, since even the liquid or gaseous condition of, say, Derrida's *differanced* signifiers and the mobility of Lyotard's *differends* is established as a new antifoundationalist foundationalism for subsequent theoretical inquiries. If, on the other hand, we understand knowledge not as a reflection of a noumenal or meta-epistemological reality but as a construction, we have no problem in admitting that whatever is built requires a firm basis, even if the aim is no longer arriving to any absolute truth. Theory is not about building perfect temples for Truth to abide, but houses for our mind to dwell. It is definitely architectonic, as Kant has taught us. Thus a viable and productive interpretation that permits an acceptable degree of understanding is firm enough. We cannot be free either of some metaphysical claims, if not any longer "the metaphysics of presence" denounced by Derrida, at least a metaphysics of ongoing, unfolding processes. Where are we going to begin from if not, precisely, the basics of these processes, namely those that occur in the nucleus of a cell, the hub of life? As all experience and the very primordial processes among live creatures depend on concrete meaning exchanges throughout the whole spectrum of life, we cannot but start from semiosis.

Semio-aesthetics and aesthesio-semiotics

The exploration of aesthetics through a semiotic methodological approach began with the incipient efforts of the Prague School, particularly Jakobson and Mukarovský, to understand what could the "poetic function", "aesthetic function", or "aesthetic

102   *Everyday Aesthetics*

posture" be defined in the linguistics context. This semiotic-aesthetics relation was taken by Morris, Lotman, Rossi-Landi, and Searle as well, each contributing valuable concepts along the way. Barthes, Todorov, Eco and Shapiro, the semiological school from Greimas, Metz, Floch, and Fontanille also had a significant say to this effort. Presently, *Groupe μ*'s work on rhetorics and visual signs, Sonesson's on painting and Tarasti's on music among others must be mentioned. These works may diverge over the particular semiotic approach taken, but they all coincide on the understanding of aesthetics as almost synonymous to art, whether they refer to literature, film, music, or visual arts. In this sense, one could better define them as poetic-semiotics or artsemiotics.[1]

On the other hand, from a partly Greimasian approach, Herman Parret argues for an "aesthetization of semiotics", redefining them as a universe of passions where the interpreter is not only cognitive but emotional and 'sentimental'. (Parret 1995, 6) In another work (2003), he elaborates a very detailed semiotic taxonomy to analyze taste and sound, specifically the aspectualization of wine and voice. Although the author denominates his approach "semio-aesthetics", it is worth using the habitual terminology (bio-semiotics, phyto-semiotics, antropo-semiotics or zoo-semiotics), so that his exploration would be better coined "pathosemiotics" if it refers to passion or "aesthesio-semiotics" as a semiotics of the senses.[2] Along this line Fontanille's recent book *Soma et sema* (2004), exploring the semiotics of the body both as represented and representing, must be mentioned.

Other non-semiotic approaches to signification and symbolism such as Clive Bell's (1977) idea of "significant form", Susanne Langer's "symbolic expression", and Cassirer's "symbolic form" often assume a purely mentalistic idea of meaning that ignores the material side of semiosis, its incarnation or its in-corporation. These approaches contrast with Dewey's remarkable contribution asking for the biological conditions of possibility, energetical as well as material, of aesthetic phenomena.

Up to here we have three connections between aesthetics and semiotics: one is art-semiotics (poesemiotics) which deals with meaning and communication in art; the other is senso-semiotics or aesthesio-semiotics referred to the senses; and the third is pathosemiotics as the semiotics of passion (even if Greimas's aesthetic examples are always artistic, Parret does make a difference).

What I will elaborate here is a fourth possibility, a semio-aesthetics that connects semiotics and aesthetics from two sides: by the target observed and as a methodological approach. On one hand, prosaics examines social communication

---

1   A new field of inquiry could thus emerge from this distinction that would analyze art not as a means for communication, but as an artistic elaboration whose main theme is semiosis. As there are artistic genres such as landscapes and portraits, still life and interiors, we could consider semio-art as a new genre of all paintings dedicated to semiotics. In other words, semio-art is the artistic game with signs and symbols, as all artworks are, but whose topic is precisely semiotics or signification. Among these, the most typical are Duchamp's *Fountain* or *L.H.O.O.Q.*, Malevitch's *White Square on White Background*, Kandinsky's first abstract watercolor paintings, Velazquez's *Meninas*, most of Magritte's work, particularly *This is not a Pipe,* and some conceptual art. All these artworks explore semiosis from one angle or another.

2   Parret did not agree to this terminological adjustment when I remarked on it.

Semio-Aesthetics 103

and interchanges (socio-semiosis) in terms of their character as aesthetic phenomena by how such character involves or affects participants' sensibilities.[3] On the other hand, since aesthetics and semiotics have a Möbius-strip relation, for aesthesis to come about (in perception or experience) there must be semiosis.[4] In other words, for something to be aesthetically significant it must have semiotic signification (in Morris's 1974 significance/signification distinction). We therefore require semiotic tools which at least may allow us following along one clear direction. Moreover, between semiotic signification to the aesthetic significance, an excess occurs whose clarification is almost the cherry on the cake.

One finds peculiar, to say the least, Rossi-Landi's contemptuous tone by which he refers to aestheticians who use semiotic tools "... a semiotic aesthetician can in any case be only a man of the past that tries to modernize himself adopting a certain language, and that language is at the risk of degrading itself at the level of a mere unskilled jargon." (Rossi-Landi 1976, 63) He contrasts them to semiologists who happen to apply semiotic methodology to art and aesthetics (among many other objects of research). His opinion surprises me because, if art is certainly a precious object for semiologists to test their methodological tools, semiosis can be also an object for aestheticians' to test their tools in the application of aesthetic analyses. What is art if not a communicative process? And what is semiosis if it does not cross through at least one of the senses?

From my somewhat embarrassing position (according to Rossi-Landi) of using semiotic tools for aesthetic studies, I will try to explore this mysterious faculty of sensitivity as it is materialized and objectified in and through communication; any communication, not only artistic. Instead of trying to understand how signs operate in artworks (cf. *Groupe μ*, Sonesson, Tarasti), or how our senses and emotions are involved in the production of the meaning (Parret's aesthesio-semiotics), I will center in those processes that exceed semiosis to the aesthetic dimension. Communication is not merely an automatic information transfer between emitter and receiver; it involves persuasiveness, vehicles to capture attention, to captivate. It not only tries to inform and convince but to fascinate and seduce. How it manages to do so is the marrow of prosaics.

---

3   On the variations in the relation between aesthetics and communication see Mandoki 2006c.

4   This contrasts to aesthesio-semiotics as a semiotic approach to aesthetics or pathosemiotics as the study of the semiotics of desire and passions as in Parret (1986, 1987, 1988).

Chapter 14

Thresholds of Semiotic Perception: Sensation, Discernment and Regard

> In one and the same human being there are cognitions that, however utterly dissimilar they are, yet have one and the same object, so that one can only conclude that there are different subjects in one and the same human being. (Franz Kafka[1])

As there is no aesthesis without semiosis, no opening of the subject to the world without the mediation of meaning, there equally is no semiosis without aesthesis either, since no meaning production is possible without opening to the world. Semio-aesthetics is thus complementary to aesthesio-semiotics. Semiosis unfolds in each of the three autopoietic orders defined by Maturana and Varela (1992) namely, the cellular, the pluricellular or individual and the pluri-individual or social (as I mentioned in Chapter 5). It initiates as a porosity or receptivity to the environment acquiring diverse degrees of diversification in each individual and species. In first order units, aesthesis takes place at the cellular membrane, whereas in second order units of more developed animals, it is enabled by membranes such as the skin, ears, eyes, mouth, and nose by which organisms are exposed to their surroundings. Aesthesis in third order units or social organisms in human societies occurs in the interactions among identities and roles within social matrixes. Third order membranes acquire a different structure depending on each matrix (in the State matrix, the membrane would be equivalent to the country's borders, as in the family matrix to the limits of the family's property, whereas in the school matrix to the list of matriculated students, as in the military matrix to the record of enrollment, as in a gang its members would be those who exhibit the same tattoo and so on).

This aperture to the world is, nevertheless, not enough to generate a semiosic process. An impulse or energy input and a material substratum are required. This *matter-energy stratum* can be denominated "mattergy" and is directed towards the survival of the organism. Mattergy also requires a particular conformation to not dissipate and to acquire meaning for an organism. This conformation is its *formal stratum*. The distinction that Hjelmslev (1969) establishes between two strata—*form* and *substance*—and two planes—*expression* and *content*—can perhaps be borrowed beyond the strictly linguistic and semantic domain where it was originally located and apply it to a wider biosemiotic spectrum focused upon relational terms between form and substance. The co-dependency between both strata may also help explain a system as con-formed by a structure (form) and activated by its organization (mattergy). Thus in a living unit, survival dynamics (mattergy) depend on its

---

1 http://www.bartleby.com/66/36/31836.html 2/3/2006.

Table 14.1 Types and Strata

Type	Formal Stratum	Mattergy stratum
System	Structure	Organization
Live unit	Contour	Dynamics
Organism	Membrane	Metabolism
Semiosis	Signs perception (perceptor)	Action (effector)

contour (form) or morphology, as metabolism (mattergy) depends on the organism's membranes (form) isolating it from and connecting it with its environment. By the same token, in semiosis, energy-matter (effectors) depends upon perception of forms (perceptors), as in the cycle proposed by Uexküll (1982). (See Table 14.1.)

At the level of antroposemiosis, these two strata increasingly diversify, particularly through the development of language, although survival always remains the basic direction of all semiosis. It is necessary to start off, therefore, from this double perspective towards aesthetic and semiotic phenomena, namely, their mattergy condition and formal articulation. For that reason I will focus aesthetic phenomena from the impulse and substance that gives them existence and from the conformations they acquire.

It was Kant who, trying to distinguish different forms of mental processes, defined sensation as "the effect of an object on our representative capacity, being affected by it". Indeed, *sensation* affects the subject, but it precedes any representative activity since it is totally corporeal. A stomach ache, a slight chill, the sensation of a momentary shade can be organically detected before being consciously represented. Sensation belongs not only to the human species but also to any live creature, whereas representation already implies a system of cultural mediations between percepts present in sensation and certain categories of classification absent in it. When a stimulus is collated with a repertoire of previous experiences, when there is a degree of conscious or unconscious memory, sensation is structured to become a percept by relating it to phylogenetic and ontogenetic codes.

The second level of perception can be designated as *discernment*. Although related to sensation that impels it, discernment goes beyond the immediacy of sheer reaction and becomes more selective. If subjects are relatively passive in sensation, in discernment they organize percepts transforming their experiential inventory. At this level of perception the subject establishes finer distinctions and attends to regularities by a more dynamic and flexible code. As sensation corresponds to the purely corporeal being, to their individuality, discernment concerns identity and depends on training and experience. A mathematician is able to discern numerical patterns and a musician discerns acoustic patterns as a painter discerns chromatic patterns or mothers discern the needs in our baby's weeping with much greater precision than other people. As an activity of trained, specialized understanding, discernment is totally matricial and depends on a social field of meaning.

A third level of perception is *regard* where subjects formally observe group conventions and unfold them in terms of their particular roles. Regard responds to the necessity of impersonal interaction in a collective order that regulates action

Thresholds of Semiotic Perception: Sensation, Discernment and Regard 107

according to circumstantial location in a group. It is purely ethological because it has to do with collective dynamics.

Let us take for example the case of a dog. At the level of sensation, it perceives pain when it is hurt or water when it is soaked, but discerns between its master and a stranger, as between particular substances' smell according to its training.[2] In a pack, dogs perceive themselves as part of that group maintaining, by regard, a short distance waiting for the others to keep themselves within the group. Bees perceive light at the level of sensation when trying to escape from a closed place, but do not discern the glass until they bump against it. However they discern between an open flower and one closed, between flowers with or without pollen and they can discern distance and direction for an appropriate place to nourish themselves or for building another honeycomb by the diameter and movement of other bees' dance. (Sebeok 1963, 1969) But in the interior of the honeycomb and in the division between workers and the queen, bees are guided by regard as collective perception. Something similar happens among birds which can hear other birds' song by sensation, but can only discern its meaning as a song dialect within their own community, whereas their regard is quite spectacular in the perfect form of birds' group flight.

The vastness of semiosis begins from sensation in its most elementary level (as heliotropes moving towards the sun or paramecia reacting merely by eating or evading obstacles). Discernment occurs in more developed animals that already distinguish new aspects from the environment by learning and is relative to each species (the cat miaows to its master at the door as a request to open it). It is possible to conjecture that collective suicides in some species like penguins and whales may have something to do with group regard controlling the individual's sensation in its impulse for survival and its discernment of danger. These examples from zoo-semiosis do not attempt any more but to illustrate the distinction here established between the three thresholds of perception.

These perceptual distinctions inevitably bring to mind Peircean semiotic phaneroscopy (phenomenology), where sensation would in a broad sense correspond to Peircean *firstness* inasmuch as "the mode of being of that which is such as it is, positively and without reference to anything else". Discernment would match *secondness* as "the mode of being of that which is such as it is, with respect to a second but regardless of any third". Regard would be compatible to *thirdness* understood as "the mode of being of that which is such as it is, in bringing a second and a third in relation to each other". (Peirce "A Letter to Lady Welby" *CP* 8.328, [1904]) For Peirce, firstness is determined by the inherent qualities of something; secondness by the relation or reaction directed towards something else, and thirdness by the mediation established in a relation between multiple organizations. Regard, then, implies a general character that is not only individual (as sensation) or interpersonal (as discernment) but also impersonal in a group context.

---

2   In the investigation of animal behavior, it has been discovered that the dog, by the sense of smell, is a privileged interpreter of symptoms like autism, cancer melanoma, tuberculosis, Ebola, and is able very insistently to alert about critical states of epilepsy and diabetes indicating alarm to the person at risk. The dog perceives abnormality and verifies the degree in which semiosis transcends the human species.

108 *Everyday Aesthetics*

Table 14.2   Phases, Thresholds, Interactions, Processes and Attributes

Phases of Subjectivity	*Thresholds of Perception*	*Personal interaction*	*Processes of Semiosis*	*Basic attribute*
Individuality	Sensation	Intrapersonal	Firstness	Immediacy
Identity	Discernment	Interpersonal	Secondness	Intermediacy
Role	Regard	Impersonal	Thirdness	Normativity

Recollecting the distinctions established in Chapter 6 relative to the phases of subjectivity, we may now link them to the thresholds of perception, the processes of semiosis and their basic attribute. (See Table 14.2.)

This scheme can partly illustrate Kafka's idea quoted at the beginning of this chapter, because it shows the existence of different unfoldings of perceptual subjectivity in each person. Although semiosis impregnates all levels of subjectivity, for the analysis of prosaics, located at the relation between subjectivity and identity, we are going to take the second threshold of perception, discernment, as dominant, although connected to sensation and regard.

Chapter 15

The Axis of the Signic

For Saussure, *semiology* was to become "the study of signs in the midst social life" implying the objective existence of the signs and their confinement to the human sphere. *Semiotics*, although much broader, is the term used by the school of thought initiated by Charles Sanders Peirce who defines the doctrine of the signs in the following way: "Logic, in its general sense, is, as I believe I have shown, only another name for *semiotic σημειωτική* [sémeiötiké] the quasi-necessary, or formal, doctrine of signs." (Peirce *CP* 2.227, c. 1897) Both, Saussure and Peirce, updated a very old debate that began at least since the ancient Greeks and continued through the Middle Ages with William Occam, Saint Thomas Aquinas, Duns Scotus following Jean Poinsot in the seventeenth century, among others. (Cf. Deely, 1990)

Charles Morris ([1938] 1994, 27–28) proposed a distinction between *semiosis* as the *process* in which something works as a sign and *semiotics* as the *study* of ordinary objects in the measure by which (and only in the measure by which) they participate in semiosis. In other words, it is necessary to distinguish *semiosis* as a process and *semiotics* as its study in equal sense as in Part Two we defined *aesthesis* as the *condition* of aperture of all live beings and *aesthetics* as the *study* of such condition.

Semiosis, as aesthesis, is not exclusive of the human species alone but constitutes processes throughout the whole biological spectrum.[1] In antroposemiosis, energy directed to human survival passes from the biome to the culturome involving the construction of personal and collective identities because surviving in socially constructed realities requires surviving as a social identity.[2] From here we can understand better the crucial role that aesthesis plays in cultural semiosis as a device for persuasion, seduction, and adhesion in maintaining and legitimizing such identities and realities (as we will see in Part 5).

We are going to approach semiotics from two basic axes, each corresponding to a particular semiosic stratum: I will designate as *axis of the signic* the frame of reference whose dominant stratum is *form* and as *axis of the symbolic* the coordinate where the *mattergy* stratum dominates.[3] It is worth insisting once again that without intentionality or impulse (energy) and a material basis to communicate and interpret,

---

1   As it was initially explored by Uexküll (1957, 1982), followed by Sebeok (1963, 1969), Krampen (1981), Hoffmeyer and Emmeche (1991), Hoffmeyer (1996), Merrell (1994), and other biosemiotists.

2   On the concept of "culturome", I refer the reader to Mandoki 2003.

3   I define the analysis of the formal stratum as "the axis of the signic", since being purely differential, it is indirectly inherited from Saussure's conception of the sign. The "axis of the symbolic", on the other hand, is material-energy related, closer to Goux's broader idea

110 *Everyday Aesthetics*

Table 15.1   Strata

Strata	Formal	Material–energy
Semiotics	Signic axis	Symbolic axis

there is no semiosis. Also, without the formal or conformational activity, neither interpretation nor communication are possible. The distinction of strata, however, does not imply that the symbolic axis lacks form or that the signic is immaterial, but that in each mode of semiosic operation, one of these elements predominates. (See Table 15.1.)

Therefore, by *sign* we can understand the basic element on which the *axis of the signic* depends. This axis, as established by Saussure with respect to linguistic value, is of a purely conventional and differential character based on its form and not motivated by its matter. Its development has been historical and acquired greater sophistication and formal complexity in a process of progressive multiplication and diversification. Such differential character is established with respect to other socially contextualized and intertextualized signs.

Similar dichotomies have been proposed in different times. From the beginnings of the theory of signs among the stoics, a distinction between "indicative signs" and "reminder signs" was established, one that Occam later developed in his differentiation between "natural sign" and "conventional sign" (the first related to Peirce's "index" and the second to his idea of "symbol"). There is something in this dichotomy that makes it persist and reappear until today, although with diverse hues, because the mind apparently works by binary operations. Kant, for example proposes the distinction between two forms of exhibition or hypotyposis: the "symbolic" (indirect and analogical) and the "schematic" (direct and demonstrative) (*Critique of Judgment* § 59). He ends this distinction saying, "This subject has been, until now, still little analyzed, although it deserves more a deeper investigation." I could not agree more with him in this respect a quarter of a millennium later.

This dichotomy will be retaken to explore semiosis, as we did in regards to aesthetics in Part 2, always in relation to a subject. Then "something is a sign if, and only if, some interpreter considers it sign of something". (Morris [1938] 1994, 28) The medieval definition of the sign as *aliquid stat pro aliquo* is reformulated by Peirce as "a sign, or *representamen*, is something that stands to somebody for something in some respect or capacity. It addresses somebody, that is, creates in the mind of that person an equivalent sign, or perhaps a more developed sign." (Peirce *CP* 2.228, c. 1897; 1955, 99) Unlike Peirce, who establishes a trichotomy between sign, object and interpretant, here I do not understand semiosis as beginning from the sign (addressing the subject) but in the subject signifying its surroundings as a "perceptor" (Uexküll 1982, 32–33) and reacting as "effector". The subject connects one thing with another, *aliquid* with *aliquo* (which does not imply that such subject is necessarily human).

---

of symbols. In a previous work (Mandoki 1994) I called this axis "semiotic" but I now realize that the term signic is more adequate, since both axes belong to semiotics.

The Axis of the Signic 111

Except for expert peirceologists, Peirce's doctrine is dangerous in its literal application to disciplines different from semiotics, because it is prone to misinterpretation not only by its complexity but its relative blurriness. For that reason and out of loyalty to Occam's razor, I have preferred to start from Saussurean theory, although with the perhaps unforgivable betrayal to Saussure of pragmatizing his approach and injecting a Bakhtinian dose to it.

Signifier

According to Hjelmslevian terminology, in addition to the two strata (substance and form) it is possible to differentiate two planes (expression and content). We can therefore link the concept of signifier to the plane of expression in the signic axis. For Saussurean linguistics, signifiers are distinguished not by their implicit meaning but by their oppositions and differentiations within a code. He defines signifiers as "cuts made through of the mass of thought", but who "cuts" and whose "thought" is pierced?[4] This implies a subject, consequently by the term "signifier" I understand the signifying agent (perceptor in Uexküll) in any order (cellular, pluricellular or pluri-individual): not the object, text, word, or sound, nor "acoustic image" as defined by Saussure from an anthropocentric linguistic perspective.[5] Consequently, there is no signifier without signified and vice versa, since there is no percept without effect. Texts do not speak, nor words mean: subjects make texts speak and words mean, define objects and attribute meanings to them, even at the elementary pre-linguistic biological level of the perceptor-effector focused by Uexküll (1982, 32–33). Semiosis is an activity always exerted by subjects although not exclusively human, since it can include at the level of an organism the dog threatening with its teeth or the flea that interprets butyric acid in the sweat of a mammal as a signal to jump, bite and reproduce (perhaps even at the molecular level in DNA replication).

At the human scale, the signifier as *agent who signifies* implies an act of conformation by a given subject in his function as enouncer and interpreter. A noise, a gesture, an act, a flavor would be signifiers for a subject who signifies them as denoting semiosic effects (danger, attack, edible, poison) and connoting emotional effects (fear, pleasure, disgust, relief). Every interplay of signifiers is product of an objectivation with diverse degrees of intersubjectivity. To paint a picture implies an objectivation by signifiers such as figures, lines, and colors in a given format. This configuration is necessarily meaningful, even if it means only "smeared colors". The painting can work as a game of signifiers for many subjects, but it not always and not only acts as a linguistic or an aesthetic signifier, since it also can be an economic, biographical, historical signifier according to the strategies put into play for decodification.

---

4   We can signify concepts by cuts made through thought as well as through perception or produce them by cuts made to the signifiers themselves and to statements in analytical work.

5   Both Hjelmslevian planes correspond respectively to Saussure's signifier and signified, who originally hesitated between *soma* and *sema* (later taken in Fontanille's book), forms and devices, image and concept until arriving at signifier and signified (Barthes 1971, 41).

Everyday Aesthetics

112

Allow me to insist that the signifier is not reduced, as in Saussurean linguistics, to a word or acoustic image whose meaning would correspond to a mental image or set of existing objects. Here we will examine a multitude of signifiers in many registers, not only verbal but non-verbal as well, and whose mere illocution creates realities, not merely reflects them.

Signified

The plane of content of the signic axis is constituted by the signified. Such signified is not the referent of the word in the real world, nor the thing in itself towards which the signifier points (Peircean object) or the reference (Saussurean psychic image), much less the referent but the product of a signifying act mediated by the signifier. The study of signifiers separated from signifieds, of a linguistics that expels semantics would result in an abstract morphology whose explanatory potential is too limited. For that reason I consider with Frei, Morris, Saussure, and Hjelmslev that the signifieds are part of the signs and, therefore, the study of semiosis will have to involve not only the signifiers but also their effects of meaning. Instead of expelling the signified from our analysis, I have decided to expel the referent and leave it to the ontologists.[6]

Barthes (1971) conceives meaning as a process or act that unites signifier and signified and whose product is a sign. I prefer to understand it—for the aims of our analysis and for reasons that will be clarified in their development—as a process, yes, but not of uniting signifier with signified as if they pre-existed the sign separated from one another (it is true that Barthes warned us against being interpreted this way), but where the production of signifiers is, simultaneously, a production signifieds and a transformation of subjects. The product of this process of meaning production is the subject itself as both signifier or perceptor and as signified or effector. To produce signifiers is to produce signifieds and a subject other, different from the previous one, because it has been altered in the process.

Consequently every signifier is fatally teleological (having *telos*, end) as it necessarily produces a signified; otherwise, it would not be "signifier". Being signifier only by the mediation of subjects, it necessarily puts into play strategies to produce such signifieds (even if the meaning produced is "it does not have meaning"). To the Saussurean concept of arbitrariness of the relation between signifier and signified, with Benveniste (1988) I prefer to denominate it a relation of conventionality.

Signifiers produce various signified effects depending on the matricial context. Giving flowers, for example, is festive and metaphorical of the youth and purity of the bride in the nuptial rite. In the funerary matrix it is a tribute, a metaphor of the evanescence of life. In the medical matrix, flowers mean prompt recovery, regaining the freshness of the flower. In business, flowers mean congratulations. In the family,

---

6 Against the distinction proposed by Greimas between the semantic that would correspond to content and the semiological that would correspond to expression (with what expression could such semiology deal that does not involve content?) the study of semiosis always implies semantics, although emphasis can also be syntactic or pragmatic (as in this case).

depending on the type of flower and the occasion, they can mean "home sweet home" (when the housewife arranges wild flowers from her garden), "happy anniversary" when they are expensive, arranged flowers, "I desire you" with red roses, or "I love you" when pink, white or yellow in a romantic situation. In the State, flowers mean formality of a ceremony. In sports or artistic matrixes they mean triumph or success. In juridical or educational, flowers are rare except perhaps on mothers' day that, as a ritual of enormous ideological weight, can cross for a moment even the austerity of a prison.

Chapter 16

The Axis of the Symbolic

Among the concepts that have most led to confusions in the field of linguistics and semiotics is the term of "symbol" by the variety of meanings attributed to it (not less ambiguous and complex than those around the term "aesthetic" already analyzed). Ogden and Richards (1938, 11), for example, use the term "symbol" in so lax a sense that it includes all verbal representations or processes of referentiality. Another use of the term is proposed by Bourdieu (1984) who speaks of "symbolic capital" referring to intellectual or cultural assets, distinguished from social and material capital. Nevertheless, as we will see, the symbolic is not immaterial at all and much less asocial. What distinguishes the symbol from the sign is, indeed, its material and energy stratum, namely, its weight and density, its sheer materiality.

Ernst Cassirer (1975, 163) has an altogether different sense of the term "symbol": "By 'symbolic form' one must understand here all spiritual energy by virtue of which a spiritual content of meaning is linked here to a concrete sensible sign and it is innerly attributed to it." Although Cassirer emphasizes the concept of energy in the symbol, his spiritual definition and the idea of "inner attribution" are, to say the least, problematic. For Peirce (1955, 102), symbols are a certain type of signs that are different from indexes and icons because they work in relation to legisigns, namely obey conventionality and normativity. Peircean *symbols* are similar to Saussurean *signs* in their relative arbitrariness and dense conventionality, whereas Saussurean *symbols* are similar to Peircean *indexes*. For Saussure (1967, 105), "what is characteristic of a symbol is that it is not completely arbitrary; it is not empty, there is a rudiment of natural link between signifier and signified". If this "natural link" is understood as existential proximity, it relates to Peirce's indexes, but if it is understood as resemblance, it relates to Peirce's icons. In fact, Saussure is recorded by his students proposing the following example: "the symbol of justice, the scales, could be replaced by any other, a car, for example" that in last instance, by this same arbitrariness, appears more akin to Peirce's "symbol". Saussure never managed to develop his concept of symbol and ended up integrating it to the sign in spite of its inconsistency with his First Principle of the arbitrariness of the sign.

Berger and Luckmann (1986, 59) understand that "any significative subject that in this way crosses from one sphere of reality to others can be defined as a symbol, and the linguistic mode by which this transcendence is achieved can be denominated symbolic language" (they refer, for example, to crossing from the oneiric sphere to everyday reality). Although I share with these authors their constructivist approach to the sociology of knowledge, this version of the symbol seems mistaken, exhibiting perhaps a psycho-spiritual inheritance from Cassirer, Eliade, or Jung. That "crossing" from dream to reality is simply performed by the metalinguistic function of language (in terms of Jakobson) when the subject translates his personal language of dreams

116   *Everyday Aesthetics*

to social language in daily life, and therefore uses signs as much as symbols. I consequently also differ from these authors in what they understand as "symbolic universes" (1986, 120–163), (referring to religion and science) which they define as "the matrix of all socially objectified and subjectively real meanings; all historical society and the biography of an individual are seen as facts that happen within this universe". (Berger and Luckmann 1986, 125) Religion is indeed a meaning and meaningful matrix, but as the family or the nation, it is constituted as much by signs as by symbols, as I will argue later.

The variety of meanings attributed to the term "symbol" is endless, a list to which we could add many other authors like Carl Jung for whom the symbol is existential (as the index of Peirce) and Wallon and Hegel (for whom the symbol is analogical and motivated).[1] I present this repertoire of definitions of the symbol so that the reader may realize the degree in which this concept, as that of the aesthetic, is far from having settled upon a common and consensual meaning.

Partially along the line of authors who find in the symbol processes of analogies, motivation, and existential proximity, I understand the *axis of the symbolic* as a process of production of meaning that operates by *associations* involving a *load* of *time*, *matter*, or *energy*. Although Cassirer also finds energy in the symbol, his concept of energy is purely spiritual. In prosaics, on the contrary, I understand "energy" in material and concrete terms, located in space-time and involving affection, effort, vitality, impetus. In contrast to the sign in which the signifier depends basically on the form as the main stratum to differentiate it from others, in the symbol the form import weighs less than the substance stratum, mattergy-time, to define its meaning.

The penis of Napoleon jealously kept by the Squire Urological Clinic of New York has less interest from the axis of the signic (a penis among others and in opposition to other organs) than from the axis of the symbolic, because it is associated with an archetypal virility of having belonged to this almost mythical individual. The relics of churches and convents associated to the life of some saint or martyr, Jimmy Hendrix's guitar associated to his undeniable musical skill and premature death, all function as symbols. Also a Rolls Royce associated to expert manual work and its aristocratic connotations, in addition to the time invested in its manufacture, its scarcity, and great pecuniary value, makes it circulate as a symbol. By the same token, Lenin's corpse associated with the 1917 revolution and its dreams of proletarian emancipation, or the Holy Sepulcher, the Kaaba of Mecca, and all those objects or places whose time, energy, and material load are affectively strong for a determined social group acquire the function of symbols.[2]

The concept of symbol (loaded of time, matter, and energy) here proposed totally diverges from the Peircean symbol (abstract and conventional), and includes index and icon of Peircean terminology depending on each particular case. Juan Diego's *tilma* with the image of the Virgin of Guadalupe is associated to the affective load of the millions who believe in her and to the time since its appearance at Tepeyac (500 years ago), as well as to the belief in the miraculous energy and power of the Virgin

---

1   Barthes (1971, 40).
2   On symbolic weight of places, see Mandoki 1998.

The Axis of the Symbolic   117

Table 16.1   Strata, Planes and Axes

STRATA	FORM	MATTERGY
Planes	Expression	Content
Axes	Signic	Symbolic
Signic axis	Signifier	Signified
Symbolic axis	Symbolizer	Symbolized

for the Guadalupans. As such, it is a symbol in the sense here elaborated, but it is also a Peircean index as a miraculous mark of her existence for the believer, a Peircean icon of her image, and a Peircean symbol of a particular manifestation of Christianity denominated "Guadalupanism". We may understand it as well as sign from the axis of the signic by opposition to other devotional figures like saints and Virgins such as Remedios, Lourdes, and so on. Even if the same object is sign, symbol, and index, there is no ambiguity in the application of these categories. Objects are not one or another category of semiotics: they function differently according to each code or axis.

"In the symbol there is always something archaic" says Lotman (1993, 49). Perhaps he is referring to that weight of time that remains in the memory of single or collective subjects. The price of an original in the art market is purely symbolic as an exchange-value representing a piece of life of the artist, in addition to the affective load that the author invested and crystallized in that work.

The mystic only can resort to the axis of the symbolic to articulate an intense and personal emotional situation of an irrational and not wholly conscious character, and expresses herself by analogies and metaphoric projections. The symbol, being cryptophoric and polysemic, condenses emotions and articulates sensations better than the sign. That is why, for the Cabalist, in the reverse of words as signs for social communication and of numbers as measures, there are symbols of God's attributes associated to concentrations of divine energy.

Chapter 17

Comparative View of Both Axes: The Symbolic and the Signic

In his book on symbolic economies, Jean Joseph Goux explored semiosis from a lax economic approach whose main contribution was not only including apparently diverse phenomena into a common perspective, but also the recognition of the materiality of symbols.[1] He first distinguished "on the one hand, the social process of *symbolization* (that is the process of exchange in the general sense of the term, of substitution of vital activities) and, on the other, the intertwined processes in diverse domains of *signification*, that is just one form of symbolization". (1990, 30) In short, for Goux, symbolization is exchange, and signification is a form of symbolization. In this symbolization process, he includes all practices of exchange, be they linguistic, economic, libidinal, political, or legal. He looks for the logical structure of this process common to all these practices of exchange to detect the specific ways in which this structure is manifested. For Goux, economy, language, desire, the State, and individual identity are all symbolic processes. "My thesis is that *all* the practices involving exchange or substitution tend to be geared to a single phase, a single form, of the logical dialectic of the symbolization process, but at the same time, the logic of this process is specific to each sphere of exchange." (Goux 1990, 93)

Deriving from Goux's wide view of symbolization, I do not, however, conceive the sign as a form of symbolization. In fact, what Goux understands as "symbolization process" is what is understood as *semiosis* in general which exceeds the human dimension to include the molecular and cellular levels, whereas the symbolic and the signic approached here are exclusively anthroposemiotic. Economy, language, desire, the State, and personal identity are, from the perspective of prosaics, as much symbolic as they are signic. Thus, the economy of a country from the axis of the signic refers to its currency, per capita income, the GIP, and so on by opposition to others in the system of worldwide economy, and will be symbolic from what it extracts in energy, time, emotions, and matter from the society in which it is examined. Language as an abstract exchange of signs in a system of oppositions and differentiation will be seen from the axis of the signic (Saussure's *langue*), but inasmuch performative discourse (*parole*) involving material, temporal and affectively charged acts such as promises, passionate expression of emotions, declarations, production of knowledge, establishment of contact, and human solidarity (the conative, expressive, aesthetic, referential and phatic functions according to Jakobson 1963[2]) will be seen from the axis of the symbolic.

---

1 I have been speaking of the materiality of symbols since Mandoki 1994, 1997.
2 On this performative dimension, I refer the reader to Mandoki 1999a.

120 *Everyday Aesthetics*

Unlike Goux, I understand signs to be incommensurable with symbols, although both are part of the general process of semiosis. The fact that gold as a symbol is at the basis of the monetary code that is signic does not imply that it must necessarily be part of the symbolic order as interpreted by Goux. What it indicates is the permanence (and not a substitution) of the axis of the symbolic as an indispensable coordinate, along with the signic, in all processes of human communication.

For the author, there are stages where the sign replaces the symbol (in economy we see how bills and credit cards have replaced gold as money and do without its endorsement). It is as if, for Goux, the sign were the evolution of the symbol, although remains bound to it. (1990, 49) He sees a linear process in economy that goes from the instrument to the fetish, from the fetish to the symbol and from the symbol to the sign. I maintain, on the other hand, that signs do not necessarily replace symbols (although it can happen in some cases, as when bills replaced metal coins) but evolve and replace other signs, not the symbols, because these remain loaded with time-mattery, without dissolving into signs.

A coin, for example, is sign and symbol: sign in differential relations with other currencies; symbol by its affective connotations, the investment of energy by labor to acquire it, or antiquity for numismatic collectors. Diverse currencies replace one another qua signs according to conventions established by the Mint. The credit card is sign in relation to other cards and other forms of pecuniary circulation and is symbol by the signature implying a commitment to pay by investing energy in socially relevant work to endorse it. For that reason, Goux's linear vision where signs replace symbols is inoperative. In any case, we can speak of periods of different meaning regimes as in fashion, artistic styles, and scientific paradigms that change throughout time and where some signs are displaced by others.

In libidinal economy, the axis of the signic can be observed in the so called "sex symbols" that operate rather as sexual signs, since these celebrities are defined by differences and oppositions to one another. But from the axis of the symbolic, celebrities invest a great deal of energy in their shows to libidinize their fans; a great deal of money in advertisement, special effects and costumes and lots of time in organizing these shows. Their fans also invest a great deal of affective energy towards them as these simulate investing enormous erotic energy to seduce them. We symbolically want to see celebrities spend in sweat, tears, and saliva during their show the equivalent to our laboral, monetary, and emotional effort invested in the purchase of the ticket—as Barthes succinctly pointed out in *Mythologies* (1980, 110–12).

The importance of both axes for prosaics' analyses is manifold, and allows differentiating between aesthetic *latching-on* in relation to the symbolic and that related to the signic. Collectors, for example, find aesthetic value in each object by signic discrimination of the differences, as well as by symbolic correlation in the effort to acquire each object and the anecdotal and affective connotations of each piece. From the axis of the symbolic, the subject appreciates the antiquity of the object, its originality and luxury, as well as its material or sentimental value. Da Vinci's *The Last Supper* has lost a good part of its perceptual or sensorial signic value by the damage of time on the pictorial material, but its symbolic value has grown by surviving half a millennium, and by the fact it was done by the hand of the great Renaissance genius and dedicated to a topic of enormous affective load.

Comparative View of Both Axes: The Symbolic and the Signic 121

While the sign has a differential value in relation to other signs and in function to the context, the symbol has an associative value. In the plane of content, symbols produce associative *significance*, as signs generate differential *signification*.[3] When discovering differential operation of signs, Saussure found that words do not carry an immanent meaning with them as one may suppose from using a dictionary. It seems a regression, therefore, to affirm that symbols are indeed loaded with significance. However, while a sign is negatively differentialized (since it is what no other signs are), the symbol is distinguished positively by integrating or accumulating what other symbols (associated with it) are.[4]

In the symbol there is an existential trace of what it represents, as in the Peircean index; for that reason it is not arbitrary. The direct material relation or existential contiguity that the index has (as in the hole of a bullet, the trace of a footstep, a barometer or a weathercock for Peirce) extends towards and includes also the affective, mental, and corporeal spheres in the symbolic axis. For that reason the mark left by a bullet will be a *signic index* when by *opposition* it differentiates the caliber of one particular weapon from another, or the attack by firearm instead of by a sharp weapon, and will be a *symbolic index* by *association* to a violent act, to an affective or historical event for the interpreter. Thus also, a palace as symbol is *index* of the amount of work invested in it by its abounding space and opulence, but it is also a Peircean *icon* by similarity in its monumentality and luxury with the lifestyle of monarchies. Whereas all processes of mental semiosis (signic or symbolic) are necessarily material-energetic being neuronal, for the symbolic axis materiality itself becomes symbolizer by the evocations and connotations it generates.

It is possible to conjecture that the axis of the signic activates the left hemisphere of the brain (where the centers of language and mathematics are located) by operating through keen differentiations, while the symbolic activates the right hemisphere as it functions by analogies and images, since the centers of creativity, of musical and space perception are located there. For our aims, however, the difference between both axes is less neurological than theoretical and heuristic, a conceptual tool for establishing distinctions that may help explain semiosic phenomena related to the aesthetic. Without a symbol concept as the one here proposed, it is difficult to explain how an old and not particularly elegant dress that Marilyn Monroe once wore could be auctioned at higher prices than a package of Microsoft or Coca Cola stocks. It charms because it is symbolically charged of connotations, a significance derived from its association to the diva.

From the signic axis we distinguish between a chair and a table, between a griffin and a centaur by oppositions and differences. We are not concerned here with the material existence of the object but with its distinction by proximate and distant terms, gender and species, its location within the system or code. From the symbolic axis, on the other hand, items are associated to other items and they acquire significance only from that association. Thus a clay tile floor is distinguished in the

---

3 I am using Morris's (1974) distinction mentioned above.

4 In German the difference between *Nacht* and *Nächte* operates negatively by a game of oppositions in the system, whereas a golden crown with diamonds, rubies and emeralds is positively distinguished by the value of its materials in addition to being a crown.

signic axis from a linoleum floor in their chemical composition, dimensions, color, texture, form of production, and so on, but from the symbolic axis clay tiles are associated to the earthy, its texture, the rustic, the tellurian, a certain warmth and freshness related to nature, whereas linoleum is associated to artificiality, modernity, functionality, hygiene, low cost. While the signic axis triggers denotation, the symbolic axis triggers connotation.

Let us emphasize that, as in the case of the "aesthetic object" that is such only in relation to a subject, we cannot speak of signs and symbols with their own independent existence separated from any subject. On the contrary, it is the axis from which a subject enunciates and interprets an object what will establish whether it will work as sign or as symbol. Although Peirce denotes by sign and symbol different aspects from those elaborated here, I share the idea that: "A symbol is defined as a sign which is fit to serve as such *simply because it will be so interpreted*." (The emphasis is mine.)[5]

The crown of the monarch as a *sign* is an item worn on the head that differs from the hat of a farmer, the bonnet of a buffoon, or the tiara of a Pope by its form. As *symbol* it is an object made of gold and precious stones, with a big investment of time and energy in labor and perhaps also an historical and affective charge stemming from tradition. The cross is *sign* of Christianity in differential relation with the Star of David of Judaism and the crescent moon and the star of Islam, but it is *symbol* if associated with the death of Christ and his sacrifice for humanity's sins. Military uniforms and religious attires, flags, Coca Cola, and other brands or logos, credit cards, and paper money, work predominantly from the signic axis by differential and combinatory elements as letters in an alphabet or combinations of 1–0 in the binary system. Flags are signs when they only operate from a differential code representing countries or determined groups. For the members of the group it represents, however, the flag acquires a significance or energy load by association with historical, collective, and personal facts. The Mexican flag as symbol is associated with Monday mornings when all children must dress in white for school and render solemn tribute to it, with the historical narrative of the hero child Juan Escutia wrapping himself in it and jumping from the Castle of Chapultepec in 1847 to defend it from the invader, with solemn political or military moments, with sport nationalism, with the central point of the *Zócalo*, center of the center of the center of the country.

A finely carved table, a meticulously embroidered dress or sewn of spangles, an immense mansion made of marble and granite will have symbolic value according to the human energy and the work invested and coagulated in them. From the signic axis each may mean Spanish table of the eighteenth century, holiday dress, or mansion of General López, because they circulate from particular signic syntaxes. From the axis of the symbolic, however, enunciated and interpreted by the energy invested in carving the table, embroidering the dress, building the mansion and extracting its materials, the time demanded in its accomplishment and the energy involved are the processes by means of which symbolic value is loaded. Neither the signification of the sign nor the significance of the symbol are universal or spontaneously interpretable anywhere, since both are contextual and intertextually constituted.

---

5   Peirce "New Elements", *EP* 2:307, 1904.

Comparative View of Both Axes: The Symbolic and the Signic

Table 17.1 Axes

Signic Axis	Symbolic Axis
Production of signification	Production of significance
Oppositions and differentiations	Associations and loads
Sinecdoquical intervention	Metaphorical intervention
Digital operation	Analogical operation
Hard conventionalized codes	Soft more intuitive codes
Denotational	Connotational
Exchange value	Use value

The sign is extensive because with greater qualitative differentiations, a quantitatively more elaborated and diversified code can be produced. The symbol is intensive; it does not require variation but concentration, as in a Zen story where by the contemplation of a mere pebble one may discover the secret of the universe. This explains why mosques were built over Jewish or Christian sanctuaries (as the cave of Macpelah, the temple of Jerusalem) and churches over mosques (as in Cordoba, where it was also initially San Vicente Cathedral). Mesoamerican pyramids also were constructed over other pyramids and churches over such pyramids. The symbol is cryptophoric, cumulative, and polysemic whereas the sign reproduces by parthenogenesis expelling ambiguities.[6]

From this point of view, use value of commodities is symbolic since it is incarnated and depends on the energy, time, matter with which it is loaded, whereas exchange value is signic since it obeys to a system of equivalencies and differences. Signs are sold at the New York Stock Exchange, whereas symbols are auctioned at Sotheby's and Christie's.

Summarizing, signs are defined by a process of differentiation within a hard or strongly conventionalized code functioning mainly by denotation. Symbols, on the other hand, generate significance and are established by associative processes keeping material-time-energy traces of their origin and function mainly through connotational operations. While signs are diversified in a centrifugal process of multiplication, symbols are loaded in a centripetal process of implosion in which value is accumulated in layers saturating greater density by the investment time, labor, and affective energy.

In addition to being semiosic, signs and symbols participate in the aesthetic dimension whenever a flag, a crown, the cross of the Christianity, or the image of the Virgin are elements to which the subject may become affectively *latched-on* attributing an emotional value to them. From his or her sensibility the subject is moved or touched by the objects, captivated by them, but the primary condition for such *latching-on* is always semiosis. There is no *latching-on* without a subject who attributes significance to its object.

---

6 An example of this expulsion of polysemy is in the distinction I previously made between "prosics" and "prosaics", as well as between "poesics" and "poetics" here proposed in a process of "semiogenesis" (another invented term, differentiated to parthenogenesis).

Chapter 18

The Non-Axis of the Obtuse

As obtuse as a whole chapter of barely more than one page is the non axis of the obtuse. Outside the symbolic and signic axes, this non axis of the obtuse demands attention despite the fact that it lacks conventions, associations, oppositions, differentiations, or loads. Roland Barthes discovered or invented this peculiar sense at the margin of what he calls meaning and information, and decided to denominate it "obtuse sense":

> The sense of the obtuse seems as if it were made manifest outside of culture, knowledge, information; from an analytical point of view it has a jocular aspect; in the measure that it opens to the infinite of language, it becomes limited for analytical reason; it is of the same race as games of words, jokes, useless expenses; indifferent to moral or aesthetic categories (the trivial, the futile, the phony and "pastiche"), it belongs to the sphere of the carnival. So that *obtuse* is the suitable word. (Barthes 1986, 52)

If the obtuse belongs to the sphere of the carnival, as Barthes affirms, then it cannot be foreign to the aesthetic and the moral (since the carnival takes the former to subvert the latter) although it can ignore their categories incapable, as they are, of apprehending it. We all have encountered the obtuse, that element out of place, abstruse, and touching. The obtuse may not be well captured by semiotics, but it is linked to the aesthetic because it depends on sensibility for grasping it and *latching-on* to it: "I believe that the obtuse sense entails a certain *emotion*; within the disguise this emotion never becomes sticky; it is an emotion that is limited *to designate* what is loved, what we want to defend; it is about a value-emotion, a valuation." Evidently, by valuation and emotion, we have landed right into the field of the aesthetic. Since for Barthes the obtuse sense is outside language, it cannot be sticky, and cannot be communicated. "One could consider *an accent*, the proper form of an emergence, of a folding (of a wrinkle) that has been marked in the heavy rug of information and meanings." (Barthes 1986, 59–62)

This emergence of which Barthes speaks of is indeed an epiphany in aesthetic *latching-on*. The accent or fold that he mentions is the interruption of discernment in an intransferable appreciation. This sudden cut subverts habitual semiotic recognition by the unexpected appearance of aesthetic dis-covery. For that reason, the obtuse is not significance generated by the symbolic axis, but a no-sense. It is neither symbolic nor signic since it does not signify or symbolize anything beside or beyond itself; it is simply appreciated without the hope of sharing this feeling with somebody. We sense it outside any order, namely, through the axes as an outside, a transgression, an alterity. It is more than absurd when the absurd becomes already part of a signic and a symbolic order. Marcel Duchamp's *Fountain* could have been obtuse to an accidental and lucky visitor at the museum, before becoming a codified and perfectly inventoried signic and symbolic object as a "ready made" in the artworld.

In order to illustrate the obtuse, Barthes presents the case of a strange character with a little hat in a scene of one of Eisenstein's films. I am going to risk an example knowing full well that the reader probably will not have a clue why precisely this, rather than any other example, occurred to me (as Barthes's reader does not have it either with respect to his example): I heard my five-year-old son defensively say to a friend: "It was not me, it was God!" The obtuse is unique and its degree of intersubjectivity is minimal: it can hardly pass degree 1, namely, the same subject of this epiphany.

Although Barthes compares the obtuse to jokes and games of words, it is not equivalent to the humorous, because humor already belongs to the signic and the symbolic and depends on them for its effect. The comic punchline is based in the signic when altering an expectation (the unexpected end of a joke) established beforehand by a code of oppositions and differentiations, namely, by habits and conventions. Humor can also be anchored in the symbolic, as in the carnivalesque spirit of blasphemy, demystification, obscenity, and eschatology, which generates laughter by the emotional discharge of mocking affectively charged objects like the Pope, the king, the Church, the body, God, sex, death. The obtuse, however, is unqualifiable: it can give laughter, sadness, melancholy, anxiety, or all at once.

What would characterize the no-sense of the obtuse is that it cannot be enunciated; *it is only apprehended, caught in the air*. Trying to enunciate this no-sense of the obtuse turns it into a sign and empties it from this obtuse character. Despite its fortuitous and intransferable character and its unusual slant, the obtuse does not escape semiosis, even if it jumps both axes to take a shortcut to aesthetic *latching-on*. Its passage through semiosis is by its interstices.

Chapter 19

Beyond Semiosis to Aesthesis

Deeply intertwined, aesthetics and semiotics maintain nevertheless important characteristics that distinguish them. As a meaning production process, semiosis is the necessary condition for aesthesis, but not sufficient. For the aesthetic to occur something else is required beyond perceptual activity, what Sánchez Vázquez lucidly indicated when he writes:

> It is difficult to believe that prehistoric man was not aware that, when introducing *excedent* formal elements, he was going beyond the practical-utilitarian limit thus opening a new space: exactly the one that we call aesthetic. Also, when certain formal elements were taking place—not by pure chance—that *exceeded* functional exigencies, a certain conscience had to occur of his own capacity to create them. (Sánchez Vázquez 1992, 100 emphasis added)[1]

Sánchez Vázquez (101) refers to such "capacity to imprint into the material an 'excedent' form [that] is symbolic, magically put, to the service of the practical purpose of hunting wild animals" and describes that "excessive form" as "good form", the result of "good work". In such appreciation of the good form and the good work, something beyond the re-cognition of the object by perception has occurred, namely, the dis-covery and appreciation of that "excessive form".

Through semiosis, the subject detects or re-cognizes its object and decodifies it by signification or symbolization according to the context in which it appears. Semiotic re-cognition offers data that subjects relate to the great number of categories by which they organize their understanding of the world. It thus acquires an informative import. But something else can happen: the object is perceived beyond its purely informative import and generates an additional value that makes it transcend to the aesthetic dimension. The question that arises is at what moment can we say that semiosis is transformed into aesthesis? When does a symbol or a sign acquire this additional aesthetic value? At the moment in which they radiate for the subject this excess of meaning that involves valuation, namely, when a semiosic event symbolizes beyond the symbol and signifies beyond the sign, exceeding itself in appreciation.[2]

---

1 On the relation between aesthetics and excess, see Mandoki (2001).

2 There is a quality of excess, says Goux (1990, 27) that determines the selection of the generalized equivalent in exchange relations. In gold there is excess, as well as in phallus, the monarch, God and the image of the father for the child. Such excess is of matter, time or energy that are projected as symbols.

The generalized selection of the equivalent in the libidinal, pecuniary or political economy belongs to the axis of the symbolic, although it works in the axis of the signic as a point of reference. While in the axis of the signic everything is exchangeable—there is no reason to

128   *Everyday Aesthetics*

Table 19.1   Semiosic and Aesthesic Processes

Phases of the Subjectivity	*Thresholds of perception*	*Semiosic process*	*Aesthesic process*
Individuality	Sensation	Detection	Pleasure/pain
Identity	Discernment	Distinction	Appreciation/ depreciation
Role	Regard	Observance	Deference/disdain

If we represent the semiosic dimension in a diagram as a plane with two axes, the symbolic and the signic, in which a semiosic event occurs by re-cognition, this event becomes an aesthesic event when, by dis-covery and appreciation, it radiates to the dimension of the aesthetic. This aesthesic event can occur in each one of the three phases of subjectivity. From individuality open to the world by sensation, aesthesis presents itself as sheer *joy* or pain. In the phase of the identity, occupied in appearing and therefore socially open to the world by discernment, the aesthesic occurs in a more selective *appreciation*. Being anonymous and predominantly collective does not mean that the role lacks elements for aesthesis, because from regard as opening threshold, *deference* arises when we become part of a collective subject. Sensation is required to be present; discernment to be discriminating, whereas regard implies to be situated. Sensation is almost epidermic and reacts spontaneously, discernment examines and distinguishes, regard observes its place and is positioned. (See Table 19.1.)

Let the ingenuous reader not be misguided by the supposition that we go through the world sometimes unfolding our identity for appreciation and others our role to show deference. This is merely an analytical scheme to help us understand some misconceptions that have clogged traditional aesthetics in the construction of its theory. From this perspective we may perhaps understand the limitations of hard analytical aesthetics located exclusively at the level of discernment exercised by the identities of *connoisseurs* pertaining to the *artworld*. For this school of thought, only the expert or *connoisseur* discerns the properties of the aesthetic object and appreciates its qualities, as Sibley's (1987, 42) idea of the art critic capable of extending the use of the five senses to exercise taste. With this gesture, aesthetic theory has excluded from the field of its interest all the other levels in which *latching-on* occurs.

---

choose an object instead another as universal referent—in the axis of symbolic the election of each object it is thoroughly motivated. For Goux the gold, the phallus, the father and God have been the foundation of symbolic value. The reason why it is gold, and not coffee or cotton, that became foundation of pecuniary value in Western civilizations derives from the axis of the symbolic by the effort to obtain it from the entrails of the earth. Gold is loaded with energy, it is coagulated working time. The phallus is the patriarchal horn of abundance; its generation of millions of sperm is absolutely excessive for the fertilization of only an ovum (as was mentioned by Bataille (1987) in the economies of the excess). The abundance of God exceeds good and justice to generate everything, from the infinite generosity of creation to the horror of demanding the sacrifice of Isaac, creating deluge and destroying Sodom and Gomorra. The monarch is personally responsible for harvests and famine, eclipses and epidemics. For a son, his father is responsible for the sacred object of desire, source of life and nourishment: his mother.

Beyond Semiosis to Aesthesis 129

The leap from semiosis to aesthesis happens when the subject surpasses its quasi automatic re-cognition of habitual perception and reaches the dis-covery of the unexpected. By "dis-covery" I mean to literally pull away the cover imposed by routine and the economy of perception: an epiphany occurs that makes the object appear to us in a novel way, unexpected or fascinating. I do not mean Dewey's "an aesthetic experience" but something more common and frequent than that, a *latching-on* to a perception for its delight import. Consider, for example, the sensation of a humming bird that can take us from discernment of re-cognizing it as a humming bird to dis-cover in appreciation its fabulous green emerald feathers and *latch-on* to the miracle of the existence of so astonishing a bird. As I said, we could also have ignored the sensation and remained in the signic re-cognition of the percept "hummingbird" missing this ephemeral opportunity for aesthetic *latching-on*.

If joy and appreciation do not need further explanation because they are common concepts in aesthetic theory, it is necessary, however, to examine the concept of deference as an aesthetic manifestation. Since deference depends on the role that is impersonal and anonymous, it is difficult to understand how sensibility can be active at this level. I mentioned before that the relation of the subject with his or her role corresponds to morality. It nevertheless does not exclude the possibility of understanding it as a sensible opening to circumstantial collective conditions. Deference happens in a collective context, and consists of a rhythmical movement of interaction that manifests itself as a collective choreography through courtesy and care for customs defined by the situation. Its aesthetic character resides in the preservation of harmony within the group by a sense of balance and rhythm. Deference is collective sensibility, and although it always starts from each particular subject who unfolds it, the configuration it achieves depends on the group.

Deference is the symmetrical opposite to carnivalization; it points to collective order as carnival to collective chaos (even if, in the last instance, carnivalesque chaos reproduces such order). Both are forms of play in the sense indicated by Caillois's distinction between *paidia* (chaotic game) and *ludus* (orderly game). In carnivalization the masses cancel distances and, with them, deference, to create a collective body that annuls identities and roles. As a fluid, the mass invades everything in its convulsion, and since personal identity requires distance, it is lost in the conglomerate itself as collective euphoria, inebriation, and rapture.

Through all these processes, not everything is sweet as honey. Sensations can be joyful, but also painful. Discernment can be appreciative, but also scornful, and regard can be deferential, but also offensive. Sensibility is open to the delightful subtleties of life, but also to aesthetic violence. Unlike a simple physical aggression against which each defends oneself as one can, by "aesthetic violence" I understand the laceration targeted exactly at the subject's aperture or vulnerability to the world.

In sum, sensation is passive to stimuli, discernment is active in organizing perception, whereas regard is observant of tacit social agreements. Sensibility is evaluative and can spring forth exceeding all and each of these processes. The subject unfolds its individuality in the world by sensation constituting its identity in discernment and observing its role in regard. From any phase or process, the subject is exposed to valuation. It is also exposed to pain and suffering, to scorn and offense, because the subject is vulnerable in all thresholds of sensibility. What characterizes sensibility as openness (in sensation, discernment or regard) to the world is facing novelty not as a danger but trustingly, coming closer to and *latching-on* to the object, because the subject feels safe. Not a strictly adaptive function, this valuation is biological excess for the subject since it alerts and sharpens its senses against the habit of automatic reactions.

Chapter 20

Aesthetic Enunciation
and its Dialogical Character

In the previous chapter we analyzed the condition of aesthesis from the interpretative receptivity of a subject. In the present we will focus it from its enunciative activity. Against the generalized idea that aesthetic enunciation is exclusive of artists, the fact is we daily display this activity throughout the diverse matrixes in which we are located. It is necessary to insist that aesthetic enunciation is not restricted either to the human being, because we find it unfolding through the animal kingdom in the proud step of the peacock when extending its fabulous feathers, in the bower bird that adorns its nest to attract the female, and in mating rites among diverse species.

As was explained in Part Three, the term "prosaics" is derived from the Latin *prosus*, participle of *provertere*, meaning to spill to the front. This is precisely what aesthetic enunciation is, related to "expression" (of Latin *expressio*, to press outside) by objectivation and its inverse "impression" (of Latin *impressus,* pressed inwards) by subjectivation. In both cases, to press outside/inside, we are dealing with the impulse that con-forms and articulates practices of exchange and communication through which the aesthetic is displayed.

Sensibility is not, therefore, a mere fantasy of an isolated individual in its inner world, or a quality of certain objects, and much less an enigmatic and inapprehensible human faculty, but a deliberate activity performed through concrete social exchanges. The task of aesthetics is thus to find conceptual tools for understanding how it operates and is displayed, since it always is sensibility of somebody in relation to something or somebody, in some place and time, and in some respect or capacity; it does not exist in the void. There is, as Bakhtin would say, a dialogic subject (not monadic) who stands as a node within a network of social relations. For that reason aesthetic communication can be understood from Bakhtinian dialogism establishing a relation between what can be said with what cannot be said, what has been said before with what can be, or not, said later. Sensibility listens even what words do not pronounce. What one shares in aesthetic communication is enunciated as vital loads, energies, materials, temperatures and temperaments, concepts, fluids, percepts, feelings and sensations that are directed from and to the subject as enunciator and interpreter in a dialogical relation.

Linguistics has separated language (*langue*) as an abstract system of combinations and rules on one side and speech (*parole*) as the individualized concrete statement on the other. Bakhtin criticized Saussure's depersonalized conception of speech and his erroneous supposition that a statement (*parole*) is totally individual. He argued that no statement in general could be attributed exclusively to the speaker; since it is the product of an interaction and of a complete and complex *social situation* in

132 *Everyday Aesthetics*

which it happens. (Voloshinov1987, 118)[1] It is true that every act of communication is located between the author of the statement and his addressee, and that it is always destined, as Bakhtin indicated, whereas "words and phrases are impersonal, do not belong to anybody and are directed to nobody". (Bajtín 1990, 285) In the study of prosaics where statements are not only verbal (lexic) but also corporeal (somatic), visual-spatial (scopic), and sonorous (acoustic), we must distinguish these different registers as well as cut them in more concrete elements. In spite of the risks of combining incommensurable visions, I will try to integrate the Saussurean with the Bakhtinian vision to have a perspective of the aesthetic communication that includes both concrete social exchanges through statements, as well as the axes from which they are formed.

Prosaics, as a particular place of observation of aesthetic processes, focuses on enunciation and interpretation and is thus located between identities; for that reason it depends on speech (*parole* in Saussure). Hence "every statement is a link in the chain, very complexly organized, of other statements". (Bajtín 1990, 258, 261) and it is also "not a conventional but a real unit, accurately delimited by the change of the discursive subject, who finishes by yielding the word to the other, a species of quiet *dixi* that is perceived by the listeners [as signal] that the speaker has concluded". In aesthetic communication, not only the author of a statement but the addressee or interpreter are both active since "all understanding of live speech, of a living statement, has an answering character (although the degree of participation can vary); all understanding is pregnant with an answer and in a certain way it generates it: the listener becomes speaker". (Bajtín 1990, 257)

Applying a semiotic model to the analysis of aesthetic phenomena does not mean that the aesthetic is reduced to language, but that language serves as a vehicle for sharing aesthetic processes. This fact partly explains why aesthetics has chosen art as its privileged object, since poetics is always an act of communication, more or less differed, between the artist and the spectator: artworks are basically acts of enunciation/interpretation. Literature is an objectivation not only in the sayable through language but indirectly also in the perceivable through it by ekphrasis. We perceive spaces in Kafka's castle and water lilies in Monet's brush strokes. In one case visibility is generated by ink printed in a paper, in the other by colors smeared on a canvas. The production of visibilities is more complex than the object that stimulates the retina. The word is not blind nor is sight mute. The yellow butterflies following Mauricio Babilonia in Gabriel Garcia Marquez's *Cien años de soledad* are totally visible. There are sonorous paintings like Delacroix's *Liberty Guiding the People of France* or Renoir's *Bathers*. To see them is to hear them, sometimes even smell them. The senses are not isolated: "Cataracts of images in the midst of words, verbal lightnings that pull out drawings," Foucault once wrote.

---

1   Although signed by Voloshinov, the authorship is attributed to Bakhtin.

Aesthetic Enunciation and its Dialogical Character

Aesthetic syntagm and paradigm

When analyzing language, Saussure considered only its linear character "that excludes the possibility of pronouncing two elements simultaneously". He consequently defined the syntagm in the following way: "These combinations that have extension by support can be called *syntagms*. A syntagm is always made up of two or more consecutive units (for example: *to reread; against all; the human life; God is good; if the weather is good, we will leave* and so on). Located in a syntagm, a term only acquires its value because it stands against that which precedes or follows it, or both." (Saussure 1967, 173)[2]

While for strict linguistics terms can only follow one another in linear syntagmatic chains, in prosaics there is a multitude of simultaneous syntagms intertwined in a single statement, since sensibility is expressed not only in what is said verbally (lexics) but by the pitch, intonation and volume used (acoustics), the gestures and postures (somatics), and the stage, costumes and props (scopics) that complement what is said. Also, while Saussurean analyses are monoglottal (one language) and monophonic (one voice), Bakhtin made us aware that we must consider statements also as heteroglottal (several languages or several registers), hybridized (interaction of two or more consciences), and polyphonic (several voices or attitudes), as they occur in prosaics. Instead of the Saussurean concept of *syntagmatic chains* that only operate by the linear succession of linguistic terms, in prosaics we will deal with *syntagmatic networks* because syntagms not only follow one another sequentially but also are interlaced in a multidimensional space of various registers and modalities.

The paradigm is the frame of reference in relation to which a statement or syntagm means by differentiation and symbolizes by association. I will not understand paradigms as purely linguistic and abstract entities in Saussure's sense, because they always emerge from concrete matrixes and are projected by exporting certain aspects unto others or import some of its patterns. Both axes, the signic and the symbolic, function paradigmatically by association and/or differentiation derived from the social matrixes. Also, both types of paradigms (signic or symbolic) operate by convention, the former depending on its formal and the latter on the material stratum. A paradigm is a social product generated from negotiations between different identities, fractions of class, ways of life, and so on by means of enouncing specific syntagms.

Syntagms such as the disappearance of the drawing contour and chiaroscuro, the use of pure colors, the visible brush stroke, the representation of light and the ephemeral as main subject of a picture characterized impressionistic statements. From such syntagms the paradigm of impressionism was constituted to evaluate diverse works associated to it. Art history is thus the production and registry of the selected artistic statements to be legitimized, codified, and hierarchized, it is the inventory that testifies the winners in the fight of syntagms' and paradigms' legitimation within

---

2 By "value", Saussure exclusively understands the linguistic effect created by oppositions and differences. It is possible to distinguish this meaning, as well as Marx's distinction between use value and exchange value from the one proposed in regards to the aesthetic dimension, namely value with respect to *latching-on*/*by* effects.

the artistic matrix. This apparatus obeys as well to its own discursive syntagms and rhetorical paradigms from which it confers or not artistic signification and significance to particular statements The man of the street, nevertheless, can *latch-on* with enthusiasm to a painting out of joy for the bright red of its watermelons, or to a religious painting by sweetness of its chubby-faced angels without there being anybody owning the right to question or judge such aesthetic preference.

PART 5
OCTADIC MODEL FOR AESTHETIC ANALYSIS

In Part 4 we examined how semiotics can function as a methodological tool for analyzing prosaics. We will now develop a cartographic guide of two coordinates, (as a grid of letters and numbers in common maps) to examine everyday life from an aesthetic perspective. I hope the reader will have patience for the neologisms here proposed and find them justified as mnemotechnic clues in this adventure. In case of emergency, I suggest the aid of the glossary.

The question of why analyze prosaics from the point of view of subjects and interactions rather than the usual in aesthetics, namely, the objects, must be answered. Interactions are the processes by which subjects exchange a variety of things with others and with the environment. Metabolism, the essential condition of survival for any live being, is basically an interaction between the creature and the environment. Thus in every interaction, an exchange of something is always at stake, be it words or substances, money or energy, power or fluids, signs and images. Hence, for Levi Strauss, exchange is the common denominator of a great number of apparently heterogeneous social activities. Among these, the most typical are economic and linguistic exchanges, which for Goux implied: "The history of societies shows a complex objective correspondence between forms of economic exchange and forms of signifying exchange [...] such an 'analogy' is and has been practiced unconsciously. Its coherence, its organic rather than accidental nature, enables us to speak not simply of an 'analogy' but of isomorphism." (Goux 1990, 110) This isomorphism explains why, indeed, despite their radical differences, both Saussure and Marx often made comparisons between these two activities and used the concept of "value" for both objects. It is not random that Feruccio Rossi-Landi (1970) considered and understood language and economy jointly through the concepts of "linguistic work" and "linguistic market". Since aesthetics also depends on the concept of "value", we can extend this isomorphism with precaution to our field of inquiry. Aesthetic value is accordingly linked to language, as it passes through semiosis, and to economy, because it involves a load, the exchange of something concrete and material, as well as affective energy or very skilled and talented work in the case of artworks.

As its conditions of possibility, exchange has the concepts of substitution, equivalence, value, identity in difference and ideal continuity through perceivable changes. In general, we can speak of diverse types of exchange according to each approach: economic in strict sense (of goods and work), mathematical (of numerical values), communicative (of messages or statements), libidinal (of sexual desires and sensuality), and aesthetic (of sensitive perceptions and activities). These forms of exchange are not pure, since elements of one type of exchange can be found in

136 *Everyday Aesthetics*

another; the distinction here is merely analytical. From prosaics such exchange is made not only through products or signs, but also involves emotions, acts and forces, what is said and done or silenced and destroyed.

By "aesthetic exchange" I will understand these processes of substitution or conversion, equivalence, transformation, and continuity in the relations that subjects establish with themselves, with others, and their environment involving their sensibility through statements or acts that put into play individual and group identities generating valuation or appreciation (both negative and positive). Such exchanges begin with "face to face" interactions which, for Berger and Luckmann (1989, 46), are the most important experiences we have with others and the prototype of all social interactions.

The projection of the semiotic axes to the aesthetic

Aesthetic exchange, as semiotic exchange in which it is based, unfolds through a dual coupling: the material or energetic (mattergy) stratum that comprises it and the formal stratum that articulates it. This formal-mattergetic coupling somehow mirrors Goux's isomorphism between linguistic and economic exchanges. It also recalls Hjelmslev's strata analyzed in Part 4 where I applied the concept of stratum of form to explain the articulation of the signic axis and the stratum of substance (matter-energy) for the symbolic. Every semiotic enunciation/interpretation process includes these two strata: the energetic or material that impels it and the formal as its objectivation device. This is consequently the node where we can project semiotic decoding to aesthetic valuation. Such projection can only happen, as previously mentioned, when a semiotic event acquires for the subject a value beyond habitual re-cognition of signification by *latching-on* to its significance via aesthetic discovery. In such case, the signic axis that allows us to differentiate one thing from another through oppositions and differentiations is exceeded by rhetorical strategies that not only signify and transmit information but also persuade towards valuation making it significant. Equally the energy-time-matter substrate in the symbolic axis acquires an exceeding weight that not only symbolizes an event but also relates to an attitudinal value on the part of the enouncer that depends on the substantial stratum.

Sensibility is phenomenologically perceived by subjects as their individual disposition and, by extension or analogy, as a disposition also of others through concrete acts of aesthetic exchange. As currency circulating in economy acquires value by exchange processes, or signs circulating in language acquire value based upon differences and oppositions within a code, identities circulate in social matrixes and their valuation depends on the aesthetic games displayed through these exchanges to produce *latching on/by* effects. In such acts there is always an attitude that I will denominate *dramatics* and a vehicle to communicate it and persuade, namely, *rhetorics*. While rhetorics articulate dramatics, the latter impels the former. In other words, aesthetic communication is the result of a coupling between dramatics' impulse and its rhetoric configuration.

Table 21.1   Strata, Axes and Coordinates

Strata	Form	Matter–energy
Semiotic	Axis of the signic	Axis of the symbolic
Aesthetic	Coordinate of the Rhetoric	Coordinate of the Dramatic

The axis of the symbolic will hereon be the instrument to map the display of dramatics, since it relates to the energetic and vital import of communication. For the analysis of rhetorics, we will use the axis of the signic, since it deals with the formalization and articulation of such impulse by differentiations and oppositions. The energetic level in which the coordinate of dramatics is focused upon acquires significance by the attitude of the speaker, namely, the impulse, force, weight, direction, intensity, dynamism, control, appropriation, cost, and consumption of energies in a social exchange. The level of con-formation and articulation that the coordinate of rhetorics deals with objectifies such energies so that they acquire signification through interactions. The difference between the term "axis" denoting semiotic operation and "coordinate" to designate aesthetic processes is exclusively methodological to distinguish a semiotic from an aesthetic focus.

Both coordinates will enable us to analyze aesthetic exchanges in processes of construction and exchange of personal or collective identities that are always persuasive in their quest for credibility and appreciation. In "face to face" interactions, the subjectivity of the other is accessible to me by means of a maximum of symptoms (Berger and Luckmann 1989, 47) and I may add that such "symptoms" in which I enunciate myself and interpret the other unfold by means of the coordinate of the rhetoric in its four registers and the dramatic in its four modalities.

Chapter 21

Rhetoric and its Registers

Since aesthetics does not deal only with perceptions and feelings that the subject passively "undergoes" in Dewey's sense but implies a deliberate activity for the production of certain effects, it is appropriate to speak of "aesthetic games" or "aesthetic strategies" rather than of "aesthetic experiences". Such games in social exchanges attempt to produce latching effects in the processes of negotiation of identities. What the enouncer intends to obtain through such games and strategies are effects of credibility, authority, affection, confidence, tenderness, and power that the addressee can grant, negotiate, or deny.

The horizontal coordinate from which I will analyze aesthetic exchanges and games I will denominate *coordinate of the rhetoric*, since in its original meaning rhetoric denotes persuasive speech or the act of influencing the thought and conduct of the addressee. I understand rhetoric exactly as the sum of semiotics plus aesthetics, since it not only transmits information but does so in a particular form or manner to persuade or seduce. The rhetoric coordinate refers to the art to move and arouse others' emotions (in its classical sense of oratory). Yet persuasion, from a prosaics perspective, is not displayed through verbal speech only, but, as we shall see, is also exhibited by the body, sounds, objects, spaces, and images.

I consequently do not understand the term "rhetorics" by its common use as "the art of the feigned word", since it would imply a discussion on fiction and reality or on sincerity and falsity that is not pertinent to our topic here. A speech in a funeral is rhetoric without being untrue or simulated. The words are real because they have been said, independently of their intention or sincerity conditions.[1] Rhetoric not only ex-presses the dramatic or attitude but can also constitute it to produce latching effects in the addressee as well as in the enouncer. Language expresses who the subjects are and produces their individual or collective identities, even if not all language is verbal.[2]

---

1 Following Searle, Vanderveken (1985, 185–88) speaks of the degree of force and conditions of sincerity of a statement. This problem does not interest here, because it implies a psychological approach.

2 The role of rhetoric has been more than clear to me as the initial assumption for the analytical model with which I studied everyday aesthetic interactions (cf. Mandoki 1991, 1994, 2003). Michael Herzfeld's (2005, 183)—professor of anthropology at Harvard—also insists on the importance of rhetoric in everyday interactions. Note that rhetoric does not depend only on ciceronian categories such as *inventio* in chosing what to say, *dispositio* in arranging it, *elocutio* in how to present it, *memoria* in linking it to other perceptions and *pronuntiatio* or *actio* by the tone and attitude of the body. In addition there is *ethos* or credibility of the speaker and, much more importantly, *locus* from where he speaks.

140 *Everyday Aesthetics*

In prosaics, four registers or channels for the exchange of aesthetic statements constitute the rhetoric coordinate: the *lexic* register (by verbal syntagms, oral or written, also numbers and other graphic signs), the *acoustic* (or sonorous as in intonation, volume, pitch of voice or sound), the *somatic* (gestures, postures, facial expression, body smell, moisture, size, and temperature), and the *scopic* (visual, spatial, topological). This coordinate can be referred to by the acronym LASoS from the four registers (lexic, acoustic, somatic, and scopic).[3]

Recent rhetoric studies by Barthes (1977), Peninou (1965), Durand (1983), *Groupe μ* (1993), and Perelman Olbrechts-Tyteca (1989) (who have applied it to fashion, marketing, advertising, art and design) have rescued this field from the disrepute in which rationalism confined it (inherited from Plato's attack against the sophists), but have not yet recognized the importance of aesthetics as a basic constituent of all rhetorical processes, since to persuade it is necessary to fascinate or intimidate, to seduce or to capture, not only convince by the logic of the arguments.

The archetypal example in rhetorics is Mark Anthony's speech after Caesar's murder in Shakespeare's *Julius Caesar*: "Friends, Romans, Countrymen, lend me your ears; I have come to bury Caesar, not to praise him ...." This is a strategy of enunciation in lexic rhetorics persuading the Romans over Brutus's culpability. It clearly illustrates aesthetic resources because it has been taken from poetics, and exhibits rhythm, alliteration, irony, and other rhetorical figures masterfully displayed. Remember Hamlet's reply to the queen using lexic and acoustic alliteration:

Queen: Hamlet, thou hast thy father much offended.
Hamlet: Mother, thou hast my father much offended.
Queen: Come, come, you answer with an idle tongue.
Hamlet: Go, go, you question with a wicked tongue.

Yet in everyday life, rhetorical speeches also exhibit a particular emotional energy for the sake of eloquence. No rhetoric can function without at least producing a credibility effect and some kind of emotion that justifies the speaker's impulse to speak. In Mark Anthony and Hamlet's case, the dramatics of rage and indignation at Caesar's and the king's betrayal and murder were articulated by verbal speech. Yet in scientific argumentation, usually considered as remote from the aesthetic domain as can be, the procedure is the same: enouncers must negotiate their credibility by the form in which syntagms are displayed according to the conventions established by their scientific community. These conventions demand dramatics of equanimity, rigor, competence, and neutrality for credibility effects on their authority and identity as scientists (*ethos*). At the same time they must convince the audience by obeying precise rules of coherence in configuring the *logos*, and conventions of the scientific community for the desired truth effects. A degree of *pathos* is also necessary in the eloquence that emphasizes the importance of what is communicated. This partly explains the

---

3   Verón (1974) considered a "misunderstanding" putting the verbal on the same semiotic level as images or gestures and argued that we must separate "codes" and "matter". He argues that language is already a code, whereas gestures are mere matter. I do not agree with his position because, to be recognized as such, gestures and images are already codified. For an extensive explanation and justification of these four registers, see Mandoki 2004.

Rhetoric and its Registers 141

temptation in which some scientists fall when fixing their empirical results to make them seem more elegant and persuasive. Broad and Wade (1982, 215–216) argue that this was the case with Mendel's peas and many other well-known scientists.

In less serious contexts, clowns usually produce comical effects through the somatic register with clumsy movements, grotesque falls, and hyperbolic gestures. In the scopic register they wear absurd costumes with strident colors and bizarre combinations, long shoes, a painted face, and a wig. By the lexic register they tell jokes and describe funny situations, and in the acoustic register the tone and pitch of voice will be exaggerated and reverberate the sound of punching.

Consider cosmetics' saleswomen at department stores who unfold profuse lexic production upon the virtues of products that supposedly eliminate wrinkles and cellulitis, affirm the bust, and mold the figure. A saleswoman filmed by *Primetime* once affirmed that her product had gained the Nobel Prize. Some cream producers even declare that their products have caviar by a curious mechanism of prestige contagion in which the status symbolism of caviar is magically transferred to the cream. Cosmetics' saleswomen are aided in their persuasive strategies by the scopics of their young and impeccable presentation, complexion, clothes, makeup, and hairdo, in addition to the attractive design of products' packaging, all accompanied by assertive and seductive somatics and acoustics. Through an apparently mere semiotic exchange of providing information about a product, most marketing campaigns basically display aesthetic strategies geared less towards explaining the product's real assets than to creating an imaginary identity for the product through style that will generate a whole chain of calculated connotations.

In relation to his theory on micro sociological analyses, Goffman ([1959] 1981) indicated how in job interviews, the candidates make an effort to display a dramatics of affability, self-confidence, order and diligence, punctuality, and subordination according to the position solicited. If we focus more specifically on the aesthetics of such dramatics, we will realize that they are articulated by strategies in the rhetoric coordinate through the scopic register by costumes prescribed for the aspired identity and hierarchy, in the acoustic by the adequate volume, pitch, tempo of voice, pronunciation and intonation, in the lexic by the coherent unfolding of disposition or expertise in the field in question and in the somatic by the gestures adequate to the position desired, authoritative if the position is high or submissive if low. These presentations of the self are, as Goffman accurately indicated, stagings, dramaturgical acts in the full sense of the term and therefore of enormous interest for prosaics. From this dramaturgical model, Berger and Luckmann (1986, 95–104) also analyzed the function of roles and the way in which agents make objectivations of their identity in daily life according to socially available typifications. As these authors affirm (1986, 98) "every institutionalized behavior involves 'roles', and these share the controlling character of institutionalization" although I would add that, rather than roles, what is at stake here are identities, because roles are assigned from outside and they do not depend on the subject of the enunciation. These stagings or representations make use of aesthetic resources to produce the credibility and adhesion they crave. In addition to symbolic interactionism and sociological or ethnographical studies, prosaics will allow us to examine the materials and configurations with which identities are constructed.

Lexic register

I have chosen the term "lexic" to designate this register because it is displayed mainly through words (of Greek *lexicos*, word) organized in phrases or syntagms up to discourses. Verbal communication is a process that can produce not only semiosic but aesthesic effects as well. The lexic register of rhetorics refers to the particular form in which verbal speech is displayed, what type of language is used, what attitude is implied in speaking and in the selection of terms. In synthesis, the lexic register concerns the form, games, styles, and languages that a subject deploys through verbal syntagms.

One assumes that there are many ways to transmit a package of information, or that a certain synonymy exists at level of statements. But prosaics would deny it since meaning, as an effect of signifying strategies, is determined by these and by their relations. In aesthetics, the order of the factors does alter the product: when using one signifier rather than another at a particular point and not another, a certain meaning is produced and not another. Therefore, the relation of arbitrariness or contingency between signifier and signified postulated by Saussure in linguistics does not operate in prosaics. The signifier fatally determines the signified.

In the diverse discursive genres analyzed by Bakhtin (Bajtín 1990, 248–293) different lexic rhetorics can be traced that obey paradigmatic rules of construction for producing specific effects according to the case: public declarations, scientific texts, military orders, bureaucratic documents, corporations managers' memoranda, everyday conversations among friends or lovers, juridical contracts and testaments, personal and official letters. Each paradigmatically projects a particular style according to the matrix from which they are emitted. These lexic genres not only transmit information but, as Bakhtin indicated, they are structured with criteria of style and composition that, I may add, are partly aesthetic criteria to produce an image of the enouncer.

The latching effects by the lexic register are not exclusive of poetics in literature and poetry. They are also found in prosaics through everyday political, legal, journalistic, academic, familiar, erotic, even scientific language. The logical-mathematical language implicitly conveys effects of neutrality, objectivity, and connotations of impersonality, and exactitude. (Broad and Wade 1982, 215–216) As an aesthetic strategy, this logical form, its neatness, order and simplicity, is in itself already persuasive of objectivity, rationality, and impartiality. An apparently neutral, barren and rational text, such as *The Chicago Manual of Style* that simply establishes rules for the presentation of manuscripts, is nonetheless full of syntagms that have nothing of neutrality and much of persuasion when selecting terms such as "it is preferable to", "it is necessary to avoid", "it must be kept", "do not try to", "one must not", "in descendent order of desirability", "it is permissible", and so on. Note the persuasive effect of using this same impersonal style and of syntagms like "one must", "do not try" as if they were the result of unquestionable laws from the beginning of the universe. The impersonal and distant tone of bureaucratic documents and their protocol style are deliberately intended to produce effects that connote a stable reality, unmistakable hierarchies, and established obligations and rights that cut across the social order as sharpened knives in clearly specified places.

The lexic register is constituted by subregisters on diverse scales, such as languages, dialects, jargons, idioms.

Acoustic register

When speaking, we not only use words to transmit meaning; we also emit sounds that entail their own semantic wealth and complement or contradict the lexic register. The tone of voice when saying "yes, my love" can be altogether antithetical to lexic signifiers and actually mean "no way, you hateful stupid!" For that reason acoustics is not only a paralanguage, as denominated by Trager (1958), but also properly a register of communication with full rights. Words can be pronounced in different ways; speeches can also be intoned and modulated in diverse forms.

The term "acoustic" is derived from the Greek *akouazesthai*, meaning "to listen". The acoustic register refers to sounds, human or animal, and all the range of the audible. As a means of human communication, acoustics is mainly modulated energy through voice and thus indexical of the subject's dramatics. What the subject says is one thing, but how he says it, or the selection of words and style (lexic register) and the tone in which he says it (acoustic register) provide not only additional information on his credibility but also hooks for latching onto the identity displayed, as voice can seduce or frighten. Since the acoustic register is closer to the subject's energy and relatively less regulated by hard conventionalized codes than the lexic register, it exposes the dramatics of the enouncer with more transparency. That is why in daily life we often trust more the acoustic than the lexic register to guess the true intentions and character of the enouncer.

Acoustic signifiers are mostly cultural and socially acquired, as can be noticed by the intonation and pronunciation of a same language in different geographical regions. There is, however, a certain genetic determination in the individual qualities of the voice that is evident in voice similarities among family members. Music is a kind of speech elaborated by sounds that operate through different sets of codes. Hymns and military marches imitate the lexic register of solemn speeches in the acoustics of their rigid rhythm, firm tone and high volume, tactical ascents and descents typical of martial ceremonies.

For a more meticulous analysis of acoustics, Trager's (1958, 1–10) work was a pioneer in offering categories to analyze height, tone, extension and qualities of voice: vocalizations that consist of vocal frame, vocal qualities such as intensity and extension of the sound as well as intonation height, and vocal characterizers like shouting, sobbing, yawning, laughing, and so on. These are all acoustic syntagms organized by the modulation of voice.

Taking Trager's (1958, 1–12) qualities of the voice, we can consider the following sub-registers for acoustics:

1. Pitch range (spectrum of tones used).
2. Lip control of vocalization.
3. Glottis control (thickness of the quality of the tone).
4. Intonation control (sharpness or smoothness in the intonation transitions).
5. Coupling control (degree of precision and force in the pronunciation).
6. Rhythmical control (smoothness or hardness in the phraseology).
7. Resonance (degree of fineness or vibration in the voice).
8. Tempo (speed when speaking, faster or slower than the norm).

144   *Everyday Aesthetics*

To which we could add Parret's (2003):

9. Volume (loudness-range).
10. Pitch-movement.
11. Continuity.
12. Phonatory register.

For a more detailed analysis of this register, Herman Parret (2003) offers a very rich variety of descriptive categories for voices based on Laver (1991) who distinguishes between impressionistic and phonetic labels. Less technical and more relevant to aesthetics are the impressionistic voices, among which three types of characters can be found: segmental (whistling, clear, precise, opaque, disfigured, nasty, and embarrassing), those that refer to vocal dynamism (9–12 above), and those that are physiological. Among these, there are types of voice for singing (tenor, soprano), physiological location of production (nasal, sarcastic, relaxed), muscular tension (stupid, metallic, delicate, sweet), mode of vibration of vocal cords (birdlike, harmonious, whistling, weak, thin), and so on.

His phenomenological and metaphorical descriptions of various types of voices (soft, velvety, brittle, liquid, rough, silky), and predications like booming, rumbling, staccato, tinkling, twittering or the French *chuchotant, soufflant, grinçant, belant, sifflant,* and so on enrich the analysis of the acoustic register from a semiotic perspective. Many of these categories go beyond the semiotics of senses intended by the author, and involve the aesthetic not precisely in Parret's implied definition (referring to the senses) but related to sensibility and its *latching-on/by* effects. Some voice qualities listed by Parret are the equivalents in acoustics to the rhetorical topics that qualify emphatics (the cavernous, the torrential, the sparkling, the oneiric, the passional, the theological, and so on). Others are related to fluxion depending on how the sound is let to flow, while proxemics and kinetics are traceable in other varieties that are worth organizing with more precision.

Somatic register

By "somatic register" I understand the rhetorical use of the body (of Greek *soma,* body) to captivate, express, or appeal to the addressee's sensibility. The somatic strategy would largely correspond to what has been denominated "body language", "face expression", "kinesics", or "non verbal communication" in the last few decades.[4] I, however, prefer the term of "somatics" because there is a variety of non-verbal communication that is not somatic, namely, acoustic and scopic, in addition to the fact that face expression is only one part of somatics, as there are others like posture, hand, body gesture, and so on. Moreover, the body is expressive not only through movement, as the term "kinesics" implies, but also by smell, temperature, moisture, size, texture, and so on. The somatic register is displayed everywhere all

---

4   Scheflen (1972), Druckman (1982), Bosmajian (1971), Kendon (1994), Ekman and Friesen (1975), Matsumoto and Ekman (1989), Knapp (1972) among others.

Rhetoric and its Registers 145

the time in human communication: the male who dances to seduce a woman or unconsciously projects his pelvis forwards to persuade her of his virility is part of this register. Somatics, moreover, is not only human but animal as well.

Quoting Derrida, Goux (1990, 10) asks why and how are "facial expressions, gestures, the whole of the body and the mundane register, in a word, the whole of the visible and spatial as such" excluded from meaning (*bedeuten*) in favor of the signs of language alone? Also, Berger and Luckmann (1986, 52–3) recognize the importance of "a variety of corporeal indices: the aspect of the face, the general position of the body, certain specific movements of arms and feet".[5] Indeed, in social relations, we often rely more on this "mundane register" of somatics to orient ourselves with respect to others than on the acoustic and lexic, because being a relatively weak or soft code, we suppose it has greater immediacy with respect to the enouncer; we trust it as an indexical sign. Despite it, somatics have been indeed excluded from most linguistic and aesthetic studies until relatively recently. Ray Birdwhistell (1972, 381–404) was a pioneer in this field, and his classic study known as "the cigarette scene" discovered the unconscious choreography though arms and legs movements, glances, gestures and facial expressions that run parallel to the verbal chat between the subjects involved.[6]

For prosaics, this register has enormous importance not only because body movement is probably the first form of human communication and the most common, but because of its great eloquence and aesthetic impact. The traditional rhetorical figures usually found in verbal oratory are also displayed in this register. We can thus find *alliteration* expressed by the repetitive movement of the head, hands or feet, as when we manifest agreement by a repetitious motion of the head or show impatience by tapping on the table with our fingers. The *anacoluthon* is an unexpected, abrupt movement. A case of *catachresis* would be to unconsciously caress the arm of an armchair or a near object expressing desire to be caressed. The somatic *ellipsis* is common among political figures by maintaining gestuality to the minimum (perfectly illustrated by somatic fixity and expressive under-performance of George W. Bush, actual President of the USA). *Hyperbole*, on the opposite, is over-performance, the exaggerated gestuality, as mimes, clowns, some singers, soap opera actors, and political leaders such as the actual president of Venezuela, Hugo Chavez. The somatic *irony* works, for example, by maintaining a serious expression to provoke laughter, or laughing to express anger. Somatic *periphrasis* consists in evading a gesture or turning aside to elude a social taboo, for example, to avoid looking at genitals or naked bodies. A case of somatic *suspension* is to delay visual or tactile intimacy at the beginning of a seduction game.

For the sub-registers of somatic rhetorics, some of the categories proposed by Hall (1963) for his proxemic behavior system of notation may be useful, except with some modifications, as the following:

---

5 They forget, however, this register when they exaggerate the importance of verbal language in the social construction of reality by particularly focusing the lexic register.

6 In homage to Birdwhistell I originally denominated this register "kinesics" in Mandoki (1994). However, because of its similarity with kinetics I decided to replace it by the term "somatics", whose reference to the body is more explicit.

146   *Everyday Aesthetics*

- Postural
- Haptic
- Thermal
- Olfactory
- Ocular.

This means that our body communicates through its posture, its way of touching or presenting itself to touch, by its temperature, smell and eye contact. In addition to Hall's, other sub-registers as body moisture, body gestures, facial expressivity, and body size by obesity or skinniness are worth considering.

- Moistural
- Gestual
- Facial
- Size.

Among these sub-registers, some are more deliberate and conscious than others, some more physiological or psychological, others more social and local, but they are all significant to aesthetics. Posture, for example, according to the classification system proposed by Hewes (1957) proves the degree in which it is a cultural and local phenomenon, rather than biological.

When enouncers try to achieve with this register something more than the transmission of information, when they try to persuade, offend, intimidate or fascinate, we are basically in the aesthetic dimension. For that reason the body is displayed not only as an image in its appearance, clothing, make-up, or by the present obsession with size and proportion dedicated to body fitness (body scopics) but as a conscious or unconscious vehicle of semiotic and aesthetic communication and exchange in its gesture, facial expressivity, its bearing or hexis, its smell, texture, and temperature for generating appreciation or disgust, attraction or repulsion in daily interactions.

Scopic register

The word "scopic" is derived from the Greek *skopía* that means to observe, to see, to watch. For that reason, I chose this term for referring to the construction of syntagms by spatial and visual components in an interaction. The scopic register is deployed by the use of costumes, props, make-up, hairstyle, spaces as a stage or scene (*setting* in terms of Goffman) to construct visual images for their sensitive effects.[7] Thus, for a given subject, furniture is symbolic and signic when denoting status and lifestyle, but it also has aesthetic connotations when valued and appreciated. Architecture, prosaics staging par excellence, is a symbol when functioning as coagulated energy through matter. It also participates of much elaborated signic and symbolic codes by

---

    7   In the previous version of this model (Mandoki 1994), I labeled this register "iconic", but due to the semiotic use of term related to resemblance, I decided to use "scopic" instead.

Rhetoric and its Registers 147

the use of materials, sites, and forms to signify lavishness, neatness, sensuality, or sobriety by differential or associational relations.

Among other syntagms that belong to the scopic register are handwriting (hybrid with the somatic gestural movement and lexic for its meaning), face or body image in visual terms (not gestural), gardens, gadgets and visual arts, utensils of daily life as furniture and equipment, settings like streets and neighborhoods, weapons displayed in military parades or wars, trophies and medals, emblems and logos (hybrid scopic-lexic), tattoos and piercing (also hybrid scopic-somatic as indexical signs of physical pain).

The decoration of domestic spaces, of a bank or office, a church, or school constitutes strategies of scopic enunciation in prosaics by the selection of components, style, and disposition. The classical components of oratory are typically displayed through the scopic register namely: *inventio* in the selection of objects and location (what objects to choose among all possible furniture, colors, textures, plants, dresses, accessories, adornments), *dispositio* in how to organize them, (how to use contrast, seriality, parallelism, or complementarity), *elocutio* to communicate them and *actio* as performance through scopics.

We can thus find *alliteration* when placing a round lamp on a round tablecloth on a round table on a round carpet. The display of collections of decorative frogs or eggs, ashtrays or bells is also scopic alliteration. The *anacoluthon* (an abrupt, unexpected movement) would be in locating a Tiffany lamp over a rustic coarse table. *Catachresis* (to transfer an act from one object to another) is typical in trying to express the desire of opulence through cheap imitations of Louis XIV furniture. Japanese decoration would be, to the eyes of Western culture, truly *elliptical*, because syntagms are elaborated with minimum elements. Scopic *hyperbole* by augmentation is typically expressed by king-size beds for a single person, in the well-known Mackintosh style chair with very high back, or in the huge dining room for 12 to 24 places for a nuclear family who uses it at most two or three times a year. The now fashionable heavy, polluting suburban trucks used as vehicles for nuclear families (most often used to transport a single person) are also hyperbolic. *Antiphrasis* is an ironic resemantization of objects, like using an old rusty coal iron as decoration in a single's ultramodern home. An example of *periphrasis* is hiding the TV set behind a door or panel in the bedroom instead of locating it at the center of the living room, as was customary among other social classes years ago. The figure of rhetorical *suspension* is established by means of corridors and halls for delaying access to a house's main room, or in locating a special anteroom to avoid allowing uninvited guests to more private family spaces.

In the scopics of costumes, the classical style resorts to *ellipsis* (eliminating superfluous elements such as abundant jewelry, embroideries, ribbon bows, printed fabrics, strident colors) whereas the eccentric and the bohemian styles resort to *hyperbole* (using all possible accessories as hats, belts, necklaces, vests, scarves, and so on), and *alliteration* (bohemian style women love to wear a ring on each finger, or diverse necklaces, earrings, bracelets). The conservative style usually uses *periphrasis* and *reticence* as the deflection of the neck and shape of a blouse to avoid pointing to the breasts, or the shape of the skirt to evade expressing the lines of the waist, hip, and thighs. A provoking décolleté works by *alliteration* when following

148 *Everyday Aesthetics*

Table 21.2   Registers and Sub-registers of Rhetoric

Lexic	Acoustic	Somatic	Scopic
Languages (English, Spanish)	Pitch, pitch-movement	Postural	Geographic: country, city
Idioms (British English,–Argentine Spanish)	Lip vocalization	Haptic	Scenographic: props, setting
Dialects (Pidgin English, Cockney)	Glottis Volume	Thermal	Topographic: Costumes, Makeup, Hairdo, accessories
Jargon (Technical: medical, semiotic, logic)	Intonation Continuity	Ocular	
Argot (lunfardo)	Phonatory Register	Olfactory/ Moistural	
	Articulation	Size	
	Resonance	Gestual	
	Tempo	Facial	

similar curves as the breasts. To use a necklace that goes down to the breasts is *catachresis* indicating the desire of being touched in that anatomical part, even if only by sight. I wonder if men's ties are also catachresical.

Also in the scopic register we can trace sub-registers at diverse scales, going from: 1) the geographical (country, city, zone, neighborhood, street, climate, and flora), 2) the scenographical (architectonic, house and garden, furniture and decoration, domestic or professional props, or equipment), and 3) topographical namely, one's sense of place expressed by grooming and visual appearance (costumes, jewels, hairdo and make-up). To a certain degree, where one lives in the geographical scale partly displays one's identity, as well as how one lives in the scenographical and one's sense of place by self-grooming and style in the topographical.

In sum, the scopic, acoustic, somatic, and lexic registers, when used for persuasive purposes are rhetorical and therefore aesthetic devices. They are not only aids of verbal language but also altogether distinct means of communication that can intertwine in harmonic, dissonant, or cacophonous combinations. A phrase can complement an act such as prohibiting (by saying "I forbid you"), and be contradicted by a playful or ironic tone in the acoustic, as much as a scopic syntagm can complement or contradict a somatic syntagm (grasping a weapon and using it to caress someone), or a gesture may cancel a lexic statement (saying "so nice to see you" with a facial expression of disgust). (See Table 21.2.)

Chapter 22

Dramatics and its Modalities

I will denominate *"dramatics"* the other coordinate of this model consisting in the deployment of the subject's attitudes, impulses, and thrust directed to the destinator's sensibility. I have chosen the word "dramatics" because it is related to acting and action "… and for this reason such works are called dramas, because in them one imitates men in action … also the Doric give acting the name of δραν". (*Poetics* Aristotle 1448b) Dramatics comes from the term *dromenon*, "something acted". By dramatics, then, I am not referring to fictitious performance, as in the theater, but to action and display of energy in daily life towards the production of aesthetic effects.

Dramatics constitutes the *ethos* or attributes of the orator as stated by Barthes: "the character that the orator must show the audience (with little concern to his sincerity) to cause a good impression: they are his spirits". It is also *pathos*, the passions and feelings of both, those who speak and those who listen, and therefore the two great psychological tests of rhetorics. A statement's *logos*, on the other hand, depends more on its rhetorics while its *ethos* and *pathos* depend on its dramatics.[1] In addition to logical tests, any enunciation process requires the orator to incessantly say, "follow me" (*fronesis*), "appreciate me" (*arete*), and "love me" (*eunoia*). (Barthes 1974, 63–64) These three statements are emitted through the dramatics of the enouncer by rhetorical strategies to obtain appreciation and adhesion from the public.

To further specify prosaics' analysis of attitudes and actions, we will apply four categories or "modalities" to the coordinate of the dramatic, namely *proxemics, kinetics, emphatics,* and *fluxion*. Dramatics are wholly dialogical since they not only manifest the position of the enouncers but also their attitude towards the addressee in terms of distance (proxemics), openness towards exchange (fluxion), immobility or dynamism (kinetics), and a particular intensity on what is considered more relevant at that moment and context (emphatics). Since matter, energy, and time are basic constituents of these modalities, dramatics are connected to or derive from the axis of the symbolic.

Proxemics

Proxemics (from the Latin *proximitas*, proximity) is a relatively recent field of study, developed particularly in the USA. Edward T. Hall (1963) coined the term to understand by it the use of space between individuals by cultural conventions. He analyzes the differences in proxemics between the Latin Americans, North

---

1   On these three dimensions and their relation to aesthetics see Mandoki (1999).

150   *Everyday Aesthetics*

Americans, Arabs, Germans, and Japanese and proposes eight dimensions of proxemic behavior, understanding by this term the establishment of distances or territoriality in daily interactions. These dimensions are the: 1) postural-sexual identifiers, 2) sociopethal-sociofugal direction, 3) kinesthetic factors, 4) codes of contact, 5) retinal combinations, 6) thermal code, 7) olfactory code, and 8) volume of voice. Unfortunately, Hall mixes the somatic with other registers, since voice is obviously acoustic, whereas sexual identifiers are not only somatic but also scopic (clothes, appearance, make-up) and acoustic (voice modulation, tone, pitch), whereas codes of contact, in addition to being somatic, can be lexic (to verbally touch the addressees by speaking about them or repeating their name), acoustic (to caress with the voice) and scopic (to use clothes that mean "touch me" as décolleté, tight garments, and so on). Despite these shortcomings, Hall's research detected a very important element in human communication. Proxemics is something more than body language, since it is manifested not only by the somatic, but also by the other registers of rhetorics, namely the lexic, acoustic, and scopic. By the same token, somatics are not only proxemic, as Hall understood them, but also dynamic or static and capable of expressing attitudes, moods, flexibility or rigidity in character, and so on. With the body we accumulate or expel, contract or expand energy, we emphasize or understate syntagms.

I have chosen the same term proposed by Hall although not applied in the original sense as "use of spaces" (that would rather correspond to something like "spaciatics", complementary to a "chronemics"[2]) but strictly as the establishment of proximities or social distances. Consequently, Hall's original sense is extended, since distances between individuals are not only spatial as Hall understood them, but also temporal and linguistic, acoustic and mediated by objects. In other words, we establish distances from others by the four registers of rhetorics, not only body language. On the other hand, the use that we will give the term "proxemics" as applied to distancing rather than to spacing is more limited since there are uses of space that are not exclusively proxemic (they can be emphatic, of fluxion or kinetic). While space is part of the scopic register and is consequently rhetoric, distance corresponds to the proxemic modality and is therefore dramatic.[3]

Using both senses of the term, namely as space and as distance, Pierre Guiraud (1989, 65–67) defines proxemics as what: "uses the space between the emitter and the receiver. The distance that we maintain between ourselves and our interlocutor, the place we occupy [...] around a table, and so on are other signs of our social status and constitute an elaborated code that varies according to cultures." But Guiraud, just as Hall, sees only the space or scopic register of proxemics, when, I insist, this distance can be expressed not only in space but in time: distance between a phrase and another, time that we take in responding to a letter, call or visit, as well as the form in which we address someone.

---

2   What I denominate by "chronemics" as the social use of time was initially explored by Eviatar Zerubavel (1985). See also Hall's (1988, 212–14) ideas of monochronic and polychronic cultures.

3   Other investigators, in addition to Hall, have focused proxemics with diverse results (Watson 1970, Ciolek 1983, Krampen 1998).

Dramatics and its Modalities 151

The basic categories of proxemics are *short-long* and they always involve a sense of territoriality that may be spatial as well as temporal, but also energetic or material. Proxemics participate whenever there is a gesture to invite somebody or not, for a coffee or a glass of wine, for lunch or for dinner, for a public celebration or in private, in a house or a restaurant, among friends or family, for a formal or an informal event, at noon or at midnight. From the axis of the symbolic, the significance of these attitudes is defined by their mattergetic input: to invite somebody for a coffee involves less energy than for supper; to invite a glass of wine implies greater intimacy than a cup of coffee.

There are diverse strategies for distancing oneself from someone, beginning by visually ignoring the person to explicitly saying "would you please be so kind as to leave?" even shouting "Please go away" up to aggressively screaming "get the hell out of here!" to pushing the person out (somatic) and closing the door (scopic). These differences depend upon the various degrees of illocutionary force produced by or invested upon the enunciation. Nevertheless, little is known of the aesthetic dimension that crosses these acts, since such strategies not only inform of the attitude of the enouncer, but also have an impact upon the interlocutor's as well as the speaker's sensibility and identity.

Kinetics

The second modality of dramatics is *kinetics* (from the Greek *kinema*, movement) and deals with the dynamism, stability, or solidity of enunciation in each register. Rhythm characterizes movement in kinetics by order and regularity, whether in solemn slowness or cheerful vivacity. Without this kinetic modality, the ludic as well the aesthetic are inconceivable, because as Huizinga indicates (1955, 142): "Such elements as the rhyme and the distich derive from and only have meaning in those timeless, ever recurring patterns of play: beat and counter-beat, rise and fall, question and answer, in short, rhythm."

The basic types of kinetics are *static* and *dynamic*. In Mark Twain's classic novel, Tom Sawyer unfolds a dynamic kinetics (he is always active in something and many things happen to him) in contrast to his brother Sidney who remains in his house studying the Bible (the most solid, permanent, and stable of all books) as a statement of static kinetics. This contrast between two brothers with opposed kinetics is almost archetypal. It appears in the Bible with the contrast between Esau and Jacob: Esau is a shepherd, dynamic, independent mostly away from home, whereas Jacob remains in the tent with his mother. In the classic film *East of Eden* (1955), James Dean incarnates the most dynamic of the brothers who discovers the truth, finds the mother, and obtains the money to save the family. In Steinbeck's novel, this kinetic contrast between Cal and his brother Aaron also mirrors that between their parents, which explains Cal's father's lack of love for him. Cal resembles his mother, a prostitute in Monterey, who displays the dynamic pole by abandoning her husband and children, whereas the lettuce farmer, Adam, remained at home reading (again) the Bible. In the mother's words: "He wanted to tie me down. He wanted to keep me on a stinking little ranch away from everybody. Keep me all to himself. Well, nobody

152   *Everyday Aesthetics*

holds me ... He wanted to own me. He wanted to bring me up like a snot-nosed kid and tell me what to do ... Always so right himself, knowing everything. Reading the Bible at me!"

Dynamic kinetics usually causes distrust (Tom with respect to his aunt Polly, Esau with respect to his mother Rebecca, and Cal with respect to his father) whereas static kinetics provoke disdain when connoting fear of risk or lack of vitality. Static kinetics, being predictable, also produces credibility and confidence, while dynamism can cause admiration.

Emphatics

Emphatics (from the Greek *emfatikos* energetic, strong) refers to the accent or intensity over a particular point in enunciation. In every act of enunciation or interpretation, there are elements with greater emphasis than others, those that are deployed with greater vehemence or that are singularized for having more importance than others. We can thus move within a range that goes from those devoid of accent or not emphatically marked up to the intensely emphatic or marked. Consequently, the basic categories of emphatics are *marked* or *unmarked*. Emphasis can be related to greater or smaller density or condensation of significance, ultimately referring to the investment of energy by the axis of the symbolic. In a phrase such as "I thought that you would go", for example, when varying the emphatics in each word, the meaning changes: "I *thought* that you would go" (but was mistaken), "I thought that *you* would go" (and not others), "I thought that you *would go*" (and not remain here), "*I* thought that you would go" (but others didn't think so).

The emphatic modality is directly linked to what is denominated "topic" in rhetorics which accentuates certain aspects of speech over others. Barthes mentions four topics or common places in rhetorics (or lexic register, in our case): 1) oratory topic (that includes three topics as well: a) of reasoning, b) of customs and c) of passions); 2) the topic of the laughable; 3) theological topic; and 4) the sensible topic or the topic of the imagination that operates by Bachelard's categories such as the cavernous, the torrential, the sparkling, and the oneiric (mentioned by Barthes 1974, 49–60). If these are true for the lexic register, we can find topics for the others, as in the acoustic register those mentioned by Parret in the quality of voices such as brittle, liquid, rough, soft, velvety, silky, tinkling, and so on.

Fluxion

I understand by *fluxion* the dramatic modality that refers to the opening or closing, tightening or relaxing, dispersing or containing, dissipating or controlling energy, matter or time in a social interaction. The term comes from Latin *fluxio* meaning "that flows".[4] I will characterize fluxion according to two basic directions, namely *open* or *centrifugal* when it is expansive, relaxed, and expulsive, and *closed* or

---

4   The term of "fluxion" used here does not have anything to do with Newton's method of fluxions calculation.

Table 22.1　Dramatic Modalities and their Grades

Proxemics	Long/short
Kinetics	Static/dynamic
Emphatics	Marked/unmarked
Fluxion	Closed/open

centripetal when it is contained and controlled. This category, as the other modalities, is always and only relational. In the first case, fluxion relates to the Freudian concept of "anality" that denotes the retentive or expulsive character. Collective customs and habits establish limits and rules to the manifestation of fluxion so that certain cultures encourage open fluxion with centrifugal somatics and acoustics such as the Mediterranean, (particularly the Spanish, the Italian, the Israeli, and the Greek), while in Teutonic or Nordic cultures as the German, Swedish, or Austrian, the centripetal modality predominates.

Fluxion varies according to ethnic origin and habits, in addition to class differences. Bourdieu (1990) indicates how class condition is manifested in the use of language by the tension or relaxation in verbal expression. According to the author, economically higher classes would be tenser in the care of style and etiquette characterized by a more closed fluxion in contrast to lower classes. It is as if social hierarchy would be paid by a greater enunciative restriction and control. For Bernstein (1972) the opposite is the case when he respectively defines restricted and elaborated codes in relation to low and high classes, where the former display retentive fluxion in the lexic register that is compensated with greater dissipation in the somatic, whereas higher status classes have a more elaborated lexics to manifest identity. Also Labov (1966) describes how low middle classes manifest linguistic hypercorrection due to their social insecurity, which in our terms is linked to more retentive lexic fluxion.

It is worth noting that repression and subordination are discernible not only in the economic, the political, and the social but in the aesthetic as well: dominated or excluded classes must keep a closed and retained fluxion in the lexic as one more handicap. Nevertheless, to this action corresponds the reaction of resistance by opening fluxion in the somatic and acoustic through gestuality and vocal volume, while the more privileged classes are expected to control these two registers. The stereotypes of the African-Americans and Latinos in the United States present them as displaying a centrifugal fluxion in the pecuniary, somatic, and acoustic registers that contrasts to the closed fluxion typical of wasps—the wasp stereotype. Ostentatious expenditure, whether in so-called "primitive societies" by the ritual of *potlatch* (Mauss 1990) and the *mayordomía* among Mexicans or in urban societies described in Veblen's (1974) classic text, displays the host's centrifugal fluxion in the destruction of goods combined with the centripetal fluxion in accumulating prestige until eclipsed by their successors.

Chapter 23

The Rhetoric-Dramatic Coupling

Dramatic modalities are coupled to each of the registers of rhetorics as energetic dispositions configured through each concrete enunciation. We are consequently going to explore one by one all the rhetoric articulations of dramatic impulse that unfold in certain directions, with certain concentrations, dynamism and intensity, and which are deployed from the sensibility of the enouncer to by the interpreter's. (See Table 23.1.)

Lexic proxemics

Lexic proxemics refers to the distances or proximities created by the use of verbal language between the enouncer and addressee. To speak in terms of "you" instead of "us" is long proxemics by establishing a distance between two groups. The use in Spanish of *tú* or *usted*, of the German *du* or *sie*, the French *tu* and *vous*, and the Russian *ty* or *vy* displays lexic proxemics, distancing oneself from the other or getting closer.[1]

Diminutives and nicknames are proxemic modalities generating a sense of proximity through the lexic register. Titles such as "Mister", "Your excellency", and "Doctor" are not only descriptive but also proxemic in extending distance and acknowledging a hierarchy. The use of a specialized jargon is a proxemic strategy that establishes a distance with respect to the non initiated and shortens it among those who share it. Quoting an author or a specialized concept between professionals or a well-known common reference shortens proxemics within members of a group and extends it with respect to others.

Here we see that territoriality investigated by Hall is not limited to the somatic register nor to personal space (as in the distance we take with respect to others in a conversation), but can be expressed collectively when demarcating a border of inclusion and exclusion between the members of a group by the use of language. Specialized terminology among doctors, lawyers or philosophers are also typical proxemic strategies in the lexic register. A more subtle manifestation of this same phenomenon in the academic world are bibliographical references where the reader can deduce, before reading a text, the distance or intellectual proximity he can have with respect to the author. Terminology, such as the one here proposed, lengthens proxemics with the non familiarized reader but shortens it with respect to concepts one is trying to apprehend, and glossaries are good measures to shorten it.

---

1   See Tripp (1972).

Everyday Aesthetics

Table 23.1   Rhetoric-Dramatic Coupling

Coordinate of the rhetoric	Coordinate of the dramatic
Signic cartography	Symbolic cartography
Registers: lexic, acoustic, somatic, scopic	Modalities: proxemics, kinetics, emphatics, fluxion
Function: articulation and objectivation given to dramatic impetus	Function: impulse and intensity given to the rhetoric conformation

Acoustic proxemics

The variations in volume of voice are a vehicle for acoustic proxemics since they determine the distances one must take with respect to the speaker. To use low volume shortens proxemics forcing the addressee to get near the enouncer, whereas speaking louder lengthens distance. However, a scream from a distance makes addressees approach, because we suppose that it expresses something important. However, shouting at somebody that is near turns him away, since that excess of energy may make the interlocutor feel threatened. In addition to volume, voice intonation can also have a proxemic effect: a monotonous intonation usually maintains the addressees at a distance, whereas varied intonation drives them nearer because it indicates greater energetic investment in what is being said. By reciprocity, addresses invest greater effort in paying attention to what is said.

In each context of interpretation, the volume of sound acquires diverse meanings: high volume of music in a discotheque shortens proxemics by erasing limits and identities among participants and creating the effect of a common musical bubble. Sexual desire and a craving for intimacy are often enunciated by smooth music to shorten proxemics. Silence can indicate extended or intimate proxemics depending on the interpretative context: in one case it signifies indifference or refusal of contact and in the second such intimacy that there is no need of words.

Somatic proxemics

Somatic proxemics may be displayed by making eye contact or ignoring the other person, locating oneself close or far from her, touching or not and how, smiling or keeping an expression of indifference, and so on. According to the somatic sub-registers for proxemics proposed by Hall (1963), we can consider that distances can be established at: a) a postural level by orienting the body towards the other (or crossing the opposite leg when sitting side to side with someone, creating an invisible circle), b) an haptic level by touching the other or not, c) the thermal and olfactory level by approaching someone so he or she can perceive our scent and temperature (as is customary among Arabs, but a gesture of extreme intimacy in our culture), and d) the ocular (how long and intense is the glance and which part of the body it is directed to). Some analysts of body language have observed that crossing the arms on the front denotes a defensive attitude (long somatic proxemics), whereas to project pelvis forwards, the typical macho assertive gesture, exemplifies short proxemics that can become quite offensive.

Among the categories that I added in this register, moisture during sexual intercourse expresses the shortest possible somatic proxemics whereas, in some cases, obesity may express a fear of being touched by very long proxemics. Also, facial expression can clearly indicate a desire for somebody to approach or to move away from us, as well as the gestuality by which we try to attract or reject someone.

Scopic proxemics

In the scopic register, proxemics denotes long and short distances established by spatial or artifactual means and it can be displayed through various mechanisms. Among these are styles (sophisticated or common), epochs (antique or contemporary or proximate), prices (at hand or unobtainable to most), location (scarce or easily available) in addition to behaviors expected from users in relation to certain objects (a genuine Ming vase invites to be seen, but not touched, as pictures and sculptures in a museum). Seats around a table are proxemic when establishing somato-scopic distances between the occupants. (Baudrillard 1981, 47–49) The corridors or lack of them in architecture and design of spaces, the transparency or opacity in architectonic materials, the division of neighborhoods and services according to social classes in urban planning are other means of deployment of scopic proxemics.

Lexic kinetics

Kinetics in the lexic register organizes enunciations for expressing either a static, solid character or the contrary, a flexible, unpredictable and dynamic display of ideas. The most obvious contrast in lexic kinetics can be found between the dynamism of poetry (freer, evocative, unexpected, discontinuous, and surprising) and the stability of theoretical speech (rigorous, logical, predictable, strictly methodical, and cautious). In philosophical discourse itself, we can illustrate the contrast in lexic kinetics by comparing Kant's discursive solidity and prudence with Nietzsche's dynamism in the boldness and discontinuity of his style. Formal or protocol speech has minimal kinetics established by decorum so that every move should strictly obey manners and conventions, whereas humoristic, sarcastic, or witty speech depends on dynamism and unexpected turns, as in jokes' punchlines.

A rhetorical resource to produce effects of greater dynamism is the use of the present tense instead of the past where facts already happened and the outcome is somehow foreseen in the tone of speaking. In the first case, by contrast, things appear to be happening at the time of the narration, so that abrupt changes and surprises are possible. It is not the same to say: "She is devoured by the God of noon that is only fed on old butterflies. The butterfly is an instantaneous animal invented by the Chinese" (Elizondo 1969, 9) than "The God of noon devoured her since he was fed only on old butterflies. The butterfly was an instantaneous animal that was invented by the Chinese." In this story obviously entitled *The Butterfly*, Salvador Elizondo handles kinetics in the lexic register analogous to the dynamic somatics of the butterfly, since there is nothing as dynamic, and instantaneous, as the present tense.

158 *Everyday Aesthetics*

By contrast, the lexic kinetics in Gabriel Garcia Marquez's *One Hundred Years of Solitude* is displayed in the past tense, as those hundred years are retrospective. It is a narration where time weighs through various generations in the Buendía family and the enduring gaze of Ursula: "Many years later, in front of the firing squad, Colonel Aureliano Buendía was going to remember that remote afternoon when his father took him to see ice for the first time." Time comes to rest here in layers and turns towards the past. These resources of poetic prosics are also displayed in prosaic prosics of everyday narrations. When saying "I go and tell him: don't come here or else …" in comparison to "I went and told him that he should not come here or else …" the greater dynamism and vivacity of the first narration is evident.

Another kinetic resource in the lexic register is the impersonal style used in enunciations such as "it is believed that", "it is not usual to" that produces an effect of immobility precisely by this lack of definition and delocalization from the enouncer. By this lexic maneuver an effect that something has been in a certain way from the beginning of the times and, therefore, will remain so forever is achieved.

Acoustics kinetics

Although the rhythm in speech has proxemic implications (in some cultures, speech rapidity implies proximity whereas slowness is remoteness, or verbosity implies lower status or the opposite), it can also be analyzed as a component of acoustic kinetics in the dynamism of variation in the vocalizations. Terms such as *presto, prestisimo, lento*, refer to acoustic kinetics in music. Worth noting is how acoustic kinetics has become increasingly dynamic in contemporary popular music; apparently an analogy of the present accelerated rhythm of life.

Somatic kinetics

Somatic kinetics refers to the dynamism or immobility, deftness or slowness in body movements. An excessively mobile somatic kinetics can cause distrust and may be interpreted as nervousness, lack of sincerity or of self-control. For the cultural parameters of the West, certain somatic dynamics such as inclining the head sideways, asymmetry in the position of the body, the gesticulation and moving arms and hands, as well as shaking the hips are interpreted as indexical of feminine identities whereas static kinetics in corporeal symmetry and gestural immobility are taken as indexes of masculinity. Somatic kinetics thus seems to operate indexically to distinguish sexual gender, much more than two, but also reliability and self-confidence.

Scopic kinetics

Scopic kinetics is the modality that produces effects of stability or dynamism through the syntax of visual objects and spaces. The solidity of heavy furniture is used to indicate stability and by extension, trustworthiness, of its owners. The typical middle-class living room set of sofa-armchair-loveseat implies minimal dynamism

The Rhetoric-Dramatic Coupling

because its parts cannot be easily replaced nor changed, in contrast to the choice of a more dynamic and spontaneous array of styles, cushions and benches.

In poetics, expressionistic styles such as Romanticism, German Expressionism, Lyric Informalism, or Mannerism enunciate a relatively more dynamic scopic kinetics than the classicist styles like Neoclassicism, Neoconcretism, Hardedge, Geometrism, or Minimalism. By the same token, kinetics of Impressionism are more dynamic than Academicism, precisely echoing the increasing social dynamization provoked by the industrial revolution. Van Gogh displays a more dynamic kinetics by the emotional vibration of his brush strokes and colors than Cezanne who was looking for the basic spatial structures in landscapes. For deconstructionist architecture, scopic kinetics are manifested by means of diagonals and oblique receding and descentred planes which create such feeling of dynamism that they can become quite unbearable. By contrast, neoclassical architecture deploys an overwhelming immobility, the reason why it has been the favorite style of dictators in their dream of perpetual power.

Art Nouveau is characterized by dynamic and capricious scopic kinetics through curved lines and asymmetries, but is relatively static in its heavy furniture where the mass dominates emptiness (in comparison to the lightness of modern styles). Bauhaus furniture, on the other hand, produce the opposite effect: by its strict axial symmetry and orthogonal composition, this style of design is static and reliable connoting efficiency, durability, precision, calculation. At the same time, their relative weightlessness in the composition where emptiness predominates over the mass, in addition to the use of modern materials, bold and pure colors and novel forms, all provide a sense of dynamism to the degree that this style has become an icon for modernity. The same happens in architecture: an Art Nouveau building is heavy in its mass and decoration, but dynamic in its ornamental motifs, in contrast to functionalist buildings that are dynamic in the levity of materials such as glass and steel, but static in the calculated predictability of their rational, symmetrical, orthogonal structure.

Lexic emphatics

There are diverse ways to accentuate, emphasize, or underline ideas when we speak. Lexic emphatics deals with the concentration of meaning at particular points in verbal speech when they are marked, or its dilution when unmarked. Strongly marked emphatics in everyday life usually occur whenever more emotional intensity is invested in reaching the addressee's sensibility in an interaction, as in threats, orders, or supplications in comparison to notifications, requests, or petitions. This modality is directly linked to what speech act theory denominates "degrees of illocutionary strength" (particularly Searle 1969, 1976 and Vanderveken 1985, 1990). Professional bluffers and those who tend to speak without saying anything are typical cases of unmarked lexic emphatics (even if their speech appears to be acoustically accentuated). Whoever has encountered these peculiar speech patterns in political and academic milieus will witness how talk can be endlessly extended because, to begin with, there was nothing specific to communicate anyway, no meaning import to deliver. In these unmarked lexic emphatics, no matter how much

160   *Everyday Aesthetics*

effort is put into paying attention, one always fails in trying to make sense of it. In military orders or in sports, in addition to the acoustic emphatics of volume and their impersonal tone, the concise form of the command heavily marks statements in this register (as in "on your marks, get set, go ...").

Note the graphical resources by which we emphasize some syntagms in written language, whether by font size, italics, bold, or quotation marks. Each word, as we know, has an emphatic syllable, and each phrase an emphatic word, as each paragraph a sentence that is more emphatic than another. The decisions when constructing a statement are frequently taken by criteria of lexic emphatics. For example, in this last phrase, the syntagm "lexic emphatics" placed at the end of the sentence displays greater lexic emphatics than elsewhere. A different sequence, namely: "Decisions are frequently taken by criteria of lexic emphatics when constructing a statement" is much less emphatic than the first version. Clinton's already legendary phrase: "I did NOT have sex with this woman" illustrates this particular coupling.

Acoustic emphatics

Acoustic emphatics deploy a force, an intensity, that condenses meaning in a particular point of an utterance over the rest of its parts and in a specific way. Fatigue or lack of energy are still part of the range of emphatics characterizing unmarked or disperse emphasis. In shouting, weeping, and laughing, greater emphasis is displayed than in normal voice so that this energetic investment becomes indexical of emotional import.

In poetics, acoustic emphatics can be easily illustrated by the classic example of the four initial notes in Beethoven's Fifth Symphony, which, as a leitmotiv, has greater emphasis than the other sounds, and within it, greater emphasis is placed upon the fourth note by duration, volume, and contrast to the former notes.

Acoustic emphatics distinguishes energetic speakers from lethargic ones, with enormous consequences in all the social practices, particularly in teaching. When the speaker puts little energy in speech, the interpreter acts in reciprocity with the same weak energetical investment. And, on the contrary, a teacher who unfolds speech with very well marked acoustics has greater probability of capturing the attention of students and obtaining greater affective and mental investment from them.

In Parret's (2003) qualification of voices, some sounds may be aesthetically interpreted as acoustic emphatics, like certain sweetness in a voice, or a velvety sound, a sarcastic tone, a hard pitch, a roaring volume, a tweeting mode of speaking, as well as whistling, clamoring, hissing, or ruffling voices among perhaps hundreds of others. Undefined, standard voices function as unmarked emphatics, such as Stephen Hawking's electronic voice (which stands out in contrast to our organic voices). The general sound of languages differs in part by the most frequently accentuated syllable (as in French the last one, in Hungarian the first, in Spanish usually the one before the last).The displacement of accent that characterizes the dialectal Argentinean Spanish (*che mirá, fijate, vení*) in contrast to other Spanish Argentinean speakers (instead of *oye mira, fijáte, ven*) illustrates acoustic collective local emphatics.

Somatic emphatics

Among the range of all possible gestural options, whether conscious or unconscious, somatic emphatics refers to the syntagm upon which more energy is invested and that is highlighted over the rest. We display particular emphatics through our body or face that can be quite indicative for our interpreters: a certain tension in the jaw or neck, a way of directing the eyes, of moving the eyebrows, of tensing the lips. In addition to being proxemic, eye contact is also emphatic when expressing diverse attitudes. An insistent glance, an energetic handshake, biting lips, blushing, shedding tears, kicking, the rigidity of the back illustrate this particular coupling.

A somatic emphatics' phenomenon discovered by body language analysts (Scheflen 1972, 37) is what they call "eyebrow flash" (when eyes are opened more than normal and pupils are instantaneously dilated) when people recognize someone for whom they feel particular affection or desire. Pouting lips for kissing or projecting the chest or hips forwards are not only sexual semiotic signals but also aesthetic emphatics for seduction.

The premeditated calm acoustic emphatics whereupon ex-president Carlos Salinas de Gortari calculated to project an amiable image was totally neutralized and contradicted by the unsheathed, accusatory forefinger with which he threatened his public, and which has been directly inherited by Andrés López Obrador in each and every one of his public speeches. Michael Jackson's moonwalk step accentuating his extraordinary dancing skill, as Bill Clinton's gesture of tightening the inferior lip over the upper one to express being touched or moved by something, all exemplify the variety of resources for somatic emphatics in everyday life.[2]

Scopic emphatics

We can also accentuate certain aspects in the scopic register by selecting particular kinds of costumes, staging, props, or make-up. The painted birth mark under the lips that was considered very sexy some time ago, the contour around the mouth to make the lips seem more fleshy, painting the hair platinum blond to enhance facial features, applying mascara to eyelashes for making the eyes seem larger are scopic emphatic strategies commonly displayed by women. Deprived social classes often present unmarked emphatics by discolored, opaque, and murky clothes. Anyone preparing for a romantic date triggers the greatest scopic emphatics possible. High heels and accessories like belts or scarves and hats, particularly jewels, are manifestations of emphatics in this register to accentuate or conceal the neck, breasts, waist, legs, and so on.

In domestic scopics, various degrees of emphatics can be seen according to heedfulness or negligence in a house arrangement. The coffee table in a middle-class home is usually the greatest point of scopic emphatics in the house, since the objects most appreciated by the owners are placed there. In the structures of the domestic environment, Baudrillard (1981, 37–70) detects the warm values of wood, leather, or

---

2 Matsumoto and Ekman (1989) made an interesting comparative study between Japanese and Americans in this heading and concluded that the intensity of the face expression varies culturally, contradicting the assumption of the universality of face expression.

162 *Everyday Aesthetics*

wool in contrast to the cold values of glass and plastic which, from the point of view of prosaics, are topics of scopic emphatics.

Choosing one type of material rather than another is not only a practical matter but an aesthetic emphatic as well. Wood and wool are associated with warmth and coziness; glass to loyalty, objectivity and hygiene; aluminum with modernity; gold and precious stones with wealth; cotton with freshness, lightness and naturalness; leather with sensuality and animality; plastic with vulgarity, efficiency and resistance; straw with rural country life; silk and velvet with elegance and sophistication; linen with aristocratic traditionalism; clay with rusticity. These topics of the natural or artificial, of warmth or coolness, of modernity or antiquity are all displayed as scopic emphatics.

Lexic fluxion

Fluxion basically refers to what is shown or hidden, released or retained in what direction through a personal or collective interaction. Lexic fluxion is manifested by discursive loquacity or its opposite, restraint and scantiness. We find centrifugal fluxion through speeches full of verbal images, alliterations and hyperboles. Rabelais's illustrates, in *Gargantua and Pantagruel*, the open lexic fluxion by his descriptive profusion and agglomeration of details, the use of hyperbole and alliteration, irony and other linguistic games as in Chapter 1.XLIV. "How the Monk rid himself of his keepers, and how Picrochole's forlorn hope was defeated."[3]

> ... that to some he beat out their brains, to others he crushed their arms, battered their legs, and bethwacked their sides till their ribs cracked with it. To others again he unjointed the spondyles or knuckles of the neck, disfigured their chaps, gashed their faces, made their cheeks hang flapping on their chin, and so swinged and balammed them that they fell down before him like hay before a mower. To some others he spoiled the frame of their kidneys, marred their backs, broke their thigh-bones, pashed in their noses, poached out their eyes, cleft their mandibles, tore their jaws, dung in their teeth into their throat, shook asunder their omoplates or shoulder-blades, sphacelated their shins, mortified their shanks, inflamed their ankles, heaved off of the hinges their ishies, their sciatic or hip-gout, dislocated the joints of their knees, squattered into pieces the boughts or pestles of their thighs, and so thumped, mauled and belaboured them everywhere, that never was corn so thick and threefold threshed upon by ploughmen's flails as were the pitifully disjointed members of their mangled bodies under the merciless baton of the cross.

It seems that centrifugal fluxion is contagious, and I could go on and on with examples, so allow me only one last one:

> Then smiling, he untied his fair braguette, and drawing out his mentul into the open air, he so bitterly all-to-bepissed them, that he drowned two hundred and sixty thousand, four hundred and eighteen, besides the women and little children. Some, nevertheless, of the company escaped this piss-flood by mere speed of foot, who, when they were at the higher end of the university, sweating, coughing, spitting, and out of breath, they began to swear and curse, some in good hot earnest, and others in jest. Carimari, carimara: golynoly, golynolo.

---

3   All quotations from this book have been taken from Project Gutenberg digital library.

The Rhetoric-Dramatic Coupling

Such centrifugal display of aesthetic exuberance in images, words, sounds, and actions partly explains the spell of this literary work.

By contrast, closed fluxion reduces speech to its minimum. In bureaucratic documents, enunciation may be as economic as possible and fluxion shuts any personal or emotional demonstrations. In everyday life, open lexic fluxion is common in explosive situations such as quarrels, insults or in states of euphoria and agitation, whereas its closed modality is typical of passive aggressive attitudes. In theoretical, academic and scientific works, thinking is forced to follow a single discursive line avoiding deviations and other non indispensable topics to the argument, closing lexic fluxion to the minimal. At the same time, it indirectly becomes centrifugal when referring the reader to numerous intertextual sources by references that exceed the author's discourse, but rigorously enunciated by the boring task of obeying the established style conventions and displaying closed fluxion by self control.

Jakobson's (1963) example to illustrate the aesthetic function in the slogan *I like Ike* during Dwight Eisenhower's presidential campaign shows not only the unfolding of fluxion in both modalities but their mutual dependency: the slogan is compact and reduced to its minimum elements in the lexic, but centrifugal in its potential of acoustic propagation due to its rhythm and sharp synaesthetic effects. A motto too long would not achieve this unisonous alliteration, and therefore its symbolic force, whereas compact phrases as *"este puño sí se ve"*, *"el pueblo, unido, jamás será vencido"* maintain the necessary tight lexic fluxion to balance an unencumbered acoustic fluxion. This correlation of opposite fluxion (for example, closed in the lexic, open in the acoustic) is used in commercials and political slogans.

In poesic poetics, economy in expression is indispensable for its allurement. Japanese haiku is the classic example of balanced fluxion, retentive in the lexic to open up a wealth of connotations, evocations, and meanings. The ellipsis in the poem *El Horal* by Jaime Sabines resorts to this double game of maximal verbal economy towards maximal abundance in connotations:

> The sea is measured by waves,
> the sky by wings,
> we by tears.
> The air rests in leaves,
> the water in eyes,
> we in nothing.
> It seems that salts and suns,
> we and nothing.[4]

Acoustic fluxion

Acoustic fluxion is the eruption or containment of sound that we emit in a certain situation. In subordination relations, subjects are forced to display a closed fluxion, speak in low volume of voice, and control any impulse to insult, shout or protest. Telenovela scriptwriters usually characterize their heroines as essentially centripetal,

---

4 Translation is mine.

164   *Everyday Aesthetics*

keeping the secret that will redeem them in the eyes of the others until practically the last episode, at the moment of *agnition* or recognition in which such a long retentive fluxion is suddenly reversed towards the expulsive apotheosis of free-flowing tears, and a plethora of feelings and confessions to The End—over well-deserved punishments of villains, and the everlasting kiss of the bride and groom.

As I mentioned before, differences in fluxion usually correspond to differences in ethnic, gender, or class collective identities. The British have been stereotyped by their phlegmatic character which is centripetal fluxion in several registers. Pope John Paul II characterized the Mexicans as people who love to shout, namely by their open acoustic fluxion. The movie stereotype of the Mexican *charro*, who shouts with a high-pitched tone when hearing mariachi music, who sings, cries, and curses, illustrates this fluxion. Women, on the contrary, are portrayed as self-sacrificed heroines submissively suffering in silence. These stereotypes metaphorically express in the acoustic and lexic register the somatic condition where the male is centrifugal when penetrating and the female centripetal when penetrated.

The masses go to stadiums among other reasons for the opportunity of unobstructed unfolding of acoustic fluxion while restraining somatic fluxion because they sit, rather than play, at the game they so much enjoy. Shouts of goooooool, goooya, cachún cachún ra ra… are greatly relished by team fans in their cathartic potential and collective identification.

Somatic fluxion

Somatic fluxion is expressed by gestures and corporeal movements that retain or expel energy. The body is rigidified in the neck, hands, jaws, forehead, mouth, and so on or on the contrary, energy flows freely in open gesticulation. As in other modalities, somatic fluxion is partly regulated by culture and partly by the subject's individuality and identity. Cultures where children are inculcated sphincter control at an early age usually also manifest centripetal fluxion in other situations (control of time, memory, work, goods, spaces) in contrast to societies called "primitive" that do not show a retentive modality in other spheres of community life as well. The Freudian concept of sublimation, where the libido is retained and channeled towards intellectual or artistic activities, is a modality of centripetal-centrifugal fluxion.

Scopic fluxion

As the baroque style in the literary poetics displays centrifugal fluxion in the lexic register, the same happens in the scopics of its architecture. That impressive expansion of formal elements where decoration seems to exceed the architectonic support and replicate by itself, and the profusion of components in an interminable formal alliteration, contrasts with the centripetal austerity of classicist styles. Functionalism, on the other hand, is the most suitable expression of a puritanical ethics of frugality by its closed scopic fluxion. It is not accidental that this style in design emerged precisely in industrialized and capitalist countries, because such economy of resources faithfully mirrors a spirit of containment and calculation.

The Rhetoric-Dramatic Coupling

From the writings of Derrida on the decentralization of the subject, a new so-called "deconstructionist style" in architecture arises whose main characteristic is the centrifugal scopic fluxion through totally off-centered spaces in bold diagonals. As an architectonic concept, deconstruction seems a scopic oxymoron, because it only constructs to deconstruct and welcomes in order to expel, but it is actually a post-industrial aesthetic rebellion primordially in the fluxion modality against the prudence and rationality of functionalism.

The exact opposite to deconstructionism's centrifugality is the cloister designed to retain around a center metaphorical to God. It is not by mere chance that the prototype of centripetal scopic fluxion resides in monastery cloisters with their cells and corridors organized around a central patio with a fountain at its center, corresponding to the closed fluxion imposed on celibacy or poverty and silence votes or prayer involving various registers, all perfectly expressed in the rigid control of time depicted in Zerubavel's (1985) account of Benedictine monasteries.

A style or a statement can show different fluxions in different aspects. For example, monumental architecture patronized during fascism is centrifugal in scale for exhibiting the massive power of the State, but centripetal in the repetitive control of its elements to demonstrate its dominion. Hieronymus Bosch's *The Garden of the Delights* is an exalted proliferation of fruits, vegetation, minerals, human figures, and animals in action and desire, all metaphorical of the abundance of sexual energy and its explosive manifestation. By contrast, his work entitled *The Seven Capital Sins* is one of the most contained, centripetal works ever painted, so compact and controlled in its expression that Bosch did not dare to alter even the axial symmetry and strict composition of the four lateral circles and center formed as well by four concentric circles in the middle of which the figure of Jesus appears.

Fluxion operates by this dual centripetal-centrifugal combination not only in the scopic poetics above described, but also in prosaics: the most obvious are big supermarkets displaying centrifugal circulation of commodities produced in various parts of the world and the surplus of supply of late Capitalism economy. In this transition from productive to consumptive Capitalism, contemporary Western societies exhibit this accelerated centrifugal fluxion in superstores with an impressive variety and amount of consumer goods. Yet such centrifugal fluxion in commodities for consumption depends on its opposite, a centripetal, controlled fluxion to control costs of production. Consumers are expected to centripetally earn money and control their time to be productive enough for maintaining the reproduction of economy. They must also spend bountifully and almost religiously obey consumerist periodical open fluxion to counterpoint the overproduction of superfluous goods.

This tendency of overproduction-consumption corresponding to a pendular centrifugal-centripetal fluxion is sharply antithetical to the minimalism in some traditional Japanese and other ethnic cultures that value compact, almost empty spaces of multiple uses. Cultures of Eastern Asia are great experts in balancing scopic fluxion through the practice of Korean *fengliu* or *poongryu*, Japanese *furyu* and Chinese *feng shui*. (Min 1999, Too 1996) Although these traditions include other modalities as well, scopic fluxion has greater relevance based on a conception of mobile energies that must be retained or expelled according to a meticulous

Everyday Aesthetics

Table 23.2   Scheme of Correspondences for the Octadic Model

	LEXICS	*ACOUSTICS*	*SOMATICS*	*SCOPICS*
PROXEMICS	Lexic Proxemics	Acoustic Proxemics	Somatic Proxemics	Scopic Proxemics
Short-Long	S L	S L	S L	S L
KINETICS	Lexic Kinetics	Acoustic Kinetics	Somatic Kinetics	Scopic Kinetics
Dynamic-Static	D S	D S	D S	D S
EMPHATICS	Lexic Emphatics	Acoustic Emphatics	Somatic Emphatics	Scopic Emphatics
Marked-Unmarked	M U	M U	M U	M U
FLUXION	Lexic Fluxion	Acoustic Fluxion	Somatic Fluxion	Scopic Fluxion
Open-Closed	O C	O C	O C	O C

adjustment of space. Feng shui means in Chinese "wind and water", which indicates the importance of flowing. The term "fengliu" is made of *feng* or moral influence that extends outwards and *liu* meaning fidelity and tends inwards. (Min 1999) We see here the double movement of fluxion. According to these traditions, it is essential to take care of the flows of nature in its shapes, scales, cardinal points, landscapes, mass, and emptiness to obtain the harmony of the human being with its context. Thus, domestic space is designed with an opening oriented to attract energies and to enable them to suitably flow in a harmonious fluxion, as well as expel them when they are harmful.

Scopic fluxion can be expressed by colors also. In contrast to many African customs that freely display a fascinating chromatic and decorative wealth, the paradigms of European good or bad taste conventions in regards to color favor restrained chromatics (brown, gray, cream, black, white, navy blue). These combinations are strangely interpreted in relation to credibility, correctness, solidity, modesty and sobriety, whereas bright and vivid colors are associated with vulgarity, low class or low morals.

To conclude, I want to indicate that these 16 categories only record in discreet terms processes that are basically continuous and mixed. A common spectator—not a specialized art critic or an art historian—nevertheless perceives with all clarity in Van Gogh's *Cypresses* the short scopic proxemics of the visible texture, the dynamic kinetics in the flaming cypresses and undulant clouds, the vigorous emphatics of brush strokes and the centrifugal fluxion of the painter's emotions. Such a spectator does not need these categories to appreciate the picture, but the student of aesthetics does require them to better understand why this work affects us as it does. In addition, this picture illustrates the concept of excess that characterizes the aesthetic dimension, because from semiotics' perspective, one simply decodifies it as "picture", "cypresses", "a Van Gogh", "painting", "modern art", "post-impressionism", and so on depending on the code applied (what thing, theme, author, technique, period, style, and so on), whereas from the aesthetic dimension of interpretation, it not merely means the above, but affects us.

Sixteen combinations are thus possible (LP, AP, SoP, SP; LK, AK, SoK, SK, LE, AE, SoE, SE; LF, AF, SoF, SF) which could be multiplied to 48 when considering three possibilities of short-neutral-long; dynamic-neutral-static; marked-neutral-unmarked; open-neutral-closed (LPs, LPn, LPl, up to SFo, SFn SFc). Since all these

The Rhetoric-Dramatic Coupling

categories are relative, it is necessary to specify in each case with respect to whom or what the modality unfolds. Jargon, for example, show long lexical proxemics with respect to other people foreign to the group and shortens it in relation to its members. Also, a verbal unfolding can be centrifugal in relation to its public including the greater amount of receivers possible and centripetal in relation to the emitter when talking only about himself. It must be remembered also that registers and modalities combine among them, so that we may find somato-lexic or acousto-scopic statements. In fact, handwriting is a lexico-scopic-somatic manifestation, since it uses words to be visually perceived and displayed by a body gesture. Speaking out loud is a lexico-acoustic expression, while deaf's signal language is lexico-somatic communication. It is advisable to put first the dominant register in the interaction, followed by the complementaries. The same can be done in respect to modalities, as when shouting "be careful!" can be an emphatic-fluxive-proxemic-kinetic lexic-somatic expression to prevent an accident. In this case it is not always clear in which order these modalities should be placed.

Chapter 24

Con-Formations
of the Rhetoric-Dramatic Coupling

The rhetoric-dramatic couplings intercross one another in various ways for the production of aesthetic meaning in every social interaction. For example, according to greeting conventions among the Wolof people (Irvine 1974, 167–191), this minimum exchange between two persons already involves a question of status and hierarchy that is expressed in the form in which this interaction takes place. Persons of inferior status denote their subordinated position by using a high pitch and strong volume (acoustic emphatics denoting inferiority), taking the initiative of greeting (open lexic fluxion), by the wordiness when speaking with hasty tempo (fast lexic kinetics) and thus settling down their social distance (long somatic proxemics). The semiotic dimension to signify and symbolize in this exchange the place that everyone occupies in the community is satisfied.

But there are situations that go beyond this semiotic dimension involving the participants' sensibility in a greater degree. Consider the following: The primordial function of a funeral is basically to get rid of the corpse. To this practical function, cultural tradition adds a second level in semiotics to symbolize and signify such event according to its customs in relation to death. But there is a third level in which strategies are deliberately unfolded towards the sensibility of the participants. This level, namely the aesthetic, can be clearly exemplified in military funerals where all modalities and registers are aesthetically geared towards a ritual that grants some kind of meaning to the death of a soldier and attempts to comfort the relatives and legitimize the military matrix. The goal is that, despite the loss of life of a loved one, the family and peers of the deceased will still remain adhered to this matrix so that it may legitimize itself and, with it, the death of the soldier too. This strategy is constituted by tactics such as slow lexic kinetics at the funeral speech to confer a sense of solemnity to the ceremony, in addition to the lexic emphatics on the virtues of the deceased. The scopic proxemics of military uniforms and the somatic proxemics in the presence of hierarchic military figures at the ceremony define a long distance with respect to common funerals and shorten it with respect to the relatives who are thus integrated as members of the matrix. The slow and rigid somatic kinetics of soldiers marching carrying the coffin, as well as their perfectly controlled centripetal somatic fluxion, contribute to the somatic emphatics of solemnity. The centripetal acoustic fluxion of the relatives in their effort to maintain composure and avoid impulses of weeping, cursing the army, or accusing those responsible, is canalized and released through the centrifugal acoustic fluxion of trumpets. The scopic emphatics of the flag that covers the coffin symbolizes by analogy that the victim has been covered by glory and wrapped by his fatherland. The flag is then carefully folded by the soldiers

170   *Everyday Aesthetics*

Table 24.1   Military Funerals

MILITARY FUNERALS	LEXICS		ACOUSTICS		SOMATICS		SCOPICS	
PROXEMICS	*Lexic Proxemics* Long verbal proxemics through a solemn, ceremonial speech		*Acoustic Proxemics* Long acoustic proxemics of military music		*Somatic Proxemics* The presence of hierarchic military figures shorten proxemics with the family including them in the military		*Scopic Proxemics* Long scopic proxemics in military uniforms and military cemetery	
Short-Long	S	L#	S	L#	S# family L# others		S	L#
KINETICS	*Lexic Kinetics* Slow verbal rhythm in the funeral speech for grave effect		*Acoustic Kinetics* Slow music for a solemnity effect		*Somatic Kinetics* Slow and rigid somatic kinetics of soldiers who march carrying the coffin		*Scopic Kinetics* Rigidly symmetrical placement of graves to enhance discipline and order	
Dynamic-Static	D	S#	D	S#	D	S#	D	S#
EMPHATICS	*Lexic Emphatics* Enhancement of the virtues of the deceased (heroism, loyalty)		*Acoustic Emphatics* Trumpet sound emphasizing the military character of the funeral		*Somatic Emphatics* Solemn poses and gestures		*Scopic Emphatics* Flag covering the coffin	
Marked-Unmarked	M#	U	M#	U	M#	U	M#	U
FLUXION	*Lexic Fluxion* No spontaneity in speech		*Acoustic Fluxion* Centripetal acoustic fluxion of no weeping, cursing or screaming		*Somatic Fluxion* Controlled centripetal fluxion in marching, and sitting according to ceremony order		*Scopic Fluxion* Closed scopic fluxion in the homogeneity of tombs and strict order of all elements	
Open-Closed	O	C#	O	C#	O	C#	O	C#

and given to the family as a symbolic body by this indexical relation of contiguity. (See Table 24.1.)

Heteroglossia

The previous example illustrates how enunciation/interpretation in the military matrix is displayed through several coordinated aesthetic registers and modalities to produce the effect of solemnity and purposeness of that death. We have, then, a case of heteroglossia (of Greek *heteros*, different and *glossa*, tongue) since verbal, somatic, scopic, and acoustic "tongues" or languages have been used in this statement.

Bakhtin, from whom this term has been borrowed, defines heteroglossia as follows:

> The novel orchestrates all its themes, the totality of the world of objects and ideas depicted and expressed in it, by means of the social diversity of speech types (*raznorecie*) and by the differing individual voices that flourish under such conditions. Authorial speech,

Con-Formations of the Rhetoric-Dramatic Coupling   171

the speeches of narrators, inserted genres, the speech of characters are merely those fundamental compositional units with whose help heteroglossia (*raznorecie*) can enter the novel; each of them permits a multiplicity of social voices and a wide variety of their links and interrelationships (always more or less dialogized). (Bakhtin 1988, 263)

He criticizes scholars of stylistics in the novel for transposing a symphonic (orchestrated) theme on to the piano keyboard, thus losing all depth and complexity of their object. This criticism is equally or more pertinent in prosaics than in poetics. We can witness how linguistic studies, whether in semantics or pragmatics, also neglect the diverse links, contradictions, reinforcements, namely the multidimensionality of social interactions. To reduce an interaction to the verbal register is like reducing a symphony to a keyboard. That is why we need at least a tetradic model.

Although there seems to be a certain ambiguity between the "multiplicity of voices" (polyphony) and the diversity of types of speech mentioned by Bakhtin in regards to the novel (prosic poetics), for the aims of our analysis applied to prosaics we are going to understand *heteroglossia* in its etymological sense, namely, the diversity in discursive vehicles or registers in enunciation. In fact, there is almost no statement that is not to a certain extent heteroglossic, because speaking already involves not only the lexic register of emitting words, but the somatic and the acoustic as well in modulating air from the lungs through the throat, mouth, tongue, teeth, lips, and writing implies not only the lexics of words, but also the somatics of the gesture and the scopics in handwriting or printing the text. All this in addition to the sub-registers implied.

Thus monoglottic syntagms (a single type of speech or register) are found in an ambulance's siren but opera, cinema, and human communication is heteroglottal as it deploys not only various languages and genres, but semiotic registers as well. A restaurant menu is heteroglottal since the names of the dishes use the lexic register, the photographs of some dishes the scopic, in addition to which the interpreter adds the somatic by synaesthesia associating flavors, scents, and textures to the dishes offered.

We can verbally refer to other registers by denotation using the lexic as dominant: "I saw John (somatic) today: he looked quite handsome in his velveteen navy blue coat (scopic); I shouted (acoustic) and yelled "hello!" (lexic) greeting him with my hands (somatic)". Here we must not conflate the (relative) monoglossia in the Hjelmslevian plane of expression having a dominant lexic register (although the acoustic or the scopic are involved in the elocution or writing) with the heteroglossia referred to in the plane of content. So when analyzing an utterance, we must make explicit which plane is analyzed. This book in your hands, for example, is obviously of a lexic dominant in the plane of expression. It includes the scopics of typography, but this is the publisher's statement, not the author's. In the plane of content, however, I refer to the four registers. Consequently it is monoglottic in the plane of expression (lexic register) and heteroglottic in the plane of content by denotation (since it refers to images, gestures, etc.). Bakhtin's texts are also monoglottic in expression and heteroglottic in content because, even if they all refer to written language in the novel with the lexic dominant (that would make them monoglottic in terms of register), he analyzes various lexic genres. Genre heteroglossia, to which Bakhtin is

172   *Everyday Aesthetics*

referring, combines epistolary and evangelical speeches, everyday conversations, mythological references, local dialects and styles or professional jargon, and so on. In everyday life we can also find genre heteroglossia say, at a university class where the professor mixes theoretical, colloquial, political and institutional language, with a joke here and a moral reprimand there. Each of these genres somehow demands a different style in language. Television is a typical plural genre heteroglossia, and with cable TV it becomes also multilingual heteroglossia, in addition to being multiregister. In fact, even if displayed through a single register, most enunciations are heteroglottic at the level of sub-registers. For example a somatic syntagm of sexual desire can be expressed in the temperature, odor, humidity, and gestuality of the body, each complementing or contradicting one another. In the scopic register of personal appearance, statements can be made by costumes, hairdo, props and make-up, so this question can be analyzed across various scales. For the sake of analysis we can extend Bakhtin's concept of heteroglossia to examine any enunciation that is constituted by various "tongues" or communicative devices including registers, sub-registers, and genres.

Polyphony

If we are able to detect heteroglossia, we have everything necessary to understand polyphony, which refers to "diverse voices" (from the Greek *poly*, many, and *phonetos*, to speak) in Bakhtin's quotation above. If heteroglossia occurs at the level of registers, sub-registers, and genres, namely of rhetorics, polyphony unfolds through dramatics. Polyphony in prosaics typically occurs in cases such as when a woman enunciates a prudish scopic emphatics by wearing modest clothes and long scopic proxemics hiding the contours of her body, but at the same time displays provocative somatic emphatics in gestures and positions, as well as sensual acoustic emphatics through a deep and gasping voice, all contrasting her long lexic proxemics and a closed lexic fluxion refusing contact. Another case that illustrates polyphony are fake orgasms where pleasure is feigned by the acoustic register and even the somatic at the postural and gestural sub-registers, but at the level of moistural, olfactory, and thermal sub-registers, the message differs.

If in great literary works social polyphony is injected into the body of the novel establishing a dialogical background, this same process also happens in collective enunciations in prosaics. Polyphony is manifested not only between the diverse registers (as when saying "go away" in the lexic but seducing by the acoustic and the somatic) but also within a same register by heterogeneous enunciations in each sub-register (an architecturally hypermodern flat decorated with Louis XIV style furniture in the scopic).

Cases of polyphony are very common in daily life due to the heterogeneity of identities that we continuously display. A dress with a soft, thin and sensual fabric that shows the contours of the body enunciates the intention to be attractive, but when used with coarse and masculine shoes indicating the purpose of comfort and aplomb it creates polyphony. Mexican President Vicente Fox's elegant Armani (or similar) suit denoting urban cosmopolitan jet set, but worn with his cowboy's boots related to his ranch in Guanajuato create a curious polyphony. Examples are abundant, since it is more likely to find dissonances among various registers than the contrary because we do not constitute our messages by strict logical coherence. So in everyday dramaturgical displays, polyphonic enunciations are common which turns interactions even more fascinating for an observer.

Hybridization

Another important concept inherited from Bakhtin for our analysis is "hybridization":

> What is the hybridization? It is a mixture of two social languages within the limits of a single utterance, an encounter within the arena of an utterance, between two different linguistic consciousnesses, separated from one another by an epoch, by social differentiation or by some other factor. (Bakhtin 1988, 358)

By hybridization I will understand the encounter between two different linguistic consciousnesses, not of two languages (which is heteroglossia) although there is no consciousness without its own discursive production whether in words, images, or corporeal sensations. Therefore, hybridization would generally, although not necessarily, imply both a degree of heteroglossia and polyphony. In a novel's prosic poetics, this hybridization of two consciences occurs between the author or re-presenter and the character or re-presented. In prosaics, the enouncer's conscience of the interpreter's presence and the probable interpretations to his or her utterances influence how the statement is displayed. This is part of what Bakhtin understood by "dialogism". For that reason, every process of enunciation/interpretation in prosaics is hybrid and dialogical, in addition to being polyphonic and heteroglottal (even if only at the level of sub-registers).

Hybridization operates at a level deeper than the explicit statement, as is the case of internalization of identities imposed by the subject's family during childhood. Alfred Hitchcock managed to portray in his film *Psycho* a case of extreme, even pathological hybridization where the character internalizes his mother's identity. Also, Gregory Bateson's (1972) "double bind hypothesis" with respect to the origin of schizophrenia within the family, can be partly explained by a process of hybridization where schizophrenics end up assuming the identity that their mother has unconsciously assigned to them in order to keep a peculiar pathological balance within the family, even if tremendously painful. Great actors and actresses are those who achieve some kind of hybridization with their character to the degree that their performance on stage becomes almost monophonic, totally identifying with the character, as in Stanislavski's method of acting.

Ex-pression, im-pression, com-pression, de-pression

There are four additional concepts that may have some heuristic value for analyzing the rhetoric-dramatic coupling. What these concepts mark is the direction for the flow of energy through a social interaction. We have thus: 1) "ex-pression" as pressing outwards from dramatics to rhetorics akin to the process of objectivation; 2) "im-pression" from rhetorics to dramatics related to subjectivation; 3) "com-pression" as a blocking that results from a confrontation between dramatics and rhetorics; 4) "de-pression" as an emptying or dispersion of both coordinates in every direction.

Rhetorics *ex-presses* dramatics when the subject of enunciation searches for the adequate means of "pressing outwards" what he feels or thinks and lets it flow, articulating what best mirrors his or her attitude or emotions. Here enunciation arises from the dramatic towards the rhetoric. The inverse process happens when the individual presents himself in a particular role (as in the interaction rituals and presentation of the self analyzed by Goffman), that not necessarily corresponds to his attitude or desire at the moment. The subject guesses the correct style and form of enunciation according to the code in certain situations, and displays them in rhetorical terms so that the interlocutor may infer a corresponding dramatic. In this case rhetorics generate an *im-pression* of a supposed attitude or implicit dramatics. Rhetorics press inwards towards dramatics by *im-pression* as dramatics presses outwards towards rhetorics in *ex-pression*.

In raising children, parents often correct rhetoric aspects in all registers, as a bad posture in somatics, a whiny tone in acoustics, coarse language in lexics, or a mess in the room in the scopics to affect the dramatics of the child by *im-pression*. We also orient ourselves by the *ex-pression* in regards to the inner life of our children, taking their rhetoric as indexical of their dramatic.

Sometimes the rhetoric and dramatic in the enouncer are totally disjointed, although the addressee may link them as a rhetorical illusion. Those known as "con-artists" fabricate a particular rhetoric to persuade upon a supposed underlying dramatic that not only does not exist, but totally contradicts the attitude of the enouncer. Somebody pretends to offer something when in fact tries to grab. They do not display *ex-pression*, as no attitude is articulated by their rhetoric, but they deploy *im-pression* since the addressees infer from rhetorics the enouncers' supposed dramatics.

Another modality in this peculiar dramatic and rhetoric coupling is *de-pression*, understood literally as voiding or emptying of pressure. We recognize a melancholic or depressive dramatics by means of unmarked or languid emphatics, slow kinetics, long proxemics and centripetal fluxion in all registers.

The last category, *com-pression*, consists in the total closure of subjectivity to all hybridization. *Com-pression* maintains subjectivity blocked in a monological speech constantly repeated to itself. It is common to find this state among puritanical, self-righteous personalities that never doubt their ideas, no matter how much evidence is provided. Fanatics are *com-pressive* individuals since they manage to permanently exclude other people's perspective. This type of subjectivity, impermeable to any inter or cosubjectivity, produces the peculiar effect of objectivity by the apparent assurance by which it enounces its positions.

In spite of certain affinity between centripetal fluxion and *com-pression*, let us not confuse them, because while fluxion refers to the flow in social exchanges, the latter is the interruption of intersubjectivity and hybridization, and therefore of any possibility of inter-action. Unlike *de-pression* in which the subject feels empty, in

Table 24.2 Types of Pressure

Ex-pression: Dramatics→Rhetorics
Im-pression: Rhetorics→Dramatics
Rhetorics→*Com-pression*←Dramatics
Rhetorics←*De-pression*→Dramatics

com-pression the subject is full of himself, blocked by the pressure of dramatics against rhetorics squashing him between both. In *com-pression* there is no polyphony nor heteroglossia or hybridization, reason why these forms of subjectivity are eminently sterile and immutable. They constitute the reverse of Socratic or Cartesian subjectivity open to wonder and doubt for playing philosophical or everyday *peripatos* games. Nevertheless, the subject of *com-pression* is tremendously persuasive when confronting weaker or more volatile subjectivities, and therefore very dangerous. In fact, there is no autocrat or dictator who does not exhibit a *com-pressive* subjectivity. (See Table 24.2.)

In these couplings sometimes only one of the registers expresses the dramatics (or rather, exposes it), while others hide it. To suppose that each individual maintains a single voice and is always monophonic is to believe in the single identity of the person. This only happens in cases of *com-pression* where the subject exerts such violence against his other identities that he represses his alternative forms of subjectivity for the sake of a dominant one, or in cases of *de-pression* when he feels he has none. The *com-pressive* subject not only represses others, but also compresses any emergent polyphony within himself by the insecurity and fear of disintegration of his identity which, paradoxically, is interpreted as firmness. I believe that, as a result of Goffman's studies in sociology, Freud's in psychoanalysis, Bakhtin's in literary discourse and even of Derrida's textual deconstruction, it is no longer possible to continue speaking of The Intention, The Attitude or The Identity in singular and univocal terms except, perhaps, in cases that could be denominated as pathological stiffening of identity by *com-pression*.

To conclude this analytical model, I must remind the reader that we are dealing here with social interactions and communicative exchanges where the aesthetic function is dominant because they strongly depend on the form of how the message is displayed and interpreted (in Jakobson's terms). As secondary functions, we find the *ex-pressive* coupling when the enouncer's impulse to objectify an idea or feeling is in the first plane (as Jakobson's expressive function), or the *im-pressive* coupling whose main point is causing an effect upon the addressee (broadly corresponds to Jakobson's conative or comissive function). In addition we find two types of couplings negatively related to the phatic function as lack of contact: the *com-pressive* where dramatics and rhetorics are neutralized one against another, and the *de-pressive* that, lacking direction, loses contact.

PART 6
MATRIXES AND IDENTITIES

The matrixes, from the Latin *"mater"*, are literally and metaphorically the places where identities are bred, sustained, and cultivated. A matrix is to the collective subject what a body is to the individual subject, namely, its indispensable material and morphological condition. As a disposition that dyes social exchanges and makes them possible, subjectivity is perceivable only when it is objectified in any of the registers and across their modalities. For that reason, the matrixes establish the conditions of possibility in this con-formation of subjectivity and its unfolding through individual and collective identities. Here we will explore some matrixes and identities as *types*, namely, as an analytical abstraction in relation to the actual matricial and identitary practices we display as *tokens* in our everyday life.

To deal with matrixes in prosaics evidently implies a systemic perspective, and thus the conception of social systems initiated by Bertalanffy, Bateson, Berger and Luckmann, Maturana and Varela among others, stands in the background. It is, however, necessary to indicate that the approach proposed here differs from the systems theory developed by Niklas Luhmann (1991). The most obvious reason is than in Luhmannian systems there is no place for the subject, in addition to considering the human being as part of the surroundings which significantly diminishes its role as agent or constituent of reality, in addition to reducing its depth and multidimensionality.

The concept of matrixes intends to observe the subject as constituent of and constituted by such matrixes, and not the "analysis of the real systems in the real world" as in Luhmann (1991, 35). This doesn't mean that matrixes are unreal, but rather that they are socially constructed by us, and only for that reason we have access to them. It is we who have built them, if not with a conscious overall plan, perhaps in a manner akin to bees' construction of beehives. Although there is necessarily an angle divergence among the versions that each subject may have of each of the social matrixes, it does not imply that shared configurations of perception cannot be established. The version here elaborated can be confronted with any other, but one can predict that coincidences with other observers will occur insofar as the observers' *a priori* conditions are common (similar space-time, relatively shared cultural conventions, almost equal corporeal morphology, even if a degree of vitality may differ). In addition, a significant part of what constitutes the matrixes is imaginary, aspects not considered by Luhmann. That is why from prosaics' perspective, Luhmann's universalistic pretension when affirming that "the theory of the social systems tries to include all the field of the objects of sociology and to constitute itself, in that sense, into a sociological universal theory" (1991, 37) seems off mark. The reason, I insist, is that the matrixes here elaborated are observed only

178 *Everyday Aesthetics*

from the subjective dimension that constitutes them, not as independent systems from the observer with their own ontic existence.

Unlike the structural functionalism of luhmannian systems, the matrixes are, as its name indicates, fertile, live and dynamic organisms. They, in turn, procreate other matrixes as the religion and national matrixes derive from the family or tribal matrix or as the juridical, the educational, and the artistic develop, as we shall see, from the religion matrix. Luhmann speaks of sharply differentiated "psychic systems" and "social systems" when operating by conscience and communication respectively, but it is difficult to understand how one can happen without the other (consider, for example, Wiley's 1994 semiotic self-derived from Mead and Peirce). A non communicated "psychic system", namely a subject without intersubjectivity, cannot exist, even in the extreme case of the wolf girls found in India in 1922. Isolated from all human contact, these girls nursed by a family of wolves developed a lupular psychic and social life to the degree that the youngest could not survive in human society and died shortly after "being rescued" (ages five and eight) and the older one only survived ten years. These young girls were quadruped and lacked any facial expression; they ate only raw meat, and were in a perfect state of physical and mental health in lupular terms of survival according to their pre-capture context. (Maturana and Varela 1992, 128–9) Their intersubjectivity was lupular.

Luhmann defines, begging the question, three dimensions: the objective, the temporal, and the social. Why these, rather than others, say the subjective, the spatial, the biological or the cultural remains a mystery. The dimensions considered for prosaic analyses are, conversely, the economic, the political, the semiotic, the technological, the ethical, the physical, the environmental, the aesthetic among others, all of them part of the complex socio-cultural organization since they intercross one another and penetrate all matrixes.

Chapter 25

The Matrixes: A General Approach

From the perspective of the sociology of the knowledge, Peter Berger and Thomas Luckmann (1986) have argued that individuals collectively produce everyday reality through objectivation, institutionalization, and legitimation processes. Inasmuch processes, the analyzed by these authors are applicable to all the matrixes, but it is necessary to emphasize that their components vary significantly in each case, and are not as homogenous as it appears from their perspective. In this part we will analyze these variations that define the specificity of each matrix and therefore, the particularity of the identities that are constituted from and by each of them.

One of these processes, namely legitimation, is explained by these authors as an indispensable requirement to obtain plausibility for the instituted reality. Legitimation implies cognitive as much as normative aspects to coherently integrate it with other segments of reality. Such legitimation begins, according to Berger and Luckmann, with linguistic objectivations in the first level, with explanatory schemes in the second and explicit theories in the third inasmuch a body of differentiated knowledge. In the fourth level, legitimation constitutes "symbolic universes" defined as "the matrix of *all* the meanings socially objectified and subjectively real; all the historical society and the biography of an individual are seen as facts that happen *within* that universe." (1986, 125) For the authors such "symbolic universe" constitutes the cosmic context of legitimation for all actions and defines the activities of each of the roles that participate in it. They define a "symbolic universe" as a unitary, almost monolithic form, although they recognize the plurality of universes in contemporary society. Nevertheless, from our perspective, these universes only seem unitary when seen from outside, so to speak, because by penetrating them it is evident that they are conformed by complex figures that resemble more an organic configuration of multiple networks, some of fractal similarity across diverse scales, than a geometric Euclidean sphere. For that reason they speak of "the symbolic universe" in singular. The matrixes, on the other hand, incorporate segments of other matrixes and of previous stages of the same matrix, whether alive or dead.[1]

There are other divergences between the concept of matrixes elaborated here from the one proposed by Berger and Luckmann. In the first place, these legitimation processes are not only linguistic, implying exclusively the lexic register, but rhetoric

---

1   For that reason, I am not going to use the concepts "world" of primary socialization and "subworlds" of secondary socialization proposed by Berger and Luckmann (1986, 174) since they all remain in the subject, nor will I restrict the concept of "roles" to the latter sense, since they operate also in the family matrix, like the roles of father, mother, son, grandfathers, and so on

180   *Everyday Aesthetics*

throughout the four registers.[2] Moreover, it is not always the case that legitimation depends on explicit explanatory schemes and theories, as their second and third level, but on practices that can be explicit (as theory in science) or implicit, affective, connotative and not totally conscious activities. By the same token, the third level indicated by these authors as "body of differentiated knowledge" requires to be understood in terms of each particular matrix with its own practices and conventions (among which we may find cognitive practices, but also economic, political, semiotic, and aesthetic). Finally, such "symbolic universe", which for Berger and Luckmann refers to religion, is only one matrix among others whose differences are strategic rather than a question of essence and not only symbolic since it integrates also signic processes (according to our distinction developed in Part 4). In other words, the religious matrix is comparable to the family matrix, the school, legal, or medical matrixes since each one constitutes its own universe with its body of practices, beliefs, conventions, habits albeit they often partly overlap one another. All matrixes are phenomena of the same nature having blurred borders, coincidences, and projections among them, without losing the specificity of their matricial body.

Berger and Luckmann stress the importance of legitimation and individuals' adhesion to the constructed matrixes, but they do not fully explain how this adhesion is achieved. This sends us to the land of rhetoric in its four registers and, consequently, to aesthetics, for an answer. At this point prosaics can explain non conscious, non explicit and deeply affective aspects where fascination and seduction are a determining factor in the social construction of reality. Accordingly, the matrixes are not only cognitive and normative, as Berger and Luckmann define institutions, but above all they are persuasive through rhetoric, seductive, and even abductive displays for their addressee's *latching–on*. Here, as in its constituent function, resides the importance of exploring them social institutions the perspective of prosaics.

When the authors state that "reality is defined socially, but the definitions are always *incarnated*, namely, the individuals and groups of concrete individuals serve as definers of reality" (1986, 149) it is worth emphasizing that such *incarnation* is of an aesthesic and semiosic character. Reality's concretion is accomplished by acoustic, scopic, somatic, and basically lexic rhetoric through eloquent and suggestive unfoldings, without which unfolding, no *latching–onto* occurs and therefore, no adhesion takes place nor the intersubjective legitimacy that such institutions require. Each matrix is therefore an experiencial, corporeal and affective world for the subjects it encompasses. Each maintains its own rhythms and tensions that distinguish one from another and requires maintenance procedures, as Luckmann and Berger indicate with respect to the institutions. Matrixes do not exist by themselves, automatically, without the intervention of the subjects who, in order to inhabit them, must construct, develop, re–elaborate and protect them (for example from heresy, madness, delinquency, and so on) by deploying some of the seclusion strategies pointed at by Foucault.

There is a paradox in Berger and Luckmann's thought: on the one hand, they recognize the active agency of subjects when making them responsible for the

---

2   The authors mention also representative rituals, ceremonies, physical objects and gestures where somatics and scopics also participate.

The Matrixes: A General Approach 181

construction of the reality, but on the other, they reduce them to a process of identification and internalization of roles, diminishing their constitutive capacity. For that reason it is important to consider the enunciation–interpretation dyad in which internalization is already active and creative in some way, as identification is constitutive. Contrary to what has been mistakenly supposed by orthodox structuralism, vulgar Marxism and antihumanist Althusserianism for example, the matrixes do not necessarily determine the subject, since it is we the subjects who have constituted the matrixes (even if, at the same time, we are constituted by them). Nevertheless, matrixes end up prevailing over us ossifying and ridigizing with time. The margin of creativity and flexibility by which the subject can operate in most matrixes is limited, in spite of their relative plasticity. There is a process of reification of the matrixes inherited from one generation to another, as mentioned by the authors, which seems to me that somehow resembles the process of fetishization of commodities denounced by Marx, namely that institutions appear to exist as part of nature, independently of human beings, instead of as social creations embodying human relations. The subject nevertheless has options, and his freedom essentially resides in the combinatory from which novel configurations can emerge. Therefore, we not only internalize or are identified with the matrixes in which we are articulated enabling cosubjectivity, but we can alter them through enunciation and interpretation by being, as individuals, in a place unique and different from all others at a microlevel, able to project a singular perspective.

If "the self is a reflected entity" as Berger and Luckmann claim (1986, 167) and since we construct our identity in relation to others, we can maneuver, although with great limitations, among expectations when simultaneously located in several matrixes. As subjects we accept prescribed roles, but we can choose between one identity and another at certain level, (for example in the most determining of all matrixes, the family, we can choose between being the obedient or the rebellious child) without refusing to accept the matrix as a whole. At the same time, we can alter the matrix (constituting, so to speak, a family in which there is a rebellious child or one in which there is none). Identities are crystallized with and from the matrix, but the matrix is also crystallized with and from the identities (as the Christian matrix was radically altered by the vision of Saint Paul in the way to Damascus, but Saul of Tarsus was also radically altered by the emergence of Christianity).

The problem of "adhesion" to the matrix that Berger and Luckmann ask themselves (1986, 183), namely, that a constructed reality must be sufficiently reasonable and convincing to be adopted and reproduced by the subjects, would depend in our terms on the aesthetic strategies displayed. These involve rhetorical eloquence (*pathos*), authority (*ethos*), and coherence (*logos*). Without a "strongly affective identification" of individuals with the matrix, as the authors recognize (1986, 197), we will not be able to participate in it nor constitute our identity from it. Here lies precisely the basic function of the aesthetic in recruiting the affective and sensorial dispositions of the subject towards their adhesion.

What is very debatable is the symmetry between objective and subjective reality proposed by the authors (1986, 185). There is no objective reality except as cosubjective reality, a shared reality whose total configuration is impossible to know from a supposedly "extra–real" outsidedness, since everyone comes from a place and a version of reality that is intersubjective, and consequently also subjective.

This impossibility of the existence of an extraneous reality does not mean that we are condemned to personal solipsism, but that our access to an objective reality is shared in different portions with the others and depends upon subjectivity. In fact, we go through life trying to share realities, and in this process we insert ourselves with others in the diverse matrixes and submatrixes. Children and parents as well as teachers and students continuously maintain processes of negotiation of shared realities. As we only count on these more or less partial or ample intersubjective realities, there is no such possibility of verifying any symmetry.

The matrixes are live units constituted by live elements, namely the subjects, maintaining a relative autonomy one from another. In the matrixes *the individual ontogenies of all the participating organisms occur fundamentally as part of the network of co–ontogenies that they bring about in constituting third order unities*" (Maturana and Varela 1992, 193, italics in the original text). This constitution depends on communication, defined, by these authors, as "the coordinated behaviors mutually triggered among the members of a social unity". For that reason we can consider them as autopoietic units according to their definition: "We are proposing that the mechanism that makes living beings autonomous systems is autopoiesis." (Maturana and Varela 1992, 48) This means that they self–reproduce as units maintaining their own organization. The product of this organization is the organism itself, without separation between producer and product. As mentioned in Chapter 5, for these authors there are three orders of autopoietic units: cellular, pluricellular, and social (primates, bees, birds, termites, humans, and so on). All three orders depend one on the other (cells depend on collective cellular organizations and individuals on the social and vice versa) and subjectivity may exist at any of these three units.

First order units or cells have a membrane as a morphological border that allows autopoiesis and a center in their nucleus; in second order units of pluricellular individuals the membrane is constituted by the skin with sensorial and nervous terminals and the center by the brain. In matrixes as third order unities, such membranes are borders discursively, ritually or legally defined and the center resides in their symbol. So in the family matrix, the membrane is located at the limits of their property or apartment, as in the national matrix at its territorial borders, and in other organizations by their norms and rules.

In sum, the matrixes are live organisms intersubjectively and collectively constituted that can be projected upon each other and overlap partially (the State matrix with the military and the juridical) or totally (in totalitarianism all matrixes are dominated by the State or the military). Inasmuch autopoietic organizations, one of the conditions of possibility of these matrixes is intersubjective adhesion by the exchange of rhetoric–dramatic strategies. We will analyze the interactions that enable such adhesion and the processes by which identities are captivated by or captured in various matrixes from a Western contemporary middle–class perspective.

Matrixes and paradigms

We already distinguished in Chapter 15 between syntagm and paradigm in terms of Saussure and Barthes's theory as a network of sequential or simultaneous

The Matrixes: A General Approach

combinations (syntagm) and a system of selection from which they are constructed (paradigm). We must now distinguish the paradigm from the matrix. The matrix is a social organism or autopoietic third order unity at a human scale that constitutes collective identities throughout a period of time and in certain locations by shared conventions and practices. The paradigm, on the other hand, is the bidimensional projection of a matrix. Paradigms consequently are always a derivative of the matrix like photographs of three-dimensional objects or a keyboard version of orchestra music, losing a good part of their complexity while maintaining some family resemblances or a relation of iconicity (in Peircean terms) with their source. Thus a paradigm is a partial synchronic cut of a dynamic changing matrix at a certain point and time, as a photogram from a film.

I asked myself: Why insist in using the same term "paradigm" that Barthes used to refer to Saussurean linguistic "systems" and Kuhn (1970) to scientific models? Why not simply call them "matricial projections" to simplify things? The reason is that it seems to me that Saussurean linguistic paradigms are themselves projections from particular social systems. For instance, a language seen as "*la langue*" is a projection of the activities and beliefs proper to a social matrix. We can say the same about painting: if we take cubism as an art paradigm, it is a projection of a section of the art matrix in a certain point and time, namely, of a group of painters in Paris during the first half of the twentieth century, who projected a view of reality of a certain social group where multiperspective, dynamism and fragmentation were very significative. As models, Kuhnian paradigms in science do not differ that much from Saussurean: Newtonianism reflects what scientists considered most significant at a certain time and place of scientific evolution. Paradigms are like an instantaneous photograph taken of a live organism that renders an image of it at a given moment, a view of what was significant enough to be named or studied.

Matrixes determine particular combinations of dramatics and rhetoric, and paradigms project them and transmit part of their structure to other matrixes. Paradigms are the traces of matrixes and as such are indexical by existential contiguity signs of them. The relation between the matrixes and paradigms may be, consequently, not only metonymic (by existential contiguity) but also sinecdoquical (the part for the whole) and metaphorical (by analogical projection) as well. In other words, it is metaphorical when what a paradigm projects is another matrix by structural similarity, and it is sinecdoquical when it projects a sector of the matrix that stands for its totality.[3] So the paradigm is experienced in terms of the matrix and vice versa. These mechanisms of projection somehow resemble what Lakoff and Johnson (1999) designate by "metaphorical mapping" hiding certain aspects and outlining others that seem more pertinent to the analogy. All metaphorical projections happen, according to these authors, from the most concrete and immediate experiences towards the most abstract. For that reason, projections always begin from the matrixes, because they are perceived and practiced concretely by subjects in their daily materiality.

---

3   I understand by "metaphor" what Lakoff and Johnson proposed in their cognitive approach, namely "*the essence of the metaphor is to understand and to experience one thing in terms of another*". (1999; 1980, 5; italics in original)

Social matrixes such as the family, juridical, school, military, religion, or medical are defined by the phylogenetic and ontogenetic experience accumulated in the collective and individual subjects. What characterizes these matrixes is that they not only reproduce their own paradigms but are also simultaneously crossed by diverse paradigmatic elements that intertwine them with other matrixes. Consequently, we will be able to distinguish paradigmatic regularities in diverse contexts, since matrixes define paradigms and particular syntactic rules in the construction of statements. The mother who reads the Bible to her children when laying them down to sleep makes a statement in the family matrix by the projection of the religion paradigm. And to the inverse, God seen as a father of humankind or the Virgin Mary as the holy mother, as well as the priest who is addressed precisely as "father", all project the family paradigm to the religious matrix.

We all participate diachronically and synchronously in diverse matrixes throughout our life and in a same day or moment. As daughters or mothers we are located in the family matrix, as students or teachers in the school matrix, as patients or doctors in the medical, as Catholics or Moslems in the religious, as Arabs or Gypsies in the ethnic, as umpires, public or players in the sport matrix. This multiplicity of matrixes can occur in two ways: *overlapping* or *sequentially*. It is sequential when the subject goes from a matrix to another on a day or a lifetime (from the school to the professional in diverse stages, or from business to the touristic during annual periods). It is overlapping when a person participates simultaneously in several matrixes (familiar, sexual, professional, and religious). Overlapping can be total or partial: *Total overlapping* occurs because we are simultaneously located in sexual, generational, national, professional, global, familiar, and class matrixes. Partial overlapping are paradigmatic projections in a same matrix of others, as when in school we practice sports, march as soldiers, and commemorate national or religious festivities. The matricial sequences can be reversible or irreversible. They are reversible when they obey a schedule and irreversible when they depend on life cycles. In sum, matrixes and paradigms can be overlapping (partial or totally), and sequential (reversible or irreversible).

While the matrixes are collective, the combination of their paradigmatic traces is unique in each individual. To have a more graphic idea of this concept of paradigms, consider the following example. If we would paint different images in each of several transparent glasses and superposed them, we could see a complex drawing with certain depth. Something similar happens to subjectivity. At first sight it seems that subjectivity is unitary, single, interior, and particular to each individual. What happens is that it is conformed by several layers as superposed glasses in which, although the effect can be unique and individualized, the components are shared with other subjects all determined by common *a priori*. These layers are the identities in relation to which subjects enunciate and interpret their experiences. Such identities are projected from social matrixes inasmuch the subject has deep roots in them, and stands on or is planted in them. Subjectivity is a unique combination of collective conditions.

Chapter 26

Diachronic and Synchronic Perspective of Cultural Matrixes

One does not feel the same being three years old as 80, being a man or a woman, Mexican or Japanese, growing up in a conservative or an anarchistic family, in wealthy or marginalized classes, being Moslem or Taoist, a scientist or a plumber, living in a lumpen or a luxurious residential neighborhood, in a deformed or an attractive body, with an assertive or a timorous character, being loved or being ignored. What constitutes the aesthetic subject is this unique combination of elements from diverse matrixes. There is something in common among women in being so, or among Eskimos as such, in being ill, professing the Mennonite faith, playing in an orchestra, and so on.

Depending on how complex a society may be, we can distinguish a variety of matrixes. In many Western societies we can trace the highly differentiated medical, juridical, educational, religional, bureaucratic, touristic, athletic, family, financial, national, mediatic, military, funerary, even urban gangs and as many groups sharing conventions one may find in a given society, on a macro or micro scale, clandestine or official, formally constituted or spontaneously generated. Whenever certain practices and perceptions become stabilized in a certain group to generate a shared identity, it is possible to speak of a social matrix. Each matrix has its own rules for rhetorical production, rules that may be relatively flexible and change, but established by a struggle for legitimation among diverse social sectors. The gender matrix, for instance, tacitly or explicitly assigns in particular cultures ways of dressing and behaving according to gender, as in the military matrix according to rank, or in the educational according to the role of student, director, prefect or teacher.

Matrixes, however, are not equal to institutions. An institution is only a segment of a matrix in which certain practices ossify by habit and become officialized by explicit norms, as a Constitution, a penal code, a school statute, and so on. Institutions fix behaviors, whereas matrixes generate them with more flexibility and less predictability. All institutions are therefore part of the matrixes, but not all matrixes are institutional. A gang, a sect, a hippie commune are matricial without being institutional. While matrixes are bio-cultural and their traditions are transmitted informally by imitation, institutions are official and their conventions are inculcated by formalized education. The educational matrix, for example, has matricial zones where play and discovery are possible as in alternative pedagogical models, and institutional zones that impose grades, discipline, and schemes of behavior for the acquisition of homogenized informative packages.

Diachronic perspective of the matrixes

Cultural matrixes are neither universal nor permanent. They have been products of a slow process of diversification that branched off from an integrated cultural zygote. This matricial zygote begins from Paleolithic stages where the tribe was the matricial unit in which all other communal acts converged and overlapped. The tribe is the origin of family and religion, of medicine and work, of painting and magic, hunting and dance. In magic practices, the shaman-artist-leader places himself at the root of social division of labor that will develop both vertically through stratification and horizontally through diversification. Cave paintings are indexical of this original zygote matrix from which one can infer primordial fascination by the human ability of visual mimesis, the origin of gestural, acoustic and verbal languages, of hunting as collective labor, of curative rites and symbolism, territorial exclusivity, and so on.

If the mother of all the matrixes is the family, the matriarch of all matrixes is religion. In addition to presenting human values, the Bible provides images of gender roles and teaching, of the State, the military, the juridical, the artistic, of the idea of nation and religion, of the heroes (incarnated particularly in the identities of David and Solomon), and the God.

In Greek classical antiquity, the *polis* or city-state was the original matrix around which the others gravitated, namely, the medical, religious and artistic, the family and laboral through slaves, later imitated at another scale by the Roman Empire where the State, the military, and the legal matrixes predominated. The Middle Ages were characterized in Western civilization by the domination and institutionalization of the Christian and Moslem religious matrixes and their projection on others, specially the military. By the beginnings of the Renaissance, the gradual secularization of diverse matrixes enabled greater autonomy of commercial, artistic, and scientific matrixes. With the development of the bourgeoisie, each of these matrixes diversified even more and progressively acquired a specific character until the present, when sub-matrixes ramify in greater and greater degrees of specialization. In totalitarian systems this process of matricial diversification reverses and implodes by merging all matrixes within the State: the juridical punishes deviations from the State's official doctrine, the medical builds sanatoriums for ideological dissidents, the artistic represents the official ideology and is forced to become propaganda, the academic watches that the production of knowledge does not deviate from political doctrine, that in turn operates as a substitute of the religious matrix.

This regressive process of matricial implosion seems to be taking place in the dark side of the process of globalization with a very amiable face in the TV screens, but not as much in industrial assembly plants. What was a process of matricial differentiation is now stickily agglutinating around a single one that seems to be the new matron of all matrixes: the financial-corporational matrix. This matrix no longer only projects its paradigm onto others but seems to be progressively absorbing them so that diverse matrixes operate as branches or affiliates of the global financial matrix. This appears to be happening with the State and national matrixes, as well as with the educational and sports. Such matricial agglutination is made even more evident in the promotion of politicians, doctors, artists, religions, and universities

Diachronic and Synchronic Perspective of Cultural Matrixes 187

as commodities, and in the promotion of commodities as pseudo-persons. If during the bourgeois era the degree of civilization (not of culture) of a certain society could have been measured by the variety and autonomy of its matrixes, at the present globalization stage the process appears to be reversed into a generalized entropy: on one hand homogenization at the macrosocial scale of technological and financial supremacy and on the other heterogeneity at an infinitesimal signic order of brands and minutely diversified products.

Synchronic perspective of the matrixes

I will very schematically illustrate some matrixes that without doubt deserve a more detailed study, but this brief overview will at least suffice for a simultaneous comparative approach. In the chapters that follow, we will examine other matrixes in a more elaborate way.

The *State matrix* is not only an abstract system of functionaries and administrators that perform their duty like bees in a beehive. To maintain the basic cohesion and legitimation for a social matrix as big and expensive as the State, a powerful *latching-on* symbol is necessary, something strong and attractive enough to pull people in and keep them functioning towards its reproduction. The apparent symbol on which this matrix is based as object of appeal is *responsibility*. In a democratic State, the leaders are exclusively elected to assume the responsibility of decisions and operations that affect the well-being or the misery of society. Unfortunately, this symbol is almost always only apparent and substituted by another whose pull is much stronger: that of *superiority* because its operational function of administration is confused with a situation of rank or hierarchy. The State matrix is invested with an auratic quality to disguise its bleakness, and is made to appear as the most exciting agonistic game one can play beyond sports. Consequently, instead of evaluating civil employees by how they perform, they are valued by the place they occupy. There are many who do have a vocation for public service, but the upper levels of this matrix are mainly occupied by people who *latch-on* to the symbol of superiority and its agonistic game.

This craving for superiority, an object of the most intense passions and trophy for a sometimes insatiable voracity (and which does not equal to power, since there are many kinds of power: the power to cure, to speak, to love, to solve problems), defines the political profession of a great number of the members of this matrix, to the degree that the mechanisms to verify responsibility remain blurred, whereas those signs that exhibit superiority are quite conspicuous, aesthetically conspicuous. Thus the State becomes what Andras Hegedüs denominated as a "system of organized irresponsibility" (mentioned by Bahro 1979, 132) but unlike the Hungarian motto of "better not do anything than do it wrong" what often prevails is "better do anything than do it well", just for the sake of appearing to be active and dramaturgically justifying a job. Trivial declarations are constantly made and minutely analyzed, whereas many crucial actions are casually ignored. Of course philanthropy and vocation for service are not wholly absent in the State matrix, but these virtues do not seem necessary at least for a political career (for more elaboration on the State matrix, see Mandoki 2007).

To inspire respect and credibility, a State requires not only semiotic syntagms but aesthetic displays in every register also. Its semiotics may be diffuse, often ambiguous and vague, but its exhibition of aesthetic strategies to establish its collective identity is indispensable. Accordingly, we always find somatic rituals (official celebrations of independence, receptions, elections); public speeches (presidential reports, harangues and oratory in Congress, messages to the Nation, candidates' public debates, appearances before the Senate); scopic and acoustic emblems (flags, national anthems, emblems, the presidential band, monuments to heroes); as well as symbolic spaces (Palace of Government, House of Representatives, historical sites) no matter what tendency or regime is in control at a given State.

Since Hamurabi's code and Roman law, the *juridical matrix* has been linked to the State and to the religious matrix, in some cases remaining tightly bound to religion until today (as in Islamic law by the *Qur'an* and *Sunnah*). All identities constituted by the juridicial matrix are organized around its symbol, *legality*, which is administered, weighed, and calculated by those who produce and exercise their professional identity in this institution against those who acquire the undesirable condition of defendants or prisoners. The main stratagem played here is proxemically dividing identities between those who remain on one side and those on the other of the juridical border. On one side are the judges, lawyers, and judicial agents, police, prosecutors, guards, detectives, juries, witnesses, and plaintiffs. On the other side are the suspects, defendants, accused, sentenced, appealed, imprisoned, exonerated. To play this deadly serious game in which no less than the life of individuals is at stake, aesthetization is necessary to make the legal seem also legitimate. How this is done is nicely described by Foucault, particularly in the beginning of *Discipline and Punish* through the public dramatization and rhetoric exhibition of punishment against the regicide Damiens. (Foucault [1975] 1983, 11–13)

In the lexic register, Roger W. Shuy (1987, 43–56) examined almost a thousand hours of secret tape recordings made by the FBI of cross-examinations to obtain evidence from the declarations before a jury. Giving testimony is a linguistic event of unequal powers where the person questioned can only aspire to have some control over his or her own declaration, not easily achieved. Shuy analyzed the tricks and tactics that agents use to intimidate, persuade, and even entice witnesses. A person's future may depend on the nuances of the words said, on the precise selection of terms for the construction of syntagms in testimonies and their persuasive effect. The lexics of the juridical matrix lie in this infinite discursive construction of jurisprudence, specialized jargon, and forensic rhetorics whereupon legal and official documents and practices are deployed. The metallic acoustics of the iron against iron in prison gates and doors is characteristic of this matrix. In addition, the voice of guards and public prosecutors to intimidate and control the defendants and prisoners, who in turn present submissive or desperate intonations, the neutral and composed tone of the judges, the vehement inflection of the plaintiffs form part of this matrix.

Why put on such hilarious wigs and gowns to perform a deadly serious act such as a condemning or exculpating a defendant? Do Dutch and English judges, as well as many of their postcolonial colleagues in Africa, really need those funny costumes to be fair and impartial? These weird scopic emphatics certainly illustrate what symbols are about, as explained in Part 4. The temporal weight of tradition on

Diachronic and Synchronic Perspective of Cultural Matrixes 189

which the authority of the judge lies, acquires here a dominant role. Such garments appear ridiculous and old fashioned, as an imperial French wig worn today by an African judge or prosecutor, but it seems as if the wig would have a magical power to symbolize the weight of law, tradition and justice, as it would by itself inspire credibility and respect. These symbols are part of an aesthetic ceremony for the conferral of authority that is designed to endow this position with an emotional meaning, a social legitimation, and an adherence to what it symbolizes. Other more practical scopic proxemics such as distinctive clothes in jails function to separate prisoners from guards, workers, and visitors. The watchtowers, the panoptic disposition of prison cells, the height of walls that surround it, the barbed wires, corridors without windows that twist and prevent to see beginning and end (as the one leading from the entrance at the *Reclusorio Femenil Oriente* in Mexico City), the iron doors, the austere cheap style of chairs and tables, of bunk beds and toilets within the cells constitute, as a whole, a specific scopics in the juridical matrix. Yet among all registers, it is the somatic that the juridical matrix most arbitrates: what must be decided is whether, how and when should the body of the indicted be tortured, secluded, evicted, or killed. In Kafka's *Penitentiary Colony*, the body has to endure the inscription of the felony on its very skin; this symbolic somato-lexics of justice is the perfect metaphor of the aesthetization of Law.

The symbol or adhesion core of the *military matrix* is exhibited as *honorability* strictly depending upon a code of honor and courage. Its predominant lexic emphatics is displayed in slogans of loyalty and patriotism, of strict obedience to order and military rank. Acoustics are deployed by rhythmical marches, shouted orders, drums and trumpets of military bands to explosion blasts. Somatic emphatics unfold here by characteristically solemn gestures and the kinetics of rigid postures, fast, compact and vigorous greetings, unison marches and military parades. Somatic fluxion in this matrix is retentive in relation to the superiors in rank because it demands a total discipline and control, and expulsive to the degree of being allowed, if not forced, even to kill. Its scopic emphatics are displayed through uniforms, short haircuts, warfare technology, flags and emblems of military rank, and so on. This matrix is projected onto others: schools imitating marches and the pledges to the flag, or the entertainment industry portraying battles and wars in film. It also imports the artistic matrix for representing itself through paintings, statues, and monuments of Generals and other hierarchical figures.

The *tourism matrix* is defined by the symbol of *transitoriety* (from the Latin *transitus*, crossing and *transitorious*, fleeting) in the double sense of passing and of brevity. The scopics of this matrix generate what Marc Augé denominates "non-places". "If a place can be defined as identity place, relational and historical, a space that can be defined neither as space of identity nor as relational nor as historical, will define a non-place." (Augé 1998, 83) Thus there are tourists who look for "authentic places" journeying through non-places such as airports, bus terminals, and hotel chains from Chicago to Cairo craving for aesthetic diversity but keep themselves in almost identical styled settings of Holiday Inns and McDonald's. Subjects in this matrix are temporarily freed from their habitual identities and transit in their role of tourists. Lexic proxemics in this matrix unfolds through tourist maps and travel manuals, tourist guides' speeches, narratives that the travelers exhibit to impress their

190   *Everyday Aesthetics*

friends and relatives back home. In the acoustic register, this matrix uses the typical lobby style music and airport's often unintelligible but constant flight announcements. The somatics of tourism is focused towards a relaxed and comfortable emphatics and a dynamic kinetics with a centrifugal fluxion to include the greatest amount of places in the shortest possible time. Among the scopic emphatics in this matrix are special outfits for traveling, hotel architecture, stars hotel categories and restaurants, in addition to props and gadgets such as suitcases, camping equipment, photo and video cameras, postcards, pamphlets, local T-shirts for tourists and souvenirs, all of which is globally sold at airports but appears to be local. Since this matrix is associated to leisure and pleasure, many other matrixes paradigmatically import it for improving their own image and attracting their members, like the State, financial, and academic matrixes hiring hotels for congresses.

Based on *mortality* as its symbol, the *funerary matrix* probably derived from the religious matrix until it became independent with its own discursive style as a secular civil organization. Inhumations, burials, inurnments, corteges, incinerations, funeral services and rituals, its own professional embalmers and morticians, gravediggers, sextons, and mourners, all form part of this inevitable social matrix. Its lexic emphatics are displayed through particular speech styles in condolences, epigrams on the gravestones, epideictic speeches or eulogies that praise the deceased, obituaries, and so on. Distinctive acoustic emphatics use low tones of voice, slow funeral music, silences and weeping of relatives and lamenters or professional mourners, muffled drums, dead marches, tolling bells, requiem music, and so on. On the somatic register, hugging the defunct's relatives and processions, carrying the coffin over the shoulders, and the act of embalming are all aesthetically presented to create an effect of solemnity. The design of cemeteries and graveyards, the styles of sepultures, cremation sites and the cinerarium or the ossuarium, the funeral coach, the caskets, urns, gravestones, coffins, flowers and crowns, plates and tombstones, monuments and memorials, the clothes, make-up and embalmment of the dead for the funeral, are some instances in the scopic register in this matrix. Aesthetics helps us face death's implacable void.

When referring to the commercial-financial-corporational matrix, nobody is surprised that its symbol for *latching-on/by* is *profit*. Included in this matrix are the traveling salesman, the peddler, the sidewalk merchant, the auctioneer, street markets, shopkeepers, retailers in commercial warehouses, malls, boutiques up to managers in great commercial corporations, and stock dealers at the international centers of Stock Exchange. This matrix provokes the excitement of playing snakes and ladders. Its lexic fluxion is centrifugal because it floods the media and stalks the consumer wherever he may be. The acoustic fluxion uses particular kinds of music in commercial malls and advertisement jingles according to the customers' social status. Somatic proxemics of this matrix have significantly shortened with the introduction of self-service supermarkets offering products to sight, touch, smell, and taste, allowing also to try on the clothes before purchasing and taste new products. Its scopic emphatics have become so sophisticated creating a real poetics of sideboards and packaging, as well as incredibly elaborated evocative images in magazines to promote fashion products, often overlapping with the artistic matrix. At a corporational level this matrix displays monumental scopics by skyscrapers

Diachronic and Synchronic Perspective of Cultural Matrixes 191

such as the twin towers of New York's World Trade Center and its equivalents around the world. In its interior a precise scopic proxemics of hierarchical division by floors and office spaces is deployed, with distinctive furniture to mark ranks (as at the present PEMEX Tower in Mexico City) with particular clothes' brands for each category. We can find diverse lexic tactics and epistolary styles in executives' meetings, memoranda, e-mail and telephone relations between managers and towards subordinates. The projection of the family matrix by the emphatics of "the great family" is a common resource to obtain the adhesion of the employees to the company. But the dominant lexic emphatics in this matrix accentuates efficiency, competitiveness, productivity, calculation of investment, risks and gains, and of course, loyalty to the company. In the kinetic modality this matrix sets out the maximum dynamism without jeopardizing solidity. Financial fluxion is aggressively open in its commercial initiatives to reach consumers and closed in decision-making and concealment of risks. Dramatic modalities are displayed in company ceremonies such as promotions, birthday cakes to "personalize" the forced impersonality of employees, and "fraternal" celebrations of Christmas and New Year. This is the matrix that has been increasingly becoming dominant in the Western world paradigmatically projecting itself upon other matrixes. We are approaching a state of financial totalitarianism. Accordingly, academic and scientific circles are expected to play in this grand casino and become as competitive, efficient, technological, and successful as a multinational corporation. This aesthetics of success is consequently imposed on children at school in exclusion of other basic values such as playing other games besides *agon*, the right of difference and the valuation of the process over the result. The commercial matrix overlaps the family and religious matrixes in the massive effort of purchasing gifts for mother's day, father's day, Christmas, and so on and literally and symbolically sucks up most of their employees' energy.

It is tempting to include the *sport matrix* in the artistic matrix (as Welsch 2005 has) because it shares with it numerous characteristics such as technical excellence, the purpose of amusement, professionalization, spectacularization, and the exhibition of playfulness. Moreover, both matrixes have common origins in the archaic religious matrix in Greece until each became a secular spectacle made by professionals, no longer in honor of the Gods but for the distraction of men. Its trajectory through the Greek stadium (parallel in its origins to the Greek amphitheater) became later, during the Roman Empire, a spectacle at the Coliseum. In addition to being spectacular, sports are easy to understand, and for that reason attract the masses maintaining the agonistic spirit that characterized Greek tragedy (of *agon*, "confrontation, originating of the ritual sphere, either of action, or of word, between a choir and an actor or between two choirs, or even between two actors" Rodríguez Adrados 1983, 609).

The soccer player trains in the technique of kicking a ball from diverse angles as the painter in the technique of perspective to obtain the illusion of a three-dimensional space in a plane. Nevertheless, what distinguishes the sport matrix from the artistic has greater weight than what both share: their semantic and syntactic density. I do not intend to say that there is no meaning and structure in sports, since no social activity lacks any of them. In the sport matrix the axis of the signic is established by the rules of the game that distinguish one game from others. Its symbolism is related to patriotic or class denotations and connotations, and expresses the aesthetization

192 *Everyday Aesthetics*

and display of energy in the effort to win. On the other hand, in the artistic matrix semantics are multiple and complex, since artworks can refer to love and hate, life and death, solitude, fate, reality and dream, betrayal and loyalty. As far as the syntactic dimension, both matrixes differ radically, because in sports it doesn't really matter how a point is obtained as long as it sticks to the rules of the game, whereas in art the "how" is practically everything. For dancers, technique and meaning conveyed by body movement and gesture are fundamental, whereas for sportsmen it is enough to arrive at the goal as soon as possible. A sport match is not a spectacle constructed beforehand correcting errors before it is presented; it is improvised and performed live before the public. Sports are *praxis* rather than *poiesis*. Nevertheless, in both matrixes aesthetics are essential since we would otherwise not find such fervent *latching-on* to the triumphs and defeats of an athlete or team as we do to an artwork's mastery. Celebrities of sports and mass arts are equally adored and similarly paid. The dramatics of their rituals and ceremonies, the *pathos* of their victories and defeats, of their bets and tenacious exercising, fanatics' intense *latching-on* to their favorite team contribute to conform this matrix whose symbol (who can doubt it?) is *triumph*. The sport matrix unfolds a profuse lexic fluxion in journalistic media overflowing with sport commentators and athletes' declarations for interviews before and after competitions. The centrifugal acoustic fluxion radiates in fanfares, regulated shouts, team fans' clubs, slogans and hymns (projected from the State or military matrixes). The public outcry "oleeee" and "siquiti bum …", "hurrah", "Bravo" up to the ejaculatory "goooooooooooal" exclamations are typical in this matrix.

The somatic is the dominant register in this matrix, as everything depends on the corporeal excellence of the sportsman. Sport kinetics are infinitely dynamic and operate through a somato-technology that pushes the body beyond its limits with an emphatics of record breaking year by year. Sport scopics unfold in the monumental architecture of the stadium, tracks, rings and arenas, its uniforms and banderoles (imported from the military paradigm), sport cars, an immense collection of gadgets, and the carnivalesque make-up of fanatics at a match. The paradigmatic traces of this matrix are projected or exported to the educational matrix in sport competitions, to the tourism matrix by special costumes and sport activities offered for tourists, in business corporations when using sport figures as role models for the promotion of their products, and in the family matrix when sport becomes a basic activity for the family. This matrix today is sponsored by the financial matrix with which it totally overlaps producing enormous capital gains, as well as with the State matrix due to its effective potential of recruiting massive adhesion. In the Olympics, the sport matrix imports national matrixes and projects the military in an agonistic spectacle of a vicarious war. The projection of the State upon the sport matrix is eloquently expressed in the agglomeration of fans at national symbolic sites after important competitions (like at the Monument of Independence at Mexico City after Mexico's triumphs and defeats at the Soccer World Cup).

Although the matrixes intercross and overlap one another through their paradigmatic traces to the degree that sometimes is not easy to distinguish between one matrix and another or between a matrix and its paradigm, we can still speak of certain autonomy of a matrix with respect to others. For example, in a semiosic event as, say, vacations, the family matrix is juxtaposed with the tourism matrix, and the

Diachronic and Synchronic Perspective of Cultural Matrixes 193

commercial matrix with the sports. To celebrate Christmas has one meaning in the religious matrix (the birth of Jesus), another in the family matrix (exchange of gifts and inexcusable attendance of the family members to a special supper with particular dishes according to each tradition, namely stuffed turkey in the USA, cod in Spain, romeritos in Mexico). This event has another meaning for the commercial matrix (rise of sales, Christmas advertisement campaigns, calculated and obligatory buys of commodities to reciprocate gifts) and at the office (Christmas decorations and toasts, gifts exchange), the tourism matrix (leisure to travel), in school (vacations), for artists (creating products for Christmas sales' opportunities, Christmas cards, Christmas as a topic for music, theater, film, painting), in the juridical with special concessions on visits and food to inmates, and finally in the medical and funerary by the increase of automobile accidents, incidence of depression cases and suicides.

If we explore the meanings that a particular topic acquires across diverse matrixes, for example "blood", we will find surprising dissimilitude illustrating the degree in which contexts determine meaning. While in the Catholic faith blood is venerated in crucifixes symbolizing the sacrifice of Christ and symbolized by the wine during the mass, for Judaism is the origin of tribal descendency but is considered impure in food and in menstruating women; in the military, blood means heroism, whereas in the medical matrix it can indicate hemorrhage and risk of death, as in the artistic it serves to enhance horror genres, particularly *gore* films, or the raw expressionism of artworks like Andres Serranos's *La Morgue* photographs or Joseph Beuys use of it as a material together with felt, fat, and honey. This variation of effects by a single scopic-somatic syntagm according to the context makes it impossible to find a general inventory of aesthetic forms, reason why we must proceed to analyze each matrix in particular.

Chapter 27

The Family Matrix

Matrix of all matrixes, the family is unequivocally the origin of culture. From that simple albeit infinitely complex act of procreation a great diversity of matrixes unfold throughout human history. Within the family matrix emerges not only the first step that takes us from the biome to the culturome. The aesthetic dimension also is born as the first, and from this most intense act of *latching-on*: the infant's to the mother's breast that will be culturalized through various vehicles of aesthesis as joy or agony (see Chapter 8).

Each matrix is based on a particular symbol from which it is constituted and to which its members adhere, although it may be historically transformed. Such symbols are the social or collective nipples for aesthetic *latching-on* by the weight in time, matter, and energy deposited on them. For the family matrix, the symbol is *maternity*, since the minimum unit from which it can be constituted as such is simply a female and her offspring. This is the case from the most archaic groups that did not yet associate reproduction to the male, until the present Western societies which, in cases of divorce, still privilege the rights of the mother over those of the father. Many will consider this ginecocentric approach to the family matrix politically incorrect, questionable and yet, the commonest, most universal game in this matrix is still girls playing mothers with their dolls. Some feminists attribute this fact to sheer cultural conditioning, without which, they assume, we would find more boys playing father with their dolls; but given a different somatic constitution, there is certainly a bio-psycho-chemico-morphological difference we are reminded of at least monthly.

In every matrix, there is usually one register that becomes more salient than the others (in sports it is somatics, in the juridical, political and academic it is lexics, in the funerary and military, somatics). In the family matrix, the dominant register is the somatic. Consequently, it may not be accidental that its symbol is basically corporeal related to the uterus and the hymen. The family unit is established in all registers from the engagement and the wedding which socially legitimizes the loss of hymen and intimate somatic proxemics between the couple, their cohabiting and procreating and the resulting responsibility for their offspring. Contrary to Sperber's (1996) claims that we are not speaking of the same thing when we refer to a marriage in different cultures, the wedding is the most universal aesthesic and semiosic statement, as it occurs in all cultures and is displayed by both aesthetic coordinates and semiotic axes. This ritual is, however, meticulously designed in a particular way in each culture, and the symbols and signs that unfold in each case vary, but the emphatics (of fidelity), the proxemics (the closest possible in the sexual act and mother-child physical relation), the fluxion (centripetal as a couple, centrifugal in its descendants), and the kinetics (hopefully stable, even beyond the death) are relatively the same across cultural differences. A dowry and the transactions of goods between

196 *Everyday Aesthetics*

both families is a common cultural custom that culminates in the great *potlatch* of nuptial celebration. It is all symbolized and aesthetically displayed by the material investment through the scopic register on the bride's expensive dress and jewels, the decorated stage set with flowers and ornaments at the ceremonial site, the somatics of the banquet and the nuptial act, the acoustics of nuptial march which in Western societies it is often Wagner, Haydn or Mendelssohn's music, and the ritual lexics by statements such as "do you accept X as your ...", "I declare you husband and wife ..." that constitutes a new reality for the couple in their social context.

Maternity as a symbol emerges from the ancestral time load connecting us to the very origins not only of culture but of life through human and animal species by the physical somatic link between mother and child, the strong affective weight of pain and joy in giving birth, as well as the intensively vigorous acts of conception, labor and parturition. However, as Engels argued in *The Origin of the Family, Private Property and the State*, patriarchy takes over matriarchal configurations in a given social group by the establishment of monogamy related to the principle of private property; and thus maternity as a symbol is substituted by virginity. From there on somatics and scopics become increasingly linked, the woman's body becomes part of the husband's material property and the matrix revolves around mater-paternity. When the affective symbolic load turns from maternity to virginity, what becomes more significant is the anxiety of losing it, the commitment to the nuptial oath, the expectations—generally on side of the fiancée—around the wedding ceremony and so on. The material load lies in the acquisition and property of the woman with her virginity as a guarantee seal symbolized in some traditions by the ring metaphorical of the vagina or of the male's money. As its dominant modality, proxemics establishes the difference between "we" as members of the family and "them" or "we" the couple and "them" the forbidden sexual partners.

The registers of rhetorics in the family matrix

It is through rhetorics where we establish marked differences in the practices of each culture in regards to the family. For Western cultures, the lexic act of the bride changing her last name from her father's for her husband's is not only signic but symbolic in the lexic register. Other typical lexic proxemic changes occur when spouses begin calling each other names such as "darling", "my dear", "sweetheart", "honey", and so on. Lexic emphatics and fluxion also change when the first baby arrives, so that its burping or defecating become important subjects of conversation. The interaction becomes totally centripetal in regards to the couple and around the baby, and lexic kinetics stabilize in repetitive syntagms by routine and elliptical expressions of implicated meanings.

As the distance between the couple shortens, new ranges of acoustic communication are allowed to express intimacy or cohabitation, from whispering and murmuring to each other's ears to panting, snoring, whining, bellowing, etc. that are strictly forbidden in other matrixes. When the baby appears in the family scene, a peculiar acoustic emphatic intonation never used before unfolds: that high pitched tone called "baby talk" used by parents when addressing the child, and that

The Family Matrix 197

the infant probably finds irritating, accustomed to more subtle, low keyed sounds of intrauterine life.

Family somatics range from sexual intercourse and penetration between the couple and pregnancy, childbirth and breast feeding for the female. This matrix establishes the sensibility we may likely have towards our body throughout our lifetime, enjoying it, enduring it, being ashamed or proud of it, open or closed to tenderness or cruelty. Somatic strategies during infancy will also regulate to a significant degree nurturing and self-confidence, as well as aggression by or rejection of physical contact. The scents that the family kitchen gives off when the stew boils, the aroma of fresh bed sheets, the smell of bread in the oven, of boiling milk, the taste of home seasoning are all somatic opportunities for *latching-on* in this matrix. Although certain aspects of somatic rhetorics are partly genetic in origin (gesturing, for example) and others are acquired by unconscious imitation, the family will be in charge of pointing up how social interactions should take place such as greeting, the intensity and duration of looking at others, the catexis of the body, facial and corporeal movements, personal hygiene and self grooming.

By aesthetic strategies in the scopic register, high and middle class families in Western urban societies prepare the image they want to present of their collective identity. This look is produced by the setting of the city, neighborhood, and street chosen, together with the staging of house or apartment in the style of the living room, dining room, kitchen, bath, and bedrooms (in addition to the automobile as an extension of the house), and the use of props such as furniture and decoration as well as the costumes worn at home (pajamas, robes, slippers) and elsewhere. During pregnancies, items in the scopic register proliferate around the house, beginning with the cradle, tulle decorations and ribbon bows, mobiles, plush dolls, baby strollers, diapers, pajamas, little blankets, hats, knitted socks, dressers, cribs, armoires, car seats, swings, high chairs, playpens, bathtubs, bassinets, linens, and so on. The newborn becomes object of aesthetic latching for the parents who are moved by the scopics of its tiny body, the high pitched acoustics of its weeping, the somatics of its gestures and of its vehement search for the nipple. On the lexic register, parents are often delighted by detecting the baby's first intelligible word.

There are diverse rhetorical tactics in the relation between mother and babies such as *hyperbole* by augmentation to overprotect and overwhelm them with attention or by diminution depriving them of affective energy and comfort. In the lexic register, it is frequent to find figures such as *euphemism* when parents use other names like "wee wee" instead of penis, the usual *periphrasis* of the story of the stork and the *metaphor* of the seed penetrating the earth, or *suspension* "when you're older, then ..." as replies to children's questions about sex and reproduction. The lexic-acoustic *aposiopesis* of the sudden anger that interrupts an expression due to an abrupt change of mood is common in interactions within this matrix. In somatic rhetorics, the figure of *catachresis* and substitution often occurs, for example among single mothers who substitute the absent father by another male figure (such as a teacher, their brother or father) as an affective and masculine model. In the scopic register *catachresis* is expressed through expensive gifts to replace the lack of affection or attention. A somatic *alliteration* occurs when kissing the nose, the hand, the other hand, the little foot of the child and *periphrasis* avoids kissing the taboo points. The *anacoluthon*

198 *Everyday Aesthetics*

often turns the child's attention somewhere else during a temper tantrum. Scopic *suspension* can be displayed by dressing a boy or girl too childishly for their age thus unconsciously trying to slow down their feeling of growing up. Scopic *alliteration* is most commonly found in personal or family collections such as stamps, coins, elephants, ashtrays, and other objects displayed in the house. We can find many other examples, but these may suffice to illustrate family rhetorics.

The modalities of the dramatic in the family matrix

Each family faces the others in a manner homologous to the individual facing others according to the dramaturgical model that Goffman ([1959] 1981) applied to the presentation of the self in daily life. From prosaics, such strategy is aesthetically displayed for constitution and legitimation of the family's collective identity and of each member's role and personal identity within it. The distinction between individuality and identity indicated with respect to particular subjects in Chapter 6 extends to the next collective level in the family matrix, since personal as well as collective identities begin here. As in family rhetorics previously discussed, the context of our analyses of these strategies in the four modalities will be, broadly speaking, contemporary Western middle-class units.

Family proxemics

Proxemics in the lexic register is defined by the frequent use of pronouns like "we" and "them" to distinguish familiar territory, habits, values, and identities. Calling the wife "my woman", "my companion", "my wife", or "my spouse" always implies a lexic proxemics of different magnitudes: the implicit proxemics in "my wife" or "husband" is longer than in "my woman" or "my man", because the former stresses the formality or legality in the relation. In Spanish *"mi compañera"* enunciates a leftist lexic proxemics with connotations such as "combat partner", "equality of sexes", "comrade". The nicknames used within the family as "pumpkin", "babe", "sugar", "petkins", "hon" instead of calling them by their name before witnesses who know them, are other proxemic tactics in the lexic register.

The lexic proxemics of calling one's mother varies in a proxemic scale from "mother", "mama" or "mommy", to "ma", "mom", "mumsy", and so on. "Mother" is more distant and conservative, than "mama"; "mom" and "ma" are intimate whereas "mumsy" has a touch of humor. Calling parents by their name, on the other hand, annuls hierarchies and shortens proxemics by canceling the generational and authority distance, at the same time that extends it by replacing parental intimacy with a more friend like term. As can be seen in this case, words used not only produce meaning, but also display an attitude chosen by the participants.

Among Hungarians or Italians, Spanish, and other Mediterranean cultures acoustic proxemics allow raising one's voice at the slightest provocation, contrasting with other more acoustically restrained cultures such as the Mexican. In Mediterranean cultures, shouting means trust, short proxemics, expression of energy, whereas in

Mexico it means an intolerable loss of control that is interpreted not as proxemic modality but as aggressive emphatics and expulsive fluxion lacking self restraint.

In certain families somatic proxemics among members will be kept as long as with strangers, or as short as incestuous abuse. Social class proxemics define for each family whether the maid, the butler or the lady of the house opens the door and answers the telephone or not. The norm imposed by pediatricians to breast feed the baby according to the strict regime of ten minutes per breast every three or four hours (instead of when the baby needs and asks for it) projects the medical matrix to the family lengthening somatic proxemics with the baby. The substitution of breastfeeding by the baby's bottle and who takes care of the baby (the mother or the governess) are somatic proxemics, as well as the time that the mother takes in responding to the baby's crying. Tying babies with blankets and dressing them so tightly that they are unable to touch themselves or the contrary, letting them free to move as they please are also instances of somatic proxemics. So is caressing them or not, smiling, kissing and making frequent eye contact with them or not, carrying babies in the arms or keeping them in the stroller. Social classes generally correspond to proxemic classes where the height at the socio-economic level is usually directly proportional to proxemic distance between mother and child.

In the scopic register, family houses are surrounded by material or invisible walls marking the limits of their property, whether they allow or block strangers the view to their space. Scopic proxemics will also define the separation of the living spaces in common territories such as the living room, family room, garden, and dining room and the individual spaces such as bedrooms or personal bathrooms, between the double matrimonial bed or twin beds for the couple or even separated rooms, between the kitchen and the dining room (radically separated in families who employ servants), the bedrooms of the domestic employees from those of the family, and so on. The proxemics of interphone, of a heavy or light main door, of halls, corridors or intermediate rooms, the distribution of bathrooms in the familiar space are all comprised in this modality.

Family kinetics

Family kinetics is deployed through social mobility, family trips, the speed by which decisions are taken, the frequency in changes, the U-hauls from house to house, the dynamic or static organization of leisure, the type of activities the family enjoys and the rhythm by which these are performed. In dynamic families, lexic kinetics will tend to become elliptical to speed up interactions already saturated with common places and contextual implicatures to the degree that a member will know exactly what others are going to say even before they speak.

Acoustic kinetics at each domestic space is differentially regulated according to these two poles of the spectrum: homes where music is rarely listened to or where speaking is monotonous, in contrast with those where there is an acoustic vitality and a variety of sonorous experiences, particularly now when music has become a household commodity.

200 *Everyday Aesthetics*

The custom to hold the newborn in a tight blanket or a *rebozo* is a somatic kinetic modality of limiting its movements, although the justification that matrons give to this behavior is of proxemic character: they say that the baby requires this sensation of being tight to feel secure by its similarity with the prenatal state. Placing the baby in an open or closed place where it can look around and move through it or not, to educate children with the modality of "don't touch", "don't go" or, on the contrary, to grant them a certain freedom for exploring its surroundings and alter things at home are other manifestations of this modality. The habit of promoting static somatic kinetics for girls to spend hours sitting and playing "home" or "cooking" in contrast to boys' dynamic games with balls and scooters participate in the conformation of somatic kinetics in this matrix. Families of dynamic somatic kinetics enjoy camping and traveling to different places and will use every opportunity to go on a trip, in contrast to those who maintain it stable, rarely travel and if so to the same places. The rhythms by which activities are performed vary in each family; in some the preparation of food will take the whole morning, while in others only a few minutes. Some families will often need to entertain themselves away from home, whereas others prefer to remain home and enjoy reading books or are busy inside the house.

Conservative scopic kinetics in this matrix will tend to acquire conventional and solid furniture, faithful to the golden rule of the complete living room set of couch, sofa, coffee table, and love seat. In more extreme cases, families that display static kinetics will have embedded furniture fixed to the walls to express permanence. A more dynamic kinetics unfolds in families where each object is acquired independently (a chair from the flea market, the table from a cable spool, another chair by exchange with a friend, a crafted vernacular bench acquired in some trip, another inherited from grandmother, and so on) and there is total flexibility to change their location.

Family emphatics

Although a family's identity depends on all dramatic modalities, the particular emphatics that a family chooses are what constitute its identity. In capitalist societies where the family has stopped being primordially a unit of production turning towards consumption, where in addition available products have exponentially multiplied and meticulously diversified, family emphatics works as a compass for its members to orient themselves in the selection of commodities. There is therefore a complete repertoire of stereotypes to choose for constructing a particular family identity in terms of the products that it consumes. In the contemporary repertoire of Western middle-class families, one can distinguish the yuppie families (modern and successful) from the moralistic, the intellectualist, the New Agers, the massmediatic, the gay family, the athletic, the bohemian, the "autistic" family (where each member stays in isolation), the hippie, the extended family (with live-in in-laws, aunts, godmothers and grandparents), the brutal (battering husbands, raping fathers or stepfathers, mothers who prostitute their daughters or allow abuse of their children), the junkie family, the honeyed (target of the sentimentality market of hallmark cards and cute gifts), the hypochondriac (where members relate to each other on the basis of diseases that opportunely appear when attention is required), the sacrificial

The Family Matrix

(based on the reiterated sacrifice of one of its members for the sake of the other), the parasitic family (that depends on another familiar unit clinging economically to it), even the schizophrenic described by Bateson (1972) and as many categories as the reader can think of.

The imaginary stereotype presently promoted most by contemporary Western standards is the *yuppie* family. Families that try to construct their identity according to this particular emphatic will be able to distinguish with all precision among products' brands, jet set celebrities, and gadgets' know-hows relative to their status. For constituting their credibility under this emphatics, its members must be perfectly up-to-date in the fashion signic axis. Their acoustic emphatics will always be friendly and nice. They will vacation on cruises, in summer houses, Sheratons and Marriots. Each member of the family will be apt to unfold an easygoing style in the somatic posturale and gesturale, eat in a fancy restaurant every Sunday and be member of some exclusive club to practice golf or tennis. They will require scopic syntagms as a luxurious modern apartment or a postmodern house, Nike casual footwear for weekends, private school uniforms for the children, various automobiles of recent models including the typical megamobile suburban truck, a geometrically designed garden with perfectly trimmed lawn, impeccably pruned trees and bushes, and so on. In addition, every single gadget that pops out the market will have a place in this family's home: microwave ovens of maximum wattage, the most recent video-games, super sound-systems of high fidelity in the car, TV monitors of high resolution and many inches, high speed cable internet and TV systems, video and DVDs, flat screen cellular computers and cell phones for each family member, several megapixelled digital cameras, memory watches, palms for supermarket shopping lists and so on. With an adequate income, it is not difficult to construct these identities because the commercial and mediatic matrixes offer the complete repertoire to choose from. The dominant register here is scopic, and the trick lies simply in buying.

Family fluxion

The fluxion that characterizes a family's identity is displayed by the tendency to openness or retention of emotions, objects, energies, desires, words, gestures, sounds, money. In the lexic register, centripetal fluxion will control expression of affection, communication of everyday experiences, and spontaneity in interactions. Closed fluxion does not allow bad words, expression of affection or spontaneity. The expulsive or open fluxion, on the other hand, will tolerate insults, detailed descriptions, long narratives, jokes of all colors, criticism in both ways, recriminations, open displays of affection, tenderness or sadness, continuous verbal exchanges. Aesthetic violence can be exerted in the lexic fluxion either by passive closed fluxion of frozen silence or by open aggressiveness and direct offense.

In the somatic register, expulsive fluxion is manifested by frequent hugs and affectionate kisses, open gesticulation and sustained eye contact among members of the family or their reticence when the main modality is retentive. Not only body language or gestuality becomes a means of communication, but its size as well. When obesity is exclusively psychological and not a result of metabolic problems,

202   *Everyday Aesthetics*

it usually becomes the most eloquent statement of closed somatic fluxion as index of obstructing emotions and accumulated impulses such as anger, frustrated desires, fear, affective needs, boredom, or resentment.

In the acoustic register, centripetal fluxion is expressed at homes where sound is strictly regulated or the opposite, when shouting, loud music, radio or TV are centrifugal. Cellular phones are proxemic and fluxion devices keeping the family within reach. They are, as Foucault would have said, panacoustic tools for monitoring members within this matrix. Some families express a festive spirit by consuming alcoholic drinks and humongous amount of decibels through sheer electronic wattage keeping their neighbors as acoustic hostages *latched-by* this intrusion. This new habit to express "fun" by the power of sound amplifiers makes one long for erstwhile styles of celebrating through the art of conversation in the lexic, by the host's best tablecloths, table settings, glasses and by decorating the house, wearing elegant suits and dresses in scopics, and offering elaborated dishes and the best wines in the somatics. In those gatherings, fine musicians used to be hired and everybody danced. This new fashion of wattage parties seems to attest a lack of vitality and a blockage of sensibility in contemporary urban life.

As far as the scopic fluxion in the family matrix is concerned, it varies enormously depending on each culture and social layer. A Japanese home will maintain a relatively clear and austere space, whereas the living space among Western middle-classes is often almost a warehouse saturated of props through a centripetal scopic fluxion of accumulation imposed by consumerism. It can acquire pathological degrees in many lonely people, particularly in the USA, who are unable to throw anything away.

Just by visiting someone's home one can infer not only the prevailing emphatics of their identity but its fluxion as well. Thus techno-gadgets may point to a yuppie family; the typical nuptial photo in the living room on top of the sofa to the prudish; book shelves in every corner, the intellectualistic; quartz stones, candles and talismans, the *New age*; fashion magazines, the massmediatic; Art Nouveau or Art Deco props, the gay family; ready-mades, the Bohemian; impersonal objects, the autistic; flea market items and objects from India, the hippie family; photos and souvenirs, the honeyed; and medicines, the hypochondriac.

Genet once said that the family is a criminal institution. Deplorably, he was not far from the truth. The mechanisms of *com-pression* of the rhetoric and the dramatic are common in familiar identities that impose rigid norms to the rest of the group and prevent any spontaneous interaction. Consequently, the most sensitive members of a family tend to *de-pression* when drained of affective or vital energy. Open *ex-pression* of emotions and desires, genuine or not, is also favored in the brutal, the *new age*, the gay, and junkie families. In others, it is handled by *im-pression* dramaturgically displaying socially legitimized identities from rhetorics (the yuppie, the prudish, the intellectualist, the honeyed) also for diverse reasons: insecurity, attachment to certain affective temperature, social, moral, economic or physical pressure. All in all, members of a family may be *latched-on* or *by* these rhetoric-dramatic articulations. They may love and identify themselves with the aesthetics displayed by a family or the contrary, get sick in their soul and trying to build their identities elsewhere. Whatever the case, these more or less unacknowledged strategies exhibited by each

The Family Matrix

family through semiotic and aesthetic dimensions certainly have a very strong impact upon the sensibility of their members.

Paradigmatic projections in the family matrix

The main paradigmatic projection of this matrix has been exported to the religious matrix. The Judeo-Christian tradition begins with the undergoing of a family around the patriarch Abraham from his father Tared, his brothers Nacor and Hara'n, his spouses, concubines, children, nephews, sisters-in-law, grandsons, great-grandchildren, and generations that followed them. The religious matrix also conceives the figure of the Messiah in family related terms, namely as a descendant by paternal line from King David.

Another enormously significant paradigmatic projection of the familiar matrix is exported to the State matrix, particularly monarchies and empires, by legitimizing the power of the king, emperor or monarch upon the doctrine of the divine right based on the family unit.[1] One can also find this projection through contemporary nepotisms among so called "democratic societies" where some political parties and positions are shamefully administered as family businesses. In capitalism, the projection of the traditional familiar matrix as unit of production towards the corporative matrix inasmuch "great family" is another instance of these export mechanisms where the General Manager of a corporation is seen as the patriarch and all his subordinates behave as children, spouses, and slaves within the "great family" of this unit.

I have analyzed the family matrix as it roughly appears in some Western contemporary urban societies, very different from traditional rural societies where families extend and integrate all the community by kinship relations. Thus the rural familiar matrix requires a different analysis that involves multiple consequences among which I can only mention vernacular scopics and acoustics. These manifestations, understood as "crafts" or "folklore", have been erroneously assimilated to the artistic matrix, when in their origin they were integrated to the religious matrix (agrarian cults), the mercantile (exchange of excedents with other communities) even the military (masks, ritual fighting costumes and crafted weapons). Consequently they require to be analyzed through an integrated multimatricial perspective, instead of isolating them by their products and comparing them to artworks.[2] At the moment, vernacular scopics have been exported to the tourism, commercial, and national matrixes according to their context of distribution, but their origin is no other than the extended family matrix.

---

1   See Turner (1984, 175–180) in his analysis of Filmer.
2   For example, Acha's (1996) comparative study of art, craft and design.

Chapter 28

The Religion Matrix

There is no matrix that has carved sensibilities more profoundly and displayed the aesthetic dimension so prolifically and everlastingly in the four registers and modalities than the religion matrix. This matrix penetrates deeply by *impression* into subjectivities generating personal and collective identities by the elaboration of narratives, rituals, values, and practices that have nourished the soul during millennia and inspirited sweeping passions to the degree of fanaticism, martyrdom, mystical ecstasies, sacrifice and sanctity, torture and war.

Religions have been studied from various perspectives (philosophical, anthropological, psychological, historical, and sociological) but strangely enough, their aesthetic exploration is totally absent. Art history has been the closest to this endeavor, but unfortunately it has abstracted aesthetic manifestations from their matricial context attending only to its objects as "works of art". Art historians observe religion items as stylistic, iconographic, and formal objects from syntactic and semantic perspectives, particularly iconographic, ignoring the pragmatic facet that is primordial for understanding the very origin of their production and cutural function. Without the particular assemblage of aesthetic practices, the meaning of religion would disappear since the values, duties and objects of reverence in each doctrine require all registers and modalities to seem legitimate, be sensibly concretized, and acquire subjective adherence. Also, without the fascination exerted by the symbolic locus of each religion upon its faithful, the seduction and charisma of its spiritual leaders and the enchantment of its narratives, myths and rituals, all eminently aesthetic, no religion is possible.

An aesthetic approach to the religion matrix implies several problems. One of them is proxemic in the sense that each of us is always closer to one religion and farther from others, brought up according to certain values and ignorant of others. As Weber argued in regards to the relation between Protestantism and capitalism, even if we are not religious, these matrixes penetrate our everyday life and become part of individual and collective *umwelten*. We cannot thus be impartial in apprehending the aesthetics of a particular religion, as we cannot be impartial in regards to *any* aesthetic analysis, since it is necessarily a question of subjective interpretation. All we can do is move around our object to apprehend as varied and dynamic perspectives of it as possible. We must add the fact that subjects attached to their religious matrix are rarely conscious of its aesthetic character, because they believe this link to be natural and spontaneous and identify their religion with its aesthetics as much as with its values. Besides, it is difficult to decide whether one should be placed outside or within a religious matrix to appreciate in depth its aesthetic specificity, and no observer can simultaneously be Moslem, Jewish and Christian. The place of observation of this matrix is, then, totally imprecise, but as in the family matrix, it does not prevent us from pointing out its most

206 *Everyday Aesthetics*

salient aesthetic strategies. Readers surely have their own versions of each religion, so the following must be taken just as one possible, personal and respectful interpretation. It is not necessary to be Moslem or Christian to appreciate the magnificence of their religious architecture, nor is it required to be Jewish to value the subtlety of Judaic texts. If Leonardo da Vinci's *Annunciation* or Mozart's *Coronation Mass* can be aesthetically appraised without the need of being Christian, the mosque of Cordoba without being Moslem or David's Psalms without being Jewish we can equally perform this analysis since what all religions appeal to is basically human sensibility, and being foreign to a matrix does not hinder us from participating in the emotion whereupon aesthetic statements have been elaborated to affirm such belief.

The symbol in this matrix is of course the *Divinity*, but each religion interprets it from its own particular rhetorics with diverse tones and hues. Thus they all constitute different subjectivities in both senses of the term, the supreme Subject in capital letter of the deity or God, and the small letter subject human believer. The three monotheistic matrixes of the West converge at symbolically associating the divinity with the rock, but diverge in its identity and location: the Kaaba in Mecca for Islamism, a pagan symbol consecrated by Muhammad for his new religion, the Holy Sepulcher for Christianity where Jesus resurrected after Crucifixion and the Wailing Wall for Judaism by its indexical proximity with two rocks: one is where Abraham almost sacrificed his son Isaac, and the other brought from the Sinai desert by the Hebrews, namely the Tables of the Law in the Ark of the Covenant. In this sense, the three monotheistic religions of the West expose their deeply litholatrous symbolic heritage.

All religions are basically defined by their belief in the dimension of the sacred by opposition to the profane (Durkheim 1982). In this polarity, the aesthetic mediates between both margins, and here lies its crucial role within this matrix, since the conception and manifestation of the sacred must be necessarily incarnated and materialized by the aesthetic to be apprehended. The most vehement access to the sacred occurs by the intense *latching-onto* the idea of the divinity during mystic ecstasies, but there are other more moderate religious experiences. Its opposite, being *latched-by* occurs among fanatics whose religious identity seizes all others and their subjectivity ends up dominated by the dogma sometimes to the extreme of sacrificing not only their life but others' as well to the belief they are obeying a god's or a leader's command. In Christianity, this religious being *latched-by* is associated to satanic possession which served as pretext for Inquisition persecutions and witch hunting across Europe during the fifteenth to seventeenth centuries (case in point: the massacres of women and children in Wurzburg, Germany in 1928–29).

The religious matrix directly influences our daily life by its meticulous prescriptions regarding the body, family, neighbors, and nation; it regulates what habits to cultivate and avoid, when to speak and keep silent, what and how to eat, when to sleep and wake up, what properties to maintain and get rid of, how and when to make love. Apparently, human beings can endure better the banalization of the sacred than the consecration of the everyday. Such prescriptions are set mainly by the *Halacha* for Judaism and the *Sunnah* for Islamism, whereas in Christianism, by Saint Paul's initiative, many Judaic onerous practices (circumcision and halachic rules of hygiene and cooking) were canceled to gain more adepts. In spite of the necessarily schematic approach to a subject so complex, we will explore in

The Religion Matrix   207

chronological order the three most prominent monotheistic religious matrixes in the Western world focusing their salient aesthetic deployments. All in all, religious aestheticized practices and rituals bestow certain places, artifacts and narratives with symbolic meaning by mattergical and temporal weight.

Judaic religious matrix

From its origins to the present, the Judaic religious matrix has been a tribal religion. In spite of emerging at the very source of patriarcalism, this matrix is literally matricial because it is based on the ancestry by maternal line, namely, all offspring from a Jewish mother will be part of this matrix. For that reason, evidently, Judaism does not practice proselytism and admits conversion with relative reluctance in individual cases of confirmed personal conviction. Its members assume to be descendants of the 12 tribes of Israel and tenaciously preserve their ancestors' cultural heritage. Jews do not consider that their mission is to convert the world to their faith but to encourage monotheistic ethics by their example. They believe there is only one God, but recognize that revelation can be manifested in diverse forms among different nations. Consequently, this matrix has a particularistic, non exclusivist, conception of religion, a particularism common to all archaic and totemic religions, but transplanted here to revelation itself, not to polytheism. When other religions with universalistic ambitions arose (Islam and Christianity), Judaism remained as a minority matrix, a condition dearly paid throughout the three or four millennia since its affirmation as a collective identity through ongoing persecution since the beginning of the Common Era.

Judaic lexics

Names may have, as signifiers, some degree of arbitrariness (as Saussure claimed) but once they get established and their roots remembered, the link with the signified pushes forwards conditioning its perception. The term "Judaism" comes from אודה *hodeh*, praise or thank, as the term "Hebrew" from *Eber*, apparently the great grandson of Noah's son Shem, linked to the root עבר, pass.

According to the first book of the Pentateuch, Genesis, the Hebrew God creates the world by the simple use of words: "and God said: Let there be light; and there was light". One cannot have a more forceful expression of the power of words than this conception of creation by the absolutely performative illocution. When God speaks for the first time to man and woman in the Garden of Eden, it was for blessing them and granting them the fruits and creatures of the Earth, the sea and the sky, and also to strongly forbid them tasting the fruit of the trees of life and of knowing good and evil. God spoke to Cain, Noah, Abraham and Sara his wife, and through His word, they believed in Him. Adam also exerted the power of the word at another scale, the human, naming the animals of paradise.

The word in this matrix is not only constituent of reality, and in that sense aesthetic ("and God said: let there be the light; ...") but in Jakobson's terms, also conative ("Be fruitful and multiply, and replenish the Earth ..."), expressive ("What hast thou done?

208 *Everyday Aesthetics*

The voice of thy brother's blood crieth unto me from the ground ..."), metalinguistic ("and God called the firmament Heaven ..."), referential ("the man has become as one of us ...") and phatic ("Where art thou ... Behold ...").[1] It is not surprising, then, that the Judaic matrix would develop its aesthetic mediation to the sacred from the lexic register with greater devotion than through any of the others. Its textual production is practically interminable: it begins with the Pentateuch, to which the texts of the prophets were added as well as the *Psalms, Song of Songs*, and *Chronicles*. From fifth and fourth centuries B.C.E. the compilation of the body of the *Torah* was concluded. Then its hermeneutic work developed through the *Mishna* ("to repeat" or "to study") during several generations of rabbinical discussion illustrated by the lessons of the rabbis, specially Shamai and Hillel and their disciple Yohanan ben Sakai and Rabbi Akiba. The *Mishna* covers a period of 600 years (compiled by Yehuda Hanasi c. 220), and is constituted by the *Midrash* as hermeneutic method, the *Halacha* or written compilation of laws inherited from Moses by oral tradition and the *Agada* as preaching or homily, including anecdotes and legends. The midrashic method, that means "to look for" or "to expose", tries to transcend the literal sense in Biblical texts and penetrate hidden meanings. The *Mishna* is continued by the *Gemara* ("study" or "tradition" in Aramaic) and both books constitute the body of the *Talmud* (from the root למד "to study" or "to teach") in its Babylon and Jerusalem versions, where a labor of at least ten centuries of exegetic analysis was consolidated. To this body others have been added as the *Tosefta* or the *Perushim* or commentaries (of the rabbi Rashi, for example), the *Chidushim* or innovations (twelfth and thirteenth centuries) and the *Sheeilot Vtshuvot* or questions and answers. As Sachar accurately states (1966, 88) if the ancient Hebrews created the Bible from their lives, their descendants created their lives from the Bible.

The theoretical hybridization effort to integrate Hebraic writings with intellectual work of other cultures has been continuous since then. Greek philosophy, particularly Plato's, inspired Philo Judeus or Philo of Alexandria, a Jew contemporary of Jesus, to write *De Vita Mosis* and *Legum Allegoriarum* conceptualizing the Hebraic God in terms of the Greek *logos*. Philo initiates the endeavor to combine reason with faith, continued in the ninth century by the figure of Saadia ben Yosef who considered that reason and revelation are complementary and tried to elaborate the concepts of the Judaic matrix in a philosophical system.[2]

Along this process of hybridization are the poet and philosopher Salomon ben Yehudah Ibn Gabirol or Avicebron called the "Jewish Plato" and Yehuda Halevi who in *The Cuzari* defends the principles of Judaism with respect to the Aristotelism, Islamism and Christianity.[3] Rambam (initials of Rabbi Moses ben Maimon, 1135–1204) commonly known as Maimonides elaborates the 14 volumes of the *Mishne Torah* or Second Law to codify Talmudic law and study the differences among the three monotheistic religions in the twelfth century. In his book *Moreh Nebuchim*, or *Guide*

---

1   On aesthetics as a means of constituting an imaginary or factual reality, see Mandoki (1999a) and on the power of illocution, see Mandoki (2004a).

2   Other thinkers worthy to be mentioned in this matrix are Samuel Ibn Nagdela (992–1055), Isaac Ben Jacobo Alfesi (1013–1103), and Rabbi Salomon Itzjaki (1040–1105) known as Rashi, all of them great teachers, poets, philologists and talmudists.

3   Graetz (1939, 283–323).

The Religion Matrix 209

of the Perplexed, Maimonides tries to integrate Aristotelian with Judaic philosophy under a rational spirit inherited from Saadia.[4] Kabbalistic hermeneutics were compiled in the *Zohar* or "Brilliance" by the Castilian kabbalist Rabbi Moises de Leon and in the *Pardes Rimonim* or "Garden of the Grenades" by Moises Cordovero. These mystic writings exemplify that the ardent religious emotion and aesthetic *latching-on* arises in this matrix primordially from the letter, as in methods such as *gematria*, *notarikon*, and *tmura*. The playfulness and the passionate absorption develop along all these practices through intellectual game of *peripatos* in its rich exegetics.

Judaic thought remains in the periphery during the thirteenth century due to persecutions, massacres and expulsions and did not emerge but four centuries later with Moses Mendelssohn (who directly influenced Kant's aesthetic philosophy) and Spinoza who despite having been excommunicated from this matrix by a pantheistic interpretation of his doctrine, he never disavowed his Jewish intellectual and ethical inspiration. Maimonides in turn influenced both philosophers to the degree that Mendelssohn humoristically attributed his back hump to the weight of maimonidic philosophy upon him. The Illustration (*Haskallah*) and social emancipation of Jews in Europe partly secularized their religious heritage. In the twentieth century, several philosophers have directly or indirectly been nourished by the Judaic matrix in the same eagerness of hybridization initiated by Philo Judaeus, from Franz Rosenzweig with Christianity in *The Star of Redemption*, Martin Buber with relation to existentialism, Walter Benjamin with Marxism, Emmanuel Levinas with respect to phenomenology and Hannah Arendt with political philosophy (in addition to Henri Bergson, Edmund Husserl, Sigmund Freud, and Ludwig Wittgenstein, Georg Cantor, Saul Kripke, Jacques Derrida, Jean Francois Lyotard, among a long list of thinkers).

This critical, playful and creative hermeneutics contributed for millennia by rabbis and philosophers in the lexic register is the heritage passed on from one generation to the next in this matrix. Judaism does not demand faith, peregrination, asceticism, love or sacrifice, but continuous intellectual activity for the conservation of its lexic patrimony. There is a reason why it is commonly said that the Jew always responds to a question with another question. The aesthetic and mystical *latching-on* within this matrix is not only related to the word but basically built by questions.[5] Even anti-intellectualistic trends as Hasidic groups who follow the teachings of rabbi Baal Shem Tov and emphasize emotion as the main experience for relating to God, depend on the lexic register because prayer and song constitute the bridge through which they render tribute to God.

The predominance of the lexic upon other registers in the Judaic matrix is allegorically expressed in the election between the two forbidden trees in paradise: the tree of eternal life and the one of knowledge of good and evil. The first tree refers

---

4   Yehuda Leon Abravanel writes *Dialoghi d'Amore* in the Renaissance and the doctor and philosopher Isaac Ben Solomon Israeli, Dunash Ben Tamim in addition Abraham Ben Meir Ibn Ezra, make an effort to integrate the Judaic tradition with Neoplatonism. It is worth adding the interpretation of laws by Yosef Ben Efraim Caro (s. 15 and 16) in his *Shuljan Aruj*.

5   According to a legend, the words written to the divinity by the Jewish faithful in small papers inserted between the little cracks of the Wall of the Lamentations have maintained it standing during millennia.

210 *Everyday Aesthetics*

to the body and immortality and the second to the mind whose effects were "and they knew that they were naked", "And Adam knew Eve his wife", "and the Lord God said, Behold, the man is become as one of us, to know good and evil: and now, lest he put forth his hand, and take also of the tree of life, and eat, and live for ever". Eve and her docile husband apparently chose knowledge over immortality (although the common interpretation understands it the other way around, as a sin of the body). Here is one of the several paradoxes of this matrix: a God that creates a tree by which knowledge can be acquired and demands the study of the *Torah* and at the same time punishes it by expelling Adam and Eve from the Garden of Eden for tasting it. The *Torah* becomes a captivating source of questions for the devoted Jew and a playful incentive for reflection and aesthetic *latching-on*. But it also generates being *latched-by* when this intellectual playfulness hinders the unfolding of other registers and modalities.

For Judaism, lexics are sacred, and studying the word is every Jew's religious duty.

Judaic acoustics

Lyres of ten cords, harps of twelve, bronze cymbals, silver trumpets, double cane flutes and the *shofar* or ram horn were the instruments played at the Temple of Jerusalem in Solomon's times. Of those instruments, the sound of the ram horn is still used to announce the beginning of the New Year and the end of "the Terrible Days" (*yamim hanoraim*) of meditation that culminate in *Yom Kippur*, the most sacred day of the Jewish calendar.

The importance of the acoustic register for Jewish religion is enormous if we consider that its node for *latching-on* is an invisible yet audible God, a God that communicates by the voice and the letter, never by the image or body. The Hebrew God speaks directly to His people who are forced to listen: *Shma Israel*! (Listen Israel!) Indeed by the ear alone, the people of Israel learned to believe in a God to whom they respond *Naase v'nishma* (we'll do and we'll listen). To listen is to obey. The acoustic register has had great importance for this matrix not only since the times of the second Temple, but as a mnemotechnical device in song and prayers, as well as an emotional expression of devotion through singing among Hasidic groups. The rhythmical feeling one gets when reading Biblical narratives' style and its effect of fascination is also part of this register.

Music for the Judaic matrix accompanies all festive occasions at the temple and home. The singer or Chazan is as important for intoning sacred music in the service of the synagogue as the rabbi during the ritual. The typical Klezmer music at Ashkenazi weddings and the special potential of the clarinet as an acoustic analogy of individual emotion of deep sadness or euphoria are characteristic of this matrix.[6]

---

6   The importance of music in this matrix for Jews is manifested by the number of Jewish musicians linked to it: Felix Mendelssohn, Jacques Offenbach, Ernest Bloch, Gustav Mahler, George Gershwin, Philip Glass, Darius Milhaud, Kurt Weill, Aaron Copland, Leonard Bernstein, Mario Castelnuovo-Tedesco, Arnold Schoenberg, André Previn and interpreters like Itzjak Stern, Yehudi Menuhin, Pinchas Zukerman, Joseph Szigeti, David Oistrakh, Jascha Heifetz, Itzjak Perlman, Arthur Rubinstein, Lorin Maazel, Nathan Milstein, André Previn among others.

The Religion Matrix 211

Among all manifestations in this register, the main one refers to the interdiction in the Third Commandment of pronouncing aloud the name of God "Thou shalt not pronounce the name of your God in vain". From here derive the different terms given to name God in each occasion and whose true name abbreviated in the Tetragrammaton could only be pronounced by *cohanim* or priests at the Temple of Jerusalem during certain prayers and a special event. This prohibition to bring forth the name of God to the acoustic register radically separates this matrix from the Christian and Islamic.

Judaic somatics

The primordial somatic practice in this matrix is the act of male circumcision eight days after birth, inscribing itself upon the very flesh of the infant as index of the people of Israel's pact with their God. In circumcision the axis of symbolic appears in all its eloquence, because it is the materiality of the body that expresses the alliance, and the time since Isaac's circumcision up to all and each of the generations that follow him which convey to this act enormous symbolic weight.[7]

In addition to literally incarnating the pact, the human body for this matrix has a primordial reproductive character. With their body the Jews render tribute to God through a spiritual sexual act, metaphorically described in the Kabbalah, poetically expressed in the *Song of Songs* (attributed to King Solomon), and ritually performed during the *Shabat* (or festivity celebrating the creation of the world each Friday at sunset). It is in this register where ethical monotheism's abstraction reaches concretion through rigorous laws in daily life and detailed prescriptions of practices and disciplines upon the body established by the *Halachah*. Superficially, the somatics in this matrix are distinguished by the orthodox's swinging movement of the body (*daven*) during prayers for greater concentration or intention (*kavanah*) connecting it to the rhythmical movement of the mind. The body is also a device that must be structured in daily rituals to maintain individuals integrated to themselves and their community. Somatic rituals take the form of fasting during the *Yom Kippur* celebration, the priests' washing ritual at the great Temple of Jerusalem at the time (when it existed before the Common Era), in the ceremonial meals of each festivity, and in the prohibition of eating pig, blood or animals sacrificed with suffering (according to the laws of *Shehitah*). The prohibition of touching corpses should be mentioned in this register (except in obedience to strict regulations), working or setting fire during *Shabat*, and having sexual relations with menstruating women, as well as the prescriptions of the ritual bath or *mikvaeh* for a woman after her menstrual period, consummation of the sexual act during *Shabat* if the woman is in her fertile period, separating dairy from meat products, men from women in orthodox and conservative synagogues, to bury the dead covered only by a sheet in coffins without nails, to light *Shabat* candles at a precise moment before sunset, to sit on the floor as an index of mourning in *shiv'ah*, to cover males' head and also married women's.[8]

---

7 Circumcision was a pre-Abrahamic practice, but perhaps only within this matrix does it acquire the meaning of sacred pact.

8 Covering the head is understood as somatic because it is not about the scopics of "using a cap" to exhibit it, but the corporeal act of covering oneself in the presence of God.

212 *Everyday Aesthetics*

While the human body is strictly regulated in this matrix, the body of God is absent in its absolute transcendence except in its feminine symbolic aspect of the *Shechinah*, relatively immanent but incorporeal, accompanying the people of Israel until the restoration of harmony (according to Kabbalistic tradition).

Being a tribal religion, Judaism is not racial but *ethnic*, constituted by Jews of diverse racial ancestry: mostly Caucasian, Arabic, and black African. Judaic tribes, such as the Roma or Gypsies, Druses, or Kurds, merge the extended familiar matrix with the religious and are consequently endogamous; they avoid conversion or proselytism and demand loyalty.

Orthodox Judaism's emphasis upon the lexic and its reduction of the somatic to an almost automated observance of halachic rules has generated an aesthetic severity and relative neglect of a corporeal sense of self. As a consequence, although Jewish and Greek cultures share intellectual hedonism in the pleasure of knowledge, they contrast in this particular aspect: while the Greeks believed in the sacredness of beauty, the Jews believed in the beauty of the sacred (as pithily stated by Sachar 1966, 100).

Judaic scopics

The Judaic matrix is characterized by obstinately refusing to unfold the aesthetic in the scopic register in obedience to the Second Commandment stating "Thou shalt not make image ..." Among the few scopic manifestations of this matrix are the use of a special mantle (*talit*) and phylacteries (*tfilim*) for prayer and what has been called "judaica", namely ornamented ritual metal objects like candelabra for *Shabat*, the *Menorah* and *Chanukiah*, indicators for reading the *Torah* in the synagogues, the *Mezuzah* or sanctifier for thresholds, lamps, ritual utensils, wine glasses, dishes for Passover and other festivities.

Traditional Jewish people have lived without images and with a meager visual production. For that reason, the symbolic weight in this register is concentrated not in the visual but in space itself. Thus the basic scopic manifestation and nodal point of symbolic intensity of this matrix is Mount Moriah also called Mount Zion, known today as the Temple Mount in Jerusalem (ironically, the most fervent Zionists today in the literal sense are those Arabs that claim exclusive access to and ownership of this mount). Its symbolic weight has accumulated for perhaps 3,500 years since, according to tradition, the mythological Abraham was on the verge of sacrificing his son Isaac exactly there according to Genesis 22. King David bought that estate from Arauna, the last leader of the Jebusites near the year 1200 (B.C.E.), to erect the great Temple and deposit the Tables of the Law. Four years after his death, Solomon his son ordered its construction on the same site. The Temple was sacked and destroyed four centuries later by the troops of Nabucodonozor II and after 70 years of exile it was reconstructed under the protection of Persian King Cyrus the Great. Antiochus Epiphanes desecrated it with pigs and pagan idols, but it was reconquered by the Hasmonean priests and remodeled by Herod who constructed enormous walls for laying foundations. The last Temple was destroyed in year 70 by the Roman emperor Titus after a Jewish insurrection. Since then this scopic landmark par excellence of the Judaic religious matrix has remained devastated (the Islamic Golden Dome mosque was built over it 600 years later), leaving only one of the Herodian walls

The Religion Matrix 213

on the west side, known today as the Wailing Wall, and which still remains as its primordial symbolic site.

Without this superposition of performative acts and memories upon the same locus, the importance of Zion for the Judaic matrix as symbolic implosion in space cannot be fully understood. Jerusalem is archetypal of how symbols function, and in particular sites of intense material, temporal and affective energy appear to bend them by their historical weight similar to the curvature in space-time exerted by a matter for relativity physics.[9]

One can thus partly understand what it is, besides habit, which attracts Jews to their religious matrix. This rich narrative weaving, the playful joy of biblical hermeneutics, the cyclical repetition of festivities that link present communities to their ancestors, the charisma of figures like King David, King Solomon, Debora, Sara, etc, the dramatism of stories like Cain's murder, Isaac being on the verge of sacrifice, Jacob's perseverance during 14 years for marrying Rachel, the fascinating figure of Joseph and the epic exodus from Egypt, stories of love and war, of loyalty and betrayal, of suffering and joy evidently captivate intelligence and imagination as a source for aesthetic *latching-on* and spiritual nourishment. Traditional music sung during festivities and rituals, the sense that there is a sacred dimension in the most concrete corporeal acts (eating, sexual intercourse, birth), and a sacred place (Zion) as indexical sign of the existence of God, all converge into the breeding of this form of sensibility and collective identity.

Christian religious matrix

While the Judaic matrix never managed to detach itself from the family matrix and remains a tribal religion, the Christian matrix (from Greek Χριστός Anointed One) developed as the logical consequence of monotheism, namely, universality. What unites the whole humanity for this religion is the death of the Redeemer, Christ, to expiate the Original Sin. The poignant image of this sacrifice is an object of intense aesthetic *latching-on* among Christians around the world (while traditionally Jews were *latched-by* it).

As the conditions of possibility of any live being are always another live being, the conditions of any matrix are always another matrix through a clearly organic matricial generation process. If the Judaic religious matrix germinates from the Abrahamic family matrix (and from some incipient monotheistic ideas in the Middle East, perhaps Egyptian or Caldean), Christianity germinates from Judaism. For that reason it is constituted by believers in the word, values and lessons of the Nazarene Jew Yehoshua Ben Joseph, descendant of the tribe of Levi, considered the Son of God, Messiah or Christ. Jesus and the Apostles never deserted or denied their Jewish religion nor set out to invent a new one—in contrast to the aspiration, seven centuries later, of the prophet Muhammad—but instead exercised critical and hermeneutic freedom offered by their own matrix. It was the Jew Saul of Tarsus, later known as Saint Paul who, after his mystical vision of Jesus on the way to Damascus,

---

9 On symbolic density, see Mandoki (1998).

214 *Everyday Aesthetics*

recognized him as Messiah and propagated his word until executed in Rome in the year 62. Since the conversion of Constantine, Christianity settles down as official religion of the Roman empire, later ramifying through diverse tendencies from the incipient division between Greek or Byzantine orthodox church and the Latin church (with several monastic orders) later divided by the Protestant schism in the sixteenth century into numerous versions until today generating new groups.[10]

Christian lexics

The word for Christian tradition is performed through various instances such as the homily, sermons, Gospels, Scholastic and theological texts, teaching catechism, in prayers, verbal confession and forgiveness, in the penance through supplication, and so on. The variety of speech acts in this matrix unfolds also in excommunion, cursing, blasphemy, execration, exoneration, oath, imprecation, abomination, abjuration, and so on, all lexic syntagms that lack meaning outside the religious matrix which grants them weight, value and performative force.

As the Judaic matrix prohibited images in the scopic register, for Catholicism it was the lexic register that had to bear most of the weight of interdiction. The prohibition to secular people of approaching sacred texts, the vigilance by the Inquisition on the lexic register to prevent or punish verbal heresies, the continuous monitoring on the word said and written as with Giordano Bruno or Galileo, the torture to obtain declaration of guilt and the retraction of the word, the ritual of confession and the prayers of penance all show an extremely complex relation to the lexic register in this matrix.

This conception of risk in Christian lexics is dramatically illustrated in the fate of two thinkers of the fifth century: Cyril (who provoked the fire at the library of Alexandria, incited massacres against the Jews and the savage lynching of the intelligent Hypathia destroying her work in mathematics and neoplatonic philosophy) and Nestorious (pacific man who simply argued for the divine and human duality in the figure of Christ). Cyril was canonized as a saint whereas Nestorious was condemned and excommunicated as heretic. All by the weight of the word that is condemned or exonerated with greater severity than criminal acts.

If St. John's Gospel conceives Christ from a stoic-platonic perspective of *logos* "In the beginning was the Verb, and the Verb was with God, and the Verb was God", the early Church seems to have deduced that if the word gave origin to the world, it could also destroy it. Consequently, the need for the Ecumenical Concilium, the Inquisition and other disciplinary apparatuses (in Foucaultian sense) to watch, punish and protect the word from the destructive power of heresy. This fervor in monitoring the word is not reduced to enunciation but to interpretation as well, reason why the

---

10 The Protestant Schism establishes transformations in all the registers: in the scopic register it is iconoclastic and denounces the idolatry of virgins and saints, and in the lexic register when Luther translated the Bible to German after Gutenberg's invention, he opened the possibility of reading it, and thus intepreting it directly without intermediaries. In the somatic register, Luther cancels celibacy allowing priests to marry and eliminating the conventual institution. For the acoustic register he composed several ritual Hymns.

The Religion Matrix

access to the sacred texts was strongly restricted. In his novel *The Name of the Rose* Umberto Eco beautifully illustrates this relation to the sacred word, reserved for ecclesiastical hierarchies and only to the monastic class during the Middle Ages and the Renaissance.

This matrix constructs its lexic register from Judaic sources that Jesus inherited and inculcated to his disciples, including the whole body of the *Torah* that has come to be known since then as the "Old Testament". Other stories were added as "New Testament", like the Apostles' narrations partly inspired by the *Book of Enoch* (ca. 64 B.C.E.) in its vision of the Messiah, hell and the demonology, as well as *The Testaments of the Twelve Patriarchs* (written by a Pharisee c. 109–107 B.C.E.). After the Apostles, the Epistles of St. Paul initiate the long chain of Christian lexics.

The three doctors of the Church were St. Ambrose, St. Hiëronymus, and St. Augustine. The first established the ecclesiastical conception of the Church and State; the second elaborated the Latin Bible for the Western Church, and the third inspired a good part of the theology until Luther and Calvin's doctrines. (Russell 1964, 318–335) In the sixth century the platonic Boecius writes *Consolations of Philosophy* waiting his execution for being considered a pagan. In the seventh century John Scotus of Erigena, (in *Division of Nature*) translates Pseudo Dionysius Areopagite, also considered heretic for placing reason over faith. From the eighth to the eleventh century, the Islamic matrix predominated in the Western world until the scholasticism of St. Anselm, Roscellinus, Abelard, St. Bonaventure and the monumental figure of St. Thomas Aquinas emerged under the influence not only of Aristotle but also by Averroes, Avicenna, and Maimonides. Aquinas' doctrine of direct revelation derived from the *Guide of the Perplexed*, according to the Spanish medievalist Miguel Asín Palacios.[11] The three most important philosophers of this time were Roger Bacon, John Duns Scotus, and William Occam. With the Reformation and Counter Reformation during the sixteenth century, the protagonic figures of Christian lexics were Luther, Calvin, and Loyola until the secularization process begins propelled by rationalism. Traces of this matrix remain in the philosophical preoccupations with respect to the truth and the existence of God (in Descartes and Kant) in Hegel's concept of "absolute spirit", and Nietzsche's harsh criticism of the Christian matrix, in addition to Teilhard de Chardin and Gabriel Marcel's Christian existentialism among others.

Christian acoustics

Bells are the acoustics par excellence of the Christian matrix marking the rhythm of daily life in convents and monasteries. (cf. Zerubavel 1985) One recognizes a Catholic town or city by the bells tolling their call to mass and marking significative times, activities, and events for the local community.

The acoustics of the Christian matrix have bequeathed upon us a choral and instrumental heritage of enormous beauty. The polyphony of the medieval *organum* and the songs of the nuns in convents and churches illustrate a fundamental part of Christian acoustics. Of Hebrew origin, Christian Hymns begin with the Gnostics

---

11 Cited by Tedeschi 1992, 98–99.

as in the *Odes of Solomon*, followed during the Byzantine times by the *roparies* as answers between psalms, *kontakias* and *canons* in the work of composers and poets as Aurelius Prudentius, Paulus Diaconus, Hrabanus Maurus, and later by Adrian Willaert, Giovanni Pierluigi da Palestrina, and Roland de Lassus among many others. The *Kyrie, Gloria, Credo, Sanctus*, the antiphons of Gregorian chants, the Renaissance sacred music of Josquin des Prez to the monumental religious music of Johann Sebastian Bach and his family, the magnificent work of Mozart (as *Coronation Mass, Laudate Dominum "Vesparae de Dominica"*, and *Exsultate, Jubilate*) and of so many other composers inspired by this matrix prove with great eloquence the exuberance of Christian acoustics. The particular timbre of the organ seems to project us to a sacred dimension by purely aesthetic strategies. Christian music has extraordinary curative qualities generating a sensation of serenity, order and harmony by just crossing the threshold of a church or cathedral. In listening to that music, one can't but acknowledge the existence of perfection.

In its iconoclastic rebellion, Protestant Reformation partly replaced the scopic register with the acoustic through Hymns sung by all the community. The Lutheran Hymns *Achtliederbuch* and *Enchiridion* and the compilation of *Hymns Ancient and Modern* of the Anglicans, as well as *English Hymnal* of Dearmer and William illustrate Protestant acoustics. With the conversion to Protestantism of African Americans in the United States, the Christian matrix developed musical genres like black spirituals derived from protestant Hymns (*Roll, Jordan, Roll*; *Go Down, Moses*; *Steal Away to Jesus*) and the highly rhythmical Gospel genre of the Baptist Church, which is said to make "the church swing with music". In these modalities, the whole community *latches-onto* the joy of singing in a musical dialogue of great emotivity for communal and "communional" integration.

Christian somatics

It is paradoxical that, for the sake of propagation, Saul de Tarsus or Saint Paul, originally a disciple of the Pharisees, relinquished two fundamental aspects of the Judaic matrix in the somatic register, namely the ritual circumcision and the laws with respect to food. It was all for making it more lenient and attractive for conversion, whereas, on the other hand, he incorporated ideas of the sect of the Essenians (first century B.C.E. to first century C.E.) with respect to celibacy as the ideal condition for "strong spirits". In other words, Christianity seems less strict with respect to the body by releasing their adepts from severe Judaic somatics but at the same time it reveals a much greater severity when marking the body as the origin of sin and establishing celibacy as a requirement for priesthood. These decisions certainly carved or marked Christian sensibilities in particular ways.

If the monastic and ecclesiastical class was allowed direct access to the dangerous lexic register in exclusion of the common secular people, this privilege had to be fully compensated in the somatic register. This symbolic economy of the body based on the Original Sin divides, so to speak, the population in two classes: on one side those productive in the material and corporeal sphere including the generation of goods and the reproduction of the species, and on the other those productive in the spiritual sphere, including the production of indulgences, blessings, and admonitions. The same

The Religion Matrix

Catholic vigilance of the lexic register in secular communities is reverted to the somatic register of the clergy where the fear of the word is exceeded by the fear of the body.

The severity whereupon this matrix conceived the body was expressed in its submission to penances and expiations by fasting and flagellation. The Inquisition invented meticulous tortures upon the body. To escape the temptations of the flesh, Origin of Alexandria (c.185–254), Christian philosopher of stoic and neoplatonic roots, had himself castrated by the literal reading of Mathew XIX, 12, "… and there are eunuchs that to themselves were made eunuchs because of the kingdom of heaven", the tragic reason why he was rejected from priesthood. Here we see the fragile balance between *latching-on* and being *latched-by* this matrix.

The symbolic economy of the Catholic faith shows two opposed movements: on the one hand *im-pression* of pressing from the somatic register by flagellation to affect attitudes of faith and generate a sense of purification in the dramatics. Its exact inverse is *ex-pression* of the existing faith, already ardent, that presses towards the somatic lacerating the body to make the believer's faith manifest before the eyes of the divinity. The *stigmata* are the most eloquent sample of this process of *ex-pression* as presentation in the somatic register of the dramatics of faith. In Catholic countries these expressions of faith by hurting the body are heartfelt, as carrying cactus leaves over the bare chest and back (described in Mexico by Juan Rulfo in his story *Talpa*), going on their bleeding knees to the Villa of Guadeloupe every 12th of December, peregrinations with many deprivations and sacrifices, penitents of Holy Friday carrying thorny twigs on their naked shoulders and those crowned by thorns representing the role of Jesus. In these cases, the somatic is the register where the enormous symbolic weight of religious fervor is *ex-pressed*.

For the Catholic faith, the devil dwells not only in the lexic register with the imprecations and abominations but particularly in the somatic register with the temptations. The exigency of faith in the dogma of the virginity of Mary and her Immaculate Conception symbolizes the complexity of the Catholic relation with the somatic register. The sacrifice of Christ began in the body by incarnation, the Verb made flesh, and culminated in the crucified body. For the inquisitors, the body was the device to alter speech by torture, because the culprits had to undergo in their flesh the sins of their spirit. The processions and peregrinations, the confinement and separation from the family, the votes of poverty, obedience, silence and sacrifice affect directly the body. The Catholic devotee expresses humility with her body by genuflection, and is protected from evil by crossing herself in persignation.

The aroma of incense, candle wax and flowers create in this register an aesthetic passage from profane to sacred space. The clergy scrupulously performs an elaborated choreography in each ritual so that the subject cannot less but confirm that perfection exists just by attending mass. Those movements regulated to the smallest detail do not seem to be designed by flesh and bone creatures. It is thus possible to infer that the preparation of the ministers of the Church is achieved largely on the forms, and thus becomes an implicit yet deliberate aesthetic training whereupon each liturgical act must be performed. Any clumsiness or lack of grace such as spilling the chalice, tripping or walking in a hurried manner would instantly break the enchantment and spell of the mass.

Christian scopics

No other monotheistic matrix has developed the aesthetic strategies in the scopic register with such vehemence during two millennia and throughout the entire planet as the Catholic religion. Compared with Islamism and Judaism, whose anti-scopic principles have jeopardized their development of visual figuration, Catholicism predominantly seduces by its imagery. Evangelization was imposed by force and by fascination, welcoming the faithful towards the vision of a world that is cruel in the painful destiny of Christ, but compassionate in offering love and consolation.

Its amazingly rich iconography commissioned the greatest talents in painting from the Middle Ages and during the Renaissance such as Giotto's frescoes in St. Francis at Assisi and Arena chapel at Padua or Santa Croce in Florence, Della Francesca's in San Francesco's Church in Arezzo, Masaccio's in the church of Carmine culminating in Raphael's paintings for the Vatican and Michelangelo's Sistine Chapel. Christian scopics are displayed not only by the image but also through symbolic spaces as the Holy Sepulcher in Jerusalem, the church of the Nativity in Bethlehem, the Vatican as seat of the Pope's power, as well as places of peregrination like the Romanesque cathedral of Santiago de Compostela and the grotto of Lourdes in France. The relics of saints in sites of Catholic cult constitute another particular manifestation of Catholic somatic-scopics where the material, somatic symbol of some fragment of the corpse of a saint or martyr where a church was built, charges a locus with additional indexical and symbolic meaning. (cf. Clarke 1992)

The humblest among the faithful can enter the most luxurious of cathedrals to pray without risk of expulsion. They can *latch-on* to its magnificent architecture, the splendor of its decoration, the freshness and subtle illumination, the huge scale, the plethora of images. Benevolent figures accompany the faithful and grant them existence and hope for the future. The devotees are surrounded by superb vitraux, stunning sculptures, delicate paintings, monumental architecture, illuminated manuscripts, expensive altarpieces, embroidering, marble reliefs, mosaics, enamels, finely decorated furniture, reliquaries of gold and silver, carpets, carved woods, and so on. The beauty of the sacred of the Hebrew heritage is here integrated with the sacredness of beauty of the Greek heritage.

The religious adhesion of Catholics appears to occur through the scopic register as the main incentive for aesthetic and mystical contemplation. Even exorcism is performed by the scopics of the cross, in addition to the lexics of incantation and somatics of kneeling and crossing oneself. The luxurious clothes of embroidered silk for the ritual of the mass, the scopic differentiation that mark hierarchies among parish priests, bishops, archbishops, cardinals and Popes, and that distinguish between Franciscans, Dominican, Augustinian and other orders, are instances of this register.[12] Without any doubt, the history of the most impressive Western architecture in our era almost equals the history of Christian scopic register from at least Santa Sophia Cathedral during the Byzantine empire, followed by monumental expressions of Romanesque, Gothic, Renaissance, Baroque, Rococo, Neoclassic up to the abstractionism of the church

---

12 It is worth mentioning in this register the *San Benito*, which is the tunic with the cross whereby the Inquisition marked those accused of heresy.

The Religion Matrix   219

of Notre Dame du Haut by Le Corbusier and San Francisco in Pampulha by Oscar Niemeyer, in addition to Gaudi's Sacred Family, the modern Basilica of Guadalupe by Ramirez Vázquez among hundreds of thousands of churches. Who can resist such powerful aesthetic allure? Not even God.

Islamic religious matrix

Among the three monotheistic religions of the West, the Islamic matrix (from the Arabic *al-islam*, الإسل submission) is the most recent and fastest growing of all, as it was consolidated in less than a century and, in less than three, it already occupied by military expansion a good part of the "civilized world" of its time. Since then and almost until its relapse at the beginnings of the twentieth century with the fall of the Ottoman Empire, this matrix controlled politically and militarily numerous territories in the West and East.

The Islamic matrix begins in the seventh century of the Christian era from the lessons taught by a merchant from Mecca, Muhammad, who declared himself the last and greatest of all prophets comparing himself to Abraham, Moses and Jesus. After being evicted from Mecca for his ideas, Muhammad moved on 16 July 622 to Yathrib or Medina (beginning of the Hegira), a city founded around the year 70 after the fall of Jerusalem by three exiled Jewish tribes, and unsuccessfully preached to local Christians and Jews to convert them to his new faith. He achieved much better results preaching to the pagan Arab tribes in the region. Since then, Islam has been propagating almost exponentially.

Islamic lexics

Muhammad set out to produce what for him would be a text superior to the Bible because he considered the Old and New Testaments a distortion of the true sense of the voice of Allah (meaning "the God" *Al-ilah* in Arabic). Being illiterate, he dictated the *Qur'an* to his cousin Ali Ibn Abi Taleb and his son in law, Uthman Ibn Affan according to Islamic tradition.[13] The *Qur'an* came forth when Muhammad was in a state of trance producing a monophonic text in which a single voice is heard (Muhammad's as messenger of Allah) unlike the collective production of the Gospels and the *Torah* and their resultant polyphony and diachronic inscription. As manifestation of the inner speech of Allah by *ex-pression*, the *Qur'an* is written in the language of *lugha* or classic Arabic that stands against the *ammiya*, or common language, as the sacred to the profane. Language thus constitutes a niche in which the believer is sheltered for contacting the sacred.

Islamic lexics later extended to the *Sunnah* or texts referred to the implementation of the prophet Muhammad's practices, the *Hadith* or sayings, decisions, opinions and acts of Muhammad (compiled by al-Bujari in the *Sahih*), as well as the *Shaaria* or the sacred law of Islam (the first version compiled by Malik Ibn Arias) and

---

13 There are debates in the Islamic community concerning the illiteracy of Muhammad, because for some the revelation of the *Qur'an* to an analphabet becomes even more miraculous, while for others it does not elevate the prophet.

220   Everyday Aesthetics

the jurisprudence or *Fiqh*. The methods of Islamic law and jurisprudence were systematized in the *Risala* by Al Shafi.

The main lexic manifestation of the Islamic matrix for Gibb, the Scottish Arabic scholar, resides in law rather than in theology. The fundamental questions in this matrix, according to this author, are first "why are the *Qur'an* and the *Hadith* accepted as legal sources" and second "how are their prescriptions to be understood and applied". (Gibb 1952, 82, 84) For that reason, the master science of Moslem lexics is jurisprudence systematized in the *Fiqh* "the agent of greater scope and effectiveness in the formation of the social order and the life of community of the Islamic people". (Gibb 1952, 16) Consequently diverse categories of rhetoric were introduced in Islamic lexics, such as *kiyas* or argument by analogy, *ijma* or argument by consensus and *ijtihad* or independent argument and free interpretation in addition to *taqlid* or principle of authority. Philosophy, however, was always seen with suspicion or used strictly as an apologetic instrument of Islam.[14]

Koranic lexics are systematically taught to boys in the *madrasa* or Moslem school, as the lexics of the *Torah* in the Judaic *yeshiva*. In both cases a strict memorization of texts is demanded, in contrast to the catechism of the Catholic matrix with a more anecdotal approach. As the Christian homily can refer to political and social issues, the oratory of the *imam* at the mosque affects the practical, political, ideological, familiar, legal, and military life of the community. This matrix partly shares with the Christian a fear of the malignant or destructive power of the word, so that blasphemy against any of the prophets is punished with death by Islamic law.

In The Holy Gospel of Jesus Christ, According to St. Matthew, Chapter 19 [24] it is written: "And again I say to you: It is easier for a camel to pass through the eye of a needle, than for a rich man to enter into the kingdom of heaven". In the *Qur'an* (7.40), this metaphor becomes literal: "Surely (as for) those who reject Our communications and turn away from them haughtily, the doors of heaven shall not be opened for them, nor shall they enter the garden until the camel pass through the eye of the needle." We see here how a metaphor in the Christian version acquires in the Islamic a totally different emphatics: where the former comforts the poor that at least their access to heaven will be easy, the latter uses it to threaten the unbelievers. These nuances are among the conditions that carve sensibilities differently.

The Spanish Islamist Miguel Asín Palacios claims that the *Qur'an* is a mixture of Christian eschatology and Persian angelology combined with the Gospels and the Hebrew *Torah*. On that question, Gibb (1952, 66) affirms "if we understand by originality a completely new system of ideas on God and humanity, the relation among them and the spiritual meaning of the universe, then the intuition of Muhammad

---

14 The first monumental compilation of commentaries of the *Qur'an* is *the Tafsir* de Abu Jafar Mohamed Ibn Jarir al-Tabari (c.839–923), and its *Tarikh al-Rusul wa al-Mulak* (*History of Prophets and Kings*). Three centuries later Fakhr Al-Din al-Razi writes the *Mafatih al-Ghayb* (the *Keys of the Mystery*) and the Sufi Muhieddin Ibn the Arabi (*Jewels of the Wisdom of the Prophets*). I illustrate Philosophers developed a dialectic synthesis of Greek with the Islamic matrix like Al Kindi (m. 873), Al Faarabi (m. 950), Ibn Sina or Avicena (980–1037), Al Ashari, the Sufi Al Ghazali, Ibn Bajja or Avempace (1118–1138) and Ibn Rushd or Averroes (1126–1198). In century XVIII, Muhammad Abdel-Wahhab writes *Kitab al-tawhid* (*Book of Unit*) origin of the fundamentalist movement of Saudi Wahabis.

The Religion Matrix   221

was not original in any aspect". He grants it, nevertheless, originality as a logical, rather than philosophical, evolution of monotheism. On this issue Bertrand Russell in his *History of the Western Philosophy* (1964, 427) affirms that, rather than creative thought, the greatest merit of medieval Moslem philosophy was transmission, and that Averroes and Avicenna can be considered as commentators more than as original philosophers. Certainly, the immense weight of *ijma* or consensus that became a theory of infallibility does not encourage originality or critical thought which are, moreover, not really an important value in this matrix as in others. It was also symptomatic that *ijtihad* or free interpretation declined to the degree that "the great majority of the moslemic doctors maintained that the door of *Ijtihad* had been closed for ever" in the third century from the Hegira. (Gibb 1952, 89, 90)

Nevertheless what attracts faithful Moslems to their religious matrix is not how original it is in comparison to others but the structure it provides for experience and the meaning and values it supplies for everyday life. So whether the conclusions of these authors are a result of their eurocentrism or not (no one can be impartial in these matters, this analysis included), and whether their judgment is fair or not, what is of interest here is that what is so dear to its followers as a guide and comfort for life is aesthetically constructed. Moslems have been captivated by their sacred text not only due to its semiotic dimension but mainly, I think, for its aesthetics in form and content. The great variety of rhetorical figures used in the *Qur'an* such as alliterations and hyperboles, in addition to the rhymed prose of *azoras* explains the attraction by this register:

[53.43] And that He it is Who makes (men) laugh and makes (them) weep;
[53.44] And that He it is Who causes death and gives life
[53.45] And that He created pairs, the male and the female
[53.46] From the small seed when it is adapted
[53.47] And that on Him is the bringing forth a second time;
[53.48] And that He it is Who enriches and gives to hold;
[53.49] And that He is the Lord of the Sirius;
[53.50] And that He did destroy the Ad of old

Or:

[74.21] Then he looked,
[74.22] Then he frowned and scowled,
[74.23] Then he turned back and was big with pride,
[74.24] Then he said: This is naught but enchantment, narrated (from others);

Examples like these are numerous. Also, the weight of Islamic law has an aesthetic impact in fearing disobedience and its punishments, closer perhaps to being captive-of rather than captivated-by it, or *latched-by* rather than *latching-on*. A prolifically narrated lexic topic in this matrix is the eschatology of Paradise to the degree that, according to Miguel Asín Palacios (1943) its most eloquent literary description in Western culture was inherited from Islamic eschatology, namely by Dante Alighieri.[15] The effects of such rich imagery in the description of the Moslem paradise and the horrors of hell are

---

15 Miguel Asín Palacios (1943) quoted by Tedeschi (1992, 58).

Everyday Aesthetics

so impressive that they partly explain the impassioned faith among militant Islamists that they will be rewarded with all these minutely described pleasures after death.

[44.45] Like dregs of oil; it shall boil in (their) bellies,
[44.46] Like the boiling of hot water.
[44.47] Seize him, then drag him down into the middle of the hell;
[44.48] Then pour above his head of the torment of the boiling water:

Whereas those who obey:

[44.53] They shall wear of fine and thick silk, (sitting) face to face;
[44.54] Thus (shall it be), and We will wed them with Houris pure, beautiful ones.
[44.55] They shall call therein for every fruit in security;
[44.56] They shall not taste therein death except the first death, and He will save them from the punishment of the hell.

A matrix does generate particular types of identities and carves certain configurations upon sensibility, so if Jewish lexics offer a labyrinth of intertextuality to be explored for discovering the secrets of the universe between the lines, and the Christian a predominantly emotional narrative of tremendous sacrifice and love, Moslem lexics persuade its devotees that they are on the side of the most powerful God, who will reward them for it after death. This faith appears to endow Moslems with a sense of self esteem and comfort similar to Christians' belief in God's love or the Jewish idea of personal duties and pride for their legacy.

Islamic acoustics

In any Moslem city of the world the acoustics of Islam can never remain unnoticed, since the psalmody of the *muezzin* from the minarets five times a day for the *adhan* radiates its surroundings with its touching sound. The songs of the children learning prayers that emanate from the *madrasas* and the singer that celebrates the ritual with his vocal melody are other aspects characteristic of this register. The musical genres of this matrix are the *Amda* or panegyrics, the *Tajwid* or *Tartil* that are psalmodies of the *Qur'an* and the *Inshad* or free song such as the *inshad of tab* based on two classic verses with fixed melody, *inshad* of *the Nuba* or *baytayn* with greater freedom in the meters and *inshad muwwal* still more open to improvization. Among classic verses used are those of Abu Ishaq Ibrahim Ibn Sahl of Seville, Jew convert to Islam who represents the splendor of the Al Andalus culture during the thirteenth century where the three matrixes integrated with great aesthetic and intellectual vigor.

There is debate within Islam whether Muhammad considered his mission to destroy all musical instruments and banned instrumental music or not. The *Shaaria* prohibits instrumental music as an art of the devil, but some argue that its interdiction in the *Qur'an* is not as clear or remains at least rather ambiguous. Nevertheless, music is played in the Islamic matrix which is certainly not deaf or mute.[16] The Judaic

---

16 I read the request from a young Moslem, who asks his *imam* if there would be some way to conserve his CD collection in exchange for giving a greater amount of charity;

The Religion Matrix

restraint against bringing to the acoustic register the name of God contrasts with its Islamic reiteration in political, military or domestic speech who usually speak "in the name of Allah". The phrase "there is no other God than Allah" repeated by Moslems, is in itself a phrase with acoustic charm: *La ilaha illallah*.

Islamic somatics

Bodies bowing down in religious submission, children's bodies rocking in the *madrasa* making the *Qur'an* enter the mind by sheer corporeal movement, women's bodies hidden by veils and heavy fabrics, bodies owned by sex contract, bodies circumcised during childhood and puberty, bodies mutilated by clitorotomy, bodies amputated or stoned by orthodox Islamic law, body to body combat aspired by the *muchaidin*, and bodies-bomb exploding amidst civilians for *Jihad* … these and similar manifestations point to the idea that the dominant register in the Islamic matrix is the somatic.[17] The body is weapon, hostage, gift or place where power is exerted or endured in this matrix.

The predominance of the somatic register in Islam is made manifest specially in each of the five pillars of Moslem faith. In the first, *Shahada,* referred to the belief that there is no other God than Allah and that Muhammad is his prophet, proposes in addition the creed in the resurrection of the body after death and the reward of a paradise bountiful in corporeal pleasures depending on the test of life on Earth. All three monotheistic religions mention life after death, but apparently only in Islamism this idea has such great power of evocation as to sacrifice life for it. For that reason *Shahada* also means martyrdom (as in *shahid* or martyr). Life for orthodox Moslems is only a test for the afterlife because they believe Allah did not create human beings only to live a few decades in this world, but for the one that follows where they will suffer hell by their sins along with the unfaithful or will be rewarded with eternal delight in paradise. (Ezzati 1976)

The second pillar is prayer or *Salah* in which the body inclines towards Mecca, the holiest locus for this matrix. The meaning of "Islam" as submission is bodily expressed by the gesture of prostrating oneself with the forehead touching the ground.[18] Thus the *rak'a* establishes the diverse positions of prostration for Moslem prayer, and defines with precision the seven movements of reverence with corresponding orations: 1) to recite the *Allahu al akbar* syntagm with the hands open

---

unfortunately he was refused, because "Allah Taala knows better". See http://islam.tc/ask-iman/index.php with the Mufti Ebrahim Desai. In spite of prohibiting instrumental music, the Arabic ethnic matrix keeps instruments of particular tone and texture as *ud* or laud, *dunbuk* or drum of a single head, *daf* or drum of arc, *quanun* or zither and *nay* or Arab flute of cane, and *nafir* or trumpet. The Arabic scale of 24 halftones, 30 rhythms and the 30 modes (instead of the 12 tones and the minor and major scales of Western music) generate a particular acoustic atmosphere. The incomparable Um Kultum must be mentioned.

17 It is worth noting that although these are practices common in this matrix, neither circumcision nor clitoridectomy are mentioned in the *Qur'an*.

18 Prostration is not exclusive of this matrix, because in acts of special devotion, Catholic and Buddhist monks prostrate to the ground, but only Islamic prostrations are performed everyday by everyone.

224 *Everyday Aesthetics*

to each side of the face; 2) to recite standing up the *Fatihah* or the initial *sura* of the *Qur'an*, followed of another passage; 3) to incline from the hips; 4) to straighten oneself; 5) to kneel down and make the first prostration with the face next to the ground; 6) to seat on the butts; and 7) a second prostration. (Gibb 1952, 62) The meticulousness of the commands on corporeal positions for prayer attests to the enormous importance of the somatic in this matrix.

The third pillar is *Sakat*, charity or gift and concerns the collective and individual body by the annual obligatory sacrifice of goods, particularly food, in addition to the voluntary donation as *sadaka* (related to the Hebrew *zdaka*, mercy or rectitude). It consists of the delivery of 2½ per cent to 20 per cent in harvest, cattle, money or goods sold during the year as loans to God that He will fully reimburse, and that will be delivered to the poor, prisoners, slaves and the "holy war" or *Jihad*. (Hattstein 2001, 23) From the obligatory Jewish *mitzvah* in aiding the widow, the orphan, the poor and the foreigner, and as Christian charity to the needy, Islam emulates these values through the *Sakat* to preserve the collective body in a similar manner to the modern welfare State.

The fourth pillar is *Saum* or fasting, particularly during the ninth month of the lunar year, the *Ramadan*. This pillar directly concerns the somatic register, since it prohibits eating, drinking, smoking, and perfuming oneself, having sexual relations and bathing from dawn to dusk. When the evening falls, they can resume these habits, necessities and pleasures.[19]

The fifth pillar is *Hadjj* or pilgrimage to Mecca, inasmuch test upon the body by having to cross deserts, suffer extreme climates and make corporeal sacrifices. When arriving at Mecca the faithful men must shave their head, dress only in sheets without sewing and abstain from sexual contact. The Moslem multitudes moving continuously around the Kaabah in Mecca kissing the stone at each turn constitute an eloquent somatic manifestation of the collective body in this matrix. If seeing those masses around the Kaabah is impressive, being part of them is probably even more so. The faithful must also run between Safa and Amrwa, meet at Mount Arafat on the ninth day, sacrifice ewes and camels, and throw stones at pillars that represent the devil.

Islam prescribes two types of preparation for prayer, both in the somatic register: first is *gusl* or total immersion of the body in special occasions, and the second is *wudhu*, the partial ablution immediately before prayer in which the hands, face, ears and feet up to the ankles are washed accompanying the ritual by particular phrases and concluding by the recitation of Chapter 97 of the *Qur'an*. This matrix emphasizes corporeal cleaning to the degree that even when water cannot be found, the body will have to be washed at least with fine sand.

The term that designates marriage in Arabic, *akd nika* literally means contract to copulate (unlike the Latin *matrimonium* that means condition or result relative to the mother, as the *patrimonium* relates to the father, or the Hebrew *nasa*, that means to suffer, to support, to elevate, to carry, to receive, to destroy and to forgive, namely, what is implied in marrying someone). During the sexual act Moslems must

---

19 They also fasted for the *Ashura*, which coincided with the Jewish *Yom Kippur*, day 10 of Moharran, but that custom was abolished for its too obvious affinity to Judaism.

The Religion Matrix

pronounce the syntagm *Bismila* or "in name of Allah" when penetrating the woman since sexuality should be performed according to Islamic prescriptions.

Although the description of the Islamic paradise unfolds by the lexic register, its sensoriality is so elaborate and embellished that it constitutes a predominantly somatic imaginary for pleasing the body: whoever arrives at the Moslem paradise will enter eight doors in which he will be received by beautiful young girls and angels and will enjoy the 72 *Hur Al Oyun*, or black-eyed daughters of paradise before whom men remain in perfect masculine vigor and youth.[20] There he will find the lagoon of the prophet irrigated by the rivers of paradise that are whiter than honey and more perfumed than musk, the leafy and aromatic gardens of flowers, shrubs and trees. He will eat delicious banquets with the best and most sophisticated dishes, will dress in the most luxurious clothes made of brocades and silks and will carry an abundance of pearls, gold, silver and precious stones. He will be annointed with fine perfumes and balsams of gray amber, musk, camphor, and aloe and will listen to the most pleasant music. In contrast, hell, inhabited mostly by womenand the unfaithful, offers the worst of corporeal tortures.[21] It is certainly understandable how humble peasants, shepherds and city dwellers of Moslem communities find this aesthetically drawn picture intensely alluring. But these descriptions pronounced to comfort the dying seem so poignant because what is described is precisely a chant to the marvel of being alive, what they will forever lose: life's aesthesics. Better teach the magnificent, sensuous value of this life at primary schools to those who can relish it.

One may compare the version of paradise in this matrix with that of its predecessors. The Christian paradise, congruent with the predominance of the scopic register, offers itself more to visibility than to corporeal sensuality. There Christians will be able to contemplate the Trinity of God the Father, the Son and the Holy Spirit, the Virgin, the Apostles, angels and saints, all of which have been depicted with enormous dedication and eloquence by Renaissance artists, particularly Tintoretto's *Paradise* (at the Ducal Palace in Venice, the greatest painted canvas in the world: 7.45m x 24.65m). If Christian paradise is more scopic than somatic, its hell is wholly suffered upon the body, as the Islamic. The relative low profile of the somatic register in the Judaic matrix affects also its conception of death, interpreted plainly as meeting with one's ancestors, as Moses declared before dying, even if Jewish folk traditions also have versions of heaven and hell.

A great variety of rules with respect to corporeal practices are specified in the *Shaaria* and the *Sunnah* (as rules in the Jewish *Halachah*). The body is disciplined by the *Sunnah* in the rigorous separation between the *khalal* (allowed) and *kharam* (forbidden). For that reason Moslems must ask their *imam* how to correctly perform daily activities (as shaving, nose surgeries, use petroleum jelly or soap, hair rinses,

---

20 According to Sheikh Palazzi, the Islamic tradition affirms that there are 72 spouses for each believer who is admitted to paradise, not only for each martyr, according to the *Hadith* compiled by Al-Tirmidhi in the *Sunan* (Volume IV, chapters "the aspects of the Paradise described to the Messenger of Allah").

21 For Gibb (1952, 42–43) the doctrine that influenced Mohamed more deeply was Christian eschatology of the Final Judgment, particularly Syriac.

226 *Everyday Aesthetics*

erections, ejaculations, kisses, caresses and oral sex), and how to distinguish between *mani* or sperm and *mazi* or flow from sexual excitement, on fasts, menstruation and masturbation, on the bodies allowed or prohibited for marriage (Moslem women are only allowed to marry Moslem men, but men can marry Christian and Jewish women, not Buddhist, pagan or of other denominations).[22]

It is not accidental that perfume culture bloomed particularly in this matrix. Avicenna himself discovered processes of distillation of aromatic oils. The forgotten body or submitted to strict halachic routines in Judaism, the stigmatized and celibate body in Christianity becomes for Islam a place of meticulous disciplinary practices that would have theoretically fascinated Michel Foucault. Yet for the believer, such importance attributed to corporeal practices aesthetically endow him of a sense of meaning, dignity and importance.

Islamic scopics

In spite of sharing with the Judaic matrix the iconoclastic proscription stated in the Bible's Second Commandment, the fate of Moslem scopics followed a different path. From this matrix emanate beautiful illuminated texts inherited from Persian culture and traditions, exquisitely decorative calligraphy and the arabesque style handwriting where the letter acquires a joyful sensuality and scopic exuberance. Islamic scopics are characterized also by the carved or modeled stalactites denominated *muqama* as an architectonic ornamental motif invented also by the Persians in the tenth century, and that is expressed with incredible lavishness at Granada's Alhambra. Abstractionist and geometric elegance unfolds in magnificent mosques from Sheik Lutfullah in Isfahan, Suleiman's in Istanbul, the blue mosque of the east in Shah Alam, the one in Cordoba, Ibn Tulun and Al Azhar in Cairo, mosques in Damascus and Al-Aksa and Omar in Jerusalem among many others.

In addition to monumental architecture, the main manifestation of Moslem scopics is its spatial orientation and sacred locus. In reaction to the custom among the Jews of Medina of praying towards Jerusalem, Muhammad first ordered Moslems to pray in the same direction, but then changed it towards Mecca, his birthplace. For that reason each mosque indicates the direction of Mecca through the special niche or *Mehrab* turning it into its major center of symbolic density, as Jerusalem is for the Judaic matrix.

A parallel approach to dramatics in the religious matrix

We have partly seen how these three monotheistic religions have created worlds to gain and preserve their adepts via aesthetic means of expression. Believers are captivated by a view and a way of life that fills their heart and provides them with a religious identity and a sense of direction. The main dramatics of these three

---

22 The restlessness that the members of this matrix show with respect to their body in questions to their *imam* can be testified through Internet pages like http://islam.tc/ask-iman/index.php with the Mufti Ebrahim Desai. Orthodox Jews must also consult with their Rabbi for very minute everyday practices.

The Religion Matrix 227

monotheistic religions basically coincide in their aspiration to educate and structure human beings exhorting them towards charity, self-discipline, consideration of others, regulation of daily personal and communitarian life ordering the body and the mind. They radically diverge, nevertheless, in their rhetoric strategies and dramatic modalities.

Religious proxemics

Territoriality and proximity could not be more dissimilar among the three matrixes. Judaic proxemics with respect to the divinity are infinitely long because the Hebrew God is absolutely transcendent, and yet very short, illustrated by the case of Job who argues directly with God accusing him of being unfair, of Moses who questions why precisely him, who stutters, should be chosen to accomplish the mission of convincing the Pharaoh of liberating the Hebrew slaves, and of Jonah who gets angry at God and tries to escape the task of warning the inhabitants of Nineveh, later to blame God for making fun of him. Also Sara was confident enough to laugh at her God when she was told she would be pregnant in her old age (the reason why she named her son Yitzjak, meaning "will laugh"). There are no intermediaries between the Jew and God, as the rabbi is a simple teacher (*rabbi* literally means teacher) not a mediator (unlike the high priests or *Cohanim* whose role was suspended after the destruction of the Temple of Jerusalem).

Proxemics in the Catholic matrix establishes a greater distance between the community and the divinity to legitimize the hierarchy of the clergy as mediating between the congregation and God (mediation which the Protestant Reformation tried to shorten). At the same time, Catholics are very close to their favorite saints and Virgins, appealing directly to them without any mediation on very concrete, everyday problems. The saints do not judge, but they answer prayers and do favors. The motto "Render unto Caesar the things which are Caesar's, and unto God the things that are God's", separates between the private sphere of faith and the public sphere of the State frequently violated but perfectly explicit in words of Jesus. Nevertheless, it allows a very short, almost intimate proxemics between the faithful and the Church always welcoming them regardless of the magnitude of sins or cruelty inflicted upon others. The Christian God forgives everything as long as the emphatics of repentance appear to be genuine.

Islamic proxemics are also dual, although with other parameters: long by establishing the clergy as intermediaries between Allah and the people, but short by agglutinating the diverse social matrixes in itself. In Islam, this distance between the religious and the political diminishes, so that religious authorities are in many Moslem countries political and mediatic at the same time, as well as educational, legal, and military through the *mullah*, the *imam*, and its different hierarchies from common clergymen to the supreme *Mufti*. On the other hand, Moslem proxemics in the original sense proposed by E.T. Hall as "territoriality" is not only long but also excluding since it prohibits access to Mecca, Medina (and also to the Temple Mount in Jerusalem) to anyone who is not Moslem, in sharp contrast to short Christian proxemics that welcomes all.

228 *Everyday Aesthetics*

The ambivalent proxemics of Islam with respect to its Judaic and Christian roots is worth noting, because on one side it grafts itself from them by taking on monotheist faith and a great number of narratives, ideas, values and practices, but on the other accuses them of distortion. For Islam, Christians and Jews are *dhimmi*, meaning "the protected people of the book", who for that same reason have a higher status than pagans in Moslem societies but also have been charged with onerous taxes and special proscriptions by Moslem law.

Religious kinetics

The kinetics of monotheism should be static by definition because they propose the idea of a single, eternal God and its millenarian permanence since the creation of the world. This explains why, for example, Islamism which arrived on the historical scene 14 centuries ago during the lifetime of Muhammad, claims to be eternal and at the same time to have mythologically emerged since the time of Abraham (who is believed by Moslems to have founded Mecca). This is a strategy that understands well the mechanism of the production of symbols, so it may consequently allege equal symbolic weight as the Judaic matrix established about three thousand years earlier. Every religion must renew and adapt to historical and social changes to survive, and there is a constant tension between the dynamism of renovating groups open to hybridization or social transformations and the stability of orthodox, fundamentalist, and conservative groups.

Judaic kinetics are twofold: on the one hand they are relatively static based on a narrative and historical heritage that goes back to about the second millennium B.C.E. and maintains a memory that according to its calendar marks the present time at almost a quarter to the sixth millennium, 5767 to be exact (will the Jewish world rest during the seventh millennium?). Judaism does not recognize Jesus as the Messiah but as one of its members; moreover, according to Jewish tradition, the prophetic condition for the arrival of the Messiah is the eradication of evil from the face of the Earth, a condition not yet fulfilled. In this sense it is totally conservative. Hebraic kinetics also do not accept the translation of the *Torah* to Latin or German, since they believe that the spirit and original sense of the word would be lost. On the other hand, this same respect for the written letter has stimulated a dynamic kinetics among more progressive individuals and groups in opening to other traditions by a rich cultural hybridization. From the last Diaspora two thousand years ago and in its condition as minority, the Judaic matrix maintained this twofold or contrasting strategy of preservation: on the one hand some groups have opened and established a dialogic relation with the cultures that have hosted them transforming their own culture. The Orthodoxy, on the other hand, created a common mental territory to dwell in by strict distinctive practices which can be kept in any place and unite various practitioners (the celebration of common festivities and regulations on everyday life like food and prayer), regardless of where geographically they may reside. The gap between these static and dynamic strategies is so big that orthodox defectors find themselves totally lost in Jewish secular culture, as in contemporary Israel, and need professional help for integration.

The Religion Matrix

Christian kinetics remained static for a long period of time in their strict monitoring of the written word against any deviation or heresy. Nevertheless, it managed to maintain significant dynamism by having to come to terms more or less reluctantly with some changes in the world vision, particularly the scientific, that threatened its theocentric vision. Apart from various religious orders and since the Protestant Schism, Christian kinetics have been dynamized generating hundreds of groups, from Calvinists, Baptists, Evangelists, Lutherans, Presbyterians, Anabaptists, Anglicans, Methodists to Mormons, Unitarians, Quakers, Millenarists or Alethians and Christian Scientists. Consequently kinetic tensions at the interior of the Christian matrix are today considerable, because there are voices that struggle to welcome emergent movements like Marxism, liberation theology, feminism, and gay and lesbian rights, while the most static oppose them. This matrix's vitality placed it at the vanguard of conquering the so called New World, together with the military and State matrixes.

Islamic kinetics were spectacularly dynamic with the support of the sword and the *Qur'an* during its expansion, since in less than a generation Islam consolidated a State and in a century a whole empire in Asia, Africa, and Europe. Muhammad began to preach in Medina in 611 and by 711 Tarek Ibn Ziad arrived at Al Andalus expanding its domain. In a century and a half this matrix achieved its intellectual apogee and during the golden Islamic age it had great cultural development. As incredible as this dynamism was, its opposite static tendency was no less remarkable, since Islamism was paralyzed during the following 300 years and has been since. This relative staticity in the development of scientific and humanistic theory may perhaps be partly attributed to the paralyzing weight of *ijma* or consensus, in addition to the rejection of hybridization and polyphony and the inability to tolerate other voices and learn from other cultures, scorning any form of alterity, as well as to its emulsion of religious, political, legal, and military powers that have since dominated this matrix's kinetics.

Religious emphatics

Evidently, what these three religious matrixes share is their emphatics upon the existence of one single God. Nevertheless, a belief that should actually link all creatures towards a common deity has radically segregated one group against the other for religious reasons, often with boundless brutality. Detailed exclusion strategies have been fabricated to define the collective subject as "us" in opposition to derogatory "others", most often its minorities who dare not recognize such interpretation or such rites.

Emphatics of the divine Subject

The emphatics of the Judaic deity presents it as a single, unpronounceable, invisible, and omnipotent Being in Whom the past, present, and future implode (the meaning of the Tetragrammaton) and from Whom the creation and the progression of history emanate. He demands the observance of the Law, the perpetuation of memory and therefore the expression of gratitude. God is anthropomorphically personified by human characteristics such as jealousy, revenge, fidelity, and generosity. On these Judaic emphatics of the Subject depend also the emphatics of individual and group

230 *Everyday Aesthetics*

identities in their effort to reach fundamental ethical values attributed to their God such as loyalty, gratitude, generosity, discipline, and, more importantly, a sense of justice. Significantly, the Jewish God can tolerate questioning, incredulity and rebellion, since the main value in this matrix is justice. This is why Job challenges God's injustice to him, and explains the belief that God will save the world as long as there are at least 36 hidden just men, the *Tzadikim Nistarim* or *lamed vavnikim*. If in February 2006, furious Moslems ignited protests throughout the Arab worlds when Danish cartoons portraying Muhammad and Islamists as being violent were published, for the Judaic matrix it is injustice, rather than pride, which most provokes indignation.

The emphatics of the deity in the Christian matrix is considerably different: it accentuates love and forgiveness. Jesus preached to love our neighbors and control violence when offering the other cheek. Christian emphatics highlight grace and humbleness, particularly Catholicism where the deity is interpreted as being extraordinarily generous, merciful, and compassionate. The concept of Trinity, by which God is believed to be One and Three simultaneously, and demands unconditional adhesion to this dogma of faith, is unique to this matrix. The Christian God calls for religious fervor, humility and blocks rational explanations.

At the beginning of the *Qur'an*, in *Al-Fatiha*, Allah is described as the [1.1] Lord of the Worlds, [1.2] The Beneficent, the Merciful, [1.3] Master of the Day of Judgment. Allah is generous with the submissive but enraged with the unfaithful, threatening impiety with the horrors of punishment in hell if they do not obey, but promising great rewards and compensations if they do. Allah knows everything and watches it all. The emphatics of the deity in the Islamic matrix demands total obedience to the Almighty, omnipresent, master and creator of everything.

Emphatics of the human subject

We see how monotheistic emphatics on the uniqueness of God from a common Hebraic source underwent significant metamorphoses through Christian and Moslem versions, which in turn had various consequences in carving the image of the individual and collective subject. In Judaism what was tested upon Abraham, the first Jewish patriarch, was his faith in a single, invisible and only audible God when demanding the sacrifice of his loved son Isaac. And yet, it is not by faith alone that the Jew belongs to his religious matrix, but by maternal line (although his kinship to the lineage of Levi and David, from whom according to tradition the Messiah will descend, depends on the paternal line). Jews may curse, question and dissent, as the biblical Job did, but their belonging to their religious matrix is basically irrevocable by its tribal rather than voluntary condition. The subject of this matrix not only has free access to Scriptures, but obligation to study them, in addition to some freedom to interpret them.

Being the most benevolent in its discourse on love and forgiveness, in its rites of absolution and exhortation to mercy, the Christian matrix is paradoxically ruthless when establishing the condition to belong to the community based upon the pure emotion of faith. Having faith is not a voluntary act, as neither is love, but a gift that does not belong to the devotee: it simply occurs or not, as an epiphany. This explains how, in order to *latch-onto* the dramatics of faith, one depends on the aesthetics of rituals. These

The Religion Matrix   231

ceremonies and sacraments must entertain the mind with narrations and gratify the senses with stimuli such as smelling incense, flowers and wax, hearing sacred music, touching the Rosary's beads, vicariously tasting the communion wafer and consecration wine and particularly appreciating its finely elaborated scopics in all its forms.

The emphatics of the subject for the Islamic matrix lies in the fundamental principle of faith in the *Shahada*: "There is no other God than Allah and Muhammad is its prophet". In this sense, Islam shares with the Christian matrix an imperative of belief. It is not enough for the Moslem to pronounce *Shahada*; he must believe it at heart. By the obligation of prayer five times a day and obedience to the five pillars, the subject in this matrix constructs his or her personal identity as a Moslem. According to the Islamic doctrine, human beings are basically good but can be taken by ingratitude, avarice, and laziness against which one must fight in the existential sense of *Jihad* (quite different from its Islamist version as "holy" war against the infidels). Thus the Moslem devoid of faith is, according to the *Qur'an*, a loser. He misses the first and most important of the five pillars, but still has the other four left to fulfill. By contrast, the lack of faith in the Jew has no serious consequences; he still belongs to his tribe. The Catholic without faith is in dis-grace (excluded from divine Grace) while still having faith in the faith that he does not have.

Such *pathos* of faith and the deeply tragic character whereupon the subject of each of these three matrixes is constituted is, to say the least, poignant. It partly allows one to understand how particular forms of sensibility have been carved, aborted or thrived in each religious matrix which is not only a system of beliefs but of subjectivity production. The Jew is given the letters in the *Torah* where he believes lies the mystery of the universe, a discursive *Big Bang* whose enigma he must discover without hope of full understanding (as the hopelessness of the Buddhist with 108 sacred texts, impossible to study in a single life). Projected to the future of interpretation and to the past gravid with meaning, the subject of the Judaic matrix perpetually sacrifices the present, so precious for Eastern matrixes as Hinduism, Tao, and Zen. Perhaps this explains why Jews always seem to be in a hurry, worried by the monumentality of a task that escapes them in the finiteness of a single lifetime. He is also burdened by 613 duties which separate them from non Jewish neighbors, provoking hostility. To the Catholic, the test of faith is presented as a perfect contradiction in the dogma of the Trinity and of the Immaculate Conception. What Catholics are forced to sacrifice for belonging to their congregation is not the present but reason, their right to understand. Their production of a religious identity must unfold more in the affective side of faith than by intellectual exegetics, with the exception at high levels of the clergy, perhaps theological debates. Western science has been painstakingly built from this divergence, as illustrated by the paradigmatic figures of Galileo Galilei and Giordano Bruno. Finally, for Moslems individuality ended with Muhammad, the last ring of the prophets represented by the *imam* in turn, to whom they must submit, as the woman to her husband, for maintaining *ijma* or consensus and the community together. The schism between Sunni and Shiite is not as much a question of interpretation of the *Qur'an* as of legitimacy of the *imam*'s power, justified in one case by social or political merits, and in another by relation to Muhammad's family. Who has the right to command and who does not is hardly a small issue in this matrix.

232   *Everyday Aesthetics*

Emphatics of the collective subject

All matrixes, not only those monotheistic here examined, but also totemic and polytheistic like the Aztec or Mayan, have in common the emphatics of their collective identity as "chosen people" by their gods. They all construct the image of their deity projecting it from a communitarian conception and invert, as Feuerbach well understood it, the election of a God by the community into the election of a community by the God. Each totem or god "chooses" its tribe to fulfill its needs and grant its favors, as Huitzilopochtli chose the Aztecs to protect them and establish Tenochtitlan, the Jewish God chose the people of Israel for delivering the Law at Mount Sinai, Jesus chose followers for his congregation, Allah chooses obedient Moslems for the Islamic paradise, and the Virgin of Guadeloupe chose Juan Diego and the Mexicans to erect her temple at the mount of Tepeyac.

This idea of the chosen collective subject is presented in each congregation by different aesthetic strategies. The Christian collective subject assembles during the communion to be purified through the Eucharist. Christ was sacrificed for the sins of humankind and this unbearable weight, this guilt, has been historically transferred to Jesus's own kin, constituting Jews as a deicidal collective identity through an inexplicable paradox of worshiping a Jewish personal identity in the figure of Jesus while simultaneously stigmatizing his collective identity.

As chosen people to receive the Pact at Mount Sinai, Jews were burdened, rather than privileged, by 613 duties ascribed to the *Torah* (becoming more elaborate throughout tradition, especially by the *Halacha*). The collective subject in this matrix is Israel (not denoting the present nation-state but the biblical and historical community), expressed by the daily prayer "Listen Israel, God our Lord is One" which addresses it collectively. This subject remembers every Passover that "God set *us* free from slavery in Egypt" which obliges promoting cohesion and solidarity beyond two millenia. From the outside, however, this collective subject has been singularized to carry burdens much heavier than the 613 duties, having been blamed for all evils from Jesus's crucifixion, the bubonic plague, witchcraft, poisoning wells, the "Protocols conspiracy", Germany's defeat in World War I, Palestinians' perpetual condition as refuges, Capitalism, Communism, the Holocaust, WTC Twin Towers' attack, the invasion of Iraq, Danish cartoons, and so on.

Among Moslems, the collective subject is the *umma* preserved by Islamic law in the *Sunnah* and the *Fiqh*. The spectacular military and political successes of Islamism during its territorial expansion contributed to the reinforcement of such collective identity, because it implied not only to being aligned with the victors but also the certainty that Allah the most powerful and merciful was on their side and against the enemy. By the same token, this is not an individualistic religion—in contrast to Christianity in its Saints and martyrs or to Judaism with its prophets and rabbis. What Islam fundamentally proposes is a social morality prescribing capital punishment to those who question the Law or the five pillars. This severity is explained less by the transgression itself (as blasphemy in the Christian matrix) than by its consequences of breaking the *ijma* and splitting the *umma*.

These modalities generate particular forms of sensibility and values, certain types of subjects and peculiar links to their congregations. That is why, as a social

The Religion Matrix 233

construction and a collective subject, each matrix is wholly accountable for the violence, weaknesses, brutality, and vulnerability it brings forth, as well as honored by the contributions it bestows upon humanity. It is easy to understand how deep these matrixes penetrate a subject's identity, not only in the monastic way of life but in the secular as well. With such significance given to the smallest details, to temples and texts, prayers and ceremonies, disciplines and beliefs during day and night, every week and month of every year, it is almost impossible to imagine another reality or a different identity from that collectively played within their group and so carefully woven by aesthetic strategies.

Religious fluxion

Approximately 2,000 million Christians, 1,400 million Moslems and 13 million Jews today constitute the population of the three matrixes here analyzed. Islam is presently gaining the greatest number of adepts and its population reproduces more rapidly. These quantitative differences can be partly explained by the collective fluxion of each matrix.

In the Judaic matrix the collective fluxion is centripetal by its tribal character that rejects proselytism. Its world community grows only biologically in congruence with the matrilineal principle and radically shrank by half during the Holocaust (which would amount to the extermination of one billion Christians; as two out of three Jews in Europe were murdered). Except in Biblical times, this matrix did not deploy territorial invasions to convert conquered people (around the year 800 the Khazar King Bulan converted to Judaism followed by many Khazarim, but not as a result of conquest). For that reason, as minority within other nations, this matrix has been for millennia object of repeated persecutions in political and military defenselessness until 60 years ago, with the establishment of a sanctuary and homeland granted by the UN on about a third of the geographic Palestine Mandate accorded to Great Britain at the fall of the Ottoman Empire.[23]

From the platform established by the Roman Empire, Christianity was the first monotheist matrix to fully understand monotheism's logic and deploy centrifugal fluxion by pacific evangelization as well as military conquest. Christian missionaries have been flowing for two millennia to all the corners of the Earth preaching the word of Christ and the salvation of souls. Nevertheless, as far as the internal groups of this matrix by the institution of priesthood, the fluxion becomes centripetal when meticulously selecting the candidates for monasticism (because few are apt for the rigors of religious life, as stated by Saint Paul with respect to the celibacy of "strong spirits"). As an instance that illustrates fluxion in the opposite direction of the Catholic Church is today's (and probably yesterday's) hermetism in the concealment of and complicity with numerous cases of pederasty among the ministers of the Church.

Islam arrived farther still in its interest for universality by decreeing that all human beings are born in Islam and that to practice other religions is to incur sinful deviation. This centrifugal Islamic fluxion is deployed together with military-political strategies

---

23 By the 1920 San Remo Conference, this zone was granted to the British Mandate.

234 *Everyday Aesthetics*

imposing Islam as official religion throughout 57 countries in Asia, Africa, and Europe (among 191 countries at the UN).[24] Thus Christianity and Islam have competed in their centrifugal fluxion for converting the masses to their faith and increasing the number of their communities for many centuries throughout their history.

Final considerations of the religious matrix

We have traversed these three matrixes that were established upon the same founding principle of the single God, albeit radically dissimilar materializations. The universe created by each religion or collective *umwelt* thus constitutes the religious identity of its members by concrete aesthetic strategies such as the scopics of temples and symbolic sites, the acoustics of their hymns and prayers, the lexics of their benedictions and narratives and the somatics of their rituals. The *latching-on/ by* that Moslems, Christians, and Jews have in relation to their matrix aesthetically constitutes them as individual and collective subjects by captivating their skin, ear, mind, sight, sense of smell and taste from birth to death. Specific practices in each matrix configure tangible, audible, visible, and intelligible aesthetic realities towards which individual subjects *latch-onto/by* with delight, fear or absorption. The border between the profane and the sacred is established in two dimensions: by space through the threshold of mosques, churches, temples, and synagogues, and by time through the rituals of Shabat, Passover, Christmas, Easter, and Ramadan.[25]

Each of these three matrixes leans predominantly on a particular register: the Judaic in the lexic (not arbitrarily the Jews have been called "people of the Book"), Catholicism in the scopic, and Islamism in the somatic. Acoustics are present in all three, but incomparably stronger in religions of African origin, some of whose elements have been transferred to Christianity like the black Baptist Church through the strongly rhythmical genre of the *Gospel*, because it is the sound, and particularly the rhythm, the way to approach the divinity and intone body and mind, the individual, and the collective, by the cadence and movement of rituals.

---

24 In the United States, for example, where there are approximately 6 million Moslems (and 6 million Jews), Islam is the religion of greater growth at the present time.

25 The main obligation for Jews is the conservation of the *Shabat* consecrating one of every seven days in obedience to the Fourth Commandment "Remember the Sabbath day, to keep it holy, Six days shalt thou labor, and do all thy work; but the seventh day is the Sabbath of the Lord thy God; in it thou shalt not do any work, thou, nor thy son, nor thy daughter, thy manservant, nor thy maidservant, nor thy cattle, nor thy stranger that is within thy gates." By the lexic register not only special prayers are said in that day, but also the mind is focused upon thoughts different from profane preoccupations. In acoustic emphatics special songs are sung and the coming of the *Shabat* was announced by six blasts of the ram's horn or trumpet blown from the Temple two thousand years ago. In somatic emphatics, devoted Jews feel particularly dignified during this weekly celebration, walking slower and moving things in a characteristic manner. In scopics, they dress clothes of better quality, and prepare the table with the best set of dishes and in the best place of the house. As the *Shabat* "is not a date, it is an atmosphere" (Abraham Joshua Heschel quoted by Zerubavel 1985, 117) and atmospheres are created by aesthetic mediations.

The process of generation of religious fervor is double: it works by *im-pression* of rhetorics upon the attitude, and by *ex-pression* when dramatics of faith demand rhetoric articulation by various means such as bodily sacrifices (fasting, peregrination) or dancing in the somatic, singing in the acoustic, interpreting and speculating in exegetic inspiration in the lexic and painting, or constructing temples and caring for symbolic places in the scopic. It also occurs by *de-pression* when subjects of deeply religious sensibility feel devoid of faith. It is common to find *com-pression* among fanatics, orthodox, fundamentalists and puritans whose severity rigidifies religion into a monological self-righteousness that excludes any possibility of dialogue and hybridization.

The form in which statements are presented not only *con-forms* religious attitudes but also *constitutes* the reality of the world proposed by each particular religion. When the Jew says *"Baruch Atah Adonai ..."*, the Christian *"Pater noster, qui es in caelis, sanctificetur nomen tuum. ..."*, and the Moslem *"La ilaha illallah"* they exceed the semiosis of a simply referential illocution and recruit their sensibility into affective connotations beyond ordinary speech. The vehicle through which the devotee enters the liminal dimension of faith is enabled by aesthetic strategies with a plethora of manifestations in all the registers and modalities without which no religion could exist.

But sensibility sustains not only aesthetics but ethics as well. One might consequently question the complicity of each matrix with the crimes committed in their name: Christian endemic antisemitism and its persecutions of minorities and collusion with pederasts, as well Islamist deliberate killings of civilians and criminal use of children for "holy wars". The Judaic matrix might also be questioned for not taking sufficient measures to alert its people at the abyss of nazi genocide, as today at the unambiguous genocidal declarations of Iran's President Mahmud Ahmadinejad, so ravenous for nuclear power, and for not hoisting enough the causes of persecuted minorities.

Paradigmatic projection of and in the religious matrix

As in the previous family matrix, paradigmatic projections related to the religious matrix move in two directions: they export as well as import paradigms from other matrixes. Jesus of Nazareth denounced the projection of the commercial matrix onto the religious when witnessing animals and other objects sold and bought next to the Temple of Jerusalem. Martin Luther disapproved the same projection among Christian priests selling indulgences as commodities. On the other direction, the most common paradigmatic exportation of the religious matrix lands upon the State, not only in fundamentalist theocracies like Iran, but in religious political parties, the establishment of the Ecumenical Concilium and the Vatican, the use of religious images when calling for war (as the image of the Virgin of Guadalupe by the priest Miguel Hidalgo during Mexico's war of independence, or the newly elected president Vicente Fox visiting the Basilica before attending the Congress). Presidential speeches that end with slogans like "God bless America" or the motto "God bless the Queen" in Great Britain and its inscription in coins are other projections of this matrix. Many national movements were projected having religion as a fundamental cohesive factor, as English Anglicanism, German Lutheranism, Spanish Catholicism, Scottish Knox Presbyterianism, and Dutch Calvinism and Arminianism.

Foucault recognized, although not indeed in these terms, the paradigmatic projection of the religious matrix to the medical by the substitution of the priests' confessionary by the psychoanalysts' couch. In this same sense, when trying to examine the body in religion, Turner (1984) ends up examining the body in medicine to which religious ideas are exported on the interpretation of leprosy, epilepsy, and hysteria as moral diseases of the soul by sin. The nuns' voluntary work in hospitals is another example of this exportation of the religious matrix to the medical. The medical matrix is also projected into the religious, as with the famous healer Kathryn Kuhlman and the congregation of Christian Science founded by Mary Baker Eddy. The case of the Jewish Hungarian doctor Ignaz Philipp Semmelweis who, fearing the angel of death and impurity of corpses enforced by Jewish tradition, demanded doctors wash their hands in a chlorinated solution when leaving the area of autopsies before examining the patients, thus reducing considerably mortality by puerperal fever in maternity wards.

From the medieval Islamic matrix during the eighth century, the Abbasid caliphs of Baghdad promoted the development of Western science through the great minds of Tabit ibn Qurra, Abul Wafa, Ibn al-Haytham or Aljazen, Al-Razi, Ibn Sina, Jabir ibn Hayyan, Al Kindi, Al Batani and Averroes. In the year 988, Al Azahar University was founded as an extension of the mosque of the same name. Medieval clergy established the first universities in Paris, Bologna, and Oxford during the eleventh and twelfth centuries. Philosophy from Christian medieval scholastics to the Renaissance and the beginnings of modernity (Occam, Saint Augustine, Aquinas) arises also as projection of the religious matrix, continued by Galileo, Kepler, Bacon, and Grosseteste. Today, apart from numerous schools and universities founded and maintained by the religious associations in totally overlapping educational and religious matrixes, the paradigmatic projection of religion even in secular schools is patent in the organization of religious plays, the suspension of activities during religious festivities like Christmas, the day of Guadalupe, or the Holy Week as official celebrations.

On the other hand, the religious matrix imports tourism and funerary paradigms to gather funds by using religious sites for mourning and even burying the dead. Religious tours are organized to religious places; visiting fees charged and souvenirs sold at churches, mosques, synagogues, and cathedrals. Examples of these projections are innumerable, because the religious matrix has had the gift of magically legitimizing almost any activity, particularly killing.

Chapter 29

The School Matrix

The *kathedra*, Greek word for "chair", signifies the position of authority much like the throne of a king, the *solium* of an archbishop, the Parliament curule of a Senator or the high backed leather managerial chair of a corporation's CEO. Thus the symbol in the school matrix is *authority* not only for the personal figure of the teacher but for the version of reality that he or she inculcates that will significantly contribute to mold up the students' sensibilities. Teachers acquire the right and duty to occupy this chair and exert corporeal and mental control on their students based upon an authority previously credited and conferred by other authorities. That is why authority is symbolic, since, according to our definition of symbol (cf. Chapter 15) it is sustained upon the investment of time and energy dedicated to accumulate an educational capital. When the correspondence between legitimate accreditation and its formal awarding is lacking, the result is the teacher who, being authorized, lacks authority and therefore resorts to authoritarianism for face saving.

A degree of aesthetic *latching-onto* (cf. Chapter 8) the topics in the learning experience by taking genuine interest in them, as well as in the interaction between teachers and students and within the classroom among themselves is a basic requirement for the optimal operation of the educational process. By contrast, being aesthetically *latched-by* school bullies, rigid teachers, and boring classes attests to a failure that can be so devastating to an individual's sensibility that it can go to the extreme of even pushing a child towards suicide. Aristotle clearly stated in the *Poetics* (1448b) "to be learning something is the greatest of pleasures not only to the philosopher but also to the rest of mankind, however small their capacity for it". In our terms, this pleasure derives from our *latching-on* by wonder and curiosity to the world. When learning ceases to be a pleasure, it is a symptom that the school matrix is more preoccupied with reproducing itself that in constituting an atmosphere for the generation and transmission of knowledge. For that reason its form of operation must focus upon inducing playful aesthetic *latching-on* to which students are naturally prone because when the world is taken as a ground for discovery, learning is stimulating and delightful, or what some could denote as an aesthetic experience for its "free play of imagination and understanding", as Kant would say.

Basically, the school matrix has the aim of releasing parents' time required for work, homogenizing students according to their national identities, while simultaneously differentiating them in terms of class and future job so that they will eventually cover the corresponding social and laboral niches and put their minds and bodies under the capitalist economy of time. Its function is not only to make docile and domesticate the dominated sectors of the population and aggressive the dominant classes, as denounced by the Marxist theory of the education (Labarca, Vasconi et al. 1979); it also domesticates the elite towards greater efficiency,

238   *Everyday Aesthetics*

aggressivity and competence since, in a pyramidal socio-economic order, each layer is forced to reproduce itself as such. The subject of the so-called "dominant class" is also dominated by its own ideology under the imperative of pecuniary and social success according to the expectations of its social circle.

Therefore, if "in the School not only the skills, abilities and knowledge of a job or profession are taught; also the values and attitudes linked to their exercise are inculcated in bourgeois society" (Labarca et al. 1979, 34) what interests us is which are those values and attitudes and, mainly, *how* are they inculcated, by which strategies, and by what means are they legitimized so people adhere to them. Marxist theory of the education that considers the school matrix as an ideological apparatus of State (in Althusser's sense) is basically correct given its role of "interpelating" and constituting subjects. But for focusing education towards liberation, as Paolo Freire proposed, and transforming the apparatus, it is necessary to examine the mechanisms whereupon it constitutes such subjects, and the aesthetic strategies that favor certain identities and not others.

School rhetorics

The dominant register of the contemporary school matrix in Western cultures is the lexic since, as we shall see, authority is invested fundamentally upon it. In general, school lexics consist in learning linguistic and numerical codes that distinguish each social and professional practice from another. The teacher is credited for masterfully handling lexics whereas the other registers are subordinated to it. Even modalities of the dramatic coordinate such as enthusiasm in teaching, the vocation or aptitudes to stimulate students, creativity and imagination to present ideas are not considered a priority for their pedagogical performance. What counts here is the ratio hour–blackboard, teacher–students, validated–invalidated.

The acoustics that dominates this matrix is an obligatory silence for the students unless they are addressed by the teacher, in addition to the perpetual sound of the teacher's voice in class. The sound of the bell is imported from the religious matrix—as in the Benedictine monasteries (cf. Zerubavel 1985)—to mark schedules and rhythms that segment time and interrupt activities. The morning rhythmical choral greeting of "good-mor-ning-Mis-ter-Brown" is a common practice in primary schools and earlier. Outside the class schedule, it is worth mentioning the mocking songs and rhymed acoustics whereby children early begin to exercise aesthetic violence against their more vulnerable peers by ridiculing or hurting their sensibility.

In the third register, somatics, the school conventions usually force young students to stay fixed in their desk almost the whole day, remain in a corner for a punishment, rise when the teacher arrives, form queues by heights, request permission to speak by raising their hand, constantly maintain the gaze to the front, and control the need of going to the bathroom, falling asleep, walking, speaking, jumping, or laughing until the class ends. This disciplination of bodies and sensibilities is exerted mainly by the mechanism of *im-pression* through the control of dramatics by rhetorics. (cf. Chapter 23)

The fourth register in the school matrix, scopics, is typically manifested in the setting of seriated classrooms that keep an eerie analogy to the prison or monastery

The School Matrix

identical cells, each with desks aligned towards the front in strict orthogonal composition. School props consist of notebooks, pencils, pens and rulers, knapsacks, textbooks, and erasers, printed maps and monographs, in addition to school uniforms. How amazingly destitute are school scopics considering their potential impact upon education! It is paradoxical that, having emerged from the religious matrix, particularly the Catholic which masterfully and deliberately used images to inculcate the religious dogma, the school has not been sufficiently concerned with its potential scopic wealth. Designers are employed for endless minute variations of packaging to sell commodities, whereas the State or private investments upon the imaginative creation of didactic material with an aesthetic concern is pitiable. Instead, the student could be surrounded by stimulating figures of "academic saints" like Pasteur, Einstein, Archimedes, Galileo, Descartes, Newton that could transmit them the belief in the genuine delights of conjectures, enigmas, and puzzle solving.

The lack of passion and creativity that dominates this matrix which often considers teaching as a load instead of a game, turns it into a system geared towards being *latched-by* for students who become almost captives of monological speech throughout the onerous years of their school deformation. Pupils could easily become captivated instead by the wealthy history of what human beings have been able to imagine, elaborate and understand. But for the joyful presence of their cell peers and the steadfast mental health of some teachers who do not let themselves be fully dominated by the industrial model and its empty efficientism, this stage of life would be insufferable. In spite of such adverse conditions, it is still sometimes possible to achieve aesthetic *latching* towards learning, a situation for which we remain forever grateful to the teacher who enabled it. In this aesthetic captivity, students are nourished by those few teachers who offer this *latching-on* opportunity.

School dramatics

The school matrix is always defined in opposition to and by competition with the family matrix. One of its functions in the basic levels of education is to exert a centripetal force strong enough to resist family pull, and thus to partially tear off the individual from the compelling link, sometimes even suffocating, between mother and child. Its role, then, is close to what the psychoanalyst Melanie Klein denominated "deterritorialization". This function, which would normally correspond to the father, is obstructed at the present time in Western societies by labor conditions under the industrial paradigm that demand not only the best but practically all energies that the individual can generate. School personnel thus substitute these relatively absent fathers, requiring dramatic strategies to intimidate the parents and strictly define territories while at the same time to persuading them of their credibility, efficiency, trustworthiness.

School proxemics

The strategies that the school matrix deploys to establish a distance that initially separates children from their family and that progressively links them to the laboral

240   *Everyday Aesthetics*

and professional submatrixes are numerous, reason why proxemics vigorously unfolds in its four registers. The long proxemics between study and play begins here, and will be later mirrored in the rigorous separation between work and leisure, the public and the private, pleasure and duty.

In the lexic register, the teaching-learning process consists of the acquisition of terms and vocabulary whose aim is to shorten students' proxemics towards classmates of the same generation or career and lengthen them from the younger ones or of different fields of knowledge. Each new word is a new toy, a conceptual finding. Unfortunately, this enjoyment in learning is jeopardized when presenting each term isolated from the context it emerged from and where it is applicable. This way, the essential pragmatic training of concepts for adaptive purposes boils down to superficial semantics, which will soon vanish from their memory. The school matrix wastes thus enormous mental resources due to deficient aesthetic tactics because of the false idea that exhibiting a terminological repertoire appears more impressive than the formation of mental structures.

In lexic proxemics, the impersonal, intimidating, and legalistic language used in calling parents for an appointment with directors, advisors or teachers is worth mentioning. Calling students by their last name, a common practice in this matrix, instantaneously establishes long proxemics. To record grades numerically or "by letters A, B, C, D (that do not mean anything except their hierarchical relation, an analogy of this matrix's tendency to classify students hierarchically on quite abstract terms) lengthens proxemics between student and teacher but supposedly shortens it with their expectations on future wages at the professional matrixes. In their identities' formation, these expectations are not as truthful and realistic as they pretend to be, since a high grades' report card is indexical less of the future professional success and the student's talent than of its present docility.

Acoustic proxemics within the school apparatus establishes that the intonations teachers use with their students must produce distancing effects to convey neutrality, authority, and impersonality, never of intimacy. In general, teachers worry more about keeping order in the group that in generating knowledge. For that reason they use also long somatic proxemics by being located in a different place, at the front of the classroom, for proxemic as much as panoptic reasons. Students will be partly constructing their identities as students from the somatic proxemics established with respect to the teacher: Those who are more rebellious will sit in the back rows, for example. The separation of the bathroom between boys and girls, and between students and teachers, establishes as well a distant somatic proxemics with respect to genders, ages, and hierarchies.

The dominant scopic proxemics in the school matrix imposes the strict uniform to students for establishing a clear distance between home and school, between one school and another, and between private and public schools, namely, between one social class and another. As scopic proxemics we can also consider the school's typical closed door and insurmountable wall separating prohibited spaces and times from parents and preventing students' escape from the institution. The school director will often occupy a special separate place, generally at the entrance or on the top floor of the school building, to define a long proxemics with respect to the rest of the personnel by the scopic register.

School kinetics

The school matrix implants the necessary stability and standardization of knowledge for the maintenance and reproduction of society, as was profusely argued by Bourdieu and Passeron (1981). This way the inventory of available knowledge becomes established by stationary lexic kinetics, at the time that it mobilizes while guaranteeing its controlled reproduction upon subsequent generations. For that reason the dominant kinetics in this matrix are static by its tendency to block the students' conceptual, appreciative, and interpretative initiative with respect to learning and demanding merely textual reproduction of books and class notes in school exams. If the function of the school matrix were to project students towards their future as adults, citizens, parents, and professionals, a future that is continuously transformed, its main goal contrastingly seems instead to be geared to prioritizing the serial production of proto-laboral identities rather than the generation enabling enriched, creative and more flexible and solidary sensibilities.

Evidently, the school matrix suffers from a rhythm problem. For that reason many students tend to update themselves through informal education by films, books, television, and the internet. There is no sufficient mobility and flexibility in the school curricula to relate to current events and debates, because the pace by which scientific or philosophical topics are integrated as school contents is extremely slow in relation to the production of knowledge. The reproductive inertia by habit of the school matrix may be transformed by technology, as the present digitalization of education, but often results in a mere technical ostentation that merely appears to aestheticize contents in a "light" superficial version demanding less effort and thus giving less heuristic results.

Somatic and acoustic kinetics are also rigorously regulated in the school matrix. Students have to remain in their assigned desk and not move more than the minimum necessary during each class. The teacher is forced to remain within the classroom practically all the morning except for rare and very festive occasions of museums visits and outdoors activities. The somatic *peripatos* that great teachers like Socrates and Rabindranath Tagore practiced by taking a walk with their students has been expelled from this matrix for obvious reasons in the contemporary Western mass societies. Pity, since walking in the somatic echoes the kinetics of learning and strolling through new mental places.

School scopic kinetics are manifested by the solidity and stability of its facilities. Each classroom is generally destined to a certain course, and not to a certain group throughout its trajectory in the school. This way students move every year to another room instead of appropriating one space for their generation as a learning workshop by collectively personalizing it, a more reasonable approach considering that they will spend many of their best hours, months, and years in them. Scopic kinetics become indexical of a worldview that proposes that reality is stagnant and unchangeable, and that only generations move through it; the result are passive subjects and tame citizens. This situation, that seems so natural by habit, is a not wholly deliberate aesthetic strategy that nonetheless produces a pre-established and detached image of the world, independent from the subjects, implying that there are no transformation options and therefore no responsibilities on this matter. In mass societies, the school ceases to be

242 *Everyday Aesthetics*

matricial and becomes more institutional fixing its programs in repetitive routines.[1] The apparently insignificant tactic of leaving classrooms at the end of the year exactly as they were at the beginning, impersonal and empty, ends up becoming metaphorical of the students' minds who do not recognize or are unable to acknowledge how they changed and what they learned throughout the year. This matrix provides no possibility of synthesis. By contrast, appropriating the space and allowing traces or inscriptions of the learning process could aestheticize it in favor of students' *latching-on*, creating an atmosphere full or memories directly linked to what they studied.

With all its immobility in initial stages, there is nevertheless enormous dynamism at the other pole of this matrix, namely at university level, whenever free research is tolerated or stimulated and different versions of reality are proposed and inquired.

School emphatics

Teachers can unfold various aesthetic strategies according to the professional identity they want to establish before their students. As there are several stereotypes in the family matrix, here we can mention different emphatics according to their dominant stereotypes deployed. The stereotype of authoritarian teachers implies the use of prescriptive and normative speech in the lexic to produce intimidation effects on their students whom they will address by their last names. The authoritarian scopic proxemics will require clothes that distinguish them from the students, preferably a formal suit. They will unfold rigid somatic kinetics, as well as static lexic and monotonous acoustic kinetics. Their fluxion will be centripetal expressing lack of interest upon their students' ideas and will maintain a *com-pression* process never favoring dialogical or mayeutic interactions. (cf. Chapter 23)

However, teachers who opt for a friendlier "fellowish" emphatics tend to show a more light-hearted somatics (freer gestures and movements), agile lexic emphatics with informal scopics similar to their students. Proxemics will shorten in the lexic (using every day and simple language), in the scopic (wearing jeans and tennis sneakers), in the somatic (making frequent eye contact with students or patting their shoulders), and in the acoustic (using an almost equivalent volume and voice tone as the students). Their lexic kinetics tend to be dynamic with games and turns of speech, some jokes and youth jargon. Somatic kinetics will be more agile and flexible and the fluxion in the somatic will likely be open by gesturing spontaneously.

The repertoire of teacher stereotypes is not reduced to these two, since one can find absent minded professors, Napoleons in St Helena, furious *führeren*, Don Juans, Mephistopheles, martyred missionaries. In the women's league we may find seductive catwomen, tender Snow Whites, rude pugilists, stern spinsters, matriarchs of generous udders, moaning Cinderellas, Platonic Diotimas, wonderteachers, innocent Red Riding Hoods before the ferocious group, and as many as the reader can add based on their experience in this matrix. Students also display stereotypical identities depending on their emphatics among which the most common are: the popular, the cool, the nerd, the grouch, the bully, the crybaby, the class clown,

---

1   I have dealt with the distinction between the matricial and the institutional in a paper presented at Casa Lamm July 2003, entitled "Los tejidos duros y blandos de la cultura".

the egghead, the scaremonger, the teacher's pet and so on that in some cases last for a lifetime. Note that these are not roles, even if there is some circumstantial conditioning, but identities because they are personalized and motivated in some way or other. They all, however, share their role as students.

The typical emphatics of the school matrix in the lexic register focuses on examinations and grades around which the link between parents, teachers, and students is maintained. The student credits, the teacher certifies, and the parent confirms receipt. Another aspect of lexic emphatics are the subject matters that the school matrix considers relevant to inculcate. There is, however, no sufficient reason that justifies not initiating primary school children into topics and workshops such as philosophy, toy invention and construction, imaginary houses and cities, classification and organization of things and ideas, the analysis of rights and obligations, a mimicry workshop of professions, another of gadget inventions, and imagining alternative possible worlds.

On the contrary, under the heading of "history", what is actually taught is in fact just a history of wars according to the official point of view, stuffing students with treaties and dates that obscure understanding their relevance and impact. Thus the history of the culture, of daily life, of works and trades, of children's life are simply ignored. Historically significant events in the community and students' family history such as emigrations, despoliation and persecutions throughout several generations, or their triumphs, prides and achievements are never considered pertinent, blocking their potential contribution to the class. To make matters worse, history education begins with Mesopotamia and China, and generally never reaches the present, so students never get to understand something of what is actually occurring in the world. The common practice of separating subjects in different classes and separating children from their surroundings and the real problems have the effect of jeopardizing an integrated view between learning and understanding which tends to maintain them in a civic infantile state throughout their lifetime.

These examples suffice to show the arbitrariness of school lexic emphatics in the choice of subjects that favor certain aspects of reality as pertinent and exclude others, many of which may have much greater relevance for the student and for society in general. This is the symbolic violence that Pierre Bourdieu and Jean Claude Passeron (1981, 45) denounce when they write "all pedagogical action (PA) is objectively a symbolic violence as imposition, by an arbitrary power, of a cultural arbitrary". Indeed, but such symbolic violence of imposing a cultural arbitrary is not as dangerous as the aesthetic violence that ruptures the student's subjectivity imposing derogatory identities such as the fool or the booby of the group. Like Genet's comment about the family being a criminal institution, the school can also generate serious degrees of aesthetic violence by the continuous abuse of teachers or fellow classmates against more sensitive or vulnerable students systematically hurting their self-esteem to the extreme cases of provoking severe depressions, suicide, and homicide. The recent murders in American schools are the effect of these cruel games that keep their victims *latched-by* mockery and scorn, desperate for any exit. The impersonality and therefore irresponsibility with respect to the identity and sensibility of students are among the ominous results of massification, alienation and blind institutionalization in this matrix, and particularly of neglecting the aesthetic dimension in everyday life.

244 *Everyday Aesthetics*

Scopic emphatics of the school matrix in its architectonic enunciation resemble penitentiaries, monasteries, or bureaucratic institutions. This way, students get used to store themselves in impersonal, alliterative and monotonous spaces. Serial neutrality and empty scopic emphatics is reinforced by the identical classrooms, identical uniforms, identical packages of information delivered at identical Taylorist times and motions by the fordist assembly-line expecting from students identical products and massified identities. More appropriate as models for this matrix are the emphatics of a workshop for inventions, an artist's studio, a carpentry, a den, a farm and a library combined with a ludoteque, videoteque and audioteque. Without denying the necessity that all students should share similar bases, there is no reason why such homogenization should govern the totality of the educational process.

School fluxion

Since the school matrix germinates from the religious matrix, a significant part of its mechanisms are directly inherited from it, particularly from the monastic routines whose strict time regulation prevailed in Benedictine monasteries schedules during the Middle Ages (Zerubavel 1985). What controls the school matrix and enunciates the authority of the teacher is the centripetal fluxion over the time of students and teachers alike, whereas the assimilation, understanding and application of knowledge seem accessory. It is worth noting that, for example, the State establishes education by criteria based on time (in Mexico, the school calendar of 200 obligatory days) rather than on understanding, applying and sharing learning. When students graduate they demonstrate having learned better the art of passing tests than of comprehending texts, expressing themselves coherently or analyzing a problem. Everything in this matrix revolves around this centripetal fluxion of time that counts minute by minute from the moment the door of the school closes until it opens again.

By circumscribing priorities into the schedule, rather than on the intellectual and social aptitudes of the students, a democratic exercise is certainly practiced by the school matrix in demanding what supposedly we all have in a similar measure: time. Other criteria such as creativity, a sense of solidarity, understanding, inventiveness, initiative, intelligence, and compassion, application of knowledge, insight, originality or clear communication of ideas would be, according to this criterion, deeply undemocratic since their distribution is unequal. The matrix thus cuts equivalent slices of time from each child's life from a minimum of four to six hours daily in basic education, demanding an additional investment dedicated to homework that usually takes the rest of the day. This way it keeps creating subjectivities that perceive life merely as a process of complying with requirements. There is no time for dreaming, adventure, leisure, "wasting time" with friends and relatives, playing and spontaneous learning, except when a child is shrewd enough to steal some time for herself away from schedules. It is not surprising that when one finally owns some free time during weekends or vacations, most people resort to already predesigned packages for filling up excedent time with programmed competitions, prefabricated summer courses and organized tours with a rigorous distribution of times.

This golden rule of the school matrix is applied to students as much as to teachers. The centripetal fluxion of time on teachers is clear as soon as they are employed per

The School Matrix 245

class hour instead of by piecework which would imply to stimulate active understanding by students and their relation with practical reality. The monastic regulation of time in this matrix is perhaps the greatest obstacle for being captivated by learning.

This centripetal fluxion of time is enunciated characteristically by two strategies, one in the scopic register and another in the lexic: the classroom or school door and the list of attendance. Many parents wake up with the threat of that door. The door is closed at the exact hour, not a minute more, nor a minute less, and is opened with the same punctuality. From the axis of the symbolic, that door symbolizes the ritual of passage of the child from the family to the educational matrix, from the mother's control to the teacher's, from flexible time to fixed schedules, from the private to the public sphere, from culture to education and from the matricial to the institutional regulated by the State. It is an absolutely univocal door: it is either closed or open in strict obedience to time.

The second syntagm characteristic of centripetal fluxion is the attendance list. Generally, last names in rigorous alphabetical order are pronounced as rapidly as possible to alert students. This list is a sort of *panacousticon* device that confirms only the presence or control of time day per day in school and not the students' affective, physical or intellectual condition in class. The teacher is not interested in knowing the students' condition, because they are not allowed to answer: "Richardson" "I slept terribly", "Smith" "I have a stomach ache", and "Brown" "my dad arrived drunk last night"—much more significant with respect to their receptive and emotional state and that affects their possibilities of learning. What the teacher expects is the simple "present", indexical of the accumulation of times dedicated to school.

The school centripetal fluxion not only operates on time, but also in the exigency to accumulate data, good grades, medals and full notebooks. In the lexic fluxion, traditional schools limit students' verbal expression and demand memorization exhibited in school festivals designed to impress parents and educational authorities.

The same happens in the acoustic register: shouting, laughing, and speaking aloud between friends are rarely tolerated in the classroom to maintain a centripetal fluxion. The opposite modality is exclusive in the panacoustic and monological device of the teacher's voice that must constantly be heard. It is worth noticing how, when the teacher leaves class, the group immediately resuscitates freeing contained energies. In the somatic fluxion, one must mention the prevailing custom in primary schools to expect sphincter control for prolonged periods that sometimes can even affect the health of the child. The student must request permission to go to the bathroom and the teacher is even granted the right to deny it. This fluxion demands the daily presence of students in its facilities, and disallows expansive or expressive movements of the body in class.

In coherence with the former, the centripetal scopic fluxion is manifested in the accumulation of school utensils, most of which are not thoroughly used, that switches to expulsive fluxion as soon as the course is over when students make bonfires with them or simply throw them to the garbage as a symbolic ritual of liberation. This fluxion of retaining instead of sharing school utensils, to cast them away later, seems calculated to prepare them towards their future consumer expulsive/retentive fluxion with its frenetic rhythm of spending and collecting.

The category of fluxion allows us to diagnose a fact that perhaps would remain unnoticed, namely, the failure in organizing an adequate fluxion for the school matrix: open with respect to time and energy for playing and expression, but closed to avoid wastefulness, open to the ludic potential but closed to the bureaucratic for safeguarding whenever possible its matricial over its institutional character. What is definitely lacking in this matrix is play and aesthetics.

Paradigmatic projection of the school matrix

Because of its deep social and individual significance, the suitable paradigmatic projections operating in the school matrix are of highest priority. Unlike the family matrix that maintains a relative autonomy as far as the selection of dominant emphatics in each family, the school is dominated by the State through the Ministry of Education that not only defines the "what" but the "how" of teaching and learning. The school matrix is the main prosthesis to produce and reproduce *latching-on* towards the national identity that the State apparatus requires. As Illich once said, schools are the State's reproduction organ.

If Martin Luther once denounced the paradigmatic projection of the commercial matrix onto religion, we can denounce today with greater vehemence its present projection on the school matrix. In private schools, children boast about their toys advertised by television, about the suburban truck that picks them up from school, their tennis sneakers' and clothes' brands, and even the model of their laptop and Windows version. This paradigmatic selection is not arbitrary, because the present prevalence of the economic model imposes itself upon all areas of social activity (as stated by Marshall Sahlins 1988; see also Stuhr 1997). Projections of the military (parades and marches around the flag), the scientific (labs, science festivals and contests), the religious (prayers in classrooms and religion courses), and the sport matrixes (school teams in interschool competitions, scholarships for good athletes) are also common. The projection of the industrialist-bureaucratic model previously mentioned through the massification of education by a Fordist assembly line that calculates its operation on automatic and homogenous processes is another case. It succeeds, however, in producing subjects who have learned something more important than to read and write, add and subtract: they will know to obey, be quiet, pass tests and sell their time.

Pity that the artistic matrix is only projected tangentially onto the school by the so-called "cultural extension" through exhibits and performances that merely legitimize institutions as supposedly promoters of the arts. This is another consequence of the conflation between the aesthetic and the artistic. Aesthetics applied to the inventive elaboration of didactic materials and to research playful pedagogy, on the other hand, is almost absent, since it requires from teachers only to teach exactly as they learned, based on a schedule.

Chapter 30

The Medical Matrix

From the medical matrix we face both the brightest and the darkest side of life. Here technology's peaks are dramatically associated with deep knowledge of nature's prodigies. The peculiar human disposition of taking health for granted makes evident the degree in which we equate it to life itself. We try to do without doctors until a disease seizes our body or threatens our life. For that reason the symbol of the medical matrix is not health, but *disease* only referring to health by its absence. Disease as symbol of this matrix is not, in this case, an object for *latching-on* but of being *latched-by*, not for being captivated but held captive by an illness (except for doctors who play *agon* with it). It operates as symbol by the inevitable affective, material and time loads dedicated to fight or to prevent it. It is not casual that *semeiotics*, as theory of signs, emerged in classical Greece precisely from this matrix, because the body appears to speak a language of symptoms whose understanding and decodification is a matter of life and death.

In the medical matrix one can go beyond semiosis by not only re-cognizing the meaning of the procedures, diagnoses or treatments but entering its quite impressive aesthetic universe. Being aesthetic does disqualify it as a scientific or functional endeavor, but complements its requirements for legitimation and adhesion. Its mechanisms of appeal can attract an individual to become a doctor or nurse, or incline us to choose one doctor rather than another. Aesthetic strategies in this matrix can be as powerful as to convince patients they are in good hands and even sensibly contribute to their prompt recovery, or the opposite, create in them anxiety and insecurity affecting their sensibility and aggravating their health.

Between science and art, the medical matrix is *im-presive* in its strategic deployment when skill and discipline are inferred from its rhetorics, and *ex-pressive* of the inventiveness and philanthropy of many of its members (regardless of the cases of voracious mercantilization, ineptitude, and negligence in this matrix).

Medical rhetorics

In order to present their identities as professionals with sufficient credibility, doctors must pass through explicitly scientific but tacitly aesthetic rites of initiation facing matricial authorities that certify their competence. A title means that they managed to perform in an acceptable way all the requirements and examinations that this matrix establishes, namely, that they succeeded in playing the game of *mimicry* not only as simulation but as imitation of their teachers (that, I insist, does not mean they are liars, but simply that there is mimesis). Haas and Shaffir (1982) studied this process of initiation from a dramaturgical perspective at the MacMaster medicine

248   *Everyday Aesthetics*

school in Canada. In their analysis by participative observation and interviews of students, these authors stress the props, vocabulary, and costumes, namely, the lexic and scopic registers, whereupon the legitimacy of those aspiring to become doctors is constituted. What is strange in their analysis is that they neglect to mention nothing less than the somatic. This register is fundamental in this matrix since, from the somatic, instruments are meticulously handled, the body is clinically explored and the patient is surgically intervened. In fact, as in the family matrix, the somatic is also the dominant register here. The selection of candidates in MacMaster, as in a great number of similar universities, requires a curriculum and a letter of motives in the lexic, a favorable photography in the scopic and an interview in which candidates display their competence in the lexics, acoustics, and somatics, in addition to the scopics of a satisfactory appearance.

In psychiatric medicine, the aesthetic function is especially important. Mental patients suffer a condition of being *latched-by* hallucinations, chronic emotional pain, and aggressive or self-destructive impulses. Their problem is not strictly mental, as implied by the term, but sensitive and affective as well, because schizophrenics and, specially, paranoiacs, demonstrate abilities of great mental coherence and creative imagination. As Gregory Bateson (1972, 1991) argued in his "double bind hypothesis", schizophrenics suffer of a situation generated in the family matrix, particularly with respect to their mother. This condition, of enormous aesthetic violence to the degree of breaking not only the identity of an individual but his or her subjectivity as well, is explained by Bateson as the impossibility to choose any alternative without condemning themselves: they are damned if they act in a certain way and damned if they don't. Some mothers practice cruel games altogether unconsciously to discharge their aggressive impulses on one of their children under a loving and caring *mimicry* that hurt the child's psychological integrity and identity construction. These are mothers who feed, but poison. It is the "bad breast" described by Melanie Klein that is not only polyphonic expressing one thing in one register and the opposite in the other. What is painful to the child is the trick of using one register as alibi for the other, namely, expressing rejection in the somatic register but hiding it with loving words in the lexic while twisting the direction of the rejection as if it came from the child. This aesthetic violence affects the person's sensibility irreversibly.

Among the strategies for treatment, Bruno Bettelheim (1974, 91–187) demonstrates an acute conscience of the crucial role of the aesthetic, particularly of the scopic register, in an institution for mental patients at the Orthogenic School of Vienna. Bettelheim put into play his sensibility and empathy with respect to the patients in *A Home for the Heart* as he denominated this place. He stressed the importance of a building in creating the spirit in its interior and asks:

> How should the patient see the institution? It shouldn't be too small, so that it seems confining, nor should it be so large that it appears overpowering. It should fit unobtrusively and harmoniously into the neighborhood but without any loss in individuality. It should have a character of its own, but not so much that a patient will feel conspicuous as he goes in or out. It should be sturdy and substantial enough to protect us, without seeming restrictive [...] Hopefully it will bespeak some grace in living, reassure any sense of

The Medical Matrix 249

insecurity without domination, and make a positive appeal to our esthetic feelings. It should convey unity, but it should contain well-articulated individual features. It should show an open face and convince us that within it, individual man is the measure of all things. (Bettelheim 1974, 98)

From our perspective, it would seem that Bettelheim deliberately applied prosaics' categories. In the scopic fluxion he proposes "it shouldn't be too small, so that it seems confining, nor should it be so large that it appears overpowering", or "it must show an open face to us and convince to us that in its interior the individual human being is the measurement of all these". For proxemics he proposes "it should fit unobtrusively and harmoniously into the neighborhood but without any loss in individuality", in kinetics "it must be solid and substantial the sufficient to protect to us, without seeming restrictive", in emphatics "it should have a character of its own, but not so much that a patient will feel conspicuous as he goes in or out" as well as "Hopefully it will bespeak some grace in living, reassure any sense of insecurity without domination, and make a positive appeal to our esthetic feelings. It should convey unity, but it should contain well-articulated individual features."

Having a disintegrated subjectivity, schizophrenic patients present problems in the somatic register (they feel their body as disintegrated) and require the scopics of congruent settings and props to help anchor themselves, as well as the lexics of therapeutical discourse. Also necessary are the acoustics of a reassuring voice or music to silence their inner voices in addition to the somatics of occupational therapy for an active *latching-on* to a reality that can captivate them enough to aid in releasing them from their captivity in being *latched-by* hallucinations. For that reason, in hospitals for mental patients, the aesthetic strategies must be deployed by deliberate *im-pression* as described by Bettelheim, surrounding the patient by opportunities for *latching-on* to landscapes, gardens, artistic, and sensorial stimuli.[1] Through these strategies, patients will be able to recognize their right to aesthetic dignity and balance their obsessive *ex-pression* with a benevolent *im-pression* of calm environment that do not threaten them but allow gradually opening themselves to a reality with a greater degree of intersubjectivity.

In our role of patients, we can hardly orient ourselves with respect to the credibility of a doctor. Our situation worsens when requesting a second or third opinion, one contradicting another. As we lack sufficient knowledge on the precision of the diagnosis and the success of the treatment, as well as about the professional competence of the doctor, we frequently resort to our aesthetic intuition for making a medical decision. We then assess the dramaturgical strategies of doctors by which they constitute their professional identities and convince us on the necessity to follow or resist their prescriptions.

If in the axis of the signic we recognize their legitimacy as doctors—as through the lexic register in the exhibition of their professional titles hung from a wall—in the symbolic we constitute their identities with an additional weight of hope and gratefulness for the treatment. We trust doctors with our most precious possession,

---

1   The opposite of that I once saw with horror in a psychiatric asylum at Parque Lira street in Mexico City during the 1960s, where in damp and depressing, dark spaces, patients were half-naked, seated on the floor in their feces, with an insufferable stench.

our health and life, to the degree of putting ourselves in their hands even in the state of deepest unconsciousness in anesthesia. Consequently doctors who exhibit nervousness and insecurity in the acoustic and the somatic registers, who are clumsy in clinical examinations or let instruments fall, or who show ignorance and confusion in the lexic and keep their office dirty, disordered or unpleasant in the scopic register, impel us to consult another specialist.

If a doctor would express disgust, repugnance, grief or fear with respect to the patient in a clinical examination, he would violate the rules of the game and would risk his professional identity, although he can indeed (and often does) feel disgust, repugnance, grief or fear. The construction of an identity as a doctor demands in the first instance to represent the role of professional neutrality and imperturbability. If for the patient a diagnosis such as "tumor" acquires a symbolic weight by being materially, temporally, and affectively associated to cancer, to the pain and fear of chemotherapy and the horror of death, the doctor on the other hand must exclusively stay in the axis of the signic establishing differences between benign or malignant tumors, degrees of malignity, types of cancer, stages I, II or III, alternatives of treatment and so on. These are the strategies with which doctors manage to cure themselves of the natural revulsion to disease, and that we could consider them as magical in a certain degree since they succeed in exorcising the suffering that such diagnosis implies.

In this matrix, not only doctors and nurses unfold aesthetic strategies. Pharmaceutical companies, at least in the USA (as in a report from *Primetime* in February 2002 on Pfizer) display aesthetic strategies for attracting doctors to prescribe their products, strategies such as invitations to luxurious vacation resorts or art museums with transportation, lodging, drinks and meals included, in addition to gifts, conferences, certificates, and so on. These tactics of persuasion are a masquerade, a common bribe.

Medical dramatics

Medical proxemics

To enter the medical matrix as a professional constitutes by itself a proxemic act in which students must be distanced from the non-initiated by the particular jargon they must memorize, credit, and exhibit through specific processes of legitimation. The amount of examinations that they must credit certifies their competence in lexic proxemics shortening the distance among colleagues and extending it with respect to other matrixes. Distances are established even among members of the same matrix by lexic proxemics among doctors specialized in a field with respect to others. In as much an aesthetic strategy, the lexics in the medical matrix construct a specific vocabulary which authorizes those credited by it to obtain patients' docility as regards a therapy imposed upon them, regardless of its pecuniary and often corporeal onus. As a student interviewed by Haas and Shaffir (1982, 192) states, "... you just can't survive if you don't learn the jargon. It's not so much an effort to identify as an effort to survive. People in medicine have a world unto themselves and a language unto

The Medical Matrix 251

themselves. It's a world with a vocabulary ... and a vocabulary that, no question about it, creates a fraternity that excludes the rest of the world and it's a real tyranny on laypersons who don't understand it." Nevertheless, the doctor must know how to swing proxemically to get near the patients to procure a clear understanding of their symptoms and make sure they, in turn, understand their treatment.

Acoustic proxemics in this matrix impose near and customized styles of enunciation with respect to the patient that do not hinder professional distance. Hass and Shaffir speak of this necessity of distancing that reminds us of Bullough's concept of "psychical distance" analyzed in Part 1, but that in this case implies a distance for the observation and the intervention on the body for treatment and not, of course, for aesthetic contemplation. Doctors do not maintain a disinterested attitude in the existence or not of the patient, but they must nonetheless remain impartial with respect to the diagnosis and therapy. This distance required from doctors is more compatible to Brecht's concept of *verfremdungseffekt* or distancing effect as the attempt of halting empathy and identification to acquire a more acute perspective of the situation, or the distancing of *theoria* with respect to everyday life.

Somatic proxemics in this matrix imposes such intimate contact that would be censurable in other matrixes. Clinical examination by gynecologists, urologists or proctologists is illustrative. The skill displayed in somatic proxemics is fundamental for doctors, because they must know how to explore patients more closely and minutely than the patients' explorations with their own body and at the same time generate the effect of long proxemics of absolute erotic and aesthetic indifference. The recent prosthesis in medical somatic proxemics enabled by robotic arms and stereostatic positioning systems or laparoscopes and ductoscopes is so close that they even surpass the doctor's natural anatomical possibilities.

Let me emphasize that certain practices of somatic proxemics are variable and obey to fashions and conventions of different times. The present short somatic proxemics at hospitals that allow fathers' presence at the delivery room during childbirth or mothers to hold their newborn almost immediately after birth were not habitual during the 1950s, whereas the traditional spank in the butt holding the baby by its leg to make it breathe is no longer done. These practices influence the participants' sensibilities, as fathers witness and participate in childbirth instead of waiting for the news at a bar, smoking a cigar to celebrate if it was a boy.

Among the strategies of aesthetic enunciation in scopic proxemics is the whole range of medical outfits: gowns, uniforms, hair caps, face covers, gloves, scrubs, robes that characterize and distinguish the personnel of a hospital and distance them from patients and their relatives. Scopic proxemics are also enunciated in the distribution of billing offices in hospitals altogether separate from the rooms, thus sheltering the patient from having to solve economic questions or pay for each medicine at the time it is administered while being hospitalized. It is worth noting the long proxemics used by doctors for outpatients by delegating upon their secretaries and receptionists the task of demanding and receiving payments, and thus aesthetically presenting their practice as purely philanthropic. An allopathic doctor would never take care of his patients in a pharmacy, as homeopaths do. Such proxemics would expose him as a mere publicist or distributor of pharmaceutical products.

252   *Everyday Aesthetics*

Part of the scopic and somatic proxemics in this matrix at the present time reside in the juxtaposition of medical attention offices for outpatients in private centers. Previously, the doctor's office was next to his house. Today these centers indicate a hierarchy in this matrix: to belong means to be successful and competent by contagion or tacit complicity of proximity to other colleagues (although it depends more on the economic or social capital of their family, not necessarily professional merits). These centers' monumental architecture produces the effect of solidity and firmness by analogy to medical services and professional competence that are not visible to the patient except by scopic association.

Medical kinetics

In lexic kinetics, doctors have to handle both steady kinetics by dominating fluently the terminology or jargon of their field and dynamic enough by continuously updating themselves in new concepts and techniques participating in specialized courses and congresses. In acoustic kinetics, a slow speech rhythm may allow one to suspect that the doctor would not be able to react with the necessary speed in a case of emergency, whereas someone too hasty could indicate superficiality or nervousness, and therefore the risk of error and negligence. The optimal somatic kinetics of the medical matrix must proceed with the possible celerity in painful treatments and at the same time maintain, as in the previous registers, a balance with the stability necessary to obtain the results hoped for. Patients will have to dynamize their somatic kinetics when forced to make therapeutic exercises or the opposite, become static when forced to stay in bed. In American hospitals, for example, once patients are accepted for hospitalization, they are forced to sit on a wheelchair although they can perfectly walk and move by themselves. When sent home, they are taken again in a wheelchair to the hospital door. This somatic kinetics aesthetic ritual is made to clearly establish the role of "patients" as persons requiring its services from the moment they enter until they are permitted to leave the hospital.

Scopic kinetics in this matrix are truly impressive: machines that move without friction up and down, to the sides, orthogonally and diagonally, special chairs that raise and lower us and that turn into beds and beds that become chairs, doors that do not squeak and close softly and precisely, objects that fasten, that transport, that inject, that cut, that sew, that insert, that connect, that separate, that observe, that isolate, that listen, that pump, that maintain, and that kill. Devices full of tubes and hoses, liquids and color capsules, bandages, syringes, drills, glass contraptions of a thousand forms, clamps, scissors and knives of all sizes. These props of scopic kinetics express the stunning dynamics of this matrix by the speed in which new technological inventions are constantly generated. They also prove that the human body requires something more than a hammer and a screwdriver.

Medical emphatics

Exhibiting diplomas on the walls (a habit no other professional displays) is not only meant to show their competence but to symbolize their efforts, since each certificate

The Medical Matrix 253

supposedly implied a significative investment of time and energy. For the patient this is an aesthetization of the skill and identity of the doctor, because aside from personal recommendations, one cannot otherwise infer the necessary legitimacy to submit oneself to their treatment.

Lexic emphatics in this matrix denominates diseases according to two basic strategies. On the one hand, it uses terms derived from Greek endowing them with aura of universality and antiquity, as "condrosarcoma" of *condros* (cartilage) and *sarcoma* (fleshy growth) or "osteoplastia" of *osteo* (bone) and plast of *plasein*, to model or to form. Innumerable medical terms come from the Greek (hiperkaliuria, hipogonadism, hemacromatosis, hypoglycemia, nephritis, etc.), source of many words in contemporary Western languages. This aesthetic strategy is related to the symbolic axis of a time load through an old and venerable tradition and millenarian wisdom inspiring respect and appreciation since the time of Hippocrates.

The other strategy is to name diseases by authorship, as the Syndrome of Marfan, Fröhlich's, Alzheimer, Loefflerm, Lowe, Louis-Bar, Larsen, Stein-Leventhal, Guillain-Barre, Cushing, Hallermann-Streiff, Albers-Schönberg, Hallervorden-Spatz, Addison, and Hodgkin. Also findings as the bacillus of Döderlein, or procedures as the maneuver of Celsus-Wigand-Martin or Manchester-Fothergill in childbirth, the test of Sims-Huhner, the factor of Hageman, Wagner's device for orthopedics or the operation of Marshall-Marchetti-Krantz for urinary incontinence are named after their authors. These lexic tactics in the construction of medical terminology are not only signic to establish differences, but symbolic as well by rendering homage to the contributing doctors. With this strategy the identity of this matrix is constructed as an accumulation of individual and collective contributions to which probably all doctors *latch-on* and aspire to immortalize by denominating a disease or procedure with their last name for posterity, linking themselves with the future and the past all the way to Hippocrates, Celsus, and Galen.

The predominant acoustic emphatics in this matrix is silence to denote tranquility and absence of pain. One moves through hospital halls accompanied by the agile and quiet displacements of beds and wheelchairs. This emphatics of silence is barely interrupted by the acoustically isolated gasps and bellows of parturient women during the strangely called "childbirth without pain" (for the gynecologists, I guess) and newborns weeping in the maternity ward. A suitable acoustic emphatics is sometimes more important than the lexic to convince the patient that the doctor is trustworthy, calm, that he knows what he is speaking about, that the well-being of the patient interests him in a special way and that he is capable of helping. In this modality it is worth mentioning the patronizing voice tones of doctors and nurses towards the patients and their relatives many of whom, in distress, unconsciously acquire a childish role. The idealized representation of operating rooms in films and TV series like *ER*, where only the heartbeat and breathing of the patient are heard in a sacrosanct silence, does not always reflect reality because as soon as the patient lies anesthetized, the jokes, the racket and the gossip between doctors and nurses often take over (as when in school, the teacher leaves the classroom).

Somatic emphatics are aesthetically displayed through diverse and minute technologies upon the patients' body establishing legitimized positions and ways of touching or other corporeal torments. The obscene position that the woman has to adopt in her visit to the gynecologist is inconceivable in any other matrix. This convention sharply contrasts with the traditional Eastern medicine and alternative or holistic therapies centered upon the somatic abilities of doctors to cure and to diagnose through scopic and somatic emphatics in nails, feet, ears, and so on and through their relation with the patient by relaxation and concentration techniques.

The main scopic emphatics of the allopathic medical matrix is asepsis. All the stage settings, props and costumes converge to this emphatics in the immaculate white of nurses' and doctors' clothes to show no sign of blood, in addition to their gloves, face caps and so on. Traditional surgery rooms are designed with hygienic tiles on the walls, furniture of strict orthogonal lines and disinfected non porous materials as aluminum, plastic, glass, and formic in neutral, solid colors. Baudrillard (1981) mentions these qualities on objects that he accurately denominated as "moral".

After the asepsis, the dominant scopic emphatics in this matrix is related to optics: electrical, electronic, isotopes and nuclear instruments, x-rays, infrared light and ultrasound or magnetic resonance, a wide range of stethoscopes, microscopes, radioscopes, endoscopes, ductoscopes, laparoscopes and videoscopes that not only observe but interpret results are constantly developed.

The selection of one doctor rather than another by the patient, as we mentioned above, frequently depends on the scopic emphatics by which doctors' construct their professional identity. A mature conservative doctor very likely decorates his waiting room with a framed reproduction of a landscape or a still life, discreet carpets and wears the traditional white doctor's costume. By contrast, the younger doctor who is also looking for a younger clientele, will unfold a modern scopic with colored uniforms, contemporary abstract art posters in the walls and modern Bauhaus like furniture tapestried in lively colors. Crass scopic mistake would be a doctor's office with rustic, folding chairs (as those rented for parties or cheap restaurants), or Louis XIV style furniture, because the message would respectively be that the doctor is primitive, lacks stability, or simulates wealth and is unaware of technological innovations in this matrix. Very intuitively, all the doctors handle an impersonal and modern scopic emphatics.

Medical fluxion

The traditional lexic fluxion in this matrix is centripetal, as doctors have usually hidden from patients the gravity of their situation and made it known exclusively to the person in charge, namely, the healthy hierarchical relative. Our role as patients may make us lose even the right to the truth on our situation. In contrast, an open lexic fluxion is demanded from the patient to communicate to a perfect stranger the most intimate sensations, fears, and acts such as vomiting, copulating, defecating, ejaculating, or menstruating.

In contrast to the lexic, in the acoustic register, a centripetal fluxion is imposed on the patient, having to abstain from crying or moaning from pain. Only parturients are allowed to gasp, but preferably not to shout, and enjoy privileges also in somatic fluxion because the success of giving birth depends on opening up during labor, but only after controlling the physical urge to push. By contrast, pregnant women who undergo an ultrasound test must maintain an almost unbearable sphincter centripetal fluxion. Children are taught from an early age to maintain control against their instincts centripetal fluxion in their sphincters, not to shy away from the menacing syringe, swallowing pills and syrups with unpleasant flavor, bearing the burning of disinfectants on a wound, remaining in bed even though they would rather get up and play, and allowing painful clinical examinations and treatments.

The typical tactic of this matrix to maintain the patients' somatic fluxion centripetal are the hospital nurses on guard, who watch that they do not escape without authorization to smoke a cigarette in some solitary corner or buy a chocolate. Their function is to verify that they receive their tasteless food, the cleaning, temperature reading and medicines at the specified time. For that reason, once the role of the patient is ascribed, the identity of the subject radically changes and reduced down to the role of patient who must become submissive and docile, able to wait for a doctor during hours without protesting (something we would never do in any other context, except, perhaps, the political). As patients, we know that we are trapped in hospitals with no exit except that authorized by the doctor. From our subordinated role, we tolerate excruciating physical aggressions as pinching, cutting and stretching of bones and muscles. We thus maintain a centripetal somatic fluxion strong enough to resist the natural impulse of reacting to the violence of many treatments. Our role as patients implies the almost total loss of authority over our own body and time; we must even relinquish our indispensable sleeping hours, constantly interrupted by the hospital's nurses waking us up to take our temperature.

The centripetal scopic fluxion of hospitals as reclusion institutions is designed to prevent patients from escaping from there in case one still has enough strength to do flee. For that reason hospitals' architecture reminds us of Bentham's panopticon, having only one access and exit perfectly watched for each floor or area of patients' rooms. The humiliating genderless gown with an opening on the back designed for hospital patients, female or male, has not only the proxemic function of separating doctors from patients, but the centripetal fluxion that prevents them to circulate around so ridiculously dressed. This little gown, as the uniform for prisoners, suspends our professional, gender, religious or familiar identities to emphasize that, as long as we remain dressed in this outfit, we only count in our role as patients.

Paradigmatic projection in and from the medical matrix

The traditional attitude of some doctors towards patients projected from the religious matrix has not varied so much since the Middle Ages and before: the patient was then blamed for becoming ill as if he had committed a sin. This strategy emerged from an ontological and moral vision of disease as incarnation of evil described by Georges Canguilhem (1986) and Bryan Turner (1984). The patient was morally blamed for his or her health, as today with the AIDs virus. Nowadays, this projection is combined with another two. On the one hand from the school matrix a didactic version is imported by which doctors slowly describe the actions they perform ("we are going to put a gelatinous liquid on your belly and you are going to feel a little cold" the seventh time one undergoes an ultrasound, but no word is proffered before brutally squeezing our breasts for a mammogram). On the other a paternalistic version projected from the familiar matrix infantilizes patients and treats them with diminutives ("how is our little patient today" to an adult woman) and praising the patient as one would a small child ("you behaved very well") that may be adequate for patients who fall into a state of infantile regression when feeling vulnerable, but that in others can be deeply offensive.

What is most spectacular in this matrix as matricial paradigms are concerned is the conspicuous projection of the tourism paradigm upon hospitals' design to make them resemble five stars luxury hotels so that patients can imagine that they are there on vacation. This aesthetic strategy of substituting one scopics for another is quite effective, which sharply contrasts with the aesthetic projection of the prison paradigm into the State's public hospitals for less privileged social classes, and produces the exact opposite effect: that the patient has been secluded there for the crime committed against the State by becoming ill and not only discontinue being productive but worse, generate expenses. Consequently these patients will have to wait for the doctor's sentence to which their case has been entrusted and find out whether they can leave on bail or on probation, with the additional disadvantage of not counting with any medical defense attorneys.

Chapter 31

The Occultist Matrix

Uncertainty, desperation, vanity, love, anger, envy, and jealousy are some of the motivations that drive a great number of people towards this matrix. The nucleus around which the diverse practices that constitute this matrix agglutinate is fortune, predicted, or manipulated by rituals and games that each occultist genre establishes. For that reason, the common term under which we will denominate diverse practitioners in this matrix is "fortune-tellers": white and black witches, litomantics, bibliomantics, onomancists, astrologers, cartomancists, palmists, psychics, quiromantics, botomancists, aruspices, crystalomantics, taumaturgs, coffee, tarot, runes, I-Ching, or huija readers, spiritualist oniromantics, mediums, rabdomantics, and phallomancists.

Evidently, the symbol that characterizes the occultist matrix is *fatality* which fortune-tellers claim is under their vision or control. Various genres of occultism are practiced according to deeply rooted local traditions or more recent fashions. Although these change, they display common strategies for the construction of identities and realities which enable us to identify them as a particular matrix. In fact, I have selected this matrix because it does not have any elements that allow it to become institutionalized. The medical matrix, for example, has matricial zones and institutional zones, so that it is accountable for cases of negligence, fraud, mistaken diagnosis, or faulty therapy, and so on, as there are clear and fixed regulations and established structures that protect the patient. Contrastingly the occultist matrix is viscous and its practices are quite contingent and malleable enough to incorporate the most diverse and capricious manifestations.

This matrix is fascinating because it is almost exclusively held in place by the pins of aesthetic strategies, since the semiosic dimension is quite thin. What is important here is not what is said but how it is said. Fortune-tellers are able to affect decision-making not only in the private life of its clients but in many occasions also public life when politicians depend on them for taking decisions (as the last Czarinne of the Romanovs, Alexandra Fyodorovna with Rasputin, Catherine de Medici with Nostradamus and, it is claimed, a terrifyingly great number of contemporary politicians). Esoteric props as Saint Maurice's sword and Wilhelm the First's bones as well as the legendary treasures of the Hapsburgs were searched for among others by Heinrich Himmler, Adolf Hitler and Rudolf Hess to control the destiny of the world in rituals of indoctrination of the SA, the Gestapo, and the SS. (cf. Anderson 1995; Sklar 1989)

The strategy of identity construction in this matrix must produce the effect that fortune-tellers are initiated in an esoteric knowledge and have special gifts to discover hidden symbols in a person's life, to interpret their interiority, read their past and future, influence the luck and destiny of others and in some cases even contacting the

258 *Everyday Aesthetics*

dead. One resorts to fortune-tellers with the hope that, even in fate, laws in arcane codes exist, and that by knowing them, destiny can be manipulated. This is the nodal center towards which the affective energies of clients and the discursive strategies of fortune-tellers converge. If there is some order in the chaos, why not believe the control of randomness? So both client and fortune-teller gather as accomplices to play the game of divination and by displaying proper aesthetic strategies make it seem true. The game itself is much like in other matrixes, but the playing board and its pieces are different.

Occultist rhetorics

As in all matrixes, occultism is displayed by means of four registers: the persuasive lexics of fortune-tellers and their particular codes arranged through horoscopes, tarot, and so on, their acoustics in intonation and pauses to produce the feeling that they penetrate into hidden dimensions, the fervent somatics of rituals and the rich scopics of fetishes, amulets, letters of divination, stones, and so on. Different occultist practices are thus distinguished by the predominance of one register over the others. The somatic register prevails in witchcraft through ritual dances and herbal ingestions, whereas in coffee reading, runes, I Ching and tarot, what predominates are lexics aided by scopic props. The acoustic dominates by the vocal impact in the personification of dead people during medium sessions, in addition to the convulsive somatics of the enouncer in trance.

In the lexic register, fortune-tellers generally violate what in Speech Act theory is defined as the Principle of Cooperation (Grice 1975), in particular the four maxims: Maxim of Quality (do not say what you believe is false or lacking of evidence), the Maxim of Quantity (be informative but not more than necessary), the Maxim of Relevance (be relevant), and the Maxim of Mode (be clear, without ambiguities, brief and ordered). In spite of it, clients generally obey Leech's courtesy principle and even Davidson's charity principle when suspending the doubt, even granting credibility and authority to the enouncer, despite the fact that their speech is totally vague and ambiguous. Courtesy rules often prevail in these interactions because the client becomes ipso facto an accomplice of the interaction by requesting it. It is a game that both, client and fortune-teller, would like to come true, because the former needs a certain result and the latter the faculties to achieve it. Together, they create an atmosphere by aesthetic strategies in which the spell becomes credible. Although this is a basic game played in all matrixes, namely mimicry or "as if" the "if" is often lost or forgotten and the game itself taken as truth.

Scopic syntagms of this matrix are quite astonishing, since one can find a polychromatic variety of candles and tarot cards, as well runes, old coins, talismans, ash, earth or salt figures, amulets, special herbs, crystal pyramids and spheres, beads, quartzes, magnets, incenses, garlic chains, zodiac images, bones, stones, shells, and snails in a very long list of divination props. If one prop does not work, we can always try another. The objects that are selected to operate in this matrix must, however, have some auratic quality that separates them from banal, ordinary objects: one cannot replace a candle by a 60 watt light bulb, magic herbs by spinach, or incense by a

The Occultist Matrix

room deodorant. The aesthetic strategy by which these objects acquire that auratic quality results from paradigmatic projections out of other matrixes borrowing by contagion part of their original symbolic load. Thus tarot cards, originally a game for entertainment during the Middle Ages that acquired great popularity with the invention of printing, are auratized by the load of time of six centuries. Magic herbs are projected from the medical matrix, astral cards from astronomy, talismans and amulets from alchemy and religion. The main supplier of props to the occultist matrix is religion, as a text of Confucianism known as I Ching, the Kabbalah and its numerology, or the templars' legends in Christianity.

We will analyze these registers combined with the dramatic modalities, but what deserves a more detailed analysis are the paradoxes and transpositions with which occultist rhetoric is constructed. That is why this matrix particularly depends on the pins of the aesthetic, and reflects how other matrixes function. I could find four transpositions: 1) the *ex-pressive* mechanism upon the *im-pressive*, 2) the signic axis upon the symbolic, 3) contingency upon destiny, and 4) identity upon individuality. Let me explain: being a typically *im-pressive* matrix, the first transposition of occultism consists in appearing as purely *ex-pressive*. By means of rhetorical construction, the im-pression created by fortune-tellers is that they own capabilities to penetrate the hidden and emerge from it by rhetoric enunciation. They play the *mimicry* of owning a gift to perceive mysterious processes inaccessible to the uninitiated simulating that it is an *ex-pressive* process from other worlds or realities.

The second process of transposition is still more interesting: the axis of the signic in this matrix appears as if it were symbolic. The reading of the tarot, horoscopes, runes, the palm of the hand, are strictly signic very pliable codes that operate by oppositions and differences as defined by Saussure with respect to language. A zodiac sign only has meaning against another or a tarot card against another like words stand to others in the system of language. Nevertheless, they appear as symbolic codes by attributing them hidden powers, a temporary load of arcane traditions and a material load in amulets, talismans and stones associated to each sign. The astral card or Chinese horoscope, as systems of oppositions and differences on the basis of the absolutely random fact of the moment of birth, is associated—by conventions established in each particular code—to metals, stones, colors, numbers, cardinal points, parts of the human body, natural elements, animals, letters, hours of the day and night, days of the week, flowers, angels, and so on as if such association was absolutely predetermined and by necessity. While in the axis of symbolic the relation between symbolizer and symbolized is motivated, necessary and non-contingent (the diamond acquires its symbolic value by the physical effort to extract it from the entrails of the earth, by the skill to polish it, its exchange value based on demand in the market, by its permanence in time, its desirability as a Jewel or decorative object in its use value, by its material qualities as brightness and hardness, by its affective load in the family ritual as metaphor of value in an engagement ring) in the occultist matrix this relation is completely arbitrary. This arbitrariness is not, paradoxically, arbitrary because "occultist symbols" are in fact nothing other than signs, reason why semiotic arbitrariness between signifier and signified is inevitable. Nothing links the sign of Scorpio with a topaz, water, dark red, genitals, Tuesdays, carnations or the planet Mars. Nevertheless, this arbitrariness disguised as necessary allows fortune-tellers to present their identities as experts by maintaining an appearance of consistency. The continuous practice in these associations produces an effect of sedimentation and necessity (Goebbels's conviction that repeating a lie a sufficient number of times makes it seem true). Such inventory of signs is, nevertheless, different from the game of similarities by which Foucault (1984) explained the Renaissance *episteme*, as the latter was based on a conception of analogies between macrocosm and microcosm with precise rules for acknowledging isotopies or isomorphisms. In occultist associations, on the other hand, there are no metaphor or synecdoche relations because any clear scheme of associative configuration is absent. What one finds is an indiscriminate juxtaposition of signifiers.

In sum, occultist symbolism is a game of *mimicry* that disguises a fortuitous semiotism by supposedly ineluctable analogies from the origin of times. Let us remember that for Goux (1990, 49) there is a process where signs replace symbols (in economy money, as sign, replaces gold that is symbol) as if the sign were the evolution of the symbol by a linear process going from the instrument to the fetish, from the fetish to the symbol and from the symbol to the sign. When this evolution occurs, as in gold-coin-bill-credit card process of substitution, a trace of the symbol that precedes the sign remains (coins were originally made of gold, bills like the Mexican "peso"—meaning weight, point to its motivated material meaning, credit cards are named "premium gold" and are made in plastic but appear metallic and so on) whereas occultist signs displayed as "symbols" are thinned down to being only an element that opposes another. This process operates by emptying the symbols' material density in a signifier that appears to be overflowing with meaning. When using such quantity of signs, the occultist matrix blocks meaning generation, because it saturates each symbol with all possible meanings and ends up draining them. In this perpetual game of signifiers, fortune-tellers add more and more series: they will associate a fish with luck in businesses, the angel Uriel, an emerald stone, a tarot card, a metal, a tree, a musical note. In spite of this symbol degradation, this matrix manages to preserve intact its symbol of fatality by the ardent desire to know and manipulate it. Clients invest every effort in rescuing fortune-tellers' speech from its nebulosity and eagerly apply what they make out of it to their everyday life.

The third transposition consists in that the occultist matrix, as no other, enjoys, by its same viscosity, of absolute license to capriciously establish relations between elements of the code and play with its combinatory, in contrast to the scientific matrix strictly regulated by logic and verifiability. Nevertheless, such freedom appears as if it were an intrinsic necessity of the associations based on some predetermination of fate. Fortune-tellers supposedly do not invent, only interpret according to a rigorous code. The client goes to this matrix looking for the hidden rules of such fate, which nonetheless promises the absolute freedom to act upon one's fate and that of others as long as one owns the adequate talisman or amulet.

Unlike medical psychotherapy that helps patients acquire tools for better constructing and presenting their personal identities as well as to avoid unnecessary harmful or painful situations, adepts of this matrix look for traces not of their identity but of their individuality. If both axes socially constitute identity, individuality, on the other hand, cannot be known: it is simply lived. Here is the fourth transposition of this matrix: trying to apprehend individuality in terms that belong to identity,

The Occultist Matrix 261

as are date and place of birth and the syntagms for the presentation of the self. Individuality is the condition of possibility for identities but its nature is pre-semiosic at an anthropological scale, even if not at a cellular level. Whenever a reference is made to what a person is, it will inevitably refer to identity, never to individuality since it is semiotically inapprehensible except through its inner endosemiosis.

In this game of reversals where the sign appears as symbol, *im-pression* as *ex-pression*, arbitrariness as necessity, random juxtapositions as analogical co germination, chance as predetermination, *mimicry* as secrets of initiation, symbolic vacuity as plethora and the identity as individuality, fortune-tellers must handle enunciation with enough dexterity as to produce an effect of certainty by *com-pression*. While philosophers are dedicated to formulate questions, fortune-tellers have the answers for everything.

Occultist dramatics

Rather than reading the future, fortune-tellers are expert in the interpretation of statements unconsciously displayed by the client through the four registers and modalities. They do not see more than what any moderately sensitive and perceptive person can see in a face to face interaction: if the person is lazy or active, shy or extroverted, warm or cold, tense or relaxed, lacks self-esteem or not, its frustration, rudeness, charm. In addition they have the opportunity granted by this same matrix to speak in terms that are socially incorrect in other contexts, as giving unsolicited advice on intimate matters to a stranger. Here is the profoundly matricial aspect that I mentioned before, because the occultist matrix is almost as cozy and smooth as a warm godmother to whom one goes in search of advice, approval, tranquility, and attention. With no pretensions of infallibility, it simply pampers and spoils us reverting all responsibility upon fate.

Occultist proxemics

Edna Aphek and Yishai Tobin (1983) set out to elucidate the discursive mechanisms of production of credibility in this matrix by Israeli palmists. Although they mention elements in the four registers, they left without exploring the scopics of costumes and the somatics of body language. Their work is nonetheless useful by the information provided with respect to the dramatic modalities. These authors classify palmists according to three characteristic types: (1) the "classic" or picturesque generally women cartomancists and coffee readers who use substandard, informal language, colloquial speech, and common errors, (2) the "scientific", generally men, who use a more technical, formal and syntactically more elaborated language, and (3) the intermediate between both. The authors indicate that although the language used in their study was Hebrew, their conclusions are applicable also to fortune-tellers in English and Spanish. I partly disagree, since in Hebrew there is no linguistic distinction between *tú* and *usted*, which is an important proxemic cue, so one can infer that if the fortune-tellers studied by Aphek and Tobin spoke Spanish, the classic

262   *Everyday Aesthetics*

fortune-teller would use "tú" and the "scientific" the "usted" that radically alters proxemics.

Their study can be interpreted in our terms as the "classic" fortune-teller displaying very short lexic proxemics using colloquial language, shortening long words, eliminating relative pronouns and certain syntactic markers, in addition to frequent common grammatical errors. The "scientific" fortune-teller, on the other hand, exhibits all the strategies of the Western specialist or expert, whose language is "educated-standard, usually of formal register, sometimes verging on the 'scientific'. We have also noted a marked use of English loan words in Hebrew, that are markers of professional and formal standard, educated speech, as well as the use of 'technical' terms." (Aphek and Tobin 1983, 290) Here we can notice how the selection of idiomatic terms has symbolic and aesthetic reverberations in prosaics by association to their respective imaginaries and matrixes: to use Arabic is associated to a world of the past, magical, irrational, intuitive, exotic; to use English, on the opposite, is associated to a modern, rational, efficient, technological world.

In this study the strategy displayed by a fortune-teller can be clearly seen through four paragraphs: in the first he criticizes the client by his lack of harmony (long lexic proxemics) making him feel insecure, and in the three following he praises him by his energy, structure and imagination to finish pampering him by shortening proxemics.

The authors concentrate in prosodic, extralinguistic and paralinguistic aspects as intonation, tension, pauses, hesitations and silences in 35 recordings of interviews between fortune-tellers and their clients. Although they do not interpret the results of this register, they give information on the acoustic proxemics of this matrix. In the tables of results only volume as acoustic emphatics is mentioned, but one can conjecture that "classic" fortune-tellers will unfold an acoustic proxemic not only short but intimate in order to create a confessional atmosphere for a stranger to speak about the most personal and private aspects of their life. The "scientist" will perform with the long, impersonal acoustic proxemics in imitation of the medical matrix.

In the "scientific" type proxemics are lengthened by making appointments by telephone through a secretary, who warns the client that not appearing or canceling the appointment too late will involve a fee, and calling to confirm as dentists or other doctors do. The "classic", however, keeps a much shorter proxemics and is much more informal with respect to appointments, as in a beauty parlor or visiting a close friend, and of course does not use a secretary as intermediary.

In somatic and scopic proxemics, the "scientific" covers the client's palms of both hands with a black liquid to get several prints in a white paper. The fortune-teller has special printed formats to write down the signs and informs the client of the possibility of purchasing a more detailed description in writing by an additional charge. The "classic" only takes the client's hand to read it directly with the help of a common paper clip and analyzes even the protuberances of the hand.

Scopic proxemics of the "classic" fortune-teller are so short that she receives the client in her apartment without separating the family from the professional space and, as the authors state, the place is disordered (old newspapers piled up, cockroaches, and so on). The "scientific" fortune-teller, in contrast, receives the client in an office

The Occultist Matrix

263

similar to a doctor's with modern furniture and waiting room. He sits behind a desk and everything looks impeccable.

In order to construct their identity and legitimize themselves, fortune-tellers can cook up that they spent a year in seclusion in Al-Wakra or Dashowuz to be initiated by an old wise woman who conserved a millenarian omniscience by oral tradition. They will never confess that they simply bought a booklet on amazon.com or went to a short course for a weekend in an accountant's office. That would immediately break the spell.

Occultist kinetics

Lexic kinetics among fortune-tellers are as contradictory as the transpositions previously mentioned: on the one hand they are very dynamic as they can jump from one subject to another without illation, but become static when stagnating in certain ideas to produce the effect that what is being said is of extreme importance.

Although it will be necessary to confirm or refute by empirical studies, it can be conjectured that the acoustic kinetics of the "classic" palmist will be more dynamic than the "scientific". This can be explained due to the fact that informal speech has the greater acoustic dynamism, indexical of emotion and more spontaneous, in contrast to the formal "scientific", which intends to produce the effect of a totally reasoned and intellectual process.

In the predominantly somatic occultism of cleanings or "limpias" and of spells against "bad vibes", "evil eye", or doing a "little job" to a rival in love or in money, sometimes much greater somatic kinetics than lexic are required, because the techniques are based on the corporeal movements that accompany the incantations. The auratic materials of occultist props need to project an extremely stable effect of scopic kinetics, namely, appearing to be the legacy of an arcane tradition in divination arts. A millenarian load of time is grafted from Chinese dynasties or Celtic tribes to produce effects of symbolization by these signifiers.

Here is another of this matrix's paradoxes, because fortune-tellers always display the appearance of practicing very archaic traditions, while they are kinetically very dynamic and truly aggressive as freelance entrepreneurs pioneering the use of internet for advertisement (when Netscape first appeared online, one could already find in the early 1990s occultist adds offering their services). Today they offer by this medium sanations, Reiki, astral letters, numerology, Chinese horoscopes and what have you to increase the business sales of their clients. Even new techniques have been invented as the Human Design System ("a synthesis of modern day sciences, including physics, astrophysics, bio and genetic chemistry, and at least four of the great esoteric systems of the age: Astrology, the I-Ching, the Kabbalah, and the Chakra system"[1]) and others to improve love relations, self-knowledge and sex life. This apparent desauratization maintains, nevertheless, an alibi with the arcane, because no fortune-tellers, be they as cybernetic as can be, will propose to read the future of the client by the information on their hard disk, the brand of their watch, cigarettes or automobile or their credit score, although as indexicals these may be much more trustworthy.

---

1   http://www.earthstarconsulting.com/aboutHDSarticle01.htm.

264 *Everyday Aesthetics*

Occultist emphatics

The predominant lexic emphatics in this matrix circles around topics such as the clients' love affairs, money, family, professional and social success, their recognition by the others, happiness, trips and their "inner world". In the last instance, everything revolves around the ego of the solicitor. An important resource for achieving the client's *latching-on* to this matrix is exoticism: geomancy of Kazajstan of thousands of years ago in the Kumalak, or the original podomancy of old Persia, the cartomancy of Mlle Lenormand, the Vaastu, Wicca, the Vedaic and Mayan astrology are likely to inspire interest.

In the lexic register, a fortune-teller analyzed by Aphek and Tobin (1983, 292) finds the client too stressed and advises him ".... you want everything, and you have to be a more harmonious person" in the lexic, but "h-a-r-m-o-n-i-o-u-s" in acoustic emphatics. The pauses produce suspense whereas the most emphatic words are the signifiers around which the fortune-teller arranges his speech.[2]

> You have an exceptionally good *imagination*. Most people don't have a creative *imagination*. For most people the quantity of their *imagination* is limited. Yes, the quantity of your *imagination* is exceptionally good; that can help you in all areas of life.
>
> There is no area of life where you can't decide to exploit your *imagination*. None. None. And, therefore, that's one of the reasons that you can work in so many fields. You can take ten different jobs in some industrial plant because of your *imagination* and because you're talented. You can try ten different things in some specific field because of your *imagination*. There's a fantastic *imagination* here quantity-, quality- and comprehension-wise, yes, you could even start from scratch and create something. (Aphek and Tobin 1983, 293)

In addition to the evident lack of discursive imagination of the fortune-teller, the syntagmatic link of alliterations, similar to the rhetoric *dispositio* in many texts of the religious matrix (the *Qur'an*), produces an alluring effect. "Imagination" is the key word; "you yes/others not", others limited quantity/you good quantity, help in areas of life/you can operate in all areas of the life, ten jobs/ten things continue the rhythm. These static lexic kinetics are disguised as lexic emphatics made to appear that the center of the client's fate wholly depends on his or her imagination.

These emphases are made, however, to conceal the fact that most of occultist discourses display an unmarked emphatics. Aphek and Tobin define the language of the divination as "omniscopic" (*omniscopus*).[3] By this term the authors understand the use of non precise language applicable to multiple situations in which clients can identify themselves and provide a personal meaning to wholly abstract and impersonal signifiers. Omniscopic language operates by syntagms that are mutually

---

2　The session briefed by Aphek and Tobin has 4 blocks; each one turns around syntagm emphatics: "harmonious" in first, "energy" in the second, "structures" or "study" in the third, "imagination" in the fourth, where the fortune-teller almost repeats in each phrase the word imagination, that I have marked for emphatic aims.

3　Given the meaning here used to the term "scopic" I would prefer the term "omnilexic" to what Tobin and Aphek refer to.

The Occultist Matrix

cancelled but seem to strengthen themselves such as "*or* you did it long ago *or* you are on the verge of doing it", "after it happened *or* after it happens ..." The use of emphatically unmarked qualifiers such as "perhaps", "also", "frequently", "somebody", "something" is characteristic of this matrix, as well as the use of scales as "more than", "less than" in which clients will have to locate themselves.

In face to face interactions, fortune-tellers will create by all registers an atmosphere that favors emphatic effects of hermetism and mystery. Lamentably, in Aphek and Tobin's work, the scopic register is almost missing since the costumes are not mentioned, but it is possible to infer that the "scientist" would use formal clothes as a suit and necktie, probably a white robe to emphasize the projection from the medical matrix. The "classic" probably uses informal clothes, preferably long and wide skirts of thin fabric printed with organic or floral motifs, heavy earrings and necklaces and many rings, perhaps one on each finger. Apart from imitating gypsy women (the archetypal fortune-tellers) these textiles evoke veils supposedly hiding mysteries from us, or the eternal feminine whose secrets are reserved to fortune-tellers. The heavy jewels complement the baroque, irrational and intuitive image in which stories, lives and secrets are accumulated.

Occultist fluxion

Lexic fluxion in this matrix is centrifugal in fortune-tellers, and centripetal in clients who are mostly interested only in themselves. The facility whereupon fortune-tellers can pass from one technique to another exemplifies not only the arbitrary game of signifiers we mentioned before, but their total openness for adding new techniques to their repertoire. With the alibi of stimulating internal development, an incredible inventory of techniques is offered to seduce the potential client, from chromotherapy, metamorphic, reflexology, past life readings, spells, crystal casting, tea leaf readings, sanation by archetypes, kinesiology, and so on.[4]

> Ivan Katsarov is an Expert in School Magus; he is also a Medium and a Master in energy and karmic corrections via energy pictures, target telepathy and Nial energy, as well as a specialist in removing negative energy and informational influences (also known as black magic). He is also making protections. The patient performs astral projection throughout the therapy, so he can harmonize the trinity Body-Spirit-Soul. As a result the man purifies and fills himself with health, love and universal success. Ivan Katsarov practice freely the exotic Shenu Olowu magic, Marocan voodoo, Phoenix's magic, Dolphins' magic, Mimbarri magic, Chronomagic. He is not only a Seichim master, but a Master in nearly 30 systems for energy healing and enlightment, and that gives him the honorable SATAI degree. Ivan Katsarov is giving courses and attunements in the following systems: Usui Reiki, Tibetan Reiki, Kundalini Reiki, Golden Reiki, Dragon Reiki, Purple Reiki, Rainbow Reiki, Crystal Reiki, Huna Reiki, KaHuna Reiki, Aloha Reiki, Uhane Nui Reiki, Lighterian Reiki, Stellar Reiki, Raku Kai Reiki, Fusion Reiki, Karmic Reiki, Chios Reiki, Imara Reiki, Rossari Reiki, Dolphin Reiki, OBE Reiki, Oktagonal Reiki, Aurora Reiki, Shamballa multidimensional healing, Karuna Ki, Ra-sheeba, Sekhem, Seichim, Isis Seichim, Phoenix Seichim (founder), Dolphin Seichim (founder), Sekhem-Seichim-Reiki,

---

4   http://members.tripod.com/psychicservices/psychicservices/?hop=ad2go.psychicgrl.

266 *Everyday Aesthetics*

SKHM, Atlantic healing system. Satai Ivan Katsarov is the author of "Encyclopedia on Reiki and systems of energy treatment" in three volumes.[5]

Isn't that something! Note the open fluxion of the variety of techniques offered by this versatile occultist. In televised fortune-telling, speech is totally centrifugal and impersonal because it is directed to all the potential receivers, and yet must produce the effect of speaking to every person in particular, so that when hearing the zodiac sign, each feels personally mentioned and prepares to listen to the advice and prediction. Behind the centripetal fluxion of the applicants preoccupied only for themselves, there is an eagerness to control, a desire well recorded by professionals of this matrix. "Finally, a unique method that shows how you can put anyone under your hypnotic spell and make him obey you. Start to see dramatic results in only 29 days or less, otherwise each cent will be given back to you", says an announcement on the internet.

Paradigmatic projection in the occultist matrix

In order to constitute their identity and credibility, members of the occultist matrix need to import paradigms from other matrixes, as the medical matrix in the cases of the "scientific" fortune-tellers practically copied from clinical examinations (where doctors attribute to themselves the right of scolding patients for smoking, taking too many saturated fats, and not doing sufficient exercise). The one cited above speaks not of clients but of "patients" and "therapies" clearly importing the medical paradigm, since people who ask for help feel that they are in trouble. "Classic" fortune-tellers choose instead the family matrix to project a maternal role by speaking as the client's aunt, godmother or grandmother to establish legitimacy for giving advice. However, most paradigmatic projections are imported from the religion matrix by using traditions like the I-Ching and the Tao, Nordic, Babylonian, Egyptian, Mayan, Persian, Hindu, Chinese, and Japanese cultures, as well as pagan religions. The commercial matrix also participates pointing towards financial success, as in dianetics that promises training for success and the recent "System of human design". Now even the school matrix at the university level is imported into this matrix, so that one can find sites that offer courses on occultism and confer certificates of assistance. I can clearly predict that soon "scientific" fortune-tellers will attend these courses or purchase their certificates to hang in their office, like dentists and pediatricians, or even design new ones from every part of the world and in strange cryptgraphic characters.

If this matrix has remained during millennia from the contributions of identities as remote as Joseph, biblical fortune-teller of the Pharaoh, Nostradamus for Catherine de Medici during the Renaissance, Moctezuma's magicians and fortune-tellers, Rasputin and Madame Blavatsky among innumerable others, it is because it has a great social acceptance. Perhaps for that reason it would not be absolutely preposterous to export the occultist matrix to the school matrix as a parallel technique to aid psychological therapy. The reason why I propose this bizarre projection is that teenagers' identities

---

5 http://magicaura.com/eng/authors/22/ivan-katsarov/.

are in a particularly vulnerable stage. Many disoriented youngsters, in a situation of acute anguish and loneliness, lacking communication with their parents, teachers and friends, could playfully find certain enlightment in sessions with fortune-tellers. If fortune-tellers disguise themselves as psychotherapists, why not disguise psychotherapists as fortune-tellers? Many teenagers will feel tempted to go to fortune-tellers for their luck in examinations, to attract someone, to do spells on classmates and teachers. Thus it could help diagnose desperate cases and perhaps prevent tragic outcomes as the Columbine or the Virginia Tech massacres in the United States. If fortunism cannot guess the future it can, however, provisionally palliate de-pression and encourage catharsis by *ex-pression* opening the sensibility of the teenager without the intimidation and stigma of psychological therapy. It can help palliate the sense of loneliness in which they are sunk and feel appreciated, perceived and praised by somebody. This proposal is, of course, a *peripatos* game.

Chapter 32

The Arts Matrix

Paradoxically, among all social matrixes, that which has most contributed and most obstructed the understanding of aesthetics is the arts matrix. This paradox can be explained by the dominant tendency in Western theory of art to usurp for this field a diversity of aesthetic practices and ignore others on the basis of two fallacies: 1) supposing that the art matrix is the only one in which the aesthetic is significant (as if there were no aesthesis in other activities like religion, sports, politics, and so on), and 2), reducing all arts exclusively to the aesthetic dimension (as if art lacked political, economic, and social dimensions). There must be a reason why, in spite of the tenacious efforts of philosophers of art and aestheticians to establish their concepts objectively, the categories related to the artistic still remain quite embroiled: even a suitable and consensed demarcation of the concept of "art" is lacking.

The problem, I think, partly owes to the confusion between complimenting and understanding, the evaluative with the descriptive, a result of which produces a great quantity of papers that apparently study art but in reality only praise it. It seems to me that great art needs no praising or justification, because it is supported by the appreciation of its public. So one is led to think that perhaps in some cases such justification is not as much of art itself but rather as a strategy of presentation of a professional identity as "expert in poetics" of the author to other members of the artworld.

This traditional link between aesthetics and art is not capricious: if aesthetics studies the human disposition to be captivated and art consists of the deliberate construction of artifacts that are consummated only when they captivate the spectator, this association is logical. It is not, however, exhaustive, because these artifacts are also fabricated for the economic support of the artist in addition to subsequent functions of social legitimation and distinction as well as prestige of its owners, collectors or promoters. While science creates objects to understand phenomena, religion to venerate the sacred, and the family to agglutinate and protect its members, art creates them for the amusement, fantasy, and delight of its public, including, of course, of artists themselves. It is worth highlighting that, in the artistic matrix, *latching-on* is no longer a means to achieve some ulterior goal but an end in itself.

What characterizes the Western artistic matrix is the symbol par excellence towards which all its practices converge and acquire their distinctive character as artworks. Evidently, this symbol is *fantasy* (from the Greek *phantastikós*, what can be presented or shown, equivalent to *phantazein* or making visible) by the enormous affective response that it provokes and the great material and energetic input on it, sometimes with extraordinary skill and patience, in spite of not being directly useful for survival.[1]

---

1 This energetic load of fantasy and creativity explains why an original painting, regardless of how deteriorated it may be, always has more symbolic value than its perfect

270   Everyday Aesthetics

All matrixes in some sense or another constitute imaginary realities and display certain degree of fantasy, but their imaginary nature is implicit and unconscious by appearing factual and objective. Artists, however, exhibit their creatures clearly as artifices (of the Latin *artificium*, artwork), products of their imagination in making the extraordinary visible, *phantazein*. Here the dimension of the imaginary becomes explicit to show the freedom artists take for themselves to invent and explore it. Artists do not care about convincing anyone on the truth of their statements—in contrast to the scientist, the fortune-teller or the priest who do need to persuade us— but are concerned only to amuse us by making us perceive what would be otherwise unperceivable without the mediation of their fantasy. Without the ingredients of artifice, fantasy and creativity to captivate us, there is no art; but something else is required to properly speak of artistic phenomena: its emergence in a relatively autonomous and differentiated matrix, with some sense of professional tradition.

Artifice allows the presentation of alternative versions of reality or *di-versions* (from the Latin *di-vertere* to spill or to turn to another direction).[2] If the approach to reality is direct, that is no di-version but simply version, it is not art but description, documentary. Brecht, an author committed to Marxism to the degree of considering art as an instrument for promoting revolutionary conscience among the proletariat, had nevertheless to admit that the function of the theater is, first and foremost, to amuse: "from immemorial times the mission of theater—as that of all the arts—has consisted of amusing people." (Brecht 1976, 109) That amusement or entertainment is a basic ingredient of art does not imply that everything amusing or entertaining is art, but only that for something to be considered artistic, whether refined or vulgar for some tastes, it must be amusing to someone.

Artifice permits the presentation of alternative versions of things with a degree of fabulation and another of plausibility without which there would be no *latching-on* to its artifacts. This creation of the fantastic is the artistic answer to what Roman Gubern (1996, 10) denominated "scopic pulsion" from a Lacanian concept understood as "the irresistible appetite to see" (I would add that also to hear, to taste, to smell, and to touch beyond the ordinary). The fantastic does not simply refer to the unreal, the false or the phantasmagoric as is implied in the common use of the term, because imaginaries are created and made perceivable to become intersubjective realities in the arts precisely due to their imaginary character. Thus they maintain the same persistence in intersubjectivity as the supposedly factual realities constructed in other matrixes.

What is here designated as the arts' matrix is not equivalent to what Anglo-American aestheticians (for example Danto [1964] 1987 and Dickie 1974, 1984) denominate *artworld*, which is only a part, even if central, of artistic manifestations,

---

forgeries even though these could be in much better visual and aesthetic conditions than the original, as a good quality copy of the already deteriorated Leonardo da Vinci's *Last Supper*. As long as it was Leonardo's own energy and time what was invested to paint it, and not just that of a common forger or a mediocre artist, the piece has immense symbolic value. This temporary load is also expressed in the permanence, sometimes millenarian, of works of art throughout very remote generations in time and space from its creators and original spectators.

2   The terms for a musical *divertimento* or short pieces of ballet called *divertissement* capture the playful and amused sense that spectators enjoy in arts.

namely "Fine Arts", produced/reproduced for a select group of members. It is not mere coincidence that Dickie's (1984, passim) institutional theory would demarcate art as a "candidate for aesthetic appreciation" basically implying to the artworld, whose candidacy can be rejected or accepted like a member in a private club. The artistic matrix, however, has overlapping and blurred borders with other matrixes, as in figure skating which would make sport and art coincide, or as art galleries that overlap with the commercial matrix, as well as museums like the Louvre whose origin overlapped with the military matrix since it was constructed to exhibit the trophies sacked by Napoleon to his conquered territories.

Although it is not the task of prosaics to define art (just as we have not needed so far to define the family, school or religion), it is nonetheless possible to explain how aesthesis unfolds through this matrix. By contrast to poetics which is *endo-artistic* and articulated by art practice, criticism and philosophy when analyzing poiesis from within (mainly its semantic and syntactic dimensions), prosaics is *exo-artistic* as its approach is pragmatic by emphasizing artistic practices from the perspective of interpreters (including the artist as first interpreter of his work) and its context. Also, unlike the pragmatics of the art critic who approaches his subject as a specialist in reference to the artworld and advises potential collectors how to invest their money in artworks, prosaics deals with artistic praxis from the point of view of any observer, not necessarily an expert nor exclusively in function of a single sense (for the spectator, a picture is not only visual, it also smells and has texture, it is located at a certain place like a museum which affects its reception, and can symbolize prestige).

We must distinguish also between socioaesthetics and sociology of art, as the first attempts to explain artistic manifestations among others within social aesthesis, whereas the second observes art in the social context. The sociology of art already assumes an established definition of the artistic and analyzes social influences and conditions that generate stylistic or other variations (eg. Hauser 1969, Wolff 1983). The socioaesthetics of art, on the other hand, explores all sensiblity-related manifestations of the arts, not only the virtuosity of a violinist but the manifestation of enthusiasm of its public, the elegant black and white suit and personal appearance, his expressivity when interpreting, the smell of the carpets and the scent wood of the concert hall together the spatial feeling of its architecture and illumination, lightning, that is to say, the whole sensorial experience that is involved in attending a concert.[3]

For that reason we will focus on two types of artistic phenomena which, using Lotman's (1990) terminology with respect to the semiosphere, can be denominated *centric* referring to dominant and totally legitimized forms of artistic production and *peripheral* to the relatively marginal. Although Lotman's work focuses more on the

---

3 Against the heavy tradition that totally ignores these environmental aspects of experience in the artistic matrix, Yuriko Saito (2005, 258) takes them into account and indicates that it is necessary to abstract them to focus the artistic object. It seems to me that attention is not quite as binary as implied Dickie's idea of attention I analyzed in Chapter 3. In other words, it is not a question of "on-off" dichotomy as computer bits. Rather it is a tetradimensional experience and multifaceted attention part of which is placed on remote aspects, near, latent, centric, focused, dispersed, concentrated and so on. All these factors are present with different intensity in artistic experience.

272

Everyday Aesthetics

semiotics of culture than on the artistic matrix, these concepts relate directly to the arts since it was not mere chance that Lotman would take his examples particularly from literature and use the museum as an example of the semiosphere. Without a doubt, the artworld constitutes the center of the artistic matrix whose nucleus is disputed between Paris and New York in curatorial initiative, echoed by the debate between "continental aesthetics" versus "analytical aesthetics" in art theory.

I will extend Lotman's notion of *periphery* to include a variety of phenomena that have not been recognized by the artworld but nonetheless keep family resemblances to the arts. I make this distinction because in a descriptive and non evaluative approach to the artistic matrix as the one here proposed, we cannot exclude from its field of study manifestations that share fantasy as their matricial symbol and yet remain in the matrix periphery for two reasons: one because of social class or number of its fans and the other by a traditional Western hierarchization of the senses. In the first case I am referring to genres like rock music, cabaret, music hall, vaudeville and even table dance among others. They are peripheral because they are considered too easy, sensuous, low class or sexually explicit, as well as vulgar. It is nevertheless possible to recognize that, as Lotman indicates, some types of peripheral works have been progressively moving towards the center until they become legitimized as canonical in the artistic matrix.

In the second case, I refer to the elevation of sight and hearing selected as proper senses for artistic reception in exclusion of taste, touch and smell as improper, a distinction which in a good part derives from Aristotle's hierarchical separation between distant senses (sight and hearing) and those he denominates as corporeal (smell, touch and taste)—although who could doubt that the former are also corporeal?—a hierarchy translated by Thomas Aquinas as "cognitive senses" and "noncognitive senses". Korsmeyer (2002) analyzes the sense of taste and its relevance for aesthetics and art theory and Brady (2005) eloquently argues for the inclusion of taste and the sense of smell as objects of aesthetic appreciation. The sense of touch and of kinesthesia (as muscular feeling) would also deserve, I think, consideration by aesthetic theory. As the term "contemplation" is projected from the religious matrix, it also indirectly carries social interdictions to activities that relate to the art matrix by their artifice, amusement and even creativity and fantasy, but are not assumed as such by the proscription that remains with respect to the body and sensuality potential.

Being a Lotmanian semiosphere, the art matrix is marked by mixed practices, functional asymmetries and heteroglossia found in other matrixes. As a legitimizing apparatus for the arts, the artworld credits canonical arts regulating all products according to its parameters. In that precise place remain art critics, philosophers of art and aestheticians as sentinels committed to watch over what can enter and what can not to the restricted group of the art circle (as Dickie 1984 names it). However, the periphery is dialogical and more flexible because it is where artistic hibridation and polyphony take place, where transgression and invention, the corporeal and the irreverent are most welcome. As Lotman indicates, the practices of the periphery challenge the center and end up penetrating it while other peripheral practices emerge.

The registers of the rhetoric in the artistic matrix

Various authors trace the origins of art to radically different epochs, each of them applying different tacit or explicit criteria for categorizing the artistic. The highly reputed social historian of art, Arnold Hauser (1969), for example, considers that art originates since the Paleolithic era. Others believe that art began during the Renaissance, like Juan Acha (1996), who jumps forwards many millennia when stating that it begins in 1300 with Giotto. For Arthur Danto (1987, 431) there can be no art if there is no art theory and art history, so one can deduce that art, in his terms, would begin in the sixteenth century with Vasari, the first art historian. It seems to me that Danto exaggerates the role of his profession to the degree of supposing there existed no artists until a theoretician arose and declared them such. As audacious in challenging the idea of the perennial character of art is Misko Suvakovic (2002) who argues that art did not emerge before the eighteenth century when it established a solid theoretical, critical and institutional background.

To decide among these positions, one needs to revise their criteria. Hauser considers that if the Paleolithic hunter-magician or the Neolithic farmer painted with significant dexterity, they must be considered artists. For him it is mainly the technique performed with ability and its aesthetic results that define the artistic, independently of the context. For Acha, individuality and professionalization are necessary conditions for the artistic, so art had to wait until the Renaissance for the emergence of individualized artists, whereas only Danto and Suvakovic made due emphasis upon the context for the demarcation of the artistic. Their position is more compatible to the systemic and matricial approach developed here, although it lacks a genealogical perspective that would allow us to explain where and how did modern artistic institution emerge in the first place.

From a matricial perspective, it was not in the eighteenth century or in the Paleolithic era when the artistic matrix arose, but much earlier and much later than that. It is a phenomenon in which various matrixes converge to generate it, a kind of egg simultaneously fertilized by different sperm in various wombs: the religious, military, family, and mercantile matrixes in partial overlapping depending on the particular genre. With Homer, a singer and story teller for the Court of Quios or Smirna, epic poetry and heroic songs were created from the military and State matrixes in the eighth century B.C.E. Hesiod's didactic poetry inspired by the Muses and gods from Olympus, and the lyric poetry of many early Greek authors derive from the religious matrix, perhaps related to the oracles. Although it is often spoken of the autonomy of the artistic matrix, this independence is very relative as it must always depend on other matrixes.

Theater as an art appeared in the sixth century B.C.E. as a differentiated development from agrarian rituals and athletic competitions, orgiastic music, phallic and ditirambic hymns and choirs. As Francisco Rodríguez Adrados (1983) argues extensively, these ritual and playful practices were still part of the religious matrix, but when the separation between the actor and the public occurred, between re-creation and creation, and between ritual and the imaginative work of an individualized author who begins and ends the piece to be represented, the arts emerge. Rodríguez Adrados establishes the distinction between theater and ritual, (that for our aims can

274   Everyday Aesthetics

be translated as the distinction between the artistic and the religious matrix) in the
following terms:

> The beginning of ritual action is in the people, although it is headed by its chiefs or their
> priests or wizards... But in the end, from ritual action we arrive at the Theater, and in it
> the people is not actor but spectator. [...] But definitely spectator: Theater is performed by
> professionals. Indeed, if we said that theater really existed when there was the possibility
> of changing the theme arbitrarily, without adapting even in the main lines to a fixed
> argument, it is necessary to add that this implies the existence of a public. (Rodríguez
> Adrados 1983, 550–1)

This change of theme and the freedom of not having to adapt to the fixed re-creation
of a pre-established argument and a specific date is precisely the birth of artistic
creativity. It is well known that literature and poetry typically characterize the lexic
register, music the acoustic register, pantomime and acrobatics the somatic, and
painting and sculpture the scopic register. There are in addition heteroglottic genres
that combine several registers as opera, theater, cinema and dance, among others.

Artistic lexics

Verbal language, whether oral or written, is a resourceful tool for the creation of the
fantasy. Through this medium, creatures so concrete and complex, so real and dear to
us as Alyosha Karamazov, Anna Karenina, Faust, Leopold Bloom, Orpheus, Hamlet
and the Quixote, were invented and are alive and kicking until today. Singular places
like Tlön and Uqbar, Lilliput, Macondo, Alice's Wonderland and so many others are
available for a visit thanks to words.

Yet not all literary genres are part of the artistic matrix; elegies, for example, are
part of the funerary or the State matrix, and sacred texts as the Bible, the Qur'an and
the Gospels belong to the religious matrix even if one can find passages of literary
and poetic quality in them. Epic poetry that narrates the accomplishments of heroes
to consolidate the collective identity of an army is part of the military matrix. Lyric
and erotic poetry, however, when performed by professionals with an elaborated
technique to entertain their public, belong to the artistic matrix, (yet amateur poems
between lovers for seduction and mating revolve around the family matrix).

Artistic literary authors like Alcman, Simonides, Bacilides, Stesichorus, Ibicus,
Archilochus, Sapho, Teognis, Anacreonte, Hipponax, and Pindarus generated the
lexics of the art matrix during ancient Greece. Court troubadours (as Bertrand
de Born, Marcabru, Bernard de Ventadour, Peire Vidal, Rambault de Vaqueiras,
Folquet de Marseille, Raimon de Miraval, Aimeric de Peguilhan and Guirant
Riquier) were part of this matrix during the eleventh and twelfth centuries, as
well as medieval secular poets who entertained their authors as well as audience.
Contemporary artistic lexics encompass high as well as low brow literature with
lyrics for the masses written by pop song writers like the Beatles, Bob Dylan
and an endless list of authors, composers, rappers, pink novella authors (like M.
Delly, Rafael Pérez y Pérez y Corín Tellado in Spanish or romance writers like
Jude Deveraux, Johanna Lindsey or Sherrilyn Kenyon), including movie script
and telenovela writers, all of which participate in the artistic matrix by sharing a

The Arts Matrix 275

common objective to amuse their public. There is an art for every public and taste, whatever the level of sophistication and technique, audacity or creativity, talent and acumen may be. *De gustibus non disputandum est.*

Artistic acoustics

Bach made perfect harmony audible. Chopin made us hear amorous and patriotic passion, Beethoven, intense euphoria and torment, and Mahler, infinite sadness. Playing music involves from the beginning all the formal characteristics of games mentioned by Huizinga (1955, 42). That is why it is called, precisely, "playing music". Like painting and sculpture, music is not exclusive of the artistic matrix, being part of the acoustics in the military, religious, family, State and funerary matrixes among others. Although it is as old as humanity and has been part of rituals in magic and war, music becomes specifically an art together with dancing and reciting in ancient Greece accompanying lyric poetry and theatrical spectacles from eighth to sixth centuries B.C.E. Individual hymnodists and music composers like Terpander of Lesbos (seventh century B.C.E.), Pindarus of Thebes (sixth–fifth centuries B.C.E.), and Timotheus of Miletus (fifth–fourth centuries B.C.E.) became famous in ancient Greece by participating in festivals and composing songs. In as much artistic, music is essentially secular as it is performed for the sheer enjoyment and entertainment of its audience. That is the reason why, during the Middle Ages when dominant acoustics were liturgical, the arts remained marginal and were practiced only by court troubadours, traveling gypsies, minstrels and jugglers. Musical structures like the ballad, the *rondeau* derived from French poetic forms, as in Italy the *ballata, caccia,* and the madrigal. From Guillaume de Machaut to Schönberg, artistic acoustics would acquire impressive sophistication and creativity to the degree of becoming an autonomous art. We must include in this matrix all musical genres from pop and rock, to romantic ballads, grunge, hip hop, heavy metal, techno, punk, country, reggae, western, bolero, calypso, mambo, ska, gothic and other underground genres, since each of them is professionally offered, with more or less acoustic creativity, dexterity and fantasy, for the amusement of their public.

Dealing with music does not automatically mean that we are located in the artistic matrix. As a musician, Johann Sebastian Bach offered his services to very different matrixes. His choral and organ sacred music was composed in the religious matrix for the Lutheran liturgy in the church of Saint Thomas, Leipzig. On the other hand, he composed chamber music for the amusement of Prince Leopold in Cothen or the court of Weimar. For teaching, Bach composed didactic music, namely, *The Art of the Fugue* or *The Well Tempered Harpsichord,* and he also played and invented music for family events or private celebrations. Although these matrixes are partially overlapped, the aristocratic court was the context that best favored maintaining the artistic triad of fantasy, creativity and amusement. We cannot deny that these are all aesthetically oriented works, and when today these various pieces are performed in concert halls they enter, by this very fact, under the rank of the artistic; but this matrix transplant was made much later and, in many cases, at the cost of confusing categories and contexts. It implies a semantic and pragmatic mutation.

276 *Everyday Aesthetics*

To bring a serenade to one's girlfriend or mother and to hire a musical group for a wedding or family celebration constitutes a musical statement in the family matrix, not in the artistic. By the same token, to hire musical celebrities for political campaigns becomes part from the State matrix, not of the artistic. It is also a mistake to consider folkloric or vernacular music as part of the artistic matrix, since it belongs to the extended family as a regional, local, communal tradition for ritual recreation. In order to distinguish when an aesthetic statement is artistic and when it is not it, it may be useful to take into account whether a musical piece or a painting is made for the sake of amusement or for capturing attention and transfering it for another purpose such as evoking a deity, praising an aristocrat, decorating a house, honoring the dead, or envigorating a battalion, in which case we are outside the artistic matrix. Such a statement will be able to generate effects of *latching-on* but will operate as sign or symbol of something else, *aliquid stat pro aliquo*. Only in the artistic matrix semiotic aesthetic transfer is subordinated to fantasy or what Jakobson (1963) understood as the poetic function of the language, that is to say, "the direction (*Einstellung*) towards the message in itself, the message by the message ..." This absence of transfer or delivery is also what, when observing aesthetics from the artistic model, Kant denominates "finality without end or purpose".

It is worth considering for a prosaic approach to the arts all those parallel acoustic conventions performed by spectators related to artistic reception such as obligatory silence in museums, theaters and concert halls during elite music performances, the regulated applause at the end of the whole musical piece and not of course after each movement, the whistling, the "bravos", the calls of "author, author".

Artistic somatics

Were it not for the jugglers, who maintained the spirit of the fantastic and of charm alive, the gravity imposed by the dominion of religion during the Middle Ages would have been unbearable. The nomadic juggler created the equivalent of a magic circle in space and time mentioned by Huizinga and played with his voice and body constituting an ephemeral, alternative reality.

We all experienced the variety of artistic genres where the somatic register predominates such as dancing, pantomime, acrobatics, and theater and which deploy the body as a vehicle of expression, in addition to high cuisine and perfumery developing the sense of taste and smell to acheive quite sophisticated levels. Long before their refinement as artistic genres, dance and mimics were part of propitiatory rituals for hunting, war and fertility through early tribal extended family matrixes. Some claim that acrobatics probably existed in pharaonic times and among Mesoamerican cultures, but they can consider them as properly artistic when performed by professionals for di-version of their public.

The oldest artistic somatic expression is perhaps pantomime represented in Greek vases, where mimes and jugglers appeared in humorous and satirical spectacles, sometimes integrating other registers in their acts such as masksc, choirs and music. The word "theater" means the place to see (from the Greek *theasthai*, meaning "to see" for example *theatron*); hence the intimate relation between theater and fantasy as "making visible". Theater originally derived from religious and communal rituals

The Arts Matrix

dedicated to Dionysus and mimetic performances during the bacchanals, but acquired its artistic character for di-version or entertainment by authors such as Thespis with his little itinerant cart presenting shows professionally. That sixth century B.C.E. in Greece must have been really incredible!

This rich theatrical tradition in Greek society, who so respected and needed theater as to construct amphitheaters in every important town, was partly forgotten and replaced by religious sacramental theater during the Middle Ages, with its pragmatics of re-creation (rather than artistic creation) and catechization (rather than diversion). Religious representations became didactic tools performed by the monks for rituals of re-presentation of Christ's Passion during the Holy Week and other festivities, albeit without the indispensable degree of freedom for fantasy and creativity, or the professional character of Greek *tiasos*. Calderón de la Barca wrote about 70 *Autos Sacramentales* for Corpus Christi commissioned by the clergy, but was able to produce artistic works like cloak-and-dagger pieces and, specially, his philosophical piece *La vida es sueño* for the amusement of his public.

Artistic somatics remained marginal among medieval jugglers supported by the court matrix. Philip Astley recovered part of this juggleresque inheritance and founded on 1768 the London circus with clowns specialized in surprising acrobatics acts. Great artists have emerged in this genre, like Enrico Rastelli, Kara (Michael Steiner), Jenny Jaeger, W.C. Fields among others. This tradition today has created the spectacular Circ du Soleil, receiving more recognition from the public than from the artworld that simply ignores it as a perfectly legitimate art genre (except for a few authors, Bouissac 1985, for example).

It is hard to believe that it took more than a millennium, almost two, to respond to the social demand of public spaces for the representation of fantasy after the construction amphitheaters like Epidauros in Greece. With urbanization and the progressive consolidation of the bourgeoisie as dominant class, the artistic matrix achieves somehow similar conditions for its permanence and development to those originally present at the Greek *polis*. Imitated by the Romans in Pompeii's theater (55 B.C.E.) this tradition was retaken during the Renaissance by the Italians like Andrea Palladio's *Teatro Olimpico* and Giovanni Battista Aleotti's *Teatro Farnese*. In sixteenth-century London, public theaters were finally established in the Elizabethan playhouses like the Rose, the Curtain, the Theater, and the famous Globe Theater of the Burbage family where Shakespeare presented his works. The *Commedia dell'arte* appears in Italy also in the sixteenth century, later influencing the *Comedie Francaise*, and blooms in Europe in the eighteenth century with professional companies that performed for the aristocracy and for the people in the palaces, theaters and city squares.

Dance originally developed as part of the extended family matrix through communitarian agrarian and wedding rituals. It can be considered as part of the artistic matrix only when dance was performed as a spectacle by professionals and integrated to theater in ancient Greece. Yet the modern Western sense of dance as an art does not arise but until the seventeenth century when ballet was professionalized as a spectacle on its own establishing rival schools, interpreters on salary, and special theaters, as when Louis XIV founds the *Academie Royale de Danse* on 1661. As a genre it will later become dependent on the bourgeoisie public, both capitalist and

278   *Everyday Aesthetics*

socialist, reaching an acrobatic somatic technique as that displayed by the Bolshoi ballet. With the increasing urbanization of modern society during the nineteenth and twentieth centuries, accelerated by the process of industrialization, artistic somatics ramify through diverse and more popular manifestations to include other social classes as the emerging proletariat, the bureaucracy and the petit bourgeoisie. New somatic art genres come forth like vaudeville, burlesque, music hall and table dance, or bar top dance whose sophistication loyally mirrors the taste of its public.

Daily food is part of the family matrix when one eats at home and for the sheer need of nourishment as a family ritual. When, however, food is prepared by a specialized chef who even "signs" his creations and displays them as professional cooking or *haut cuisine*, it participates in the artistic matrix. As aristocratic courts fostered artistic music and painting, there is nothing strange about it also favoring artistic cuisine. The so called "architect of French cooking" Marie Antoine "Antonin" Careme served Prince Talleyrand, and Alexander I of Russia. He is the author of the spectacular baroque pastry architecture named *"pieces-montees"*. Gastronomical art of author is consolidated in France at least since Boulanger, in Paris, opened the first restaurant by 1765 (from the word "to recover") in the modern sense. Georges Auguste Escoffier, official chef of the Grand Hotel of Monte Carlo, and later of the Ritz hotel chain, received in 1920 the Legion of Honor for his artistic creations.

Korsmeyer (2002, 21, 63–100) argues for the viability to integrate the sense of taste as a subject for philosophical tradition. She does so from the quite difficult position of cognitive aesthetics which supposes that all aesthetic appreciation requires understanding and reflection, quite problematic if one tries to prove that food is art. She employs the symbolic sense of food to justify that it is not only pleasant to the sense of taste but has a semiosic dimension (although, in terms of Goodman whose frame of reference is used, she denotes it as "symbolic"). Korsmeyer ends up denying an artistic status to *haut cuisine*, although she states that cooking could be considered as a minor or decorative art, or perhaps applied art or functional from a position that maintains the hierarchical structuring of the senses and the arts. (Korsmeyer 2002, 197) I wonder if, from the feminist position in which she approaches the problem, such hierarchical structuring of "minor" and "major" arts does not reproduce the same sexual politics that Korsmeyer denounces with respect to the hierarchical structuring of the senses. (2002, 51–60) It is not accidental that what it is known as "minor arts" correspond mainly to those practiced by women in everyday life, such as basketwork, knitting, ceramics, textiles, interior decoration, embroidery, and cooking. On the contrary Kuehn (2005), following Telfer (1996), does not have doubts in defending food as art, as did Quinet (1981) even if without convincing enough arguments. If in effect professional, creative preparation of food (that displays creativity, fantasy and is amusing to enjoy) may not be sufficiently justified as an art in the strict sense of the artworld for reasons widely discussed, nothing prevents us to acknowledge it as part of the periphery of the artistic matrix. For strict nutritional aims, we could be fed on simple pills: if we invent different forms of cooking that stimulate various senses like the visual, olfactory, touch and taste, it is because it can be a very pleasurable and satisfactory multisensorial experience.

The Arts Matrix 279

As for the sense of smell, whenever scents and incenses are used not for religious rituals, nor for the ointment of athletes, or in the medical matrix for aromatherapies, but simply for amusement, delight and fantasy, we may speak of an art of perfumes. The sense of smell had such importance that it deserved the attention of a disciple of Aristotle, Theophrastus, who wrote *Treaty on Odors*, in the fourth century B.C.E. Modern perfumes for the sake of pleasure and amusement began to be produced in the West at least by the end of the fourteenth century with the "Water of Hungary" by Queen Elizabeth of Hungary, prospering during the Italian Renaissance with Catherine de Medici. In 1656, there was already an official guild of perfume manufacturers in France. The court of Louis XV was even named "the perfumed court" due to the aromas applied not only to the skin but to clothes, fans, wigs and furniture. This genre evolves by greater variety of aromas such floral, woods, aldehydes, herbs, citruses, resins, lavender, amber, camphor and incenses until the present brands by fashion designers like Patou, Guerlain, D'Orsay, Chanel and Dior, who integrate to the art of olfactory fantasies also the scopic register by their sophisticated packaging. Olfactory creations are incredibly powerful, and they can evoke fantasies of orange groves in flower, sunny woods, wet forests , Chinese temples, and aztec rituals. In Japan, perfumery was later developed into an art named "kodo" taught in special schools, and as a paradigmatic image of the aesthetic power of perfume, Patrick Süskind's novel *Perfume* is an obligatory reference.

From the sense of smell we can pass to the sense of touch. To the human faculty of enjoying touch has been attributed a different meaning depending on the context. Whereas in business, sexual pleasures can be practiced furtively among other tactics to escalate positions in a company, in the family matrix it is engraved with values like loyalty, duty, love, reproduction, efficiency or a tacit contractual relation of exclusivity in the long term. In polytheistic religious matrixes, sexuality is dedicated to the deities and participates in orgiastic rituals of fertility, reason why it cannot be considered as prostitution (as it has been generally assumed) since sex is propitiatory, not commercial.

Regardless of how controversial it may sound, I am convinced that we must at least think about the possibility of considering certain manifestations of eroticism as part of the artistic matrix. Prostitution as a profession has existed at least since the first urban concentrations, selling sexual pleasure for money, favors or material goods, as any other merchandise. Street prostitutes that sell their body as receptacles, perform a service that almost resembles charging for the use of a public bathroom. There are, however, properly artistic forms of practicing professional eroticism, as there are forms of artistic cooking or preparing perfumes. We can all paint, dance, sing, cook and fornicate, but this does not turn us into artists. Only those who perform professionally with style, grace and dexterity and who fulfill the triad of creativity-fantasy-amusement can be considered as such. Artistic prostitutes, like artistic painters or musicians, deliberately create an atmosphere for pleasure and fantasy. Under their spell, clients cease being employees humiliated by their boss or impotent husbands and to become exciting, desired and powerful males, Adonis or Zeus. Among the Greeks, inventors of the artistic matrix, this genre was certainly present, at least in Athens since the time of Solon (seventh to sixth century B.C.E.) who regulated prostitution. Professional eroticism was practiced by specialized

280 *Everyday Aesthetics*

women, the hetaerae, trained for the diversion of masculine wealthy clients as an art with personal authorship, special techniques, creativity, imagination, and fantasy. The legendary Aspasia, lover of Pericles (who inspired the figure of Diotima of Mantinea in Plato's Symposium) could have been one of its most distinguished artists. As Greek erotic vases are at the origin of artistic scopics, hetaerae are at the origin of this genre in artistic somatics. They were also competent in good conversation and practiced their trade incorporating music, dance, singing and poetry, probably also perfumes and wine of great refinement. From the eighteenth century on, Japanese geishas (geisha literally means "artistic person") have also been professionally educated to provide pleasure to economically and politically powerful men able to afford them. Rather than artistic, it seems to me that geishas are themselves artworks embodying perfection: their finest embroidered silk kimonos, their complex hairdos, their delicate, handmade fans, jewelry and make-up in scopics, their measured words, perspicuous and opportune in their lexics, their songs and harmonious intonation, the grace and elegance of their movements, postures and gestures in the somatic, in addition to the harmony of their dance.

Although what prostitution offers is supposedly a natural product, namely the body, the artifice consists in the creation of an erotic atmosphere and metamorphosis of identities where women become exclusively objects of pleasure, as men turn into gods of virility, a Zeus or a Rambo. The art of the hetaerae never obtained artistic legitimacy because of the stigmatization imposed by the religious and medical matrixes blaming it of all evils, from capital sins to venereal diseases. Despite it, brothels of various types, tastes and fantasies have continued and proliferated up to contemporary fantasy variations from sadomasochist theatralizations (and their chains, whips, spikes and leather props) and porno Japanese *mangas* disguised characters, to all kinds of peek shows. The exhibition of sexual identities at Amsterdam's street windows or the "fishbowls" in Bangkok resemble art galleries or book stores designed to tempt costumers. Although the stigma remains nowadays, elegant harlotry is not responsible for its cheap banalization and criminal use, in the same sense that Rembrandt's paintings or Bach's arias are not responsible for obscene portraits or banal songs.

This subject is extremely controversial and I will not attempt to exhaust it or to solve it here; I simply try to be consistent with the idea that the five senses would have the same prerogative to participate in the artistic matrix. The artworld can insist on the artistic exclusivity of sight and hearing, but other social practices maintain "family resemblances" (as Wittgenstein would say) with the arts, independently of their peripheral location, and must be considered as pertinent for prosaics from the reference frame it proposes. A poetics' perspective may find *haut cuisine*, erotic arts, or perfumes not worthy to reflect upon. Prosaics, on the contrary, must observe these manifestations exactly where they are situated, in the overlapping of the commercial and the artistic matrixes.

Presently, the artistic genre has become more fashionable in the somatic register with more eloquence is performance. The list is long: from Dada to Yves Klein's naked models and the live sculptures of Gilbert and George (Under arcs 1970) or the 71 sculptures of Manzini, Kaprow and Aconci's works, Nitsch's corporeal catharsis, the physical self aggressions by Kurtycz or Serpa, pushing the body to the limits by Marina Abramovic (Rhythms 1973–74, Inspiration/expiration 1977, Potential Energy 1980, Long Walk in the Great Wall 1988) later with Ulay, Orlan's surgeries or self-mutilations by the Viennese artist Rudolf Schwarzkogler (who died at the age of 29 bleeding to death after injuring his penis during a performance).

In addition to somatics as means of artistic expression, there is the part that corresponds to the spectator, somatic complicity. Each genre of the artistic matrix determines for its public not only the lexics and acoustics but also the proper somatics to enjoy it, like remaining almost immovable in the seats at the cinema, theater and concerts, applauding the artists during determined periods, participating corporeally in eroticism or tasting slowly the delights of a chef or the quality of a wine. In the self mutilating performances of Marina Abramovic not only the artist's tolerance but of the spectator's to contemplate physical pain is tested, since on one occasion a member of the audience saved her life from suffocating on carbon dioxide when he or she interrupted the act in which she lay on the floor surrounded by a wooden star in flames. I have heard cases of innocent spectators who run to the scene to rescue the character in difficulty.

The code also establishes in each case the somatic for the artists, like bowing before the public or gestures that express success or satisfaction like extended arms and kisses to the air. I must also mention another manifestation in two registers, the famous photographs of piles of naked bodies by Spencer Tunick which seem more interesting from the playful somatic experience for the models than the scopics of the photographer. Presently, the street mimes, clowns and fire performers who pretend to be live "statue" performers incarnate the somatics of the original juggleresque spirit in contemporary cities.

Although all art is matricial, not all art is institutional, namely since it need not be consecrated from the top by hierarchized artworld authorities to be enjoyed. It can also be located in peripheral zones and be an important part of the entertainment, creativity and fantasy resources for significant sectors of the population.

Artistic scopics

Mainstream art history has been retroactively claiming for its discipline all objects considered beautiful rescued from the past, from cave paintings at Lascaux and Altamira, engravings in bone or ivory, feminine figures of the gravetian period or the Willendorf Venus, up to the sculpture, ceramics and painting of pharaonic Egypt, dynastic China and theocratic Mesoamerican cultures as alibi of the universality and eternity of art. These are spectacular and beautiful objects indeed, but not necessarily artistic. Any object from the antiquity whose syntax is conspicuously aesthetic has been appropriated by the artistic matrix as part of its inventory to reiterate the established synonymy between aesthetics and art. Here we have the most legitimized massive theft in history.

Most of these works, mistakenly considered artistic, were in fact cultural objects belonging to archaic undifferentiated tribal or familiar matrix. If many of these objects are surprising in their expressive, compositional and technical skill, they are such because of their syntax for appealing to human sensibility. That does not mean, however, that they are artistic, since the special care in their manufacture obeys to the

282 *Everyday Aesthetics*

interest of pleasing Gods rather than humans. The so-called "art" of the Paleolithic or Neolithic is tribal or communitarian scopics whose function was to protect them in hunting and war, appeal to the gods or goddesses to fertilize the land or to favor rain, certainly not to create fantasies and amuse or entertain the members of the tribe.

The Parthenon in Athens, considered archetypal of classical art, is an aesthetic strategy in the scopic register of the religious matrix consecrated to the deities of the Mount Olympus, not an art object for the entertainment and fantasy of a public. The monumental sculpture of Pharaoh Kafre, today in the museum of Cairo, is part of the matrix of State, not yet of the artistic, and so are the reliefs in the palaces of Ashurnasirpal in Nimrod and the paintings of the palace at Knossos in the Minoan civilization. The frescoes of Pompeii, for example, are part of the family matrix located in domestic spaces.

The scopics in the artistic matrix did not appear one day out of nothing through the magical brush strokes of Giotto di Bondone, as implied in the proposal of Acha (1996). For the artistic function to arise, it was necessary that the triad creativity-fantasy-diversion, and conditions such as personal authorship, professionalization and spectacularization be met. Phidias who made the monumental Zeus and Athena in the Parthenon, and Praxiteles to whom the statues of Aphrodite and Hermes are attributed, established themselves as individual authors. In this sense they are in the process of transition or overlapping between the religious and the artistic matrix: although these figures are still vehicles of religious veneration, they already begin to display personal authorship. Thus, visual arts emerge partially from religion by the seventh and sixth century B.C.E. with professional authors who sign their vases and exhibit their personal mastery, fantasy and creativity, like Epictetus I and II, Cleitias, Douris, Exekias and Euphronius. Two thousand years later, Giotto also created visual and spatial imaginaries that were still part of the religious matrix both at the semantic and the pragmatic level, but proposed a new syntax inviting the spectator to follow the painting for visual delectation in his incipient effort to create a sense of spatial context for the characters.

By the sixteenth century art was emerging from the religious and familiar matrixes with the support of patrons as the Florentines Giovanni Rucellai (patrons of Paolo Uccello and Domenico Veneziano) and Cosimo de Medici (who supported painters as Fra Angelico, Fra Filippo Lippi, and sculptors Luca of the Robbia, Donatello and Ghiberti, as well as Brunelleschi the architect). Pope Julius II, on the other hand, commissioned Michelangelo to paint the Sistine Chapel strictly for the religious matrix. Although these aesthetic practices became part of the political-economic unit of the aristocratic court or family matrix by patronage, the patrons' eagerness for diversion and enjoyment, and their economic means to provide it, attracted the most talented and bold artists of their time favoring creativity and relative freedom to invent. In fact, the artistic matrix always requires some funding, as the State matrix, and is parasitical or totally merges with the commercial.

This matrix began its process of institutionalization through the establishment of academies (the term "Academy" derives from the Greek, as in Plato's Academy) like the *Accademia di Disegno* in Florence in 1563 (under patronage of Cosimo de Medici), and the *Accademia di San Luca* in 1593 in Rome. It is not casual that also in that century art history and art criticism were initiated as disciplines by Giorgio Vasari

The Arts Matrix 283

(1511–1574), whose *Lives of the most Eminent Painters, Sculptors and Architects* began the mystification of artists based on the model of the heroes of classic antiquity. A new concept of "art" arose, regulated by its own disciplines and procedures, in contrast to the pre-artistic traditional trade of anonymous medieval craftsmen. This professionalization of artistic scopics and the beginning of their institutionalization was crystallized with the foundation of the Academie Royale de Peinture et de Sculpture in Paris (1648), the Academy of San Fernando in Madrid (1752), the Royal Academy of London (1768), and the Academy of the Three Noble Arts of San Carlos in Mexico (1781) (painting, sculpture and architecture, where I studied). Overlapping with the school matrix, art academies originally were aristocratic associations that welcomed the incipient, talented bourgeoisie to their service in the process of capitalistic and urban expansion. By the eighteenth century the artistic matrix was consolidated and already generated networks of art collectors, museums and art historians as Johann Joachim Winckelmann and art critics such as Denis Diderot.

Haut couture displays costumes as authorial creative work for the amusement of its public to touch, see, wear and move around with them. New, eccentric and frequently unwearable models as those of Jean-Paul Gautier's appear in fashion pageants for the aesthetic delight and fantasy of the *jet set*, similar to an opera performance or an art exhibit.[4] Fashion as a genre is partly scopic in the make-up and costumes exhibited, and partly somatic in the models and gestures, proportions, postures, and so on. Initially, the aesthetics of clothes required great palace celebrations and gala parties to exhibit them. Now costumes are moving from the periphery to the center when no less than the Metropolitan Museum of Art has been organizing exhibitions like Balenciaga (1973), Infra-Apparel (1993), "Orientalism: Visions of the East in Western Dress" (1994), "Jacqueline Kennedy: The White House Years" (2001), "Rara Avis" from the collection of Iris Apfel Barrel (2005), or the fashion of Chanel and many others.

The artistic matrix requires amphitheaters, museums, brothels, cabarets, restaurants, theaters, galleries or circus tents to exhibit its products. The public that attends any of these, goes for the same reasons: to enjoy and amuse themselves, to be detached from their ordinary identities and vicariously acquire others such as identifying with a literary character, feel as the singer's sweetheart, a prostitute or stripper's object of desire, a swan in love, acquire a painter's view or a musician's hearing, the taste of a chef, the skillful and vulnerable body of a circus acrobat or the invulnerable protagonist of video-games.

Modalities of artistic dramatics

The theoretical decision to propose these four modalities and not others may be better understood through this matrix because they are directly linked to categories often

---

4   *Prêt-à-porter*, however, is not art but intermatricial design (uniforms for soldiers, policemen, nurses and school, clothes for secretaries, suits for managers and bureaucrats) that solves the need to get dressed for suitably representing the assigned role. By being intermatricial, it is not part of the artistic matrix, because it contributes with the iconic outfits to very different matrixes.

284 *Everyday Aesthetics*

used in art theory. If we incorporate the categories proposed by, for example, Dondis (1976, 28–9) in his syntax of the image, we will become aware that proxemics has to do with transparency or opacity, complexity or simplicity, subtlety or the obviousness of its enunciations attracting certain type of spectators while turning others away. The categories of regularity and irregularity, dynamism and immobility, continuity or randomness, solidity or flimsiness, predictability or spontaneity, balance or instability, symmetry or asymmetry, variation or coherence, all refer to the modality of kinetics. Emphatics is manifested by contrast, sharpness, distortion, tone, accent, boldness, brightness or the opposite diffusivity, vagueness, ambiguity, indecision and neutrality in unmarked emphatics. The centripetal or closed fluxion relates to juxtaposition, contour, centrality, agglomeration and concentration, whereas the open fluxion to exuberance, dispersion or profusion, fragmentation, propagation and so on. It is therefore justified to organize this snarled range of categories according to four basic modalities.

As analytical categories for the examination of the art matrix, the dramatic modalities can be of significant heuristic value if applied to the various layers of art related phenomena. By such "layers" I mean: a) signifiers/symbolizers (instruments' timbre and pitch, colors, shapes, and gestures); b) artistic languages (high or low brow, elite or popular); c) styles and idiolects (euphuism and gongorism, satire and picaresque, naturalism and surrealism, hip hop and Dodecaphonic music, impressionism); d) genres (soap opera or opera, novel or short story, sonata, sonnets, comedy and tragedy, symphonic or chamber music, progressive rock or romantic ballads); e) codes (abstractionism, realism, chromaticism, serialism); and lastly f) the attitude in the relation between an author and its characters. There is no reason to suppose that certain features that attract us to a painting would not exert attraction towards, say, a person. The elongation in Greco's or Modigliani's characters can be equally or more touching in a real person's elongated, languid figure, or vice versa, the personal identity and material presence of Pope Innocent X also made Velazquez' re-presentation of his portrait particularly interesting.

The following view of the modalities in this matrix must necessarily be brief, as it was elaborated mainly for the purpose of enticing those interested in this matrix to further explore their possibilities in greater detail.

Artistic proxemics

In the art matrix, the difference between high brow and low brow art, as well as among genres and styles is defined in great part by proxemics. For Aristotle, comedy is close to everyday characters "of a lower type", while tragedy imitates those of "higher type", more distant to the common people, like kings and heroes. Aristophanes's comedies establish short proxemics with everyday life, mocking the political world of his time (for example, the unscrupulous Cleon), as Menander depicts everyday characters, namely cooks, slaves, and merchants occupied in daily matters. On the other hand, tragedies like Euripides' Medea, daughter of King Aeetes of Clochis or Sophocles' Oedipus Rex, depict events quite remote to common people's lives.

During the Middle Ages and the Renaissance, the religious matrix took great pains to lengthen proxemics from the people towards hierarchical figures and

The Arts Matrix

sacred texts for establishing a sense of holiness, supremacy, and solemnity. Yet once a year, the carnival shortened that distance by humor and desacralization in the carnivalesque spirit that so much interested Bakhtin. The propagation of printing in Europe also significantly shortened accessibility to both religious and secular texts. In fact, Bocaccio's *Decameron* and Rabelais' *Gargantua* and *Pantagruel*, archetypal authors of early and late Renaissance literature, shorten the proxemics of previous epic narrations towards daily erotic and humoristic stories created basically for the sake of fantasy and diversion. Today, because of the distance in time, these authors have become canonical figures removed from popular taste and thus reading them becomes often more a duty than a subversive pleasure. Younger generations definitely enjoy proximity less with the past than with the fantasies of the future, and are thus fascinated by the epics in George Lucas's double trilogy *Star Wars* and by Tolkien and J.K. Rowling's stories. Shakespearean theater was created for the amusement of the common people and the aristocracy, both of which were reflected by distinctive lexic proxemics varying in refinement, genre and style, from the common to the majestic and from prose to poetry according to their social status. Later, French preciousism, English euphuism and Spanish culteranism established long proxemics to the common public by allusions to Greek mythology, the use of hyperbaton, repeated antitheses and alliterations, complex grammatical syntax, and so on. By contrast, picaresque styles humorously depicting astute rascals remained closer to the market and the street.

In the process of proxemic shortening between authors and their characters one must mention Dostoyevsky's profound psychological and existential exploration of his characters, followed by Joyce's utmost proximity even entering his character's unconscious and most intimate thoughts.

The constitution of the modern artworld has been an attempt to select and institutionalize for its circle only those products that generally display long proxemics to the general public not only as a matter of taste but also because economic, professional, and sometimes even political interests are at stake as to the precise limits of its consecrated inventory.

At the present time, there are two theatrical genres that owe their enormous success to very short lexic proxemics with their public: soap opera and telenovela. Both are extremely localist genres that nevertheless have a remarkable impact, particularly telenovelas, among very heterogeneous audiences. Although in some cases the argument is preposterous, the dialogues sometimes remain near to everyday life because the episodes are recorded on a daily basis and it is impossible to elaborate them more scrupulously. Moreover, their relative verisimilitude and part of their artistic quality depend on the freshness and immediacy of such short lexic proxemics.[5] This success must be due to the proximity that characters acquire by

---

5   See Mandoki (2002). Immediately after the defeat of the Taliban regime in Afghanistan that had banned television for years, the new Afghan State managed to transmit 3 hours daily, one of which was dedicated to the successful Mexican soap opera *Mirada de Mujer*. The romantic preoccupations due to the difference of age between the protagonist and her lover or the problems of the anorexic daughter probably seem quite exotic in a society with serious problems of famine and that forced its women to cover themselves for decades with a burka.

286   *Everyday Aesthetics*

their daily presence in the domestic space through the TV monitor, in addition to the intimate confessions shared with the public and the adjacent information they provide on social conventions. I have heard women say that they watch telenovelas among other things for social training, namely, to learn how to dress, speak and act on certain occasions. In our terms, telenovelas have become dramaturgical schools for the construction of personal identities, as well as for emotions where many learn when it is legitimate to be angry or sad, what to expect emotionally from others, and what can be considered socially acceptable.

All music is a proxemic game of sounds: we listen how melodies and rhythms approach us while others disappear in the horizon and reappear in a slightly different form. Music is composed to create acoustic landscapes for exploration. Some musical panoramas are exciting, profound, with great mystery, intensity, luminosity or gloom, while others are simply flat and boring. Originally integrated to ancient Greek theater, acoustic proxemics developed to entertain the aristocracy by the patronage of court musicians commissioned to write and play lighter themes and amuse the guests and hosts of these splendid parties. On a technical level, artistic acoustics have never achieved such short proxemics to everyday life as today. Just by slightly moving a finger, we can hear a symphony any time, anywhere, thanks to the invention of radio and recorded music. The most intimate acoustic proxemics is in the absolute privacy provided by earphones. This short proxemics occurs not only in the consumption of music, cheaper every day, but in its creation, because anybody can now play and compose pop and rock pieces without significant training. Keyboards now have a bank of recorded rhythms and tunes with which anyone can pretend to be a composer. Consequently we find the proliferation of musical genres fabricated for immediate massive consumption by the simplicity of their codes, the stickiness of their melodies, the insipidity of their lyrics or rhythm, and their well calculated recipes for success. These contrast to the auditory training required to appreciate the work, for example, of Schoenberg's dodecaphonic music, Webern's serial music, Stockhausen and Cage's aleatory music, all of which imply a distance and an effort that attracts really very few.

At the moment music has become, like sports and other preferences, a strategy of distinction from a signic axis that marks variable proxemics between diverse generational groups, of class extraction, gender or idiosyncrasy, even political sympathies. Displaying predilection for a certain type of music constitutes by this modality one of the strategies for the construction of identity and of expressing adhesion or repulsion to particular social groups.

With the invention of ballet, somatic proxemics were extended in this elite genre of the seventeenth century becoming an art for minorities and whose interpretation required a very rigorous training, almost from childhood. On the other end, short somatic proxemics developed in genres like cabaret and burlesque as at the *Folies-Bergere* in Paris since 1869, night clubs like *Le Chat Noir* (1881, showing comedy, spectacles, half-naked women, political satire), music halls up to the present table dance, strippers bars and Chippendale male strip shows. In these genres, the attraction consists in the effect of corporeal proximity and sensuality of the performers with respect to the public. *Haute couture* and gourmet cooking are also genres that maintain a long exclusive proxemics of class as mechanisms of distinction for the elite: to consume a chef's creation or to wear unique clothes of famous designers are obviously not within the reach of majorities. In fact, the models selected to present *haute couture* creations for magazines and pageants are themselves also fabricated in their particular anatomic characteristics (some displaying an almost concave abdomen in contrast to the plump bodies of workers and farmers, therefore establishing a long proxemics of class), their indifferent, spoiled or bored facial expressions and emaciated bodies as an additional long proxemic strategy to distance them from ordinary people in the streets who own normal round bodies.

In analogy to proxemic shortening in the lexic register during the Renaissance by more humorous topics and erotic themes, painting also began to represent religious or mythological topics but with settings resembling more those known by the spectator of everyday life to generate the sensation of material proximity. Giotto painted mountains and castles to simulate a more realistic space. Chiaroscuro and perspective helped further reducing the distance of pictorial representation by the volumetric tactility of its characters and objects. The genres of Madonnas and Annunciations acquired a quality of everydayness by representing almost flesh and bone women in naturalistic environments, occupied in reading or resting at home, in contrast to the remote medieval virgins apparently nailed to a gilded flat background. Having the bourgeoisie with great power of acquisition, the Flemish school of painting shortened even more conventional scopic proxemics by selecting everyday subjects, specially in Vermeer's interior scenes and Van Eyck's and Hal's portraits, not to mention Rembrandt's.

With the invention of photography in the nineteenth century, professional painters, particularly portraitists, questioned the meaning and future possibilities of their craft. The emergence of the avant-gardes, each more elitist than the former, followed. From then on, art's scopic proxemics lengthened from non educated spectators who were increasingly required to handle radically different codes of interpretation from those applicable to academic painting. This process also shortened proxemics among members of the artworld, who could now view with disdain the frustration of common spectators for not being able to understand modern art.

By the second half of the twentieth century, painting was becoming an interesting, decorative commodity for a new public with great financial possibilities, even if with little artistic education. After the fashion boom of action painting, new artists emerged like Oldenburg, Warhol, Segal and Hanson, Rauschenberg, Lichtenstein who recuperated for their new, younger rich public the pleasure of recognizing what sculptures and paintings are about. The strategy was simple: appropriating characters, signifiers and topics of mass culture. Andy Warhol used Brillo detergent boxes, Campbell's soup cans and the big world of political and mediatic celebrities (Mao, Kennedy, Marilyn Monroe, Ingrid Bergman, Marlene Dietrich and Greta Garbo, Liz Taylor, Jackie and Elvis Presley, Muhammad Ali) with decorative, highly contrasting colors similar to commercial advertisements. Rauschenberg and Lichtenstein quoted comic strips' signifiers, Segal and Hanson everyday scenes of American life. Hyperrealism and Superrealism schools with authors like Freud (Lucian), Rustin, Fischl, in addition to Howe and Mapplethorpe, appeared to shorten proxemics even more, leaving nothing to the imagination, and thus, paradoxically, creating a new sense of remoteness.

288 *Everyday Aesthetics*

Among all the genres of contemporary artistic scopics, cinema and video-games are certainly developing the *poiesis* of fantasy to admirable degrees of creativity and technical perfection by their skillful verisimilitude in making the invisible visible, as the shipwreck of the *Titanic* or the dinosaurs running through the prairies of *Jurassic Park*. This technical virtuosity is equivalent to what Renaissance painters achieved in their time after the discovery of the novel technique of chiaroscuro and perspective. The present scopic technology has also shortened the proxemics to incorporate the somatic register in the interactivity of videogames, some of which can be simultaneously played between people in two opposite corners of the planet, as in *Warcraft*.

The acme of this process of proxemic shortening is perhaps the successful television program *Big Brother* where the everyday as such becomes a show during a confinement of 106 days. This is the new aesthetics of the hyperreal announced by Baudrillard (1978) but at levels that he himself did not imagine in the 1970s, when for the first time the intimacies of the Loud family were televised during seven months, 300 hours uninterrupted. Obscenity enters the artistic matrix when the fantasy now proposed is that of turning the spectator into a legitimized voyeur. The artists of this new genre are not, however, the inhabitants of the house of *Big Brother*, but the producers of the program who used their creativity and fantasy for inventing a show that exhibits people who spill authentic tears, snots and sweat in close up and real time as a production voraciously consumed by the masses.

Artistic kinetics

Lexic kinetics in the artistic matrix is enormously dynamic through a variety of ways, as in poetry which mobilizes the word by unusual semantic associations and evocative games. A paradigmatic novel, as far as lexic dynamics is concerned, is Joyce's *Ulysses*, sliding through diverse discursive genres, styles and planes, as well as mythological, religious, historical, psychological and philosophical references and meanings. In the opposite end of this modality are the clichés and stereotypes in genres like fotonovela, typical telenovelas and pink novels or romances whose lexics are so predictable that practically illustrate paraplegic kinetics. Given the speed of contemporary urban life, genres like mini fiction and ultra short stories are today growing with remarkable success as readers' concentration span diminishes and rhythm of experience increases.

Acoustic kinetics are indispensable in the artistic matrix since without dynamism music is impossible. Music *is* movement. The variety of kinetics in playing classical music is explicitly enunciated through terms as *allegro, andante, adagietto, vivace, ritenuto, slentando, veloce, moderato, rallentando* or in German *rasch, langsam* or *schnell*. By contrast, popular music for the masses does not require such specific directions granting more freedom to interpreters, because it lacks the complexity that composers of classical music usually endow their works.

For analyzing somatic kinetics from the point of view of the spectator, the concepts of "scene-image" and "labyrinth-image" proposed by Roman Gubern (1996) can be quite illuminating. A show is almost purely scene-image because the spectator sits and observes the performance at a theater's stage or reflected at the cinema screen

The Arts Matrix 289

or television monitor. When admiring a painting, the spectator's somatic kinetics are fixed as before a scene-image. Also, even if sculpture or Op-art partly demand from spectators to move around the work from different angles, their position is stable at every moment and thus not significantly different from a scene-image. In video-games players stay in a fixed place while characters and events pass before their eyes as scene-image. As an interactive game, however, players vicariously travel through such spaces with an electronic control generating kinetics of labyrinth-image. In addition to perfectly connecting scene and labyrinth images, video-games integrate somatic with scopic kinetics, as well as acoustic and to a lesser extent also lexic kinetics referring to imaginary worlds.

The impressive scopic dynamism of the Renaissance when pictorial representation was transformed by resources such as perspective, chiaroscuro, degradation and saturation of color, remained relatively stable during half a millennium becoming canonical in academic art. But at quarter to twelve of the nineteenth century, this stability was subverted beginning with Monet's painting *Impression: Dawn* (1872). From this picture on, scopic kinetics were resolutely dynamized in the effort to represent no longer the eternal as in traditional mythical or religious topics, but the ephemeral: light, steam, reflections in the water, the course of the day. Impressionist artists developed a pictorial style to grasp fleetingness and, for that reason, their contemporaries blamed them for leaving their paintings incomplete. We know the story: soon after came pointillism, post-impressionism, fauvism, expressionism, cubism, futurism, surrealism, constructivism, suprematism, vorticism, orphism, neoplasticism, and so on in a previously unseen swift succession and overlapping of styles.

By 1895, the dream of perhaps all scopic artists came true: the illusion of the moving image. The Lumiere brothers managed to dinamize the image in a plane producing effects so realistic that caused terror among the first spectators seeing a train quickly moving towards them in *L'Arrivée d'un train à la Ciotat* (1895). Since then, scopic kinetics progressively accelerated not only in avant-garde art, but particularly in the art of masses and its generation of scopic genres, products, and transitory celebrities.

Artistic emphatics

When speaking of artistic genres, one must inevitably refer to emphatics since they characterize the accent that artists choose to place on a particular aspect while unmarking others. The variety of literary genres in prosics (such as satiric, melodramatic, moralizing, comic, tragic, romantic or ironic, farce, and so on) and in poesics (for instance elegy, ode, pastoral, dramatic monologue, and so on) depend on where and how such emphasis is placed. Any topic, for instance a young man falls in love with a woman that turned out to be his mother, can be represented in various tones depending on emphatics, from a melodrama to a farce, a satire or a tragedy. From prosic lexic emphatics we can encounter frequent themes particularly accentuated by authors, such as woman in danger, irreversible fall of the protagonist, persecuted man, family in problems, faithful pet, the return of the prodigal son, common individual in an extraordinary situation or the opposite, the

290   *Everyday Aesthetics*

outcast or outlaw in a common situation, and so on. There is also an emphatics of roles in individual characters such as victim, victimizer, betrayer, intimate friend, accomplice, fool, rival, or in Propp's ([1928] 1989) narratological model the hero, villain, donor, magical helper, dispatcher, false hero, prince/princess and victim (as the six roles later proposed by Greimas's (1966) actantial model: subject/object of action (*sujet/objet*), sender and receiver of effects (*destinateur/destinataire*), and helper/enemy (*adjuvant/opposant*)). Genres are defined by formulas depending on their emphasis: romantic (a character is passionately obsessed by another), fantastic (familiarity with the strange or bizarre), war (the main character overcomes several tests to be accepted by the group), cops (the protagonist makes a moral activity in an immoral world), western (the protagonist takes the community to civilization), and so on. (Zavala 1997, 77)

In soap opera and telenovelas, emphatics are established around the main motivational or strongest character who displays what Gubern (1997, 35) denominated as "complexes". He adjudicates Narcissus's complex to characters that adore themselves, King Midas to the compulsion of changing everything into gold, Satyriasis to the womanizer, Brutus's complex to the initiated who destroys his initiator, Cinderella's to the social climber by a marriage without responsibilities, the complex of Diana to the virile protest of the insubordinate woman, Betsabe's complex to adultery by calculation, the complex of Circe or the compulsive seducer, Mesalina to nymphomania, Delilah's or the castrating woman and Daphne's to the permanent virgin. I would like to add to this list the complex of Medea or the destroyer of her children, the complex of Endymion ignoring the passion provoked, Acteon's complex to the captured peeping Tom, the complex of Aegistus to the adulterous accomplice in assassinating his rival, Aesculapious' complex always rescuing protagonists that relapse at the hospital, Agamemnon's to the victim of the unfaithful wife alongside Clytemnestra's or the adulterous assassin, the complex of Telemacus or the son in search of his absent father, Fedra's to the incestuous stepmother, in addition, of course, to the complex of Iphigenia or the sacrificed daughter in filial love. Among these, it is the complex of Andromeda the commonest topic of traditional telenovelas, always rescued from the monster by her Perseus and taken happily to conjugal life. (Mandoki 2002)

In classical music, acoustic emphatics or the character of the interpretation are marked by specific indications such as *piano, pianissimo, forte, fortissimo, sforzando, soave, staccato, tenuto,* and in the semantic by terminology as *affettuoso, espressivo, festive, scherzando, piacevole, dolente, agitato, spiritoso, with determination, dolce, sospirando* (in German *feierlich, ernst, ausdrucksvoll, mit enfindung, ruhig*). Yet serious musical pieces can mutate into a light emphatics by stylistic devices like mantovanization or tomitization (arrangements by Mantovani or Tomita organ), in the same way that jazzing Bach's religious music can turn it sensuous. In the *Carmen* opera song "Habanera", the character acquires still greater sensuality than Bizet's original by the seductive emphatics in Filippa Giordano's interpretation. It is possible to also imagine the inverse, singing the Habanera with such solemnity that it could accompany a funeral. Love is the topic par excellence of the music for masses, in every case accompanied by particular emphatic hues such as sadness, loneliness, jealousy, nostalgia, desire, revenge, self-pity, or schmaltz.

The Arts Matrix 291

As far as somatic emphatics, the precise gesture in theater, the perfect movement in dance, the right texture in cooking, illustrate this modality. Weightlessness or the attempt of freeing the body from gravity is a recurrent emphatic in ballet dancing as well as in acrobatic performances. For the *Circ du Soleil* this challenge to gravity seems to be its main *leit motiv*. Among other somatic emphatics manifestations in the art matrix it is worth pointing at the remarkable emphasis placed upon the foot's arch and elongated legs in ballet, and in low brow dancing, Michael Jackson's characteristic backward "moonwalk step". In high brow performance genre, and from an altogether different approach, Orlan's "carnal art" through surgical body transformation is a case in point.

Somatic emphatics is a basic component re-presented in figurative scopic arts, as Adam's gesture of covering his face and Eve's covering her breast and genitals in Masaccio's *Expulsion of Adam and Eve*, later echoed by Botticelli's *Birth of Venus*, not for shame but modesty. In his *Tribute Money*, Jesus's finger, repeated by St. Peter's, pointing to the sea where the coin was to be taken out of the mouth of the first fish, constitute the somatic emphatics of the painting. Impossible not to mention the Gioconda's keen expression concentrated in her mouth and eyes looking back at the spectator, in contrast to the traditional more elusive virgins looking down. El Greco's Cardinal Niño de Guevara's left hand and Pope Innocent X's eyebrows and fingers painted by Velazquez, as well Rembrandt's Syndics' eyes looking down at us in a self righteous attitude, or Grunewald's Christs with twitched fingers exemplify what is meant by this modality. However, the paradigmatic image of artistic emphatics in this register is the almost finger to finger touch in MichaelAngelo's *Creation of Adam*.

In painting, the most frequent scopic topics have been nature (landscapes, flowers, fruits, and still life), mother and child, domestic interiors, animals, Greek and Christian mythology, historic episodes, portraits, children, bathers, odalisques, and so on. Masterpieces in painting combine different topics, as Velazquez who in *Meninas* mixes portrait and self-portrait, in addition to the animal and domestic interiors. From impressionism's revolution, light and movement became the dominant scopic topic. Each of the avant-gardes that followed was defined by its particular emphatics, as the unconscious for surrealism, multiperspective in cubism, technology and industrialization in futurism, the decay of the bourgeoisie in expressionism, the communist utopia in socialist realism, irrationality and randomness in dada, color in orphism, and so on. Personal artistic styles and idiolects are marked by characteristic emphatics, as the feminine sensual exoticism for Gauguin, the stained gausses in Burri from his experiences as a military doctor, the rundown walls of Tapies, Matisse's flat chromatism, Rothko's mystic spatialism, and Albers's chromatic precision, the poignant brush strokes in Van Gogh and his vibrant self portraits, the geometric compositive emphasis of Cezanne, the presentation of real space in Fontana's paintings, Warhol's celebritism, pictorial essentialism in Mondrian and Malevitch. In photography, the list of artistic scopics may be endless as well, since what is photography if not a gesture of scopic empathics?

Artistic fluxion

In addition to contrasting proxemics and emphasis on quite different subjects, fine arts contrast the arts for the masses in fluxion, since, the former can be characterized by their centripetal fluxion in a series of concentric hierarchical circles (the "artworld") established to confer or not artistic status to a work and, consequently to the personal identities of artists. For the plastic arts, consecrating spaces that monopolize the rights of conferral of artistic status are the Museum of Modern Art (MOMA), the Whitney, the Metropolitan and the Guggenheim at New York on one side of the Atlantic and on the other the Louvre and the Pompidou in Paris. For the other registers we must mention the Lincoln Center for the Performing Arts in New York, Covent Garden in London, Scala in Milan, and so on. Cultural centers in smaller cities follow similar guidelines for artistic consecration to those emanated from the centers. The arts of masses, on the other hand, only need advertising and sales in the market to determine who is a successful artist, and consequently nominated or awarded for MTV, Grammy, Tony, Emmy and Oscar prizes.

Literary production depends on the centripetal fluxion that authors can generate to maintain readers adhered to their discursive weaving. Also in classical music acoustic fluxion is relatively centripetal for keeping the public concentrated in each movement during the couple of hours the concert lasts. Conventions in this matrix establish for the public a contained somatic fluxion during the interpretation, whether a concert or theater performance. When concluding the piece, it briefly allows to open acoustic fluxion by the applause or whistling and shouting "bravo", but the person who happens to clap after the first movement is seriously penalized with shushing and disapproving glances from all, hearing his own lonely applause embarrassingly vanish.

In contrast, the open acoustic fluxion in mass concerts does not demand from the public too much effort of concentration. By its volume and multiple additional sensorial stimuli as lights, costumes, dances, continuous hyperbolic movements on the stage, amplified and multiplied projections of the singer and striking special effects, these performances overflow the scene towards the spectator who can sing and shout, even dance and jump during the show. Broadly one can say that while in fine arts it is the public who makes the effort, sometimes a significative one, of approaching the centripetal fluxion of the artist (as in the conceptual work of John Cage in his experiments with monotony and radio waves receivers in *Imaginary Landscape 4* or Edgar Varese's electronic music), in mass arts it is the artists who unfold a centrifugal fluxion trying to reach the greatest amount of public possible and grab its attention. These centrifugal acoustics are becoming a threat of being *latched-by* the personal musical taste of the supermarket manager or the full power of amplifiers from a car blasting it out in the streets.

Typical open somatic fluxion takes place in *rave* events and rock concerts where the participants dance and jump against each other or are thrown over. Genres such as table dances and strippers are centrifugal to seduce all the guests as if each one in particular was the desired lover. One finds its opposite in elite contemporary dance where the public remains fixed and fully concentrated in appreciating the graceful and delicate gestures of classic ballet or the fragmentary, edgy, and even chaotic

The Arts Matrix 293

movements of contemporary dance. I mean of course Martha Graham's revolution with dancers' angularity and muscular contractions, as well as Pina Bausch's and contemporary choreographers like Wim Vanderkeybus's new body emphatics.[6]

In correlation to this tendency, the scopic fluxion of painting during the twentieth century has become progressively centripetal. After the impressionist revolution, a second revolution in this register took place by 1910, similar to Schoenberg's dodecaphonic revolution, when Kandinsky initiated abstractionism and the spectator could no longer recognize the subject of the work and was forced to attend exclusively to the chromatic and formal decisions taken by the artist. In each of the following avant-gardes, the artist became more and more absorbed in himself to the degree that the favorite subject of art became art itself, as mentioned in contemporary emphatics. Duchamp makes explicit the implicit constituents of the *artworld*, because only in the museum and with Duchamp as a judge and the signature of "R. Mutt", the urinal could be transmuted into an artwork. With *Fountain*, Duchamp played *mimicry* (when presenting an object that somehow mimetizes the "sculptoric"), *agon* (by participating in a contest), *alea* (risking the rejection of the piece), *peripatos* (simply conceiving the whole idea), and *ilinx* (by subverting many of the most cherished criteria of the *artworld*) in a single movement. No surprise that this move would inspire conceptual art, pop art, ready-mades, installations, happenings that would characterize the artworld during the second half of the twentieth century.

Art itself became a favorite topic for artists in plastic arts, theater and film, (Malevich *White Square in a White Background*, Pirandello's *Six Characters Looking for an Author*, Fellini's *8½*, and so on). At the moment, it has arrived at an impasse known as "postmodernism" by continuous recycling of previous scopic types, ironic quotes, and superpositions. In contrast, the scopics of the masses, particularly in film, have become even more centrifugal representing imaginary realities with greater technological creativity and surprising realism of special effects. The archetypal George Lucas's double trilogy *Starwars*, or Ang Lee's *Crouching Tiger, Hidden Dragon* and an endless list of other films offer the spectator unique scopic and oneiric opportunities to travel through fantasy.

It seemed that art's fluxion could not lock itself up more than in the increasing eccentricities of the avant-gardes, and nevertheless it did in the so called "trans-vangarde". The subject of art was no longer art itself, but the artist as such. Ben sitting with a sign in his chest written *I am an artist*, the live sculptures of Gilbert George, the surgeries of Orlan, and the autobiographical works of Joseph Beuys illustrate these artist-centric trans-vangarde tendencies.

Paradigm projections related to the artistic matrix

As the religious matrix, the artistic has been extremely solicited for legitimating purposes by its fascinating character and enormous prestige. Diverse matrixes have

---

6 In *Roseland* by this last author, it is possible to notice the short somatic proxemics of the dancers with daily movements, whereas in the syntax and semantics, proxemics is extended by not narrating a story as is usual in classical ballet, but is analogous to abstraction in painting.

hired artists for their service inserting them in other institutions, as the Renaissance aristocratic familiar matrix through the patronage of musicians, writers and painters not only for the properly artistic delight they can provide but to elevate the host's prestige. The matrix of State in the days of the Spanish Queen Mariana and Felipe IV projected Velazquez's genius to reinforce their court's standing. Mexican muralism is a typical case of State projection to represent ideological and political agendas. Artistic activities are also imported to the medical matrix in therapeutic exercises such as psychodrama and the musicotherapy, or into legal prisons for occupational therapy by artistic workshops or shows to entertain inmates.

Although composers depend on their own matrix to construct their professional identities and legitimize their idiolect or personal style, the matrix of State, religion, the military, or sports can also commission them. In this sense their work can be considered plurimatricial. Like Bach, Mozart also was solicited by different matrixes: being a child prodigy he was inserted in the monarchic State matrix of the court of Vienna by invitation of the Empress Maria Teresa and her husband Francis I. For the religious matrix, he composed *Coronation Mass* and other religious works, and for artistic overlapping the aristocratic he elaborated several operas such as the *Wedding of Figaro*, *Don Giovanni* and the *Magic Flute*, whereas the *Requiem* is inserted in the funeral matrix. Nevertheless, when varying the context, these works acquire a different social meaning depending on whether they are interpreted in an official State ceremony, a concert, a religious ritual, or a school festival.

The corporational or financial matrixes utilize art as advertising strategies by patronizing artistic events like painting and sculpture contests. The case of a vodka company that uses art for its promotion campaigns, in addition to cigarette announcements with classical music as a background, are cases in point. Thus, the autonomy of the artistic matrix is extremely weak and relative, because it depends on other matrixes in which artists must often insert their work to survive professionally. If formerly the court matrix and the State accumulated enough economic excedents to maintain the artistic matrix, today the great patrons of art are financial and commercial corporations, the State and, above all, the masses' consumption and ratings.

Conclusions

Matricial Symbols and Aesthetic Games

We initiated with the problems and debates circumscribed to the ivory tower of aesthetics and ended at the ordinary homes, schools, and hospitals we encounter everyday. What became manifest in this theoretical journey was that, unlike the diagnosis of descentering taking place in contemporary society announced by Derrida and other postmodernists, identities converge towards a symbolic center in each and every social matrix. Removing the center would imply its liquidation and, hence, the elimination of the identities that sprout from it. Centers vary according to what particular instance is at stake: For an individual the center resides in her organic vitality, as for each subject in his or her mental life, whereas for collective identities the center is located at each matricial symbol. Only roles are decentered since they depend on constantly varying circumstances, but these are so specific that no center is necessary: the context itself is determinant.

Matricial symbolic centers concentrate semiosic density and enable shared realities that require aesthetic strategies for their members' *latching-onto*, thus allowing these matrixes' reproduction. While individuals *latch-on* to life by instinct and subjects *latch-on* to experience for their sense of self, identity *latching-on* needs to be constructed and actively shared, and thus requires greater formal elaboration to be effective. Here stems the necessity of displaying aesthetic strategies that gravitate around matricial symbols which establish values and define borders for each personal identity, and between the "we" and "they" of collective identities. (See Table C.1.)

Aided by a route map of the aesthetic rhetoric/dramatic coordinates, we have observed aesthetic strategies displayed through diverse matrixes. Far from being an exhaustive reading, this cartography is merely a guide for any lucky reader with the opportunity of deepening further in the exploration of these manifestations. On our way we discovered how intimately the aesthetic dimension is entwined with the ludic, since what constitutes the aesthetic *latching-on* always emerges from this particular coupling: the aesthesics of playing and playfulness of aesthesics.

Games are thus necessary in all matrixes, whether they are played deliberately or unknowingly. According to the categories we developed in Chapter 12, in the family matrix we witness girls playing *mimicry* by simulating to be mothers to their dolls, and spouses simulating fidelity during adultery. *Agon* is usually the main game between siblings in rivalry for their parents' affection. Some families are also agonistic in opposition to their relatives or neighbors. *Alea* is played by families who decide to have one more baby hoping that after eight girls, the next baby will indeed be a boy, or in taking risks as to the health and condition of an embryo. Marriage itself is a game of *alea*, because we do not know what awaits us in the future with our chosen spouse. Playing *peripatos* is indispensable when educating children, as we must constantly ponder in advance all the possible "what ifs". Less amusing is

Everyday Aesthetics

Table C.1   Matrixes' Symbols

MATRIX	SYMBOL
Family	Maternity
Religion	Divinity
School	Authority
Medical	Disease
Occultist	Fatality
Juridical	Legality
Military	Honorability
Sport	Triumph
Tourism	Transitoriety
Financial	Profit
Funerary	Mortality
Art	Fantasy
State	Responsibility
National	Nationality
Global	Humanity

having to play *ilinx* when the family loses balance in states of crisis and danger, or in cases of death, disease, domestic violence or addiction. As I mentioned before, we can *latch-on* to games, and be *latched by* them as well.

Agon is practiced in the religious matrix particularly by the Christians and Moslems in their effort to compete and attract the greater amount of devotees. Followers of doctrines that believe in divine predetermination, as Calvinism, evidently play *alea* with respect to salvation. *Ilinx* is played among the most fervent who experience states of trance, or among those who suffer from the anguish of doubting the existence of God from a strongly religious sensibility. It is worth mentioning the *mimicry* played by the Catholic Church concealing pederast priests and covering up situations of child sexual abuse. *Peripatos* is played in many religions by inventing amazing apocalyptic and paradisiacal descriptions, as well as by their exegetics and theological speculation.

The most suitable game for the school matrix is without doubt *peripatos* when allowing creativity or what Peirce called "musement" by "abduction", a playful meditation different from and complementary to induction and deduction that triggers invention, conjecture and enigma solving. Unfortunately, however, the most common game in this matrix is instead *agon,* not bad in presenting challenges but ceases to be amusing whenever it ends in punishment and humiliation. It is also common to gamble *alea* in multiple choice tests, and in the fortuitous event of having a teacher that radically inspires a student's vocation or the opposite: kills it. As soon as teachers leave the classroom, playing *mimicry* is typical in students' caricaturization, or in mimicking behaviors cherished by the teachers. *Ilinx* is played in extreme situations of expulsion or admission to a school or when one's future depends on a test.

Being a matrix that daily encounters the extreme vulnerability of the human being, the medical matrix does not exclude the possibility of playing *agon*. This

Matricial Symbols and Aesthetic Games

game arises by competing against a disease or against colleagues for prestige in pioneering certain treatments as well as among researchers in rivalry to establish certain theories as dominant. Let us mention the particularly ferocious *agon* performed among pharmaceutical companies. There is, of course, *peripatos* in the formulation of hypotheses and conjectures for treatment. *Ilinx* is inevitable in dealing with life or death cases and in the effort of keeping seriously ill patients alive, as *alea* is involved in the results of an operation and its complications. Placebos in medicine research are typical cases of *mimicry*.

In the occultist matrix the main game is *alea* because what fortune-tellers promise is to affect their clients' destiny by their horoscope or other aleatory magic props. Fortune-tellers also play the *mimicry* of divination and impersonation of special powers, and *peripatos* guessing what could sound meaningful to their clients. There is *agon* against competitors and in the persuasiveness of the various techniques, while *ilinx* in confronting an important decision is the experience that frequently takes most clients to solicit services in this matrix.

In the juridical matrix, lawyers and public prosecutors typically play *agon* (and so do police and criminals when both roles are not performed by the same individuals). Defendants gamble *alea* as to whether enough evidence of their guilt is presented at the litigation or not, whether they were assigned a particular judge and jury and not another, and whether they can pay the best trained lawyers or not. During the trial, the defendant remains in the game of *ilinx*. *Mimicry* in this matrix is played when erasing fingerprints or staging crimes, planting drugs for extortion, simulating humane conditions in jails during official visits of certain Human Rights Watch guests, or in appearing with conservative clothes to create the effect of well behaved identities before the judge and juries to be exonerated. False witnesses play mimicry when shedding tears at the podium or simulating emotions. As for *peripatos* in this matrix, it is typically played by forensic detectives or in criminal investigation illustrated in literature by Arthur Conan Doyle's character Sherlock Holmes, or Agatha Christie's detective Hercule Poirot or Miss Marple.

In the military matrix the game par excellence is *agon*, although in the battlefield what is played is basically *alea* of being killed or surviving a bombing or shooting episode. *Ilinx* occurs in the vertigo of war and radical change of values and forms of life that contrast normal everyday life. *Peripatos* when imagining attack strategies is not absent, nor of course is *mimicry* to deceive the enemy, especially in the scopics of camouflage design of military uniforms and disguising tanks and weapons with foliage.

The sport matrix is the kingdom of *agon,* naturally. But *mimicry* is also played in the amazing spectacularization of wrestling or in the typical pitchers' trick of simulating throwing the ball in one direction to deceive the player at the bat. Athletes play *alea* in the accidental conditions that can strongly influence the results of a game (a wet field, having the sun in front, the phase of the menstrual cycle among female Olympic athletes) and *ilinx* by the extreme passions at defeat or triumph among players and fanatics. World cup football penalties are situations of *ilinx* for the player in front of the ball, as well as for the goaltender. As in war, there is also a certain degree of *peripatos* in planning strategies to win.

298 *Everyday Aesthetics*

In the tourism matrix *peripatos* is played in scheduling trips and venturing towards remote, unknown places. Discrete tourists play *mimicry* by dressing in imitation of local customs to merge with the environment as much as possible. Many play *agon* through trips that involve extreme and risky activities and *ilinx* when realizing one is lost in an unknown place away from daily routine and unable to communicate with others. Playing *alea* is wonderful when one travels alone and is blessed with unusual and random encounters, or when one runs into the obtuse.

The mercantile, financial or corporational matrixes ferociously play *agon* in competition for the market, *alea* in risking losses or profits, particularly in the stock market, *peripatos* when inventing new strategies for marketing and *ilinx* when trying to remain in a strongly aggressive environment and avoiding bankruptcy in dangerous conditions. *Mimicry* is a newly discovered game in this matrix now that quasi-personal identities are fabricated and simulated for products by advertising campaigns, as if instead of purchasing a commodity one buys oneself an identity.

Logical would be to think that, given its gravity, no games are played in the funeral matrix. Nevertheless, seriousness does not exclude the playful dimension; on the contrary, is part of it. *Alea* is the main game in this matrix, as we all play it by knowing that just this time we were spared, but perhaps the next will be our turn to lose. For that reason we play *agon* against death, a competition that we will only lose a single time. *Ilinx* is played having to visualize the future in the absence of a person who was fundamental to one's life. Mourners hired to weep at funerals according to customs of diverse cultures play *mimicry*, and so do relatives who simulate sorrow but feel joy at the prospect of receiving a juicy inheritance. Only *peripatos* is absent, because when facing the forcefulness of death, there is no place left for any "what if", although our imagination plays with possibilities of reincarnation and paradise, and by pondering what if our loved deceased were still alive.

The game that truly creative artists play is *peripatos* when venturing towards imaginary worlds, a game that Huizinga relatively ignored, particularly in the playfulness of plastic arts and literature. (cf. Chapter 12) Every artistic and intellectual creation is an exciting game of *peripatos* for exploring the fantastic. But artists also play *agon* in biennials, literary contests, castings and popularity competitions like the Grammy, the Venice Biennial, the Oscar, the Emmy, and so on. *Mimicry* is typical of drama and is found in music that simulates the emotions of characters in theater, film, and television; realistic genres like novels, telenovela and soap opera also mimic everyday life. There is a degree of *mimicry* in the emotional identification of the spectator or author with a character or what Coleridge called the "suspension of disbelief". A case that illustrates *ilinx* in the plastic arts is painting with watercolors, where a mistake can irreversibly ruin the picture, as well as in acrobatic arts at the circus playing precisely with vertigo. *Ilinx* is often played in high investments on mass arts' risking success or failure, being in the peak of fame and object of adoration or beneath a chasm in embarrassment (eg. Britney Spears' odyssey). One also plays *alea* in the arts when using accidental qualities of materials like wood and marble for sculpture, casual or suggestive brushes in painting, or unexpected encounters in daily life that make great stories in literature. It is a matter of *alea* to have absolute hearing for music or not, a pleasant and strong voice, a sense of rhythm or of space, talent or not.

Matricial Symbols and Aesthetic Games   299

For most statesmen, reality is constituted vertically so that the main sport practiced in the State matrix is climbing the political mountain and developing skills in *agon,* its favorite game. They must play *mimicry* because in relatively democratic regimes they need to captivate voters, so special histrionic talents are required to enounce with some degree of credibility what they suppose people wish to hear. The excitement in the game of *ilinx* that politicians like to play is directly proportional to their hierarchy, namely, the vertigo of political triumph or failure is intensified by the height of the desired position. *Alea* is also played when betting a political career in alliances that can be favored by luck or cursed. Winning or losing in the elections is often a mere game of *alea* for politicians when no real issues are debated.

The parade of heroes and villains, of victims and oppressors in the official history of every country does not leave any doubt that in the national matrix the favorite game is *agon*. It is usually presented in aesthetic terms as an epic narration where the good ones won, and the others lost because they were either bad or wrong. This matrix plays *alea* in its territorial and ethnic definition by the arbitrariness of its borders and the fortuitous character of many of its outcomes.[1] We cannot know to what extent, for example, the conquest of Mexico by the Spaniards would have been radically altered if Mesoamerican Indians would have been immune to smallpox, or if their god Quetzalcóatl would not have been bearded and blond but African black. In the national matrix *mimicry* is the selected game by presenting national heroes as role models, and children are made to swear they will die for their country just like these other heroes did. National *ilinx* vicariously occurs when the pride of a nation depends for many upon victory or defeat of national selection soccer teams and other Olympic sports. This way, sport matrixes are curiously exported to the national matrix for people to identify with particular athletes simply because of the fortuitous event of having been born in a certain point and not another of the planet earth, or for signing a lease with a particular team.

Lastly, in the global matrix *agon* is implacably played at the international forums by the aggressive competition for markets and natural resources, *mimicry* in global propaganda for all countries to imitate the imperial centers of global ideology, *ilinx* in the progressive loss of ecologically sustainable conditions with indiscriminate industrial pollution and waste growth, and *alea* in the political bets of poor countries under absolute disadvantage conditions. As in the national and State matrixes, in the global matrix the game of *peripatos* is very difficult to find. This is unfortunate given the enormous problems and challenges we must face: nuclear, military, economic, demographic and ecological threats and, above all, social devastation by the systematic exclusion from the most basic conditions of dignity and security of the world's majority population.

The separate analysis of each matrix here performed runs the risk of being misunderstood as if these would actually exist as discreet, finite and clearly limited units (similar to a reductionist interpretation of Lotman's semiospheres). It is necessary to assert, however, that matrixes are not separated from others. On the contrary, society is constituted by networks of integrated matrixes sharing a manifold of connections in a dense multidimensional fabric whose most approximate

---

1   See Gellner (1997).

image is perhaps the brain's network of synaptic connections. For that reason, the matricial model of analysis here developed may be comprehended as a metaphorical projection to the social and cultural level (target) of the neuronal cartography of cerebral processes (source) with its weak and strong circuits and mappings. (cf. Edelman 1992) The matrixes therefore are not systems in differential opposition to surroundings (as Luhmann conceived them) but complex reticular configurations of intermingled filaments constituted by statements and acts in continuous processes of signic differentiation and symbolic concentration and densification. The collective identity of each matrix is defined, as in synaptic connections, by particular maps of routes that maintain certain regularities. These maps are, on diverse scales, habits of thought and perception, rituals and conventions in everyday action and communication some of which are stronger than others.

The process of matrix generation makes one germinate from another, all from the original common stem of the family or tribal matrix. Sprouts and derivations are generated through the religion matrix and its initial tribal Judaic conception, later branching off into Christianity and Islam (or the juridical deriving from religious laws). In a process opposed to entropy, the natural tendency has been matricial progression and diversification that may remind us of universe expansion theories. This diversification can, nevertheless, be limited by degenerative processes that occur in totalitarian and fundamentalist systems when they all implode into an overlapping superposition of all matrixes upon a single one: the State.

The global matrix constitutes at the moment the broadest configuration existing of human culturomes. From a simple outer perspective, this matrix would seem like a spheroid body located in Euclidean space (hence the term "global", from the Latin *globus*, round body, sphere) but from the interior it is a fine and very complex reticulation on multiple scales of human of actions, emotions, communication and imagination in relation to planetary biomes. What maintains matricial networks in form is not only the continuous intersemiosic flow that they transmit and habitual routes in which they operate, but the sticky aesthetic textures that allow adhesion regardless of the scale or how fine the filament may be. These are the aesthetics that concern prosaics.

References

Acha, Juan. 1996. *Introducción a la teoría de los diseños*. México: Trillas.

Aldrich, Virgil. 1963. *Philosophy of Art*. New Jersey: Prentice Hall.

Anderson, Ken. 1995. *Hitler and the Occult*. New York: Prometheus Books.

Aphek, Edna and Tobin, Yishai. 1983. "On Image Building and Establishing Credibility in the Language of Fortune Telling". *Eastern Anthropologist*. 36 (4): 287–308.

Arendt, Hannah. [1958] 1998. *The Human Condition*. Chicago and London: University of Chicago Press.

Aristotle. *Poetics*. Digital version from http://www.perseus.tufts.edu/cgi–bin/ptext? lookup=Aristot.+Poet.+toc. 2/28/2006.

Armstrong, A. MacC. 1987. "Shapeliness a Clue to Aesthetics". *British Journal of Aesthetics* 27, 1: 1–8.

Arnheim, Rudolf. 1985. *Arte y Percepción Visual*. María Luisa Balseiro (tr.). Madrid: Alianza. 6th edn.

Asín Palacios, Miguel. 1943. *La escatología musulmana en La Divina Comedia seguida de la historia y crítica de una polémica*. Madrid: CSIC 1943 2nd edn.

Augé, Marc. 1998. *Los no lugares: Espacios del anonimato*. Barcelona: Gedisa.

Bahro, Rudolf. 1979. *La alternativa; Crítica del socialismo realmente existente*. Barcelona: Materiales.

Bajtín, Mijail. 1990. *Estética de la Creación Verbal*. Tatiana Buvnova (tr.). México: Siglo XXI. 4th edn.

Bakhtin, Mikhail Mikhailovich. 1988. *The Dialogic Imagination: Four Essays by M. M. Bakhtin*. Michael Holquist (ed.) Caryl Emerson and Michael Holquist (tr.). Austin: University of Texas Press.

Bakhtin, Mikhail Mikhailovich and Medvedev P.N. 1985. *The Formal Method in Literary Scholarship; A Critical Introduction to Sociological Poetics*. Boston: Harvard.

Barthes, Roland. 1971. *Elementos de Semiología*. Alberto Méndez (tr.). Madrid: Alberto Corazón.

Barthes, Roland. 1974. *Investigaciones Retóricas* I. La Antigua Retórica Ayudamemoria. Buenos Aires, Tiempo Contemporáneo.

Barthes, Roland. 1977. "The Rhetoric of the Image". *Image-Music-Text*. London: Fontana.

Barthes, Roland. 1980. *Mitologías*. Héctor Schmucler (tr.). México: Siglo veintiuno.

Barthes, Roland. 1986. *Lo Obvio y lo Obtuso*. C. Fernández Medrano (tr.). Barcelona: Paidós.

Bateson, Gregory. 1972. *Steps to an Ecology of Mind*. Toronto: Random House.

Bateson, Gregory. 1991. *A Sacred Unity: Further Steps to an Ecology of Mind*. New York: Harper Collins.

Baudrillard, J. 1978. *Cultura y Simulacro*. Pedro Rovira (tr.) *La Precession des simulacres*. Barcelona: Kairós.

Baudrillard, Jean. 1981. *El Sistema de los Objetos*. México: Siglo XXI, 6th edn.

Baumgarten, Alexander Gottlieb. [1735] 1975. *Reflexiones Filosóficas acerca de la Poesía*. Buenos Aires: Aguilar. 4th edn.

Bayer, Raymond. 1984. *Historia de la Estética*. Jasmin Reuter (tr.). México: Fondo de Cultura Económica.

Beardsley, Monroe C. 1987. "Aesthetic Point Of View". *Philosophy Looks at the Arts*. Joseph Margolis (ed.). Philadelphia: Temple University Press. 3rd edn.

Bekoff, Marc and Byers, John A. (eds). 1998. *Animal Play; Evolutionary, Comparative and Ecological Perspectives*. Cambridge: Cambridge University Press.

Beristáin, Helena. 1992. *Diccionario de retórica*. México: Porrúa. 3rd edn.

Bell, Clive. 1977. "Art as Significant Form: The Aesthetic Hypothesis". Dickie, George, Scalfani, Richard Roblin, Ronald (eds). *Aesthetics; A Critical Anthology*. New York: St Martins. 2nd edn.

Benjamin, Walter. 1968. "The Work of Art in the Age of Mechanical Reproduction". *Illumination*. New York: Hartcourt, 217–251.

Benveniste, Émile. 1988. *Problemas de lingüística general I*. Juan Almela (tr.). México: Siglo veintiuno.

Berger, Peter L. and Luckmann, Thomas. 1986. *La construcción social de la realidad*. Silvia Zuleta (tr.). Buenos Aires: Amorrortu.

Berleant, Arnold. 1986. "The Historicity of Aesthetics I II". *British Journal of Aesthetics*. 26 (2): 101–11; (3): 195–203.

Berleant, Arnold. 2002. *The Aesthetic Field*. USA: Cybereditions.

Berleant, Arnold. 1991. *Art and Engagement*. Philadelphia: Temple University Press.

Berlyne, Daniel E.E. 1971. *Aesthetics and Psychobiology*. Toronto: University of Toronto Press.

Bernstein, Basil. 1972. "Elaborated and Restricted Codes: Their Social Origins and Some Consequences". *The Ethnography of Communication*. 55–67.

Bettelheim, Bruno. 1974. *A Home for the Heart*. New York: York, Alfred A. Knopf.

Binkley, Timothy. [1977] 1987. "Piece: Contra Aesthetics" *Philosophy Looks at the Arts*. Joseph Margolis (ed.). Philadelphia: Temple University Press.

Birdwhistell, Ray L. 1952. *Introduction to Kinesics*. Washington: Department of State, Foreign Service Institute.

Birdwhistell, Ray L. 1972. "A Kinesic–Linguistic Exercise: The Cigarette Scene". Gumperz, J. and Hymes, D. (eds). *The Ethnography of Communication*. pp. 381–404.

Bosmajian, Haig, A. 1971. *The Rhetoric of Nonverbal Communication*. Illinois: Scott, Foresman Co.

Bouissac, Paul. 1985. *Circus and Culture: A Semiotic Approach*. Lanham: University Press of America.

Bourdieu, Pierre and Jean Claude Passeron. 1981. *La reproducción; elementos para una teoría del sistema de enseñanza*. Barcelona: Laia.

Bourdieu, Pierre. 1987. "The Historical Genesis of a Pure Aesthetic". *Journal of Aesthetics and Art Criticism*, 46.

Bourdieu, Pierre. 1984. *Distinction: A Social Critique of the Judgment of Taste*. London: Routledge Kegan Paul.

Brady, Emily. 2005. "Sniffing and Savoring; the Aesthetics of Smells and Tastes". *The Aesthetics of Everyday Life*. Andrew Light and Jonathan Smith (eds). New York: Columbia University Press.

Brecht, Bertolt. 1976. "El pequeño organon para el teatro". *Escritos sobre teatro*, vol. 3. Buenos Aires: Nueva Visión.

Brecht, Bertolt. 1985. "Teatro épico". *Técnicas y teorías de la dirección escénica*. Sergio Jiménez and Edgar Ceballos (eds). vol. 1: 327–345. México: UNAM GEGSA.

Broad, William and Wade, Nicholas. 1982. *Betrayers of the Truth; Fraud and Deceit in the Halls of Science*. New York: Simon Schuster.

Bullough, Edward. 1979. "Psychical Distance". *A Modern Book of Esthetics: An Anthology*. Melvin Rader M. (ed.). New York: Holt, Rinehart Winston, 347–362. 5th edn.

Caillois, Roger. 1994. *Los juegos y los hombres.; la máscara y el vértigo*. Jorge Ferreiro (tr.). México: Fondo de cultura económica.

Canguilhem, Georges. 1986. *Lo normal y lo patológico*. México: Siglo Veintiuno.

Carroll, Noël. 1986. "Art and Interaction". *Journal of Aesthetics and Art Criticism*. 45 (1): 57–62.

Cassirer, Ernst. 1975. *Esencia y efecto del concepto de símbolo*. México: Fondo de cultura económica.

Certeau, Michel de. 1988. *The Practice of Everyday Life*. Berkeley: University of California.

Ciolek, T. Matthew. 1983. "The Proxemic Lexicon: A First Approximation". *Journal of Nonverbal Behavior.* 8 (1): 55–79.

Clarke, David. 1992. "The Icon and the Index: Modes of Invoking the Body's Presence". *The American Journal of Semiotics*, 9 (1): 49–80.

Crowther, Paul. 1987. "Aesthetic Aspects". *British Journal of Aesthetics.* 27 (1): 9–19.

Danto, Arthur. [1964] 1987. "The Artworld". *Philosophy Looks at the Arts*. Joseph Margolis (ed.). Philadelphia: Temple University Press.

Deely, John. 1990. *Basics of Semiotics*. Bloomington: Indiana University Press.

Dessoir, Max. 1923. *Asthetik und allgemeine kunstwissenschaft*, in den grundzugen dargestellt. Stuttgart: F. enke.

Dewey, John. [1934] 1980. *Art as Experience*. New York: Perigee.

Dickie, George. 1965. "Beardsley's Phantom Aesthetic Experience". *Journal of Philosophy.* 62: 129–136.

Dickie, George, Scalfani, Richard Roblin, Ronald (eds). 1977. *Aesthetics: A Critical Anthology*. New York: St Martins Press.

Dickie, George. 1974. *Art and the Aesthetic: An Institutional Analysis*. New York: Cornell University Press.

Dickie, George. 1984. *The Art Circle*. New York: Haven.

Dickie, George. 1988. *Evaluating Art*. Philadelphia: Temple University Press.

304 *Everyday Aesthetics*

Dickie, George. [1964] 1992. "The Myth of the Aesthetic Attitude". *The Philosophy of the Visual Arts*. Philip Alperson (ed). New York and Oxford: Oxford University Press.

Dickie, George.1968. "Is Psychology Relevant to Aesthetics?". *Contemporary Studies in Aesthetics*. Francis Coleman. Pittsburgh: MacGraw–Hill.

Diffey, T.J. 1984. "The Sociological Challenge to Aesthetics". *British Journal of Aesthetics*. 24: 168–171.

Dissanayake, Ellen. 1996. *Homo Aestheticus: Where Art comes From and Why*. Washington: University of Washington Press.

Dondis, D.A. 1976. *La sintaxis de la imagen*. Justo G. Beramendi (tr.). Barcelona: Gustavo Gili.

Dorfles, Gillo. 1989. *Elogio de la disarmonía*. Barcelona: Lumen. Traduccion de: *Elogio Della Disarmonia*. Milano: Garzanti.

Druckman, Daniel. 1982. *Nonverbal Communication*. London: Sage Publications.

Ducrot, Oswald and Tzevtan Todorov. 1974. *Diccionario enciclopédico de las ciencias del lenguaje*. Buenos Aires: Siglo XXI.

Dufrenne, Mikel. 1973. *The Phenomenology of Aesthetic Experience*. Casey, Edward S. (tr.). Northwestern University Press.

Dufrenne, Mikel. 1987. *In the Presence of the Sensuous*. Roberts, Mark. S. and Gallagher, Dennis (eds). New Jersey: Humanities Press International.

Dundes, A., Leach, W. et al. 1972. "The Strategy of Turkish Boys Verbal Dueling Rhymes" in Gumperz, J.J. and Hymes, D. (eds).

Durand, Jacques. 1983. " Rhetoric and the Advertising Image". Theo Van Leeuwin (tr.). *Australian Journal of Cultural Studies*. 1–2: 29–63.

Durkheim, Emile. 1982. *Las formas elementales de la vida religiosa*. Ramón Ramos (tr.). Madrid: Akal.

Eagleton, Terry, 1990.*The Ideology of the Aesthetic*. New York: Blackwell.

Eco, Umberto. [1968] 1974. *La estructura ausente*. Francisco Serra Cantarell (tr.). Barcelona: Lumen.

Eco, Umberto. 1978. *Tratado de Semiótica General*. Carlos Manzano (tr.). México and Barcelona: Lumen and Nueva Imagen.

Eco, Umberto. 1991. *Apocalípticos e integrados*. Barcelona: Lumen.

Edelman, Gerald M. and Tononi, Giulio. 2000. *A Universe of Consciousness: How Matter Becomes Imagination*. New York: Basic Books.

Edelman, Gerald M. 1992. *Bright Air, Brilliant Fire: On the Matter of the Mind*. New York: Basic Books.

Ekman, Paul and Friesen, Wallace V. 1975. *Unmasking The Face*. New Jersey: Prentice Hall.

Elizondo, Salvador. 1969. *El Retrato de Zoe y Otras Mentiras*. México: Joaquín Mortiz.

Engels, Federico. 1978. *El origen de la familia, la propiedad privada y el estado*. México: Editores mexicanos unidos.

Engler, Gideon. 1990. "Aesthetics in Science and in Art". *British Journal of Aesthetics*. 30.

Ezzati, Abdul Fazl. 1976. *The Spread of Islam: The Contributing Factors*. London: Islam College for Advanced Studies Press.

References

Ferry, Luc. [1990] 1994. *Homo Aestheticus: The Invention of Taste in the Democratic Age*. Chicago: University of Chicago Press.

Feyerabend, Paul K. 1974. *Contra el Método*. Barcelona: Ariel.

Fish, Stanley. 1976. "Interpreting the Varorium". *Critical Inquiry* 2. Primavera, 465–485.

Fish, Stanley. 1980. *Is There a Text in this Class?* Boston: Harvard University Press.

Fontanille, Jacques. 2004. *Soma et sema, figures du corps*. Paris: Maisonneuve.

Foucault, Michel. 1984. *Las palabras y las cosas*. Elsa Cecilia Frost (tr.). México: Siglo veintiuno editores, 14th edn.

Foucault, Michel. 1986. *Historia de la sexualidad*. vol. 2. Martí Soler (tr.). Siglo veintiuno editores.

Foucault, Michel. 1983. *Vigilar y castigar: nacimiento de la prisión*. Aurelio Grazón del Camino (tr.). Siglo veintiuno editores.

Geertz, Clifford. 1997. "Juego profundo: nota sobre la riña de gallos en Bali". *La interpretación de las culturas*. Barcelona: Gedisa, pp. 339–372.

Gellner, Ernest. 1997. *Naciones y Nacionalismos*. Madrid: Alianza.

Gibb, Hamilton Alexander Rosskeen, Sir. 1952. *El mahometismo*. México: Fondo de cultura económica.

Giménez, Gilberto. 1991. "La identidad social o el retorno del sujeto en sociología". *Versión*. 2, UAM.

Goffman, Erving. 1963. *Stigma: Notes on the Management of Spoiled Identity*. New Jersey: Prentice Hall.

Goffman, Erving. 1967. *Interaction Rituals*. New York: Doubleday.

Goffman, Erving. [1959] 1981. *La Presentación de la Persona en la Vida Cotidiana*. Hildegarde, B., Torres Perrén and Flora Setaro (tr.). Buenos Aires: Amorrortu. (Original English version *The Presentation of the Self in Everyday Life*. Garden City, NY: Doubleday Anchor.)

Goux, Jean–Joseph. 1990. *Symbolic Economies*. New York: Cornell University Press.

Graetz, Heinrich. 1939. *Historia del pueblo de Israel* V.4. México: La Verdad.

Greimas, Algirdas. 1966. *Sémantique structurale*. Paris: Larousse.

Grice, H. Paul. 1975. "Logic and Conversation". *Syntax and Semantics, vol. 3: Speech Acts*. En Cole Morgan (eds). New York: Academic Press.

Groupe μ. 1970. *Retórica general*. Barcelona: Paidós.

Grupo μ. 1993. *Tratado del signo visual; para una retórica de la imagen*. Madrid: Cátedra.

Gubern, Roman. 1996. *Del bisonte a la realidad virtual*. Barcelona: Anagrama.

Gubern, Roman. 1997. "Fabulación audiovisual y mitogenia" in Verón, E. and Chauvel, E.L. (eds). *Telenovelas: ficción popular y mutaciones culturales*. En Cole Morgan (eds). Barcelona: Gedisa.

Guiraud, Pierre. 1989. *Semiología*. México: Siglo XXI, 16th edn.

Gumperz, John J. and Hymes, Dell. 1972. *Directions in Sociolinguistics*. Holt, Rinehart and Winston.

Gumperz, John. J. and Hymes, Dell (eds). 1972. *The Ethnography of Communication*. 66, 6, parte 2.

Haas, John and Shaffir, William. 1982. "Taking on the role of Doctor: A Dramaturgical Analysis of Professionalization". *Symbolic Interaction.* 5 (2): 187–204.

Hall, Edward T. 1963. "A System for the Notation of Proxemic Behavior". *American Anthropologist.* 65: 1003–1026.

Hall, Edward T. 1988. *La Dimensión Oculta. México.* Félix Balcno (tr.). Siglo XXI, 12th edn.

Hattstein, Markus and Peter Delius.2001. *El islam, arte y arquitectura.* Berlin: Köneman.

Hauser, Arnold. 1969. *Historia social de la literatura y el arte* I, II, III. Madrid: Guadarrama.

Hewes, Gordon, W. 1957. "Anthropology of Posture". *Scientific American.* 196 (Feb): 123–32.

Hoffmeyer, Jesper. 1996. *Signs of Meaning in the Universe.* Barbara J. Haveland (tr.). Indianapolis: Indiana University Press.

Hoffmeyer, Jesper and Emmeche, Claus. 1991. "Code–duality and the semiotics of nature". *On Semiotic Modeling.* Myrdene Anderson and Floyd Merrell (eds). 117–166. Berlin: Mouton de Gruyter.

Huizinga, Johan. 1955. *Homo Ludens: A Study of the Play Element in Culture.* Boston: Beacon Press.

Hume, David. 1757. "Of the Standard of Taste". http://www.csulb.edu/~jvancamp/361r15.html.

Hyman, Lawrence W. 1986. "A Defence of Aesthetic Experience: In Reply to George Dickie". *British Journal of Aesthetics.* 26 (1): 62–63.

Irvine, John Taylor. 1974. "Strategies of Status Manipulation in the Wolof Greeting", Bauman Shrezer. *Explorations in the Ethnography of Speaking.* New York: Cambridge University Press, 167–191.

Jakobson, Roman. 1963. *Essais de Linguistique Générale.* Paris: Minuit.

Jauss, Hans Robert. 1978. *Pour une Esthetique de la Reception.* Paris: Gallimard.

Joseph, Isaac. 1999. *Erving Goffman y la microsociología.* Barcelona: Gedisa.

Kant, Immanuel. [1781] *Critique of Pure Reason.* Digital version. Norman Kemp-Smith (tr.). http://www.class.uidaho.edu/mickelsen/ToC/Kant%20Critique%20ToC.htm 23/03/2006.

Kant, Immanuel. [1790] *Critique of Judgment.* Digital version. James Creed Meredith (tr.). http://www.class.uidaho.edu/mickelsen/texts/Kant%20Crit%20Judgment.txt 23/03/2006.

Kendon, Adam. 1994. "Do Gestures Communicate? A Review". *Research on Language and Social Interaction.* 27 (3): 175–200.

Knapp, Mark L. 1972. *Nonverbal Communication in Human Interaction.* New York: H.R.W.

Kolnai, Aurel. 2004. *On Disgust.* Korsmeyer, Carolyn and Barry Smith (eds). Open Court Press.

Korsmeyer, Carolyn. 2002. *El sentido del gusto.* Barcelona: Paidós.

Krampen, Martin. 1981. "Phytosemiotics". *Semiotica.* 36(3/4): 187–209.

Krampen, Martin. 1998. "Proxemics: the secret of a humane architecture". *The Man and the City: Spaces, Forms, Meanings.* Saint Petersburg: Architecton.

References

Kuhn, Thomas. 1970. *The Structure of Scientific Revolutions*. Chicago: University of Chicago Press.

Labarca, Guillermo; Vasconi, Tomás; Finkel Sara and Recca, Inés. 1979. *La educación burguesa*. México: Nueva Imagen. 3rd edn.

Labov, William. 1966. "Hypercorrection by the Lower Middle Class as a Factor in Linguistic Change". *Sociolinguistics*. William Bright (ed.). The Hague: Mouton. pp. 84–102.

Lakoff, George and Johnson, Mark. 1980. *Metaphors We Live By*. Chicago: The University of Chicago Press.

Lakoff, George and Johnson, Mark. 1999. *Philosophy in the Flesh*. New York: Basic Books.

Langer, Susanne K. 1979. "Expressiveness and Symbolism". *A Modern Book of Aesthetics*. Rader M. (ed.). Holt, Rinehart Winston. 5th edn.

Leddy, Thomas. 1995. "Everyday Surface Aesthetic Qualities: 'Neat', 'Messy', 'Clean', 'Dirty'". *Journal of Aesthetics and Art Criticism*. 53: 3.

Lefebvre, Henri. 1972. *La vida cotidiana en el mundo moderno*. Madrid: Alianza.

Levinas, Emmanuel. [1969] 1998. *Totality and Infinity: An Essay on Exteriority*. Alphonso Lingis (tr.). Pittsburgh: Duquesne University Press.

Light, Andrew and Smith, Jonathan (eds). 2005. *The Aesthetics of Everyday Life*. New York: Columbia University Press.

Lipps, Theodor. 1924. *Los fundamentos de la estética*. Madrid: Jorro.

Lotman, Iuri, M. 1993. "El símbolo en el sistema de la cultura". *Escritos* 9. BUAP.

Lotman, Yuri, M. 1990. *Universe of the Mind; A Semiotic Theory of Culture*. Bloomington and Indianapolis: Indiana University Press.

Luhmann, Niklas. 1991. *Sistemas sociales: lineamientos para una Teoría General*. Silvia Pappe and Brunhilde Erker (tr.). México: Alianza, UIA.

Mandoki, Katya. 1994. *Prosaica: introducción a la estética de lo cotidiano*. México: Grijalbo.

Mandoki, Katya. 1997. "Between Signs and Symbols: An Economic Distinction?". *Semiotics Around the World: Synthesis in Diversity*. Rauch Irmengard and Carr F. Gerald (eds). Berlin, New York: Mouton de Gruyter. 1015–1018.

Mandoki, Katya. 1998. "Sites of Symbolic Density: A Relativistic Approach to Experienced Space". *Philosophies of Place* III. Andrew Light (ed.). New York: Rowman Littlefield. 73–95.

Mandoki, Katya. 1999. "Terror and Aesthetics: Nazi Strategies for Mass Organisation". *Renaissance and Modern Studies*. 42: 64–81.

Mandoki, Katya. 1999a. "Aesthetics and Pragmatics: Conversion, Constitution and the Dimensions of Illocutionary Acts". *Pragmatics and Cognition*. 7 (2): 313–337.

Mandoki, Katya. 2001. "Material Excess and Aesthetic Transmutation". *Economies of Excess: Parallax*. John Armitage (ed.). 18 7 (1): 64–75.

Mandoki, Katya. 2002a. "A Host of Ghosts in Descartes' Theater". *Semiotica*. 142/1–4: 361–379.

Mandoki, Katya. 2002. "The Secret Door: Reception Aesthetics of Telenovela". *Aesthetics and Television*. Ruth Lorand (ed.). New York: Peter Lang.

Mandoki, Katya. 2003. "A Biological Mapping to Culture". *Journal of Contemporary Thought 17*. The Maharaja Sayajirao University of Baroda, India, Louisiana State University, Central Washington University, USA. pp. 153–172.

Mandoki, Katya. 2003b. "Aisthesis y Semiosis: ¿doble hélice o cinta Möbius?". *Proceedings of the VIIth Congress of the International Association of Visual Semiotics*. Mexico: ITESM, CD Rom.

Mandoki, Katya. 2004. "A Multisemiotic Model for Social Interactions". Paper presented at the *International Congress of the International Association for Semiotic Studies*. Lyon.

Mandoki, Katya. 2004a. "Power and Semiosis". *Semiotica*. 150–1/4. 151: 1–18.

Mandoki, Katya. 2006a. *Estética cotidiana y juegos de la cultura: Prosaica I*. México: Siglo XXI editores.

Mandoki, Katya. 2006b. *Prácticas estéticas e identidades sociales: Prosaica II*. México: Siglo XXI editores.

Mandoki, Katya. 2006c. *Estética y comunicación: de acción, pasión y seducción*. Bogotá: Groupo Editorial Norma.

Mandoki, Katya. 2007. *La construcción estética del Estado y de la identidad nacional: Prosaica III*. México: Siglo XXI editores.

Mandoki Winkler, Catalina Inés. 1991. *Estética y Poder*. México: Universidad Nacional Autónoma de México. Ph.D. Dissertation.

Margolis, Joseph (ed.). 1987. *Philosophy Looks at the Arts*. Philadelphia: Temple University Press. 3rd ed.

Marx, Karl and Engels, Frederich. 1968. *Escritos sobre arte*. Buenos Aires: Futura.

Matsumoto, D. and Ekman, P. 1989. "American–Japanese Cultural Differences in Intensity Ratings of Facial Expressions of Emotion". *Motivation and Emotion*. 13 (2): 143–157.

Maturana, Humberto R. and Varela, Francisco J. 1992. *The Tree of Knowledge: The Biological Roots of Human Understanding*. Robert Paolucci (tr.). Boston: Shambhala.

Mauss, Marcel. 1990. *The Gift: The Form and Reason for Exchange in Archaic Societies*. W.D. Halls (tr.). New York and London: Norton.

Merrell, Floyd. 1994. *Signs Grow, Life Goes On*. Toronto: University of Toronto Press.

Min, Joosik. 1999. "'*Fengliu*', The Aesthetic Way of Life in East Asian Culture". *Filozofski Vestnik Proceedings of the XIVth International Congress of Aesthetics*. Liubljana. 131–140.

Mitias, Michael (ed.). 1986. *Possibility of the Aesthetic Experience*. Boston: Nijhoff.

Mitias, Michael. 1982. "What Makes an Experience Aesthetic?". *Journal of Aesthetics and Art Criticism*. 41 (2): 157–170.

Morris, Charles. [1938] 1994. *Fundamentos de la teoría de los signos*. Barcelona: Paidós.

Morris, Charles. [1964] 1974. *La significación y lo significativo: studio de las relaciones entre el signo y el valor*. Madrid: Alberto Corazón. *Signification and Significance*. Jesús Antonio Cid (tr.). Cambridge, Massachussets: MIT Press.

References 309

Morson, Gary. S. and Emerson, Caryl. 1990. *Mikhail Bakhtin, Creation of a Prosaics*. California: Stanford University Press.

Mukarovský, Jan. 1977. *Escritos de estetica y semiotica del arte*. Hanna Anthony–Visová (tr.). Barcelona: Gustavo Gili.

Naukkarinen, Ossi. 1998. *Aesthetics of the Unavoidable: Aesthetic Variations in Human Appearance*. Lahti: International Institute of Applied Aesthetics.

Nwodo, Christopher S. 1984. "Philosophy of Art Versus Aesthetics". *British Journal of Aesthetics*. 24: 195–205.

Ogden, Charles Kay and Richards, Ivory Armstrong. 1938. *The Meaning of Meaning*. New York: K. Paul, Trench and Trubner.

Osborne, Harold. 1980. "Aesthetic Implications of Conceptual Art, Happenings, etc.". *British Journal of Aesthetics*. 20 (1): 6–22.

Osborne, Harold. 1981. "Concepts of Order in Natural Sciences and in the Visual Fine Arts". *Leonardo*. 14.

Osborne, Harold. 1984. "Mathematical Beauty and Physical Science". *British Journal of Aesthetics*. 24.

Osborne, Harold 1986. "Interpretation in Science and in Art". *British Journal of Aesthetics*. 26.

Parret, Herman. 1993. *The Aesthetics of Communication: Pragmatics and Beyond*. S. Rennie (tr.). Dordrecht: Kluwer Academic Publishers.

Parret, Herman. 2003. "Vino y voz: hacia una inter–estésica de las cualidades sensoriales". *Tópicos del Seminario*.

Parret, Herman. 1995. *De la semiótica a la estética. Enunciación, sensación, pasiones*. Buenos Aires: Edicial.

Passmore, John. 1951. "The Dreariness of Aesthetics". *Mind*. 60.

Peirce, Charles Sanders. 1955. "Logic as Semiotic: The Theory of Signs". *Philosophical Writings of Peirce*. Justus Buchler (ed.). New York: Dover.

Peirce, Charles Sanders. 1958. *Charles S. Peirce: Selected Writings*. Philip P. Wiener (ed.). New York: Dover.

Peirce, Charles Sanders. *The Essential Peirce. Selected Philosophical Writings*. (EP) vol. 1 (1867–1893). Nathan Houser Christian Kloesel (eds) 1992, vol. 2 (1893–1913), edited by the Peirce Edition Project, 1998. Bloomington and Indianapolis: Indiana University Press.

Peirce, Charles Sanders. *Collected Papers of Charles Sanders Peirce*, (CP) 8 volumes, vols 1–6. Charles Hartshorne and Paul Weiss (eds). vols 7–8, ed. Arthur W. Burks. Cambridge, Mass: Harvard University Press, 1931–1958.

Pelc, Jerzy. 2000. "Semiosis and Semiosics vs. Semiotics". *Semiotica*. 128–3/4: 425–434.

Peninou, Georges. 1965. "La semiologie dans la recherche publicitaire". *Gestion*. December 1965: 727–734.

Pérez Agote, Alfonso. 1986. "La identidad colectiva: una reflexión desde la sociología". *Revista de Occidente*. 56, Madrid.

Piaget, Jean. 1983. *Seis estudios de psicología*. Nuria Petit (tr.). México: Seix Barral.

Radford, Robert. 1999. "Aurel Kolnai's 'Disgust', a Source in the Art and Writing of Salvador Dalí". *The Burlington Magazine*. 141 (1150): 32–33. January.

310   *Everyday Aesthetics*

Rizzolatti, Giacomo and Leonardo Fogassi and Vittorio Gallese. 2006. "Mirrors in the Mind". *Scientific American*. November: 30–37.

Rodríguez Adrados, Francisco. 1983. *Fiesta, comedia y tragedia*. Madrid: Alianza.

Rubert de Ventós, Xavier. 1969. *Teoría de la Sensibilidad*. Barcelona: Península.

Russell, Bertrand. 1964. *A History of Western Philosophy*. New York: Simon and Schuster.

Sachar, Abram Leon. 1966. *A History of the Jews*. Toronto: Random House.

Sahlins, Marshall. 1988. "Le pensée bourgeoise". *Cultura y razón práctica*. Barcelona: Gedisa. 166–218.

Saint–Martin, Fernande. 1992. "A Case of Intersemiotics: The Reception of a Visual Advertisement". *Semiotica*. 91–1/2: 79–98.

Saint–Martin, Fernande. 1990. *Semiotics of Visual Language*. Bloomington: Indiana University Press.

Saito, Yuriko. 2001. "Everyday Aesthetics (Art and Non-art Objects)". *Philosophy and Literature*. 25 (1): 87-95 APR.

Saito, Yuriko. 2005. "The Aesthetics of Weather". *The Aesthetics of Everyday Life*. Andrew Light and Jonathan Smith (eds). New York: Columbia University Press.

Sánchez Vázquez, Adolfo. 1992. *Invitación a la Estética*. México: Grijalbo.

Sartre, Jean–Paul. 1999. *L'Etre et le Néant* quoted by Joseph 1999.

Sartwell, Crispin. 1995. *The Art of Living: Aesthetics of the Ordinary in World Spiritual Traditions*. New York: State University of New York Press.

Saussure, Ferdinand de. [1916] 1967. *Curso de Lingüística General*. Mauro Armiño (tr.). Buenos Aires: Losada.

Scheflen, Albert. E. 1972. *Body Language and the Social Order*. New Jersey: Prentice Hall.

Schütz, Alfred. 1976. *Fenomenologia del mundo social/Introduccion a la sociologia comprensiva*. Buenos Aires: Paidos.

Schütz, Alfred and Luckmann, Thomas. 1977. *Las estructuras del mundo de la vida* Néstor Miguez (tr.). Ariel Bignami (rev.). Buenos Aires: Amorrortu.

Searle, John. 1969. *Speech Acts: An Essay in the Philosophy of Language*. London: Cambridge University Press.

Searle, John. 1976. "A Classification of Illocutionary Acts". *Language and Society*. 5: 1–23.

Sebeok, Thomas A. 1963. "Communication among Social Bees; Porpoises and Sonar; Man and Dolphin". *Language*. 39: 448–466.

Sebeok, Thomas and Ramsay, Alexandra (eds). 1969. *Approaches to Animal Communication*. The Hague: Mouton de Gruyter.

Shusterman, Richard. 1992. *Pragmatist Aesthetics: Living Beauty, Rethinking Art*. New York: Blackwell.

Shusterman, Richard. 1999. "The End of Aesthetic Experience". *Journal of Aesthetics and Art Criticism*. 57: 29–41.

Shuy, Roger W. 1987. "Conversational Power in FBI Covert Tape Recordings". *Power Through Discourse*. Kedar, Leah (ed.). Norwood: Ablex. 43–56.

Sibley, Frank. 1987. "Aesthetic Concepts". *Philosophy Looks at the Arts*. Joseph Margolis (ed.). Philadelphia: Temple University Press.

Sklar, Dusty. 1989. *The Nazis and the Occult*. New York: Dorset Press.

References

Sonesson, Göran. 1988. *Methods and Models in Pictorial Semiotics; Report 3 from the Project Pictorial Meanings in the Society of Information*. Lund: Lund University.

Sperber, Dan. 1996. *Explaining Culture: A Naturalistic Approach*. Oxford and Massachusetts: Blackwell.

Stolnitz, Jerome. [1960] 1992. "The Aesthetic Attitude". *The Philosophy of the Visual Arts*. Philip Alperson (ed.). New York and Oxford: Oxford University Press.

Stuhr, John J. 1997. *Genealogical Pragmatism*. New York: SUNY.

Suvakovic, Misko. 2002. "Discourses of Hegemony". Paper presented at Congress *Hegemony in Art and Culture*. Ljublana.

Tarasti, Eero. 1994. *A Theory of Musical Semiotics*. Bloomington and Indianapolis: Indiana University Press.

Tedeschi, Mario. 1992. *Polémica y convivencia de las tres religiones*. Colección Sefarad. Madrid: Mapfe.

Todorov, Tzvetan. 1984. *Mikhail Bakhtin, The Dialogical Principle*. Godzich, W. (tr.). Minneapolis: University of Minnesota Press.

Too, Lillian. 1996. *The Complete Illustrated Guide to Feng Shui*. New York: Barnes and Noble.

Townsend, Dabney. 1992. "From Shaftesbury to Kant: The Development of the Concept of Aesthetic Experience". *Essays on the History of Aesthetics*. Peter Kivy (ed.). Rochester NY: University of Rochester Press.

Trager, George L. 1958. "Paralanguage: A First Approximation". *Studies in Linguistics*. 13 (1 & 2): 1–10.

Tripp, Susan E. 1972. "On Sociolinguistic Rules: Alteration and Co–occurrence". Gumperz and Hymes (eds). 218–233.

Tuan, Yi–Fu. 1995. *Passing Strange and Wonderful: Aesthetics, Nature and Culture*. New York, Tokyo and London: Kodansha.

Turner, Bryan. S. 1984. *The Body and Society*. Oxford: Basil Blackwell.

Uexküll, Jakob von. 1982. "The Theory of Meaning". *Semiotica*. 42 (1): 25–82.

Uexküll, Jakob von. 1957. "A Stroll Through the Worlds of Animals And Men". *Instinctive Behavior: The Development of a Modern Concept*. Claire Schiller (ed. and tr.). New York: International Universities Press. 5–80. Reprinted in *Semiotica*. 89 (4): 319–391.

Uexküll, Thure von, Geigges, Werner and Herrmann, Jörg M .1993. "Endosemiosis". *Semiotica*. 96–1/2: 5–51.

Ulrich, Herbert (ed.). 2000. *National Socialist Extermination Policies: Contemporary Perspectives and Controversies. (Volume 2, War and Genocide)*. New York and Oxford: Berghahn Books.

Vanderveken, Daniel. 1985. "What is an Illocutionary Force". *Dialogue: An Interdisciplinary Approach*. Marcelo Dascal (ed.). Amsterdam: John Benjamins. pp. 181–204.

Veblen, Thorstein. 1974. *Teoría de la clase ociosa*. 2nd edn. México: Fondo de Cultura Económica. (English original *Theory of Leisure Class*).

Verón, Eliseo. 1974. "Para una semiología de las operaciones translingüísticas". *Lenguajes: Revista de lingüística y semiología*. 1 (2): 11–36.

Voloshinov, Valentin N. 1987. *Freudianism: A Critical Sketch*. Titunik, I.R. and Bruss, N.R (eds). Bloomington: Indiana University Press.

Watson, O. Michael. 1970. *Proxemic Behavior: A Cross–cultural Study*. La Haya, Mouton.

Wechsler, Judith (ed.). 1978. *On Aesthetics in Science*. Cambridge: MIT Press.

Weitz, Morris. [1956] 1987. "The Role of Theory in Aesthetics". *Philosophy Looks at the Arts*. Margolis, Joseph. (ed). Philadelphia: Temple University Press. 3rd edn.

Weitz, Morris. 1989. "Wittgenstein's Aesthetics". *Aesthetics; A Critical Anthology*. George Dickie, Richard Scalfani and Ronald Roblin (eds). New York: St Martins. 2nd edn.

Welsch, Wolfgang. 2005. "Sport Viewed Aesthetically, an Even as Art?". *The Aesthetics of Everyday Life*. Andrew Light and Jonathan Smith (eds). New York: Columbia University Press.

Wiley, Norbert. 1994. *The Semiotic Self*. Chicago: University of Chicago Press.

Wittgenstein, Ludwig. 1958. *Philosophical Investigations*. Anscombe, G.E.M. (tr.). New York: Blackwell. 2nd edn.

Wolff, Janet. 1983. *Aesthetics and the Sociology of Art*. London: George Allen and Unwin.

Zavala, Lauro. 1997. *Permanencia voluntaria: el cine y su espectador*. Xalapa: Universidad Veracruzana.

Zerubavel, Eviatar. 1985. *Hidden Rhythms: Schedules and Calendars in Social Life*. Berkeley, Los Angeles and London: University of California Press.

Index

Abélard, Pierre 215
Abi Taleb, Ali Ibn 219
Abramovic, Marina 281
Abravanel, Yehuda Leon 209 n4
Abul Wafa 236
Academia de las tres nobles artes de San
    Carlos 283
Academie Royale de Danse 277
Academie Royale de Peinture et de
    Sculpture 283
Academy of San Fernando in Madrid 283
Acconci, Vito 280
Acha, Juan 203, 273, 282
acrobatics 283, 291, 298
Adorno, Theodor 4 n1, 16, 59
aesthesiology xi, 74, 84
aesthesis xvi, xvii, 34–35, 43, 48–51, 55,
    61–63, 65, 67–71, 73–74, 76, 78,
    84–85, 103, 105, 109, 127–129, 131,
    195, 269, 271
    anthropoaesthesis 49
    endoaesthesis 50
    exo-aestheis 50
aesthetic
    activity xvii, 51, 69, 70, 75
    adhesion 26–27, 47, 67, 77, 80, 98, 109,
        141, 149, 180–182, 189, 191–192,
        218, 230, 247, 286, 300
    appreciation 9, 11–12, 18–26, 39, 40, 54,
        58, 61, 76–77, 84, 125, 127–129, 136–
        137, 146, 149, 253, 269, 271–272, 278
    aspects 18–19, 24–25, 30, 33–34, 53 n2, 56
    attention 17–26, 33–34, 43, 47, 51, 68,
        77, 103, 160, 271
    attitude 3, 17, 22–24, 28, 33–34, 68
    categories 4, 6, 38, 125
    contemplation 15, 17, 19, 21–22, 28, 31,
        38, 40–41, 67–68, 70, 82–84, 89,
        123, 218, 251, 272
    debate 30, 32, 46, 53, 98, 272
    delight 17–19, 21, 28, 32, 34, 41, 42, 54,
        68, 82, 90–91, 129, 234, 269, 279,
        283, 294
    dignity xvi, 249, 267

dimension 5, 29, 39, 40–41, 43, 51, 74,
    77, 80, 103, 123, 127, 133 n1, 146,
    151, 166, 195, 205, 243, 269, 295
dis-covery 19, 84, 125, 127–129
disinterest 17–24, 32, 37, 41, 68–69, 82,
    98, 251
distance, distancing 19, 20, 22
engagement 18, 21–22, 32, 68, 70
enunciation xvi, 9, 31, 78, 131, 132, 251
experience 4, 10, 11–12, 17–19, 20 n3,
    21, 25, 28, 30–35, 38, 48, 61, 63,
    67–70, 79, 83, 88, 93, 129, 139, 237
intention xv, 9, 23–24, 33–34
interpretation xvi, 8–9, 23, 29, 31, 56, 58,
    65, 77–79, 101, 110–111, 132, 136,
    152, 156, 166, 170, 173, 181, 205, 286
intrusion 25, 42, 69, 202
judgment 1, 3, 8, 11, 17, 24–27, 41, 46,
    54, 67, 89, 101
motivation 23–26, 33–34
object 10–13, 17–18, 30–34, 38, 43, 48,
    53, 55–56, 81, 83–84, 101, 122, 128
perception 20, 26, 91
phenomena 1, 23–24, 28, 41, 63, 75–76,
    101–103, 106, 132
potential, potentiality xv, 30–31, 34
position or posture 23, 101–102
practices 51, 78, 205, 269, 282
presence 19, 27, 38, 41, 52, 56, 76,
    169–170
process 32, 47, 60, 77, 132, 137
qualities 13 n2, 16, 24, 26, 32–34
reception 20, 29, 51, 53, 76, 272
relation 12, 19, 26, 40, 54
strategies xv, 58, 70, 79, 98, 139, 142,
    181, 188, 197, 206, 216, 218,
    232–235, 238, 241, 247, 249, 250,
    253, 256–259, 262, 295
subject 33, 47, 53–56, 69, 185
swinging 21–22, 251
theory xv, 1, 3–5, 7–9, 12, 15, 19, 21 n4,
    23, 30–31, 35, 39, 40, 43, 45–47, 51,
    53, 62, 68–69, 75, 87, 97, 128–129,
    272

314 *Everyday Aesthetics*

value xi, 19, 23, 37, 73, 87, 120, 127, 135
violence xvi, 42, 69, 83–84, 95, 97–98,
   129, 201, 238, 243, 248
aestheticians xvii, 1, 4, 4 n1, 11–13, 17, 18,
   37, 41–42, 46, 56, 73, 83, 85, 97,
   103, 269, 270, 272
aesthetics
   analytic 4, 5, 9, 12, 18, 22, 43, 78, 83,
      97, 128, 272
   art (of, in) 29–30, 49, 51, 75–80, 269, 294
   as a communicative process xvii, 5,
      22, 30–31, 50, 54, 78, 102, 103,
      131–132, 136, 146, 175
   definition of 3–4, 10, 12, 17, 23–24,
      26–27, 29, 32–35, 41, 45–48, 51, 68,
      76–79, 84, 91, 97, 144
   as a discipline 3–7, 12, 43, 97, 99
   environmental 5 n1, 178, 271 n3
   exclusivity of xvi, 29–30, 186
   as a field xvi, 3, 5–6, 12, 17, 20, 40, 43,
      45, 48–49, 51, 53, 60, 76, 81, 85, 93,
      97, 101, 125, 128, 135, 269
   mainstream theory xv, xvi, 13, 15, 21,
      37, 43, 68
   Marxist 4 n1, 8, 15, 79
   and psychology 5, 11–12, 22, 33, 39,
      40–42, 47, 54, 60, 77–78, 98–99,
      146, 201
   transdisciplinary 5
   of violence xvi, 41
Akiba, Rabbi 208
Albers, Josef 291
Aldrich, Virgil 21, 23
Alighieri, Dante 221
allgemeine kunstwissenschaft 5, 73, 87
alterity xi, 22, 125, 229
Ambrose, Saint 215
Anderson, Ken 257
Anselm, Saint 215
Aphek, Edna 261, 262, 264, 265
Apostles 213, 215, 225
Aquinas, Thomas 5, 84, 109, 215, 236, 272
Archimedes 239
architecture 19, 89, 146, 157, 159, 164–165,
   190, 192, 206, 218, 226, 252, 255,
   271, 278, 283
Arendt, Hannah 64, 209
Aristophanes 284
Aristotle 20, 31, 64, 75, 94, 149, 215, 237,
   272, 279, 284
Armstrong, A. Mac 13 n2

Arnheim, Rudolf 4, 39
art
   art history 4–6, 46, 133, 205, 273, 281–282
   as artifice 84, 88, 270, 272, 280
   artists 9–12, 15–16, 24, 30, 54–55, 76,
      87–88, 97, 117, 131–134, 164, 178,
      193, 225, 244, 269–294
   artwork 5, 8–13, 16, 20, 22–25, 29–31,
      34–35, 43, 50, 54, 56, 73, 76, 81, 88,
      97, 101–103, 132, 135, 192–193,
      203, 269, 270–271, 280, 293
   artworld 1, 23–4, 29, 51, 76, 97, 126,
      128, 269–272, 277–278, 280–281,
      285, 287, 292–293
   conceptual art 21, 29, 102, 293
   elite art and artists 15, 80, 89, 276, 284,
      286–287, 292
Ashari, Al- 220 n4
Asín Palacios, Miguel 215, 220, 221
Aspasia 280
Augé, Marc 189
Augustine, Saint 215
autopoiesis, autopoietic 49, 80, 105, 182–183
Avempace 220 n14
Averroes 215, 220 n14, 221, 236
Avicebron 208
Avicenna, or Ibn Sina 215, 220 n14, 221,
   226, 236
Azhar Al- Mosque 226

Baal Shem Tov 209
Ben Meir Ibn Ezra, Abraham 209 n4
Ben Sakai, Yohanan 208
Bach, Johann Sebastian 216, 275, 294
Bachelard, Gastón 152
Bacon, Roger 215
Bacon, Sir Francis 236
Bahro, Rudolf 187
Bajja Ibn Or Avempace 220
Bajtín, Mijail 22, 39, 132, 142 *see also*
      Bakhtin, Voloshinov
Baker Eddy, Mary 236
Bakhtin, Mikhail Mikhailovich 16, 22, 39,
      62, 76, 79, 87–88, 91, 111, 131–133,
      142, 170–173, 175, 285 *see also*
      Bajtín, Voloshinov
Barthes, Roland xi n1, 10, 41, 102, 111–112,
      116, 120, 125–126, 140, 149, 152,
      182–183
Bataille, Georges 128 n2
Batani, Al- 236

Index

315

Bateson, Gregory 51, 173, 177, 201, 248
Baudrillard, Jean 55 n5, 157, 161, 254, 288
Bauhaus 159, 254
Baumgarten, Alexander Gottlieb xvi, 1, 6,
    27–28, 32, 37, 46, 97
Bayer, Raymond 84
Beardsley, Monroe C. 22–23, 32, 79
beauty xv, xvi, 3–12, 15–18, 25–28, 31, 37,
    39–43, 45, 47, 53, 55–56, 61, 70,
    73–75, 78, 82–83, 85, 91, 93, 97, 99,
    101, 212, 215, 218, 262
Beethoven, Ludwig van 82, 160, 275
Bekoff, Marc 50
Bell, Clive 102
Ben (artist) 293
Ben Efraim Caro, Yosef 209 n4
Ben Meir Ibn Ezra, Abraham 209 n4
Ben Solomon Israeli, Isaac 209 n4
Ben Tamiz Dunash 209 n4
Benjamin, Walter 4 n1, 16, 20, 209
Benveniste, Émile 112
Berger, Peter L. 58, 62–64, 77–78, 115–116,
    136–137, 141, 145, 177, 179–181
Bergson, Henri 64, 209
Beristáin, Helena xi n1
Berleant, Arnold 4, 5, 18, 21–22, 32, 37, 68,
    83–85, 97
Berlyne, Daniel 39
Bernstein, Basil 153
Bettelheim, Bruno 248–249
Beuys, Joseph 193, 293
Bible 151–152, 184, 186, 208, 214–215,
    219, 226, 274 *see also Torah*, New
    Testament
Binkley, Timothy 29, 34
bio-aesthetics 47, 49–52
biology, related to 5, 39, 56–58, 63, 81–82, 89,
    91, 102, 109, 111, 130, 146, 178, 233
biome 109, 195, 300
biosemiotics 102, 105
Birdwhistell, Ray L. 145, 145 n6
Bizet, Georges 290
Bloom, Leopold 274
body 46, 59, 61–64, 68, 82, 84, 91, 102,
    126, 129, 139–140, 144–147,
    150, 156, 158, 161, 164, 167, 170,
    172, 177, 179, 180, 185, 189, 192,
    196–197, 201, 206, 208, 210–212,
    215–217, 223–227, 243, 236, 245,
    247–249, 251–253, 255, 259, 261,
    265, 272, 276, 279–280, 283, 291,
    293, 300 *see also* body language

Boecius 215
Bonaventure, Saint 215
Bosch, Hieronymus 165
Bosmajian, Haig, A 144
Bouissac, Paul 277
Boulanger, M. 278
Bourdieu, Pierre 4, 51, 115, 153, 241, 243
bourgeoisie 8–9, 25, 186, 277–278, 283,
    287, 291
Brady, Emily 84–85, 272
Brands 122, 187, 191, 201, 246, 263, 279
Brecht, Bertolt 15, 20–22, 251, 270
Broad, William 141–142
Brunelleschi, Filippo 282
Bruno, Giordano 214, 231
Buber, Martin 209
Bujari, Al- 219
Bujarin, Nikolai Ivanovitch 4 n1
Bullough, Edward 19–23, 98, 251
Burri, Alberto 291
Bush, George W., 145
Byers, John A. 50

Cage, John 286, 292
Caillois, Roger 94, 129
Calvin, John, Calvinism 215, 229, 236, 296
Camus, Albert 28
Canguilhem, Georges 255
Cantor, Georg 209
Carême, Marie Antoine "Antonin" 278
Carlson, Allen 4, 84
Caro, Yosef ben Efraim 209 n5
Carroll, Noël 29
Cassirer, Ernst 4 n1, 102, 115–116
Catholicism 214, 218, 230, 234, 236
Certeau, Michel De 77
Chanel, Coco 283
Chardin, Teilhard De 215
Chopin, Frederich 275
Christ 122, 193, 213–214, 217–218, 220,
    232–233
Ciolek, T. Matthew 150 n3
circus 277, 283, 298
Clarke, David 218
Cleitias 282
comedy 75, 101, 284, 286
communication xvi, 31, 54, 78, 102–103,
    110, 117, 120, 131–132, 136–137,
    142–146, 148, 150, 167, 171, 178,
    182, 196, 201, 244, 267
com-pression 173–175, 202, 235, 242

316 *Everyday Aesthetics*

conscience 62–63, 80, 127, 133, 173, 178, 248, 270
conventions 7, 10, 15–16, 27–29, 47, 54, 58, 61, 64, 79, 83, 88, 106, 110, 112, 115–116, 120, 123, 125–126, 132–133, 140, 143, 149, 157, 163, 166, 169, 177, 180, 183, 185, 200, 238, 251, 254, 259, 276, 286–287, 292, 300
cooking 200, 206, 263, 278–279, 284, 286, 291
Cordovero, Moises 209
creativity 121, 181, 238–239, 244, 269–270, 272, 274–275, 277–282, 288, 293, 296
credibility xv, 58–59, 77, 137, 139–141, 143, 152, 166, 188–189, 201, 239, 247, 249, 258, 261, 266, 299
Crowther, Paul 4 n1, 18, 19, 53 n2
culture xvii, 26–28, 50, 61–62, 64, 90–91, 93–95, 97, 125, 147, 156, 164, 187, 195–196, 202, 221–222, 226, 228, 243, 245, 272, 287
culturome 109, 109 n2, 195
Cyril 214

Dada 37, 82, 280, 291
dance 59, 107, 145, 186, 258, 272, 274, 276–280, 286, 291–293
Danto, Arthur 5 n1, 11–12, 19, 29, 33–34, 51, 76, 270, 273
Darwinian 81–82
Davidson's charity principle 258
Dean, James 151
Dearmer, Percy 216
deconstruction 5 n2, 11, 53, 89, 101, 159, 165, 175
decoration xv, 147–148, 159, 164, 197, 218, 278
Deely, John 109
deference 128–129
Delius, Peter 224
Della Volpe, Galvano 4 n1
de-pression 173–175, 202, 235, 267
Derrida, Jacques 5, 53, 101, 145, 165, 175, 209, 295
Descartes, René 215, 239
    design in fashion 279, 283, 287
    design "Human Design system" 263, 266
design, designers 157, 159, 164–166, 183, 189–190, 195, 201, 203, 217, 224, 239, 254–256, 266, 280, 297
Dessoir, Max 5, 73–74, 87

Dewey, John 5 n1, 6, 6 n2, 8–9, 15, 27–29, 32–34, 46, 55, 61–63, 68–69, 75–76, 88–91, 93, 102, 129, 139
dhimmi 228
diachronic 184–187, 189, 191, 193, 219
Diaconus, Paulus 216
dialogic 55, 131, 149, 172–173, 228, 242, 272
dialogue, dialogism 54–55, 88, 131, 173, 235
Dickie, George 5 n1, 12, 17–18, 20–26, 32–34, 39, 51, 68, 76, 136–137, 173, 186, 218, 270–272, 300
Diderot, Denis 283
differentiation 11, 110–111, 119, 121, 123, 125–126, 133
Diffey, T.J. 3, 5
Dilthey, Wilhelm 32
Diotima of Mantinea 280
discernment 105–108, 125, 128–130
discipline 5–6, 12, 30, 42, 43, 45, 47, 78, 97, 111, 170, 185, 188, 189, 211, 225, 227, 230, 233, 247, 281, 282–283
    discipline, aesthetics as a 3–5
disposition 30–31, 41, 55, 69, 91, 136
Dissanayake, Ellen 81–82, 85
distancing 15
    artistic distance 286–287
    corporeal 156
    distance required for personal identity 129
    distance as proxemic device and territoriality 149–151
    distanced contemplation 15 *see also* aesthetic distance
    in the family 196, 198–199
    lack of distance 21
        carnivalization cancellation of distance 129, 285
    medical 250–251
    psychical distance 19, 20, 98
    religious 227
    in school 239–240
    in sound 156
    in speech 155
    visual 157
domestication 38–39, 237
domesticity
    domestic employees 199
    domestic spaces 147–148, 161, 166, 199, 282, 286, 291
    domestic utensils 89
    domestic violence xvi, 296

Index 317

Dondis, Dondis A. 284
Dorfles, Gillo 85
dramaturgical xv, 51, 58, 77, 141, 173, 187, 198, 202, 247, 249, 286
Druckman, Daniel 144 n4
Drug addiction xvi, 59, 70, 97
Duchamp, Marcel 11, 29, 102, 215, 293
Ducrot, Osvaldo xi n1
Dufrenne, Mikel 4 n1, 6, 8, 10–12, 32, 38
Dunash Ben Tamim 209 n4
Dundes, A. Leach 79
Durand, Jacques 140
Durkheim, Emile 80, 206

Eagleton, Terry 4 n1, 8, 46, 51, 62
Eco, Umberto 4 n1, 79, 102, 215
economy, economic 5, 20, 30, 45, 54, 63, 69, 78, 81, 111, 119–120, 127–129, 135–136, 153, 163–165, 178, 180, 199, 201–202, 216–217, 237–238, 246, 251–252, 260, 269, 280, 282, 285, 294, 299
Edelman, Gerald M. 62, 300
einfühlung 22, 32, 50, 53, 87
Einstein, Albert 56, 239
Eisenhower, Dwight 163
Ekman, Paul 144 n4, 161 n2
Elizondo, Salvador 157
Emerson, Caryl 76, 78, 87–88
Emmeche, Claus 109 n1
emotion, emotional xvi, 3, 8–10, 12, 18, 20, 25, 27–28, 39–41, 50, 54, 61, 63, 79, 89, 97–98, 102–103, 111, 117, 119–120, 123, 125–126, 136, 139, 140, 159–160, 163, 166, 174, 189, 201–202, 206, 209–210, 222, 230, 245, 248, 263, 286, 297–298, 300
Engels, Friedrich 196
Engler, Gideon 6
entertainment xv, 70, 189, 259, 270, 275, 277, 281–282
environment 16, 48–49, 51, 58, 61, 69, 105–107, 135–136, 161, 178, 249, 271 n3, 287, 298
environmental 5 n1, 178, 271
erfahrung 32
erlebnis 32, 53
erotic 28, 81, 120, 142, 251, 274, 279–281, 285, 287
ethics 4, 41, 47, 80, 164, 235

ethnic 16, 58, 69, 81, 153, 164–165, 184, 212, 223 n16, 299
ethos 139 n2, 140, 149, 181
Euclid 62, 179, 300
Euripides 284
everyday life xvi, xvii, 1, 13, 15–17, 21, 23, 38–41, 43, 50–51, 62, 67–68, 73, 75–91, 93, 99, 135, 139, 140, 159, 161, 163, 172, 177, 179, 205, 221, 228, 243, 251, 260, 278, 284, 286–288, 295, 297
everyday characters 284
everyday experiences 201
everyday interactions 139
everyday speech and conversations 285, 142, 158
exchange 43, 58, 101, 117, 119, 123, 127 n2, 131–133, 135–137, 139–141, 146, 149, 169, 174–175, 177, 182, 193, 200–201, 203, 222, 259
Stock exchange 190
exotopy 22
experience 3–4, 7, 9–13, 17, 19–21, 25, 27–28, 32–35, 37, 39, 48, 53, 59–63, 67–71, 74, 77, 79, 83, 85, 87–90, 93, 101, 103, 106, 136, 183–184, 199, 201, 206, 209, 221, 237, 242, 271, 276, 278, 281, 288, 291, 295–297
see also aesthetic experience
ex-pression 173–175, 202, 217, 219, 235, 249, 261, 267
expression 3, 9–10, 40, 55, 73, 111–112, 117, 119, 131, 140, 145, 153, 156, 163–165, 167, 196–198, 201, 207, 210, 217–218, 226, 229, 245, 246, 276, 291
artistic 76, 80, 281
plane of expression 111, 171 *see also* symbolic expression, facial expression
Ezzati, Abdul Fazl 223

Faarabi, Al- 220 n14
face to face interaction 54, 58, 136–137, 222, 261, 265
facial expression 140, 144–145, 148, 157, 161 n2, 178, 287
Fakhr Al-Din Al-Razi 220 n14
family resemblances 3, 46, 183, 272, 280
fantasy 21, 84, 131, 269–270, 272, 274–283, 285, 288, 293, 296

fascination xv, 24, 49, 60, 68, 180, 186, 205, 210, 218

fascism 165

feeling 3, 9, 20, 26, 28, 38, 40–41, 46, 61, 70, 90, 125, 159, 175, 198, 210, 256, 258, 271–272

feminine 63, 158, 212, 265, 281, 291

Ferry, Luc 81

fetish, fetishism 7–13, 22, 30, 42–43, 56, 84, 87, 120, 181, 258, 260

Feuerbach, Ludwig 232

Feyerabend, Paul K. 53

Fichte, Johann Gottlieb 5 n1

Filmer, Robert 203, n1

Fiqh 220, 232

Fish, Stanley 31, 54 n3, 56

Fontanille, Jacques 102, 111 n5, 274

food 83–84, 97, 193, 200, 216, 224, 228, 278

form 9, 11, 54, 56, 61, 67, 73, 89, 93, 105–107, 109–111, 116–117, 119, 122, 125, 139–140, 142, 150, 160, 169, 174, 213, 221, 235, 286

  excedent form 127

  form of the message 78, 175

  form perception 4

  form stratum 136–137

  significant form 4, 102

  symbolic form 102, 115

Foucault, Michel 31, 47, 60, 132, 180, 188, 202, 214, 226, 236, 260

foundation 13, 27, 37, 101, 128 n2, 212, 283

Fox, Vicente 172, 235

Frankfurt School 15, 38

Freire, Paolo 238

Freud, Sigmund 45, 60, 153, 164, 175, 209, 287

Friesen, Wallace V. 144 n4

fundamentalism 220 n4, 228, 235

funerals, funerary 112, 185, 169–179, 190, 193, 195, 236, 274–275, 290, 294, 296, 298

Fyodorovna, Alexandra 257

Gabirol, Yehudah Ibn 208

Gadamer, Hans-Georg 9, 32

Galen 253

Galileo 214, 231, 236, 239

games, playing 31–32, 49–51, 59, 82, 90–95, 129, 151, 164, 185, 190–191, 195, 200, 210, 240, 244, 246, 247, 255, 258–260, 267, 270 n2, 275, 276, 286, 288–289, 293, 295–299

agon 93–95, 187, 191–192, 247, 293, 295–299

alea 94–95, 293, 295–299

"free play of imagination and understanding" 32, 68–69, 93, 237

ilinx 94–95, 293, 296–299

mimicry 94–95, 243, 247–248, 250, 258–261, 293, 295–299

peripatos 94–95, 175, 209, 241, 267, 293, 295–299

Garbo, Greta 287

García Márquez, Gabriel 132, 158

Gaudi, Antoni 219

Gauguin, Paul 291

Gauthier, Jean Paul 283

Geertz, Clifford 77

geisha 280

Gellner, Ernest 299 n1

Gemara 208

gender 81, 121, 158, 164, 185–186, 240, 255, 286

genealogy 34, 47, 60

Genesis 207, 212

genesis of cultural conventions 64

  pathogenesis 123

  semiogenesis 123 n6

genocide 98, 235

genre 15–16, 76, 79, 83, 88–89, 91, 98, 102, 142, 171–172, 193, 216, 222, 234, 257, 272–281, 283–292, 298

gestalt psychology 39

gestapo 98, 257

gestual, gestuality 145–146, 148, 153, 157, 172, 201

Ghazali, Al- 220 n14

Gibb, Hamilton Alexander Rosskeen Sir 220–221, 224–225

Gilbert and George 280

Giménez, Gilberto 80 n4

Giordano, Filippa 290

Giotto di Bondone 218, 273, 282, 287

global matrix 184, 296, 299, 300

  global process 63, 186, 199

  globalization 186–187

Goebbels, Joseph 260

Goffman, Erving xv, 58, 59, 77–78, 93, 141, 146, 174–175, 198

Goodman, Nelson 4 n1, 278

Gospel 214, 219, 220, 274

Gospel music 216, 234

Index 319

Goux, Jean–Joseph 109 n3, 119–120, 127–128, 135–136, 145, 260
Graetz, Heinrich 208 n3
Graham, Martha 293
Gramsci 4 n1
Greimas, Algirdas 102, 112, 290
Grice, H. Paul 258
Grosseteste 236
Groupe μ 102–103, 140
Guadalupe, Virgin of 116, 235–236
Gubern, Roman 270, 288, 290
Guerlain 279
Guirant Riquier 279
Guiraud, Pierre 28, 150

Haapala, Arto 5 n1, n84
Haas, John 247
Hadith 219, 220, 225
Hadjj 224
Halacha 206, 208, 211, 225, 232
Halevi Yehuda 208
Hall, Edward T. 145, 149, 150, 155–156, 227
Hamlet 140, 274
haptic 25, 146, 148, 156
Hattstein, Markus 224
Hauser, Arnold 4, 28, 271, 273
Haydn, Joseph 196
Haytham Ibn al- (Aljazen) 236
Hayyan, Jabir ibn 236
Hegedüs, Andras 187
Hegel, Georg Wilhelm Friedrich 116
hegira 219, 221
Heidegger 4 n1, 5, 53, 53 n1
heresy 180, 214, 215, 218, 229
Heschel Abraham Joshua 234
Hess, Rudolf 257
heteroglossia 88, 170–173, 175, 272
Hewes, Gordon 146
hierarchy 141, 153, 155, 169, 187, 227, 252, 272, 299
Hiëronymus, Saint 215
Himmler, Heinrich 257
Hippocrates 253
Hitchcock, Alfred 173
Hitler, Adolf 257
Hjelmslev, Louis 105, 112
Hoffmeyer, Jesper 109 n1
Holy Sepulcher 116, 206, 218
homily 208, 214, 220
hospitals 251–253, 255, 290

Huizinga, Johan 90–91, 93–94, 151, 275–276, 298
Hume, David 8, 17, 97
Husserl, Edmund 4 n1, 209
Hutcheson, Francis 22
hybridization 88, 173–175, 208–209, 228–229, 235
hygiene 122, 162, 197, 206, 254
Hyman, Lawrence W. 20 n3

icon 115–117, 121, 159, 283 n4
iconic 146 n7, 283
iconicity 183
iconoclastic 214, 216, 226
iconographic 205
iconography 218
identity 52, 57–60, 76, 80, 98, 106, 108–109, 119, 128–129, 135, 140–142, 143, 148, 151, 153, 164, 173, 175, 181, 185, 188–189, 197–198, 200–202, 206–207, 213, 226, 231–234, 242–243, 246, 248, 250, 253–255, 257, 259–261, 263, 266, 269, 274, 284, 286, 295, 298, 300
ideology 8, 16, 30, 46, 56, 62, 79, 113, 186, 220, 238, 294, 299
ijma or consensus 220, 221, 229, 231–232
Illich, Ivan 246
illusion 20–21, 25, 91, 174, 191, 289
image 26, 40, 41, 98, 121, 132, 135, 139, 142, 146, 161–163, 171, 173, 183–184, 186, 190, 197, 210, 221, 230, 241, 258, 265, 279, 284
image, aesthetic 88
image, artistic 16
image, body 147
image, mental or psychic 112, 300
image, religious 123, 212–214, 218, 232, 235, 239
image, visual or acoustic 67, 111, 112, 117, 140 n3
image-scene 288–289
image-labyrinth 288–289
as object in mirror 57
imagination 9, 17, 27, 29, 32, 50, 68, 152, 213, 237–238, 248, 262, 264, 270, 280, 287, 298, 300
"free play of imagination and understanding" 32, 68–69, 93, 237
imam 220, 222, 225–227, 231

320 *Everyday Aesthetics*

im-pression 173–175, 202, 217, 235, 238,
        249, 259, 261
incense 89, 217, 231, 258, 279
individuality 39, 52, 57–60, 80, 106, 108,
        128–129, 164, 198, 231, 248–249,
        259–261, 273
industrial, industrialization 16, 38, 159, 164,
        186, 189, 239, 246, 264, 278, 291, 299
Inquisition 206, 214, 217, 218 n12
institutionalists 5 n1, 271
institutionalization processes 51, 64, 141,
        179, 186, 233, 242, 243, 246, 257,
        282–283, 285
institutions, artistic 11, 12, 29, 37, 273, 281
institutions, social 58, 70, 78, 80, 88, 180–181,
        185, 202, 240, 245, 248, 255, 294
intentionality 25, 63, 69–70, 109
interaction xv, xvi, 28–29, 43, 48–51,
        54–55, 58–59, 61, 78, 105–106, 108,
        129, 131, 133, 135–137, 139 n2,
        141, 146, 150, 152, 159, 162, 167,
        169, 171, 173–175, 182, 196–197,
        199, 201–202, 237, 242, 258, 265
International Association of Empirical
        Aesthetics 27, 39
internet 201, 226 n22, 241, 263, 266
interpretation xvi, 8–9, 23, 29, 31, 56, 58, 65,
        77–79, 101, 110–111, 152, 156, 166,
        173, 205–206, 209, 210, 220–221, 229,
        231, 236, 261, 266, 287, 290, 292, 299
        enunciation/interpretation 78, 132, 136,
        170, 173, 181, 214
interpreter 102, 107 n2, 110–111, 121,
        131–132, 155, 160–161, 171, 173,
        210, 271, 277, 288
intersubjectivity 54–58, 62, 111, 126, 174,
        178, 249, 270
intonation 87, 133, 140–141, 143, 148, 156,
        188, 196, 240, 258, 262, 280
intuition xvi, 8, 61–62, 64–65, 220, 249
Irvine, John Taylor 169

Jackson, Michael 161, 291
Jakobson, Roman 4 n1, 78, 101, 115, 119,
        163, 175, 207, 276
Jarir al-Tabari ibn 220
Jauss, Hans Robert 56
Jerusalem 123, 208, 210–213, 218–219,
        226–227, 235
Jesus 165, 193, 206, 208, 213, 215–217, 219,
        220, 227–228, 230, 232, 235, 291

Job 227, 230
John, Saint 214
Johnson, Mark 63, 90, 183, 183 n3
Joseph, Isaac 59
Joyce, James 288
juggler 275–277, 281
juridical 49, 113, 142, 178, 182, 185–186,
        188–189, 193, 195, 296–297, 300

Kaaba 116, 206, 224
Kabbalah 211, 259, 263
Kafka, Franz 82, 105, 108, 132, 189
Kandinsky, Vasilly 102, 293
Kant, Immanuel xvi, 1, 4–5, 9, 17–21, 25–30,
        32, 34, 37–39, 41–42, 46–47, 54, 57,
        61–63, 67–70, 87, 89, 93, 97, 101,
        106, 110, 157, 209, 215, 237, 276
        Critique of Judgment 17, 26, 39, 41, 46,
        54, 62, 110
        Critique of Pure Reason 46, 61
Kaprow, Alan 280
Kendon, Adam 144
Kepler, Johannes 236
kinaesthetic 25
Kindi, Al- 220 n14, 236
Klein, Melanie 239, 248
Klein, Yves 280
Knapp, Mark L. 144 n4
Kolnai, Aurel 38
Korsmeyer, Carolyn 5 n1, 38, 272, 278
Kosik, Karel 4 n1
Krampen, Martin 109, 150
Kripke, Saul 209
Kuehn, Glenn 84, 278
Kuhn, Thomas 183
Kurtycz, Marcos 289

Labarca, Guillermo 237
Labov, William 153
Lacan, Jacques 57, 270
Lakoff, George 63, 90, 183, 183 n3
Langer, Susanne K. 5 n1, 9, 102
language xvi, xvii, 3–4, 6–7, 9–10, 31, 54, 57,
        63–64, 83, 87, 90, 103, 106, 115–116,
        119, 121, 125, 131–133, 135–136,
        139, 140 n3, 142, 145, 148, 153, 155,
        160, 170, 172–174, 183, 219, 242,
        250, 253, 259, 261–262, 274, 284
        body language 144, 150, 156, 161, 201,
        247, 261
        colloquial 262

Index

institutional 172, 240
omniscopic 264
paralanguage 143
signal language 167
verbal 148, 155, 186, 274
Lassus, Roland de 216
latching-onto, latched-by 67–71, 91, 94–95,
  123, 202, 206, 213, 217, 221, 237,
  239, 243, 247–249, 296
Le Corbusier 219
lebenswelt 77
Leddy, Tom 83
Lee, Ang 293
Lefebvre, Henri 77
legitimation 64, 133, 179, 180, 185, 187,
  189, 198, 247, 250, 269
León, Rabbi Moises De 209
Levinas Emmanuel 50, 209
Levi-Strauss, Claude 135
linguistics, language xvii, 78, 102, 111–112,
  115, 131, 133, 142
Lipps, Theodor 22, 32, 50
literature 7, 49, 76, 79–80, 87, 91, 102, 132,
  142, 272, 274, 285, 297–298
locus xv, 139 n2, 205, 213, 218, 223, 226
logos 55, 122, 140, 147, 149, 181, 208, 214
Lotman, Iuri, M. 102, 117, 271–272, 299
Loyola, San Igancio De 215
Lucas, George 285, 293
Luckmann, Thomas 58, 62–64, 77–78, 115–
  116, 136–137, 141, 145, 177, 179–181
ludus 94 n1, 129
Luhmann, Niklas 177–178, 300
Lunacharsky 4 n1
Luther, Martin 214 n10, 214–216, 235, 246
Lyotard, Jean Francois 53 n1, 101, 209

Machaut, Guillaume De 275
madrasa 220, 222–223
magic 8–10, 91, 93, 127, 141, 186, 189,
  236, 250, 258–259, 262, 265–266,
  273, 275–276, 282, 290, 294, 297
Maimonides 208–209, 215
Meir Ibn Ezra, Abraham Ben 209
make up 146, 148, 150, 161, 190, 192, 280, 283
Malevitch, Vladimir 102 n1, 291
Malik, Anas Ibn 219
Mandoki, Katya 45, 84, 103 n1, 109 n2, 116
  n2, 119 n1–2, 127 n1, 139 n2, 140
  n3, 145 n6, 146 n7, 149 n1, 187, 208
  n1, 213 n9, 285 n5, 290

Manzini, Piero 280
Marcel, Gabriel 215
marketing xv, 30, 140–141, 298
Marx, Karl 9, 27, 63, 133 n2, 135, 181
Marxism, Marxist 4 n1, 8, 15, 54, 79, 181,
  209, 229, 237–238, 270
masculine 63, 172, 197, 225, 280
Mass 193, 206, 215–218
mass art and culture 70, 79, 80, 129, 192,
  274, 287, 288–290, 292–293, 298
massacre 9, 76, 206, 209, 214, 267
masses, massification 15, 19, 28, 98, 164,
  191, 224, 234, 241, 243, 244, 246,
  294
Matisse, Henri 291
Matsumoto, D. 144 n4, 161 n2
Maturana, Humberto R. 49, 105, 177, 178,
  182
Maurus, Hrabanus 216
Mauss, Marcel 153
Mecca 116, 206, 219, 223–224, 226–228
Medici, Catherine de 257, 266, 279
medicine 10, 54, 69, 182, 202, 236, 247–
  248, 250–251, 254–255, 297
Medina 219, 226–227, 229
membrane 26, 48–49, 59, 105–106, 182
Menander 284
Mendelsohn, Moses 209
Merleau Ponty 4 n1, 77
Merrell, Floyd 109 n1
Messiah 203, 213–215, 228, 230
metaphor, metaphorical 9, 12, 31, 68, 75,
  79, 81, 90, 94, 112, 123, 144, 164,
  165, 177, 183, 183 n1, 189, 193,
  197, 211, 220, 242, 259, 260, 300
  metaphorical projection 9, 34, 67, 71, 117
Midrash 208
military 49, 95, 105, 122, 142–143, 147,
  160, 169–170, 182, 184–186, 189,
  192–193, 195, 203, 219–220, 223,
  227, 229, 232–233, 246, 271,
  273–275, 291, 294, 296–297, 299
mimesis 186, 247
Min, Joosik 165–166
Mishna 208
Mitias, Michael 32–34
Moles, Abraham 38
Mondrian, Piet 291
monoglossia 171
Monroe, Marilyn 121, 287
Moore, George Edward 4 n1

322 *Everyday Aesthetics*

moral, morality 13 n2, 18, 20 n3, 40–41, 47, 90, 98, 125, 129, 166, 172, 202, 232, 236, 254–255, 290
   immoral 18, 40–42, 290
   moral, moralistic category 38, 83, 95, 125, 200
Morris, Charles 48, 102, 109–110, 112
Morson, Gary S. 76, 79, 87–88
mosques 206, 212, 220, 226, 236
Mozart, Wolfgang Amadeus 82, 216, 294
Muhammad 206, 213, 219–220, 222–223, 226, 228–231, 287
Muhammad Abdel–Wahhab 220
Muhieddin Ibn The Arabi 220
Mukařovský, Jan 4 n1, 23, 73, 78, 87 n1, 101
multidisciplinary 3, 5–6
museum 11, 13, 155–156, 19, 24, 34, 37, 50, 81, 89, 90, 125, 157, 241, 250, 271–272, 276, 282–283, 292–293
music 16, 18, 20, 22, 25–26, 28, 31, 41, 49, 51, 61, 67–69, 83, 86, 98, 101–102, 106, 116, 121, 143, 156, 158, 164, 170, 183, 190, 193, 196, 199, 202, 210, 213, 216, 222–223, 225, 231, 249, 260, 270, 272–276, 278–280, 283–284, 286, 288, 290, 292, 294, 298
mysticism 80
myth, mythology 15–35, 43, 90, 98, 116, 120, 172, 205, 212, 228, 285, 287–289, 291

Nagdela, Samuel Ibn 208 n2
Naukkarinen, Ossi 82, 85
Neoplatonism 90, 209, 214, 217
New Testament *see also* Bible 215, 219
Newton, Isaac 152, 183, 239
Niemeyer, Oscar 219
Nietzsche, Friedrich 47, 157, 215
Nitsch, Hermann 280
non-aesthetic 11, 30, 32–34, 43
novels 20, 22, 69, 75–76, 79–80, 83, 88, 129, 151, 159, 170–173, 181, 215, 279, 284, 288
Nwodo, Christopher, S. 4–7

objectivation 55–58, 60, 64–65, 111, 131–132, 136, 141, 156, 174, 179
objectivity xvi, 10, 25, 53–57, 142, 162, 174
objectual, objectuality 55–57
obtuse 41, 125–126, 126
Occam, William 24, 109–111, 215, 236

Ogden, Charles Kay 115
Olbrechts-Tyteca 140
organism 26, 48–49, 55, 105–106, 111, 178, 182–183
Origin of Alexandria 217
originality 120, 220–221, 244
Orlan 82, 281, 291, 293
orthodoxy 6–7, 53, 89, 181, 211–212, 214, 223, 226, 228, 235
Osborne, Harold 6, 21
Othello 20, 23, 40

Paetzold, Heinz 77 n2
paideia 94 n1, 129
painting 18 n2, 23, 31, 49, 54, 64, 76, 94, 101, 102, 111, 132, 134, 161, 166, 183, 186, 189, 193, 218, 235, 269, 274–276, 278, 280–284, 287, 289, 291, 293–294, 298
panaestheticism xvi, 17, 37, 73
Pangloss syndrome 37, 38, 41, 83–84, 95
pantomime 274, 276
paradigm 64, 81, 85, 120, 133–134, 142, 166, 182–184, 186, 192, 203, 235–236, 239, 256, 266, 293
paradigmatic projections 184, 203, 235–236, 246, 255, 259, 266
Parret, Herman 32, 54 n4, 70, 102–103, 144, 152, 160
Passeron, Jean Claude 241, 243
Passmore, John 97
Pasteur, Louis 239
pathos 140, 149, 181, 192, 231
pathosemiotics 102, 103 n4
Patou, Jean 279
Paul, Saint 181, 206, 213, 215–216, 233
Peirce, Charles Sanders 54, 107, 109–112, 115–117, 121–122, 178, 183, 296
Pelc, Jerzy 48
Peninou, Jacques 140
perception 3, 4, 7, 8, 11–12, 18–20, 22–26, 28–29, 31, 38, 45–47, 50, 53–57, 61–62, 64–65, 67, 75–78, 83, 91, 103, 105–108, 111, 121, 127–129, 135, 139, 177, 185, 207, 300
Perelman, Chaim 140
Pérez Agote, Alfonso 80 n4
perfume 28, 225–226, 276, 279–280
Pericles 280
persuasion xv, 77, 98, 109, 139, 142, 250
phaneroscopy 107

Index

phenomenological, phenomenology xvi, 4, 12, 32, 34, 50, 62, 67, 69, 71, 78, 107, 136, 144, 209

Philo Judeus 208–209

philosophy 3–8, 16, 46, 50–51, 63, 75, 208, 220, 243, 271
  aesthetic philosophy 209
  analytical philosophy 97
  Christian philosophy 236
  Greek philosophy 208
  Judaic philosophy 209
  Moslem philosophy 221
  neoplatonic philosophy 214

Piaget, Jean 62

Plato, platonism 5, 31, 64, 140, 208, 280, 282

playing *see* games

poesics 79–80, 123 n6, 289

poetics 49, 51–52, 75–76, 79–80, 87–88, 91, 123, 132, 140, 142, 159–160, 163–165, 171, 173, 190, 269, 271, 280

Poetics 75–76, 149, 237

poetry 7, 16, 31, 75, 79, 83, 142, 157, 273–275, 280, 285, 288

political xv, 5, 15–16, 20, 25, 30, 38, 69, 70, 77, 79–81, 98, 119, 122, 127, 142, 145, 153, 159, 163, 172, 178, 180, 186–187, 195, 203, 209, 220, 223, 227, 229, 231–233, 235, 255, 269, 276, 282, 284–287, 294, 299

politics xv, 22, 45, 78, 98, 269, 278

polyphony 88, 171–173, 175, 215, 219, 229, 272

popular, popularity 242, 259, 278, 298
  popular art 89 n2, 284
  popular music 158, 288
  popular taste 285

postmodernism 89 n2, 293

posture 23, 102, 144, 146, 174

potlatch 153, 196

pragmatics 78, 112 n6, 171, 205, 240, 271, 275, 277, 282

pragmatism 5 n1, 89 n2, 11

prayer 79, 80, 165, 209, 210–212, 214, 222–224, 227–228, 231–234, 238, 246

prejudice 70

presentation of identity xv, 52, 57–58, 76–77, 141–142, 174, 198, 217, 261, 269

Principle of Cooperation 258

props 93, 133, 146, 148, 161, 172, 190, 197, 202, 239, 248–249, 252, 254, 257–259, 263, 280, 297

prosaics xvii, 49, 51–52, 73–81, 87–91, 93, 97, 99, 102–103, 108, 116, 119, 120, 123 n6, 131–133, 135–136, 139–142, 145–147, 149, 164, 165, 171–173, 177, 180, 198, 249, 262, 271, 280, 300

prosics 79–80, 123 n6, 158, 289

prostitution 7, 151, 200, 279–280, 283

Prudentius, Aurelius 216

Pseudo Dionysus Areopagite 215

psychical distance 19, 20, 22, 98, 251

psychology 3–4, 12, 39–41, 47, 60, 78

Quinet 84, 278

Qur'an 188, 219–224, 229–232, 264, 274

Rabelais, François 88, 162, 285

racism xvi, 97

Radford, Robert 38 n1

Ramadan 224, 234

Rasputin 257, 266

rational, rationalism 25, 46, 53 n1, 140, 142, 159, 215, 230
  irrational 117, 262, 265, 291
  rational argumentation 98
  rational thinking 53
  rationalist ideology 46
  rationality 142, 165

Razi Al- 236

regard 105–108

relativism 7, 42

re-presentation 52, 72, 277, 284

revelation 207–208, 215, 219

rhetoric acts
  actio 139 n2, 147
  dispositio 139 n2, 147, 264
  elocutio 139 n2, 147
  inventio 139 n2
  memoria 139 n2
  pronuntiatio 139 n2

rhetoric figures
  alliteration 140, 145, 147, 162–164, 197–198, 221, 264, 285
  anacoluthon 145, 147, 197
  antiphrasis 147
  catachresis 145, 147–148, 197
  ellipsis 145, 147, 163
  hyperbole 145, 147, 162, 197, 221
  irony 140, 145, 162
  periphrasis 145, 147, 197
  reticence 147

324 *Everyday Aesthetics*

rhythm 32, 61, 64, 69, 91, 93, 129, 140, 143, 151, 158, 163, 170, 199, 215, 234, 241, 245, 252, 264, 286, 288, 298
Richards, Ivory Armstrong 115
ritual 89, 113, 153, 169, 191, 195–196, 203, 210–212, 214, 216–218, 222, 224, 245, 252, 258–259, 273–274, 276, 278, 294
Rizzolatti, Giacomo 50
Rodríguez Adrados, Francisco 191, 273–274
roles 59, 88, 105–106, 129, 141, 179, 181, 186, 243, 290, 295, 297
Roscellinus 215
Rosenzweig, Franz 209
Rossi-Landi, Feruccio 50, 102–103, 135
Royal Academy of London 283
Rubert De Ventós, Xavier 6 n2
Rulfo, Juan 217
Rushd, Ibn Or Averroes 220 n14
Russell, Bertrand 4 n1, 215, 221

Saadia Ben Yosef 208
Sabines, Jaime 163
Sachar, Abram Leon 208, 212
sacred, sacredness 64, 89, 128, 206, 208, 210–219, 221, 226, 231, 234, 269, 274–275, 285
Sahl of Seville, Abú Isháq Ibrahim Ibn 222
Sahlins, Marshall 246
Saint–Martin, Fernande 62
Saito, Yuriko 83, 85, 271
Salinas de Gortari, Carlos 161
Sánchez Vázquez, Adolfo 4 n1, 30–31, 40–41, 45, 68, 85, 127
Sartre, Jean–Paul 59, 59 n1
Sartwell, Crispin 83
Saussure, Ferdinand De xvii, 51, 78, 109–112, 115, 119, 121, 131–133, 135, 142, 182–183, 207, 259
Schaper, Eva 4 n1
Scheflen, Albert E. 144 n4, 161
Schiller, Friedrich 5, 83
Schoenberg, Arnold 210 n6, 286, 293
Schopenhauer 5 n1, 64
Schütz, Alfred 77
Schwarzkogler, Rudolf 281
science and aesthetics xvi, 5–7, 16, 39, 43, 45–46, 55–56, 62–64, 84, 87, 90, 94, 97, 116, 180, 183, 220, 231, 236, 246–247, 263, 269
Scotus, John Duns 109, 215

Scotus of Erigena, John 125
sculpture 49, 157, 218, 274–275, 280–283, 287, 289, 293–294, 298
Searle, John 102, 139, 159
Sebeok, Thomas 107, 109 n1
seduction xv, 55, 60, 68, 109, 145, 161, 180, 205, 274
semantic 71, 83, 105, 112, 143, 171, 191–192, 205, 240, 271, 275, 282, 288, 290, 293 n6
semio-aesthetics 101–103, 105
semiosis xvii, 19, 48–51, 60, 77 n2, 101–103, 105–112, 119–121, 123, 126–127, 129, 135, 235, 247, 261
semiotics xvii, 4, 48, 50, 78, 101–103, 105, 109–111, 115, 117, 125, 127, 135, 139, 144, 166, 169, 188, 272
Semmelweis, Ignaz Philipp 236
sensation 26, 46, 54, 61–62, 64–65, 67, 73, 76, 87, 97, 105–108, 117, 128–130, 173, 200, 216, 254, 287
senses 9, 26–27, 39, 46, 63, 67–69, 74, 84, 95, 102–103, 128, 130, 132, 144, 231, 272, 278, 280
sensibility xvi, 3, 6, 8, 10, 12, 27, 29, 38–43, 45–51, 60–61, 64, 69–70, 76–78, 88–89, 91, 97–98, 123, 125, 129–131, 133, 136, 144, 149, 151, 155, 159, 169, 197, 202–203, 206, 213, 222, 231–232, 235, 237–238, 243, 247–248, 267, 281, 296
sensorial, sensoriality xvi, 11, 28–29, 46, 51, 63, 88, 120, 181–182, 225, 249, 271, 278, 292
sensual, sensuality 10, 12, 29, 46, 83, 135, 147, 162, 172, 225–226, 272, 286, 290–291
Serpa, Carlos 280
setting 58, 93, 146–148, 189, 197, 202, 211, 238, 249, 254, 287
sexual, sexuality 25, 28, 63, 120, 135, 150, 156–158, 161, 165, 172, 184, 195–197, 211, 213, 224–226, 272, 278–280, 296
Shaaria 219, 222, 225
Shabat 211–212, 234
Shaffir, William 247, 250–251
Shafi, Al- 220
Shaftesbury, Third Earl of, Anthony Ashley Cooper 17
shahada 223, 231

Index

Shakespeare, William 75, 90, 140, 227, 285
Shapiro 4 n1
Shehitah 211
Shklovsky, Victor 22 n5
shofar 210
Shusterman, Richard 5 n1, 32–34, 89
Shuy, Roger W. 188
Sibley, Frank 53 n2, 84, 128
sign 48, 50, 109, 110, 112, 115–117,
    119–123, 126–127, 145, 213, 254,
    259–261, 266, 276, 282, 293
signic 109–113, 116–117, 119–123,
    125–129, 133, 136–137, 146, 156,
    180, 187, 191, 196, 201, 249–250,
    253, 259, 286, 300
significance 41, 77, 90–91, 103, 121–123,
    125, 134, 136–137, 151–152, 233,
    246
signification 10, 46, 51, 61, 102–103, 119,
    121–123, 127, 134, 136, 137
signified 111–112, 115, 117, 142, 207, 259
signifier 111–112, 115–117, 142, 259–260
Sina, Ibn Or Avicenna 208, 220 n14
singularity 57, 60
Sklar, Dusty 257
smell 13, 19, 30, 39, 67–68, 84, 107, 132,
    140, 144, 146, 190, 197, 234,
    270–272, 276, 279
socioaesthetics 50–51, 271
sociology 3–5, 43, 45, 77–78, 80, 115, 141,
    175, 177, 179, 205, 271
Sonesson, Göran 102, 103
Sophocles 284
space 11, 27, 61–62, 64, 69, 89, 91, 116,
    121, 127, 131–132, 139, 146–147,
    149–150, 155, 157–158, 164–166,
    177, 188–189, 191, 199, 202,
    212–213, 217–218, 234, 240–242,
    244, 249, 262, 270, 276–277, 282,
    286–287, 289, 291–292, 298, 300
space-time 27, 61–62, 64, 91, 116, 177, 213
spectacle 37, 40, 191–192, 275–277, 286
spectator 9–12, 19–24, 29–31, 34, 51, 132,
    166, 269–271, 274, 276, 281–282,
    284, 287–289, 291–293, 298
Sperber, Dan 195
Spinoza, Baruch 209
sports xv, 22, 34, 49, 70, 79–80, 84–85, 89,
    95, 113, 122, 147, 160, 184, 186–7,
    191–193, 195, 246, 269, 271, 286,
    294, 296–297, 299

standard, standards 28, 43, 97, 101, 160,
    201, 241, 261–262
Stanislavski 173
State 78, 105, 113, 182, 186–187, 190, 192,
    196, 238
Stolnitz, Jerome 17–18, 22–24
Stuhr, John J. 246
style 3, 77, 79, 87, 120, 141–143, 146–149,
    153, 157–159, 163–166, 172, 174,
    189–191, 197, 201–202, 210, 226,
    251, 254, 279, 284–285, 288–289,
    291, 294
subjectivation 56–58, 60, 65, 69, 131, 174
subjectivism 32, 42, 53
subjectivity xvi, 3, 8, 27, 31, 47–48, 53–54,
    56–60, 63–64, 80, 91, 97–98, 108,
    128, 137, 174–175, 177, 182, 184,
    206, 231, 243, 248–249
sublime xv, 30, 38, 40, 42, 55, 87
submatrixes 182, 240
sub-objectivism 53–54, 54 n3
subregisters 142, 156
substitution 22, 119–120, 135–136, 197,
    199, 236, 260
Sunnah 188, 206, 219, 225, 232
Suvakovic, Misko 273
symbol, symbolic 5, 16, 27, 41, 43, 54, 59,
    77, 78, 102, 109–110, 115–117,
    119–128, 133, 136–137, 141, 146,
    149, 151–152, 156, 163, 169–170,
    179–180, 182, 186–193, 195–196,
    205–207, 211–213, 216–218, 226,
    228, 234–235, 237, 243, 243, 245,
    247, 249–250, 253, 257, 259–263,
    269–272, 276, 278, 284, 295–297,
    299–300
    symbolic capital 115
    symbolic expression 4, 9, 102
    symbolic universes 116, 179–180
symmetry 9, 58, 94, 158–159, 165,
    181–182, 284
syntagm 133, 148, 160–161, 172, 182–183,
    193, 223, 225, 245, 264

Tabari Jafar Mohamed Ibn Jarir al- 220 n14
Tabit, Ibn Qurra 236
tactile 145
Talmud 208
Tapies, Antoni 291
Tarasti, Eero 102–103
Tarek Ibn Ziad 229

taste 3, 8, 19, 26–27, 32, 37, 39, 46, 49, 54, 56, 67, 84, 89, 97, 101–102, 128, 166, 190, 197, 222, 234, 255, 270, 272, 275–276, 278, 280, 283, 285
technology 16, 62, 189, 192, 241, 247, 288, 291
Tedeschi, Mario 215 n11, 221 n15
Teilhard de Chardin, Pierre 215
telenovela 34, 163, 274, 285–286, 288, 290, 298
television 20, 40, 85, 89, 172, 241, 246, 285, 288–289, 298
temperature 131, 140, 144, 146, 156, 172, 202, 255
temples 101, 123, 210–212, 227, 232–235, 279
temporal 62–64, 119, 150–151, 178, 188, 207, 213, 250
texture 11, 19, 24, 67, 122, 144, 146–147, 166, 171, 223 n16, 271, 291, 300
theater 15, 20, 54–55, 76, 89–90, 101, 149, 193, 270, 273–274, 276–277, 281, 283, 285–286, 288, 291–293, 298
Tintoretto 225
Tobin, Yishai 261–262, 264
Todorov, Tzvetan xi n1, 22, 102
Too, Lillian 165
topographic 148
Torah 208, 210, 212, 215, 219, 220–221, 228, 231–232
torture 189, 205, 214, 217, 225
totalitarianism 191, 300
tourism 95, 189–190, 192–193, 203, 236, 256, 296, 298
Townsend, Dabney 31
tradition 19, 82–83, 122, 169, 188–189, 193, 203, 208–209, 212, 214, 219, 225, 228, 230, 232, 236, 253, 263, 270, 271, 276–278
tragedy 75, 94, 101, 191, 284, 289
Trager, George L. 143
tragic 39–41, 57, 68, 217, 231, 267, 289
tribal 178, 193, 207, 212–213, 230, 233, 276, 281–282, 300
Tripp, Susan E. 155 n1
Tuan,Yi–Fu 82–85
Turner, Bryan S. 203 n1, 236, 255
Twain, Mark 151

Uexküll, Jakob Von 56, 106, 109 n1, 110–111
Uexküll, Thure Von 50
ugliness 6, 18, 38, 40, 53, 75, 93

Ulay 281
Ulrich, Herbert 98
umma 232
understanding xvi, 9, 12, 16, 19, 28–29, 32, 39, 41, 50, 61, 68–69, 84, 91, 93, 97, 99, 101–102, 106, 127, 129, 131–132, 140, 150, 205, 231, 237, 243–245, 247, 251, 269, 278 *see also* "free play of imagination and understanding"
uniforms 122, 169–170, 189, 192, 201, 239–240, 244, 251, 254–255, 283 n4, 297
universal, universality 25–27, 54, 81–82, 89, 122, 128, 161, 177, 186, 195, 207, 213, 233, 253, 265, 281
Uthman Ibn Affan 219

value 3, 8–9, 16, 20 n3, 27, 29, 34, 39, 47, 56, 58, 65, 68, 73, 80, 98, 101, 110, 120–123, 125, 127–128, 133, 135–136, 146, 161–162, 165, 186–187, 191, 198, 205–206, 213–214, 221, 224–225, 228, 230, 232, 238, 279, 295, 297
  associative value 121
  differential value 121
  exchange value 117, 123, 259
  expressive value 91
  heuristic value 78, 173, 284
  linguistic value 110–111, 133 n2
  pecuniary value 116, 128
  practical value 23
  sensuous value 225
  sentimental or emotional value 120, 123, 125
  signic value 120
  social value 11
  survival value 82
  symbolic value 120, 122, 128, 259, 269–270
  theoretical value 22–23
  truth value 47
  use value 123, 133 n2 *see also* aesthetic value
Van Gogh, Vincent 24, 82, 159, 166, 291
Vanderkeybus, Wim 293
Vanderveken, Daniel 139 n1, 159
Varela, Francisco J. 49, 105, 177, 178, 182
Vasari, Giorgio 273, 282
Vasconi, Tomás 237–238
Veblen, Thorstein 153

Index 327

Velazquez, Diego De 30–31, 102, 284, 291, 294
verfremdungseffekt 20–22, 251
Verón, Eliseo 140 n3
videogames 288–289
Vinci, Leonardo da 120, 206, 270 n1
violence xvi, 38, 40–42, 70, 84, 98–99, 175, 201, 230, 233, 243, 248, 255 *see also* aesthetic violence, domestic violence, symbolic violence
visibility 132, 225
visual xvi, 16, 34, 51, 62, 67–68, 102, 132, 140, 145–148, 151, 158, 167, 186, 212, 218, 270–271, 278, 282, 298
visual arts 43, 102, 147
visual mirage 19, 282
vitality 34, 61, 63–64, 89, 116, 152, 177, 199, 202, 229, 295
Voloshinov, Valentin N. 132, 132 n1

Wade, Nicholas 141–142
Warhol, Andy 11, 287, 291
Watson, O. Michael 150 n3
Wechsler, Judith 6
Weitz, Morris 3, 4 n1, 47, 68
Wellek, Rene 32, 39
Welsch, Wolfgang 84, 191
Willaert, Adrian 216
Winckelmann, Johann Joachim 283
Wittgenstein, Ludwig 3, 4 n1, 22, 209, 280
Wolff, Janet 4–5, 78 n3, 271

Yom Kippur 210–211, 224

Zavala, Lauro 94, 290
Zerubavel, Eviatar 62, 150, 165, 215, 234, 238, 244
zoo-aesthetics 49